Paint the
NATIONAL PARKS

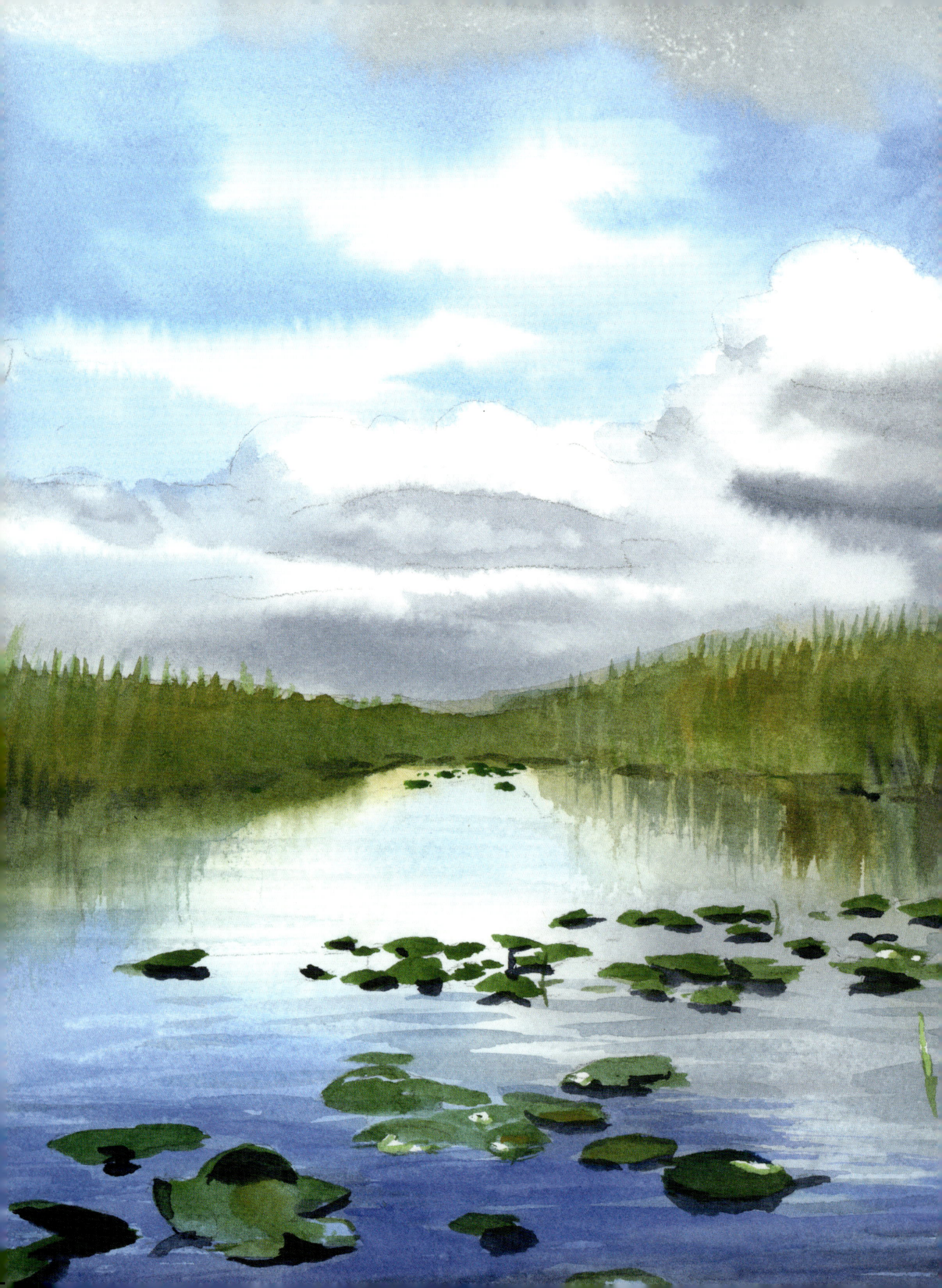

Paint the
NATIONAL PARKS

A Watercolor Journey

EMILY OLSON
Founder of Watercolor Mastery

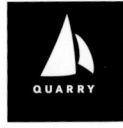

Quarto.com

First Published in 2025 by Quarry Books, an imprint of The Quarto Group,
100 Cummings Center, Suite 265-D, Beverly, MA 01915, USA.
T (978) 282-9590 F (978) 283-2742

Quarry Books titles are also available at discount for retail, wholesale, promotional, and bulk purchase. For details, contact the Special Sales Manager by email at specialsales@quarto.com or by mail at The Quarto Group,
Attn: Special Sales Manager, 100 Cummings Center, Suite 265-D, Beverly, MA 01915, USA.

10 9 8 7 6 5 4 3 2 1

ISBN: 978-0-7603-9396-3

Digital edition published in 2025
eISBN: 978-0-7603-9397-0

Library of Congress Cataloging-in-Publication Data

Names: Olson, Emily (Artist), author.
Title: Paint the National Parks : a watercolor journey / Emily Olson,
   founder of Watercolor Mastery.
Description: Beverly, MA : Quarry Books, 2025. | Includes index. | Summary:
   "Paint the National Parks takes you on a journey across the United
   States as you paint stunning scenes and subjects from some of America's
   most iconic places in glorious watercolor"-- Provided by publisher.
Identifiers: LCCN 2024062019 (print) | LCCN 2024062020 (ebook) | ISBN
   9780760393963 (trade paperback) | ISBN 9780760393970 (ebook)
Subjects: LCSH: Watercolor painting--Technique. | National parks and
   reserves--United States. | Landscape painting--Technique. | Wildlife
   painting--Technique.
Classification: LCC ND2420 .O46 2025 (print) | LCC ND2420 (ebook) | DDC
   751.42/249973--dc23/eng/20250127
LC record available at https://lccn.loc.gov/2024062019
LC ebook record available at https://lccn.loc.gov/20

Design: Sporto
Cover Image: Emily Olson
Page Layout: Sporto
Photography and Illustrations: Emily Olson; except p. 21 (all) Mitch Castor; pp. 40, 48 (left), 50 (top), 58, 74, 82, 86, 104, 108, 112, 126, 132, 136, 142, 146, 152 Shutterstock; pp. 22 (left), 48 (right), 113 (top, left and bottom, left), 118 (bottom), 119 (bottom, left) Ana Rose Bain

Printed in China

Acknowledgments

A heartfelt thank you to my identical twin—my "Womb-mate," Anna Rose Bain—for inspiring me to pursue art full-time and for gifting me my very first set of watercolor paints. Our "paintcation" adventures exploring the national parks together have given me some of the most cherished memories of my life.

Thanks to my parents, Bruce and Hollee, for always encouraging my artistic pursuits, even from a young age—despite the times when it involved permanent ink on the walls!

I am deeply grateful to Daniel Sprick, Raj Chaudhuri, and the entire Denver art group for their unwavering support of my artistic journey. Your wisdom, guidance, constructive critiques, and above all, friendship and encouragement, have meant the world to me!

To my two kiddos, Ansley and Luke—I *adore* you! You make me laugh and you inspire me every day.

My deepest thanks go to my husband, Blake. I couldn't have created this book without your patience, support, feedback, and encouragement. We truly make a great team.

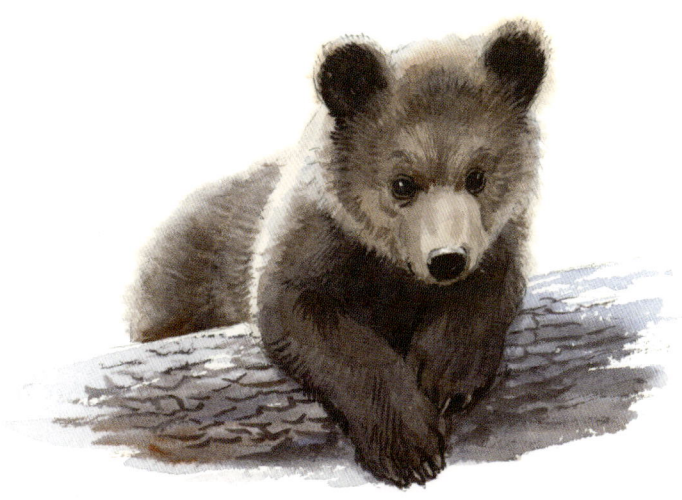

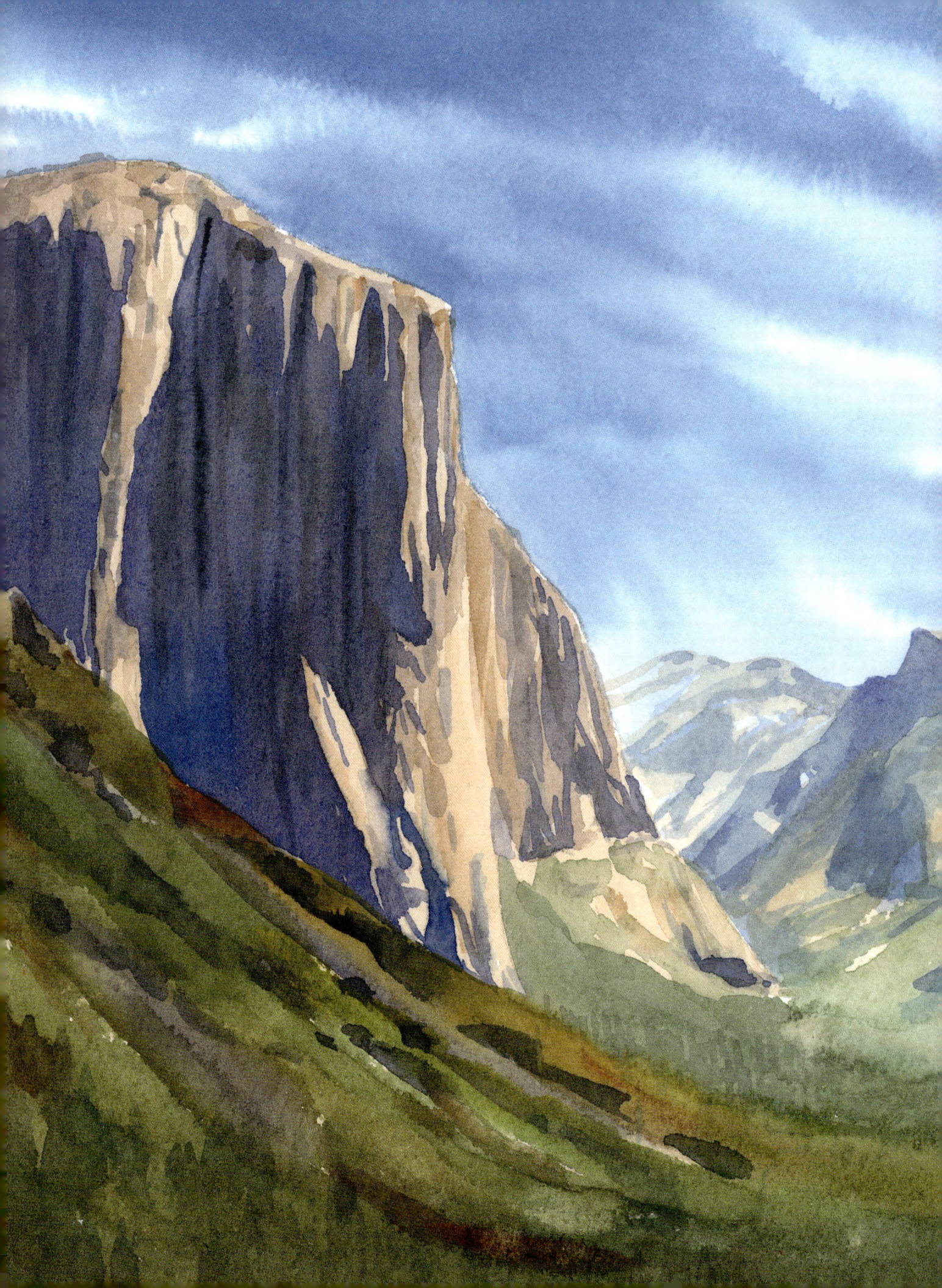

Contents

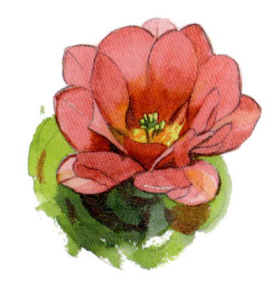

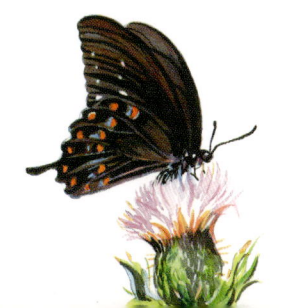

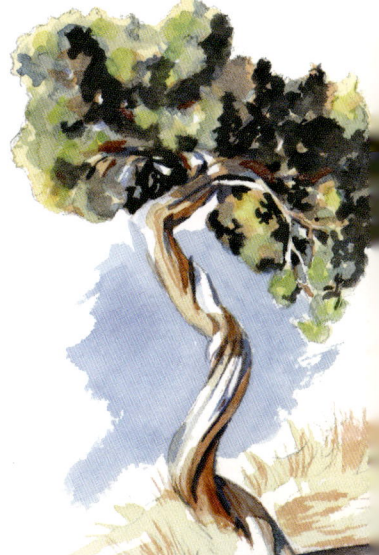

Introduction

AMERICA'S NATIONAL PARKS: A PAINTER'S PARADISE

Welcome! I'm so excited you're here! If you are delighted by nature and love to paint, this book is for you!

Over the years, America's national parks have captured the imaginations of many artists, including the great Albert Bierstadt, Thomas Moran, Carl Rungius, and others. Thousands of creatives from all over come to the parks to marvel at the wonders of creation, to feel at one with nature, and to capture the unfiltered beauty of the great outdoors on paper and canvas.

Do you remember your first divine encounter with nature?

The Grand Canyon was my first national park—I was 14 years old. I had never experienced anything remotely like it. My thirsty inner adventurer was awakened. I knew I would be an explorer for life!

It's hard to find words that adequately describe the ethereal magic of Dream Lake in Rocky Mountain National Park, the implausible grandeur of Yosemite, or the graceful balancing act of Delicate Arch in Arches National Park. Where words fail, images can succeed. As an artist, you possess a special superpower: You can view the world with a vocabulary and skill set that are unavailable to nonartists. Where a casual observer sees a "canyon," you see a jigsaw puzzle of endless compositional potential. Where others see a "mountain," you see light, shadow, color, and texture. There will always be fresh locations to explore and new compositions to discover. One could spend an entire lifetime exploring and painting just one of the national parks and never exhaust the creative possibilities. For this book, I have chosen twenty of the most visited parks, focusing on some of the most breathtaking and iconic locations within each of these.

Paint along with me! Together we will take an unforgettable artistic journey through the American national parks using my favorite medium: watercolors.

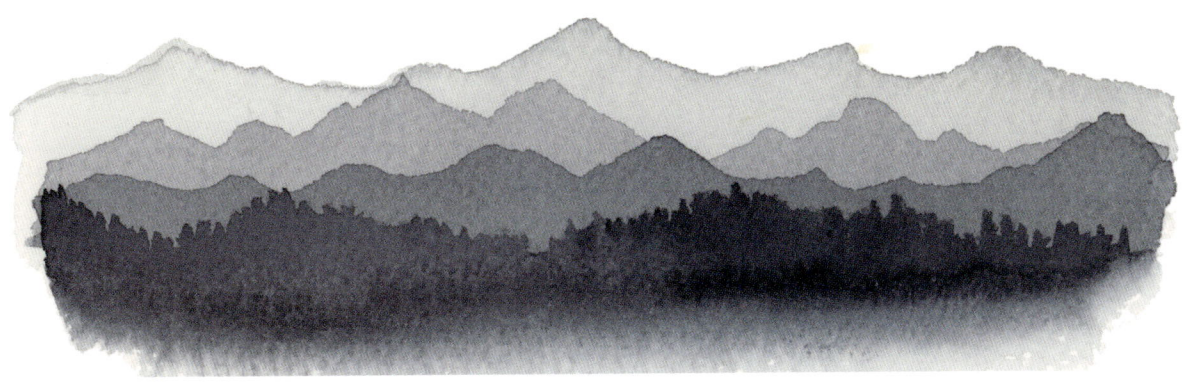

HOW TO USE THIS BOOK

If you are new to watercolor, Part 1 of this book will help you get acquainted with this beautiful and sometimes unpredictable medium. Even if you are a more experienced painter, it's a good idea to look over the materials list and review some of the techniques we will use later in the book. Part 2 includes step-by-step instructions for painting each of the twenty parks from a photo, as well as fun miniature tutorials for painting small studies of plants and animals you might see when visiting the parks. Throughout the book you will see QR codes. You can scan these with the photo app on your phone and tap on the popup link to watch short demonstration videos of each painting. By the end of this book, I hope you will have a solid grasp on how to paint landscapes with watercolors, regardless of the changing scenery, light, texture, and subject matter. You will also have a gorgeous art collection of some of the most beloved locations on Earth. So grab your paints, and let's dive in!

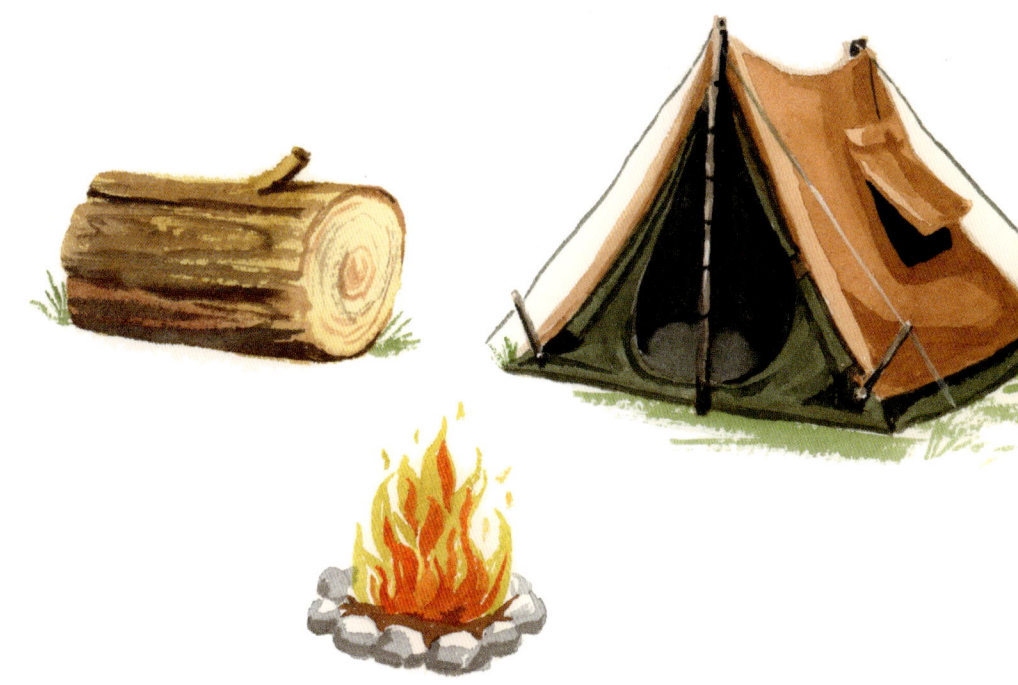

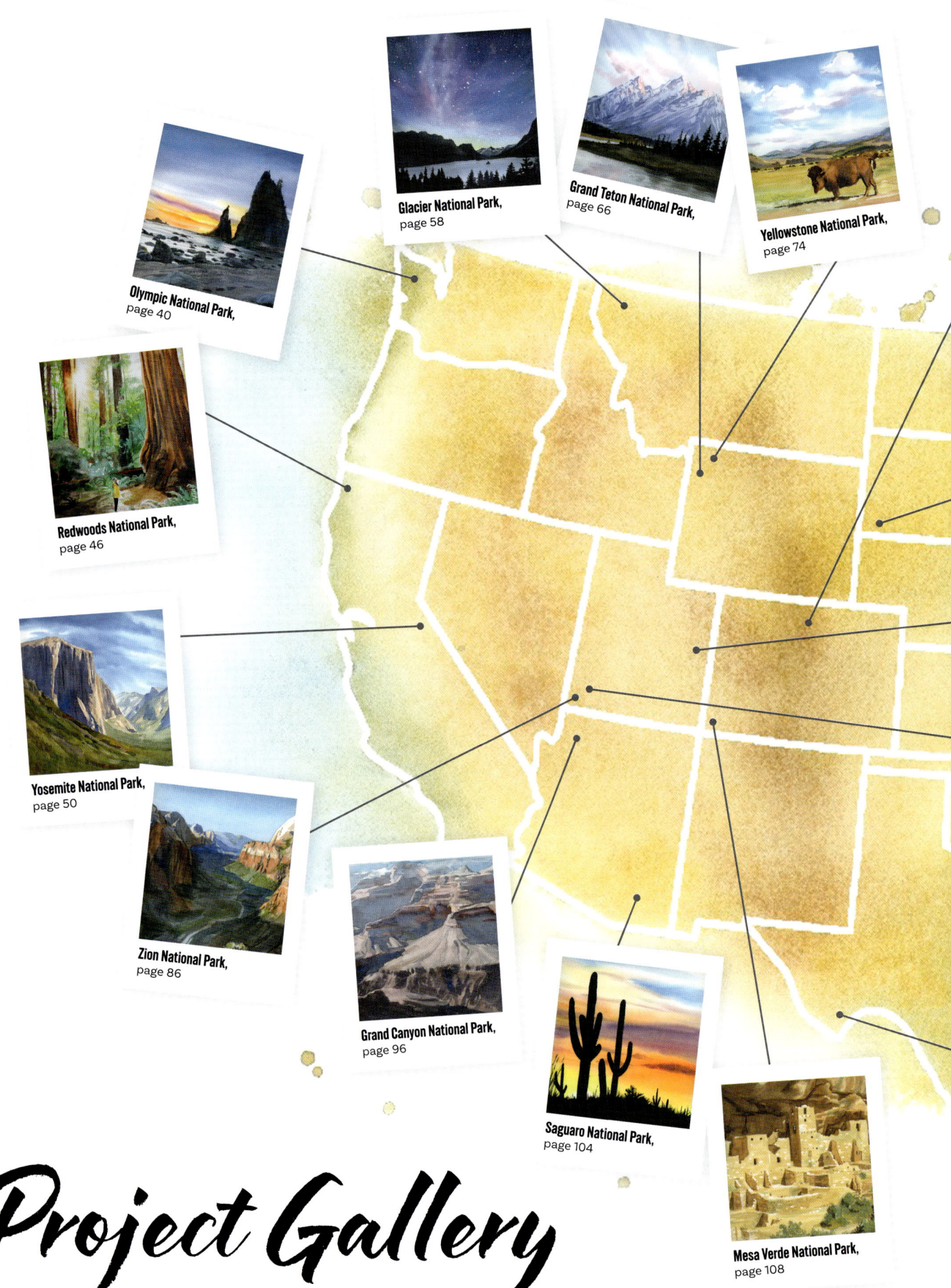

Glacier National Park, page 58

Grand Teton National Park, page 66

Yellowstone National Park, page 74

Olympic National Park, page 40

Redwoods National Park, page 46

Yosemite National Park, page 50

Zion National Park, page 86

Grand Canyon National Park, page 96

Saguaro National Park, page 104

Mesa Verde National Park, page 108

Project Gallery

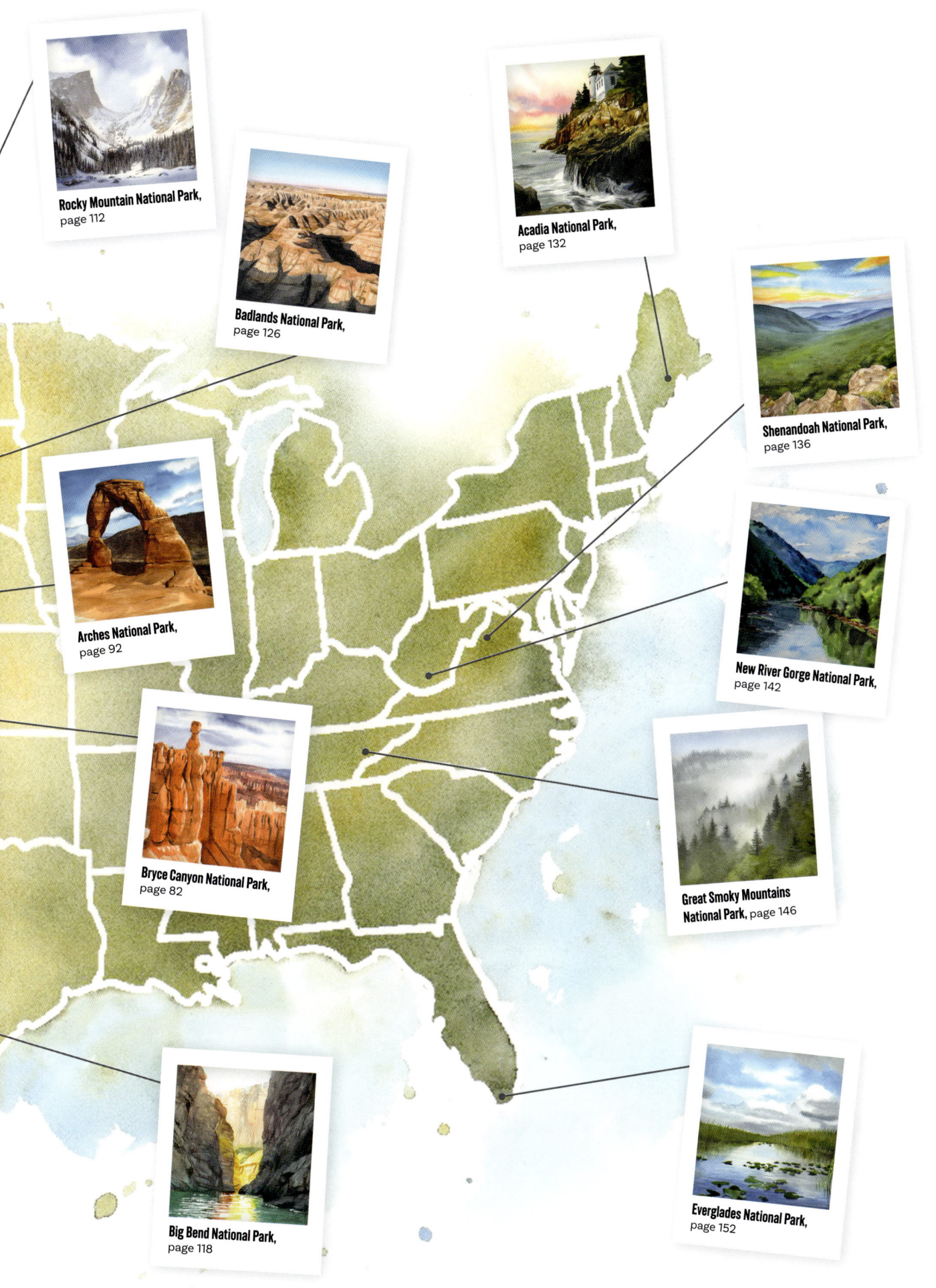

Rocky Mountain National Park, page 112

Badlands National Park, page 126

Acadia National Park, page 132

Shenandoah National Park, page 136

Arches National Park, page 92

New River Gorge National Park, page 142

Bryce Canyon National Park, page 82

Great Smoky Mountains National Park, page 146

Big Bend National Park, page 118

Everglades National Park, page 152

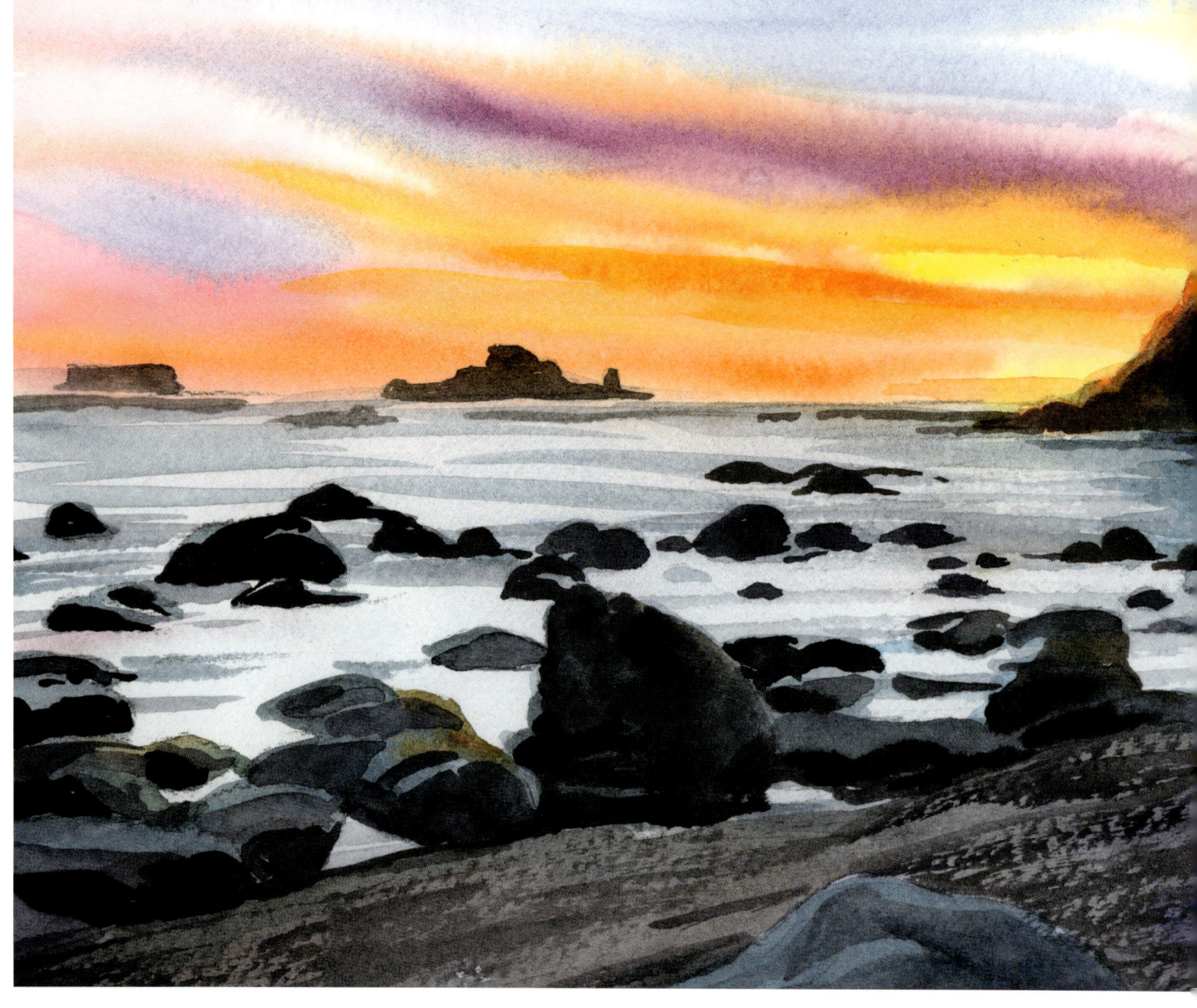

Part 1
GETTING STARTED

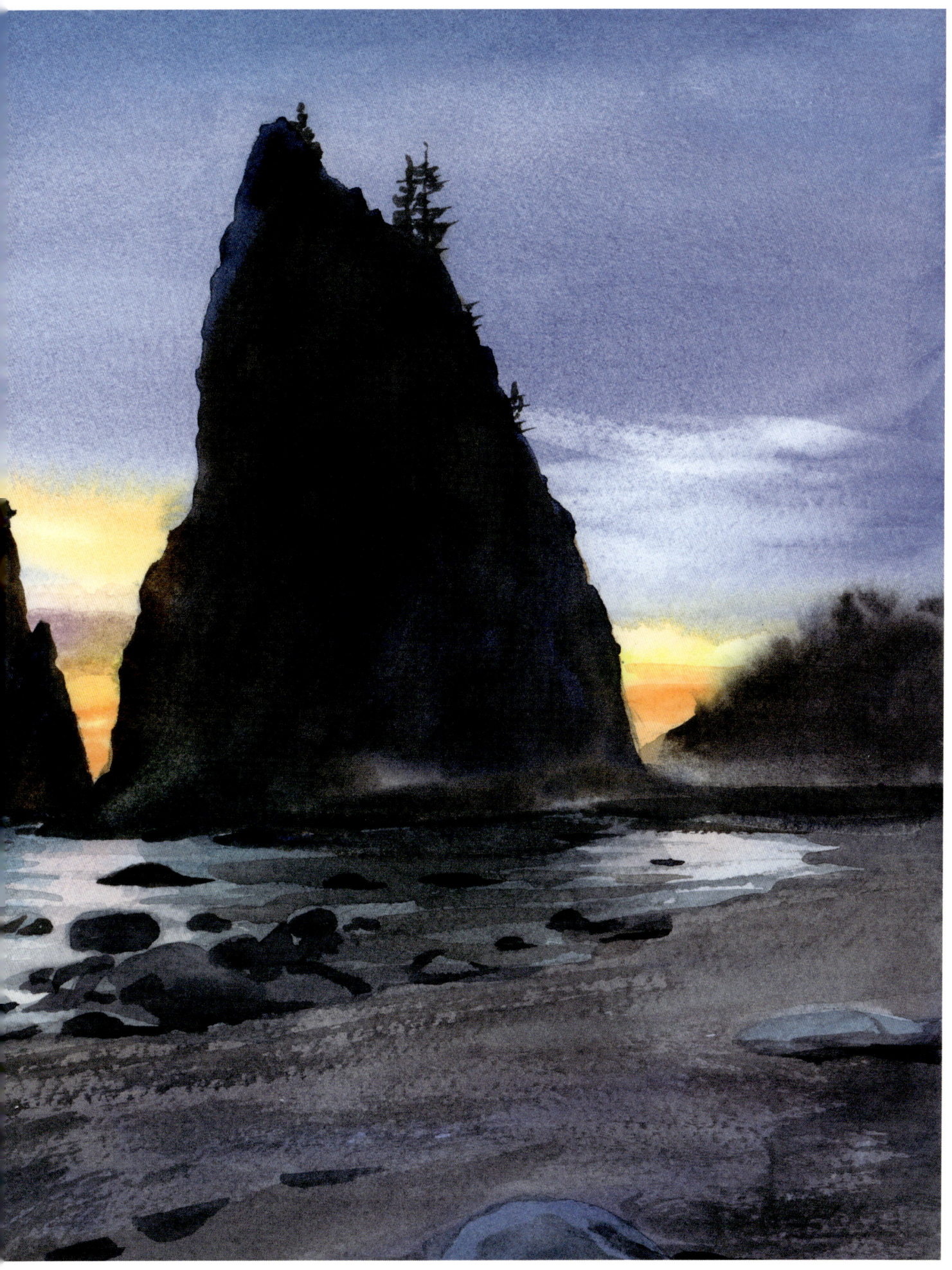

Materials

If you have done some watercolor painting, you may already have the basic supplies. If you're just getting started, it's not necessary to rush out and buy a bunch of supplies (although it can be fun!). After years of painting and experimenting with different materials, I have found what works for me and what will work for the projects in this book.

PAINTS

I have tested out hundreds of different paint colors and brands. I will sometimes rotate out paints, but there are certain colors that remain constant on my palette. A well-rounded palette should have two sets of primary colors (i.e., yellow, blue, and red): a warm set and a cool set. We'll discuss color temperature in the next section about basic color theory. You should also have a "mixer" like burnt sienna and a dark such as Payne's gray or indigo, and it's a good idea to have at least one of each of the secondary colors: green, violet, and orange.

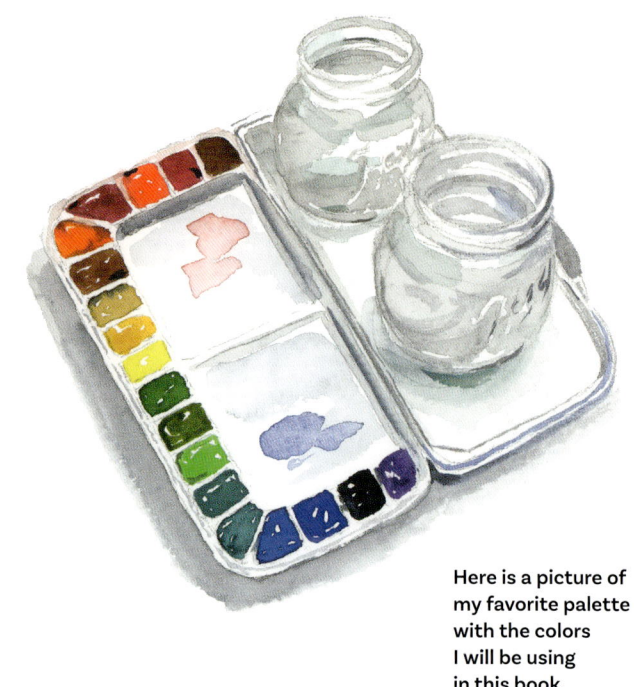

Here is a picture of my favorite palette with the colors I will be using in this book.

These are the colors I used in the projects in this book.

Daniel Smith quinacridone rose

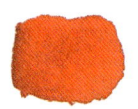
Holbein scarlet lake

Holbein permanent alizarin crimson

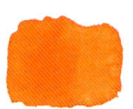
Winsor & Newton transparent orange

Daniel Smith burnt sienna

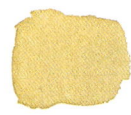
Holbein yellow ochre

Holbein gamboge nova

Daniel Smith hansa yellow light

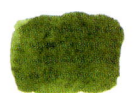
Daniel Smith sap green

Holbein marine blue

QOR phthalo blue (GS or green shade

Daniel Smith ultramarine blue

Daniel Smith indigo

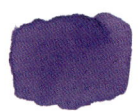
Holbein permanent violet

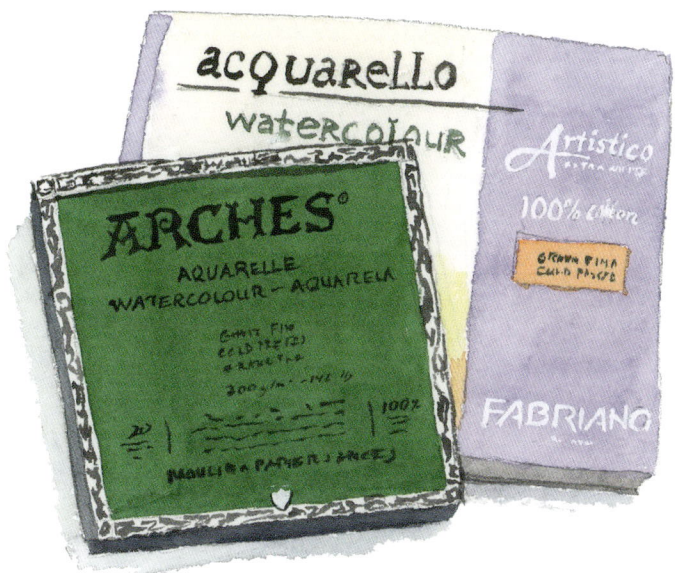

Watercolor blocks, which come in various sizes, are my favorite format for watercolor papers.

The 9 x 12-inch (23 x 30.5 cm)-sized paper can be used to create either vertical or horizontal compositions. I will sometimes also border the paper with artist's tape to create an easily frameable 8 x 10-inch (20.5 x 25.5 cm) aspect ratio.

PAPER

Every great watercolor painting starts out as a blank sheet of paper! The kind of paper you choose really matters if you want to achieve the best results. Because it can affect the way different watercolor techniques "work," paper is the most important item on your list of materials.

I recommend using 100-percent cotton watercolor paper. Cotton paper is generally more expensive than the readily available wood pulp papers, but it is a much more durable surface. Watercolor paper comes in several different textures: hot pressed, cold pressed, and rough pressed. Choosing your paper texture is really a matter of preference, but I like cold-pressed paper because it has just the right amount of "tooth."

Paper comes in sheets, pads, or blocks. In this book, I will be using two different brands and sizes: a 9 x 12-inch (23 x 30.5 cm) block of Fabriano Artistico 140-pound (300 gsm), cotton, cold-pressed paper, and a 7.9 x 7.9-inch (20 x 20 cm) block of Arches 140-pound (300 gsm), cotton, cold-pressed paper. The advantage of using a block versus loose sheets or pads is that the sides of the paper are glued down. This allows you to apply multiple washes of paint and water without worrying about your paper warping and buckling. The painting will dry completely flat, and then you can remove it from the block using a palette knife.

BRUSHES

While it's nice to have a large arsenal of brushes in different shapes and sizes, I find that the brushes I keep coming back to are round brushes. The variety of shapes, edges, and washes you can achieve with just a round brush are enough to paint almost anything! In this book, I will be using round brushes in sizes 4, 6, 8, and 10. I prefer the springy quality of synthetic or blended bristle brushes—they are also more affordable than natural hair brushes, which are typically made with squirrel or sable hair. Synthetic brushes also hold less water than natural bristle brushes, which makes water control more manageable for beginners.

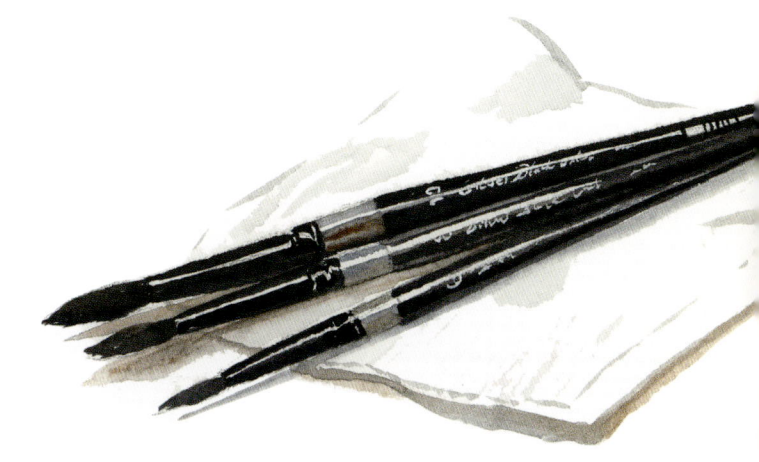

I prefer synthetic or blended bristle round brushes.

OTHER MATERIALS

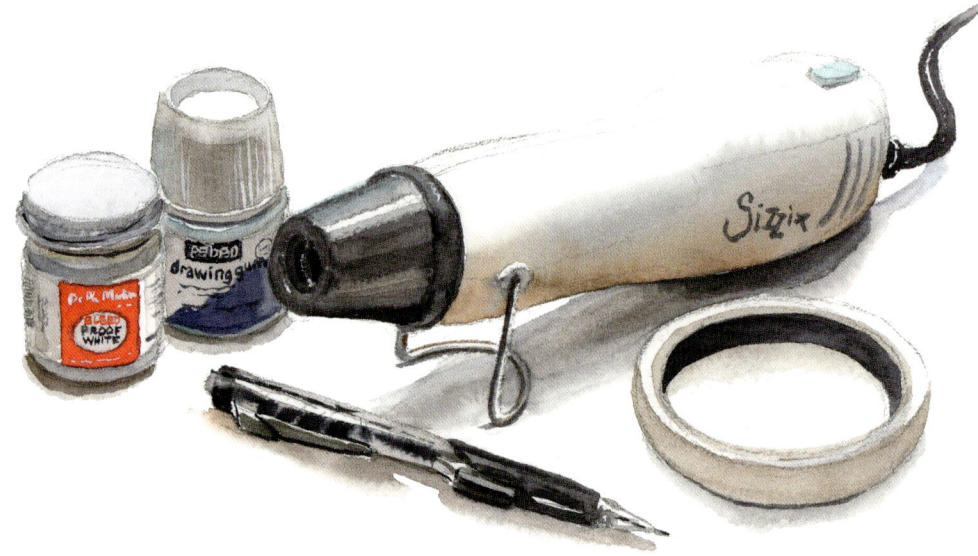

You'll need a few supplies, including opaque white paint, masking fluid, a mechanical pencil, a heat tool, and masking tape.

For the projects in this book, I list what brushes, paper, and paints I used. However, I always have a few other materials on hand, and you should, too.

Water Jars

I use glass jars, but any container will work! It's a good idea to have two jars—one for cleaning your dirty paint brush, and one for painting clear washes.

Palette

It's helpful to have a palette with large wells for mixing. I really like my Mijello airtight eighteen-well plastic palette.

Paper Towel or Sponge

This is an essential supply, not only for keeping your work area clean, but also for controlling how much water is in your brush!

Spray Bottle

A spray bottle filled with water makes it easy to wet your paper.

Masking Tape

This is a great tool for securing your paper (if you're working with loose sheets), creating borders, or even for masking straight lines like on the sides of buildings or the horizon line of a seascape.

Mechanical Pencil

If you are freehand sketching your drawing, a mechanical pencil works great! It does not require sharpening and comes with an eraser. I prefer pencils with a 0.7-mm lead.

Kneaded Eraser

This type of eraser is useful for gently removing pencil lines.

Heat Tool or Hair Dryer

I will sometimes use a heat tool to speed up drying time between layers of wet paint. To prevent scorching the paper, it's best to use this on low heat and only after the paper has dried enough so that it's no longer glistening.

Masking Fluid

Masking fluid is a liquid latex that can be painted on to mask areas of your painting and protect them from being painted over. I like the blue-tinted masking fluid because it's easy to see where you apply it.

Opaque White Paint

I use the white of the paper for most of the whites in my watercolor paintings, but sometimes it's much easier to use an opaque white to paint small highlights and tiny white details. I use Dr. Ph. Martin's Bleedproof White, but white gouache works great, too! Many watercolor sets come with Chinese white, but I've found it's not quite opaque enough for my liking and I never use that color.

Sketching
AND VALUE STUDIES

Creating an accurate sketch before you start painting is one of the most crucial steps in achieving a successful piece of artwork. A well-thought-out sketch allows you to plan the placement of elements in your painting. It helps you determine the composition, balance, and focal points of the artwork. This is particularly important in watercolor painting, where correcting mistakes can be challenging.

FREEHAND SKETCHING

For many of my paintings, I prefer to freehand sketch by closely observing my reference and carefully comparing the shapes. The goal is to accurately draw each shape and ensure it correctly relates to the surrounding shapes. This involves thinking abstractly about shapes and values, rather than labeling them.

In the example at right, to replicate this small landscape, it's important to observe the relationships between the shapes. Notice how the slope on the left reaches a third of the way up the composition. The highest peak extends to two-thirds of the total height, and the apex of the tallest tree is positioned three-quarters of the way across the composition.

These are just some examples of the mental comparisons we make while freehand sketching. Like any skill, it becomes easier with practice.

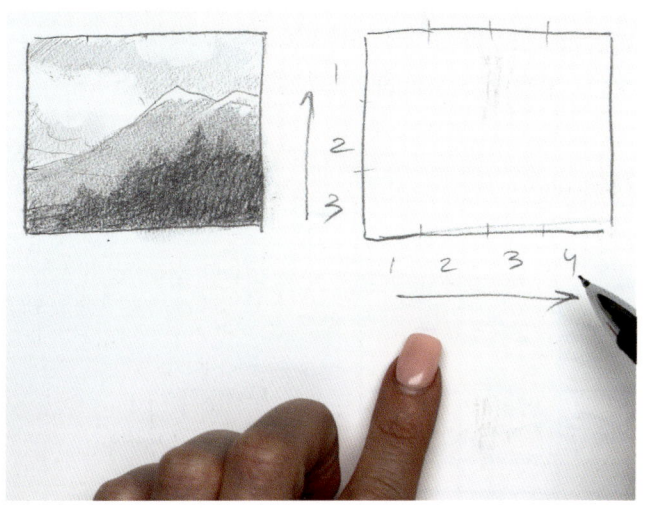

Divide the height and width of the composition so you can easily see the positions of shapes.

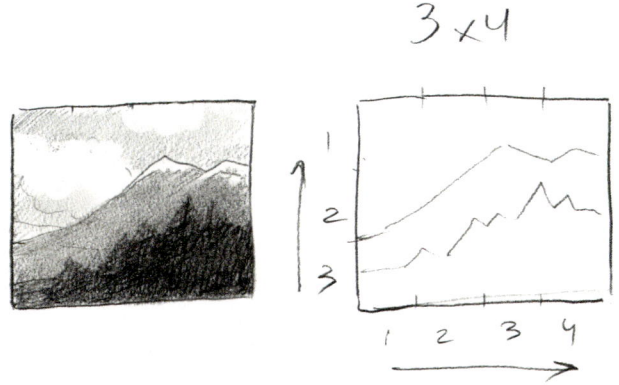

Freehand sketching the shapes becomes easier with practice.

GRID METHOD

If freehand sketching feels intimidating or you are concerned about smudging your watercolor paper, the grid method is a helpful alternative. Begin by drawing a simple grid over your reference photo, either using photo editing software or by printing the image and drawing the grid with a ruler.

Ensure your watercolor paper matches the exact aspect ratio of your reference photo. For instance, if your reference photo is 4 x 5 (10 x 13 cm), you could scale up to an 8 x 10 (20 x 25 cm) or 16 x 20 (40 x 51 cm) painting. Use water-soluble pencils or light graphite to draw a matching grid on your paper. The grid divides your drawing into smaller, manageable sections, helping you accurately judge the spatial relationships between shapes on a smaller scale.

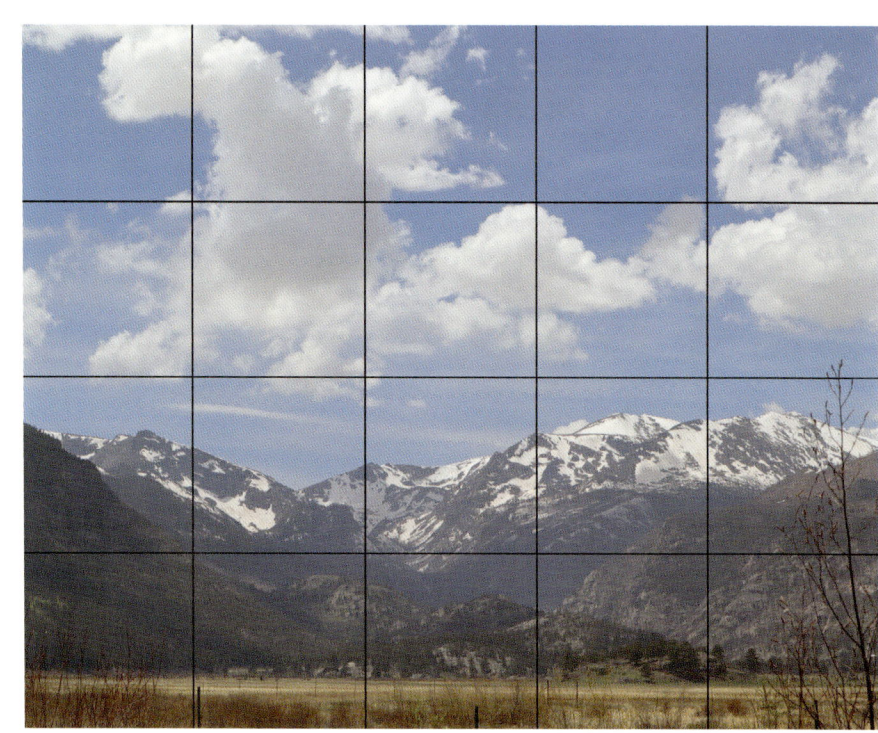

Add a grid over the photo.

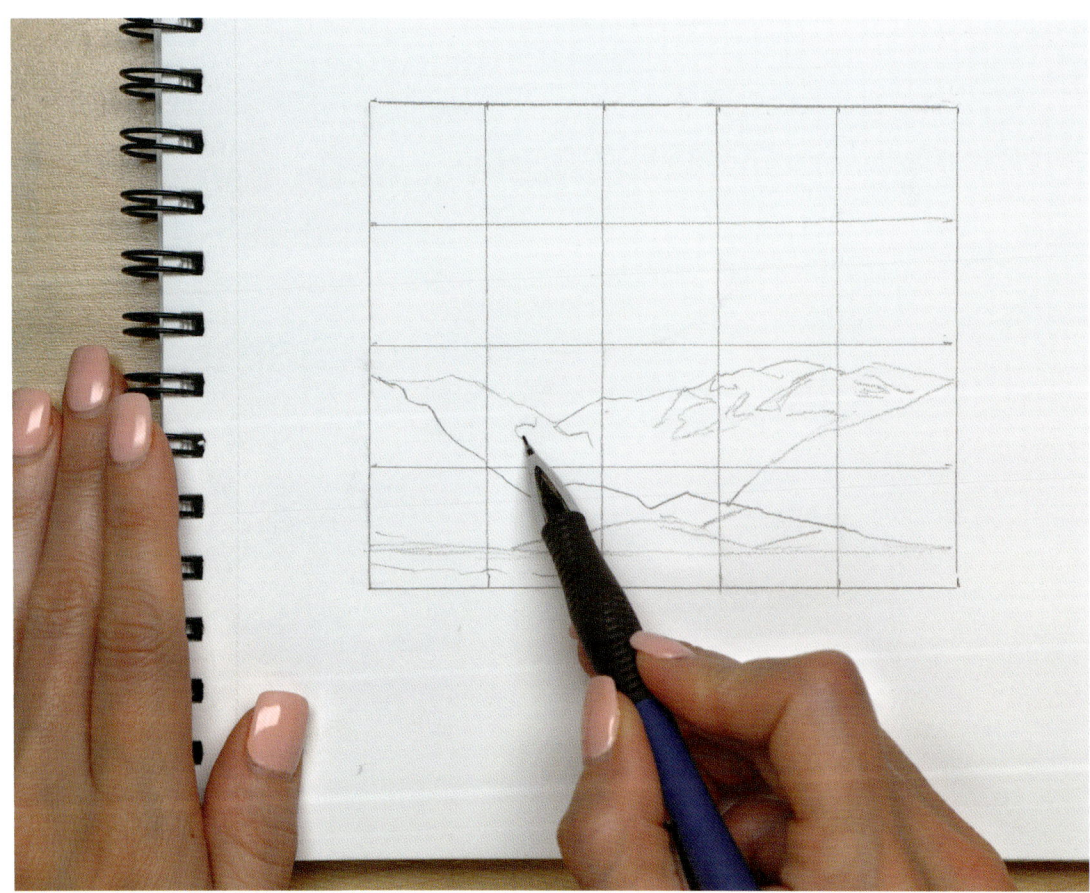

The grid divides your drawing into smaller, more manageable sections.

TRACING WITH TRANSFER PAPER

I highly recommend using transfer paper for creating fast and efficient and accurate outlines—it's the best method for achieving a clean, precise sketch. This is the method I use for getting the quickest and most accurate sketch.

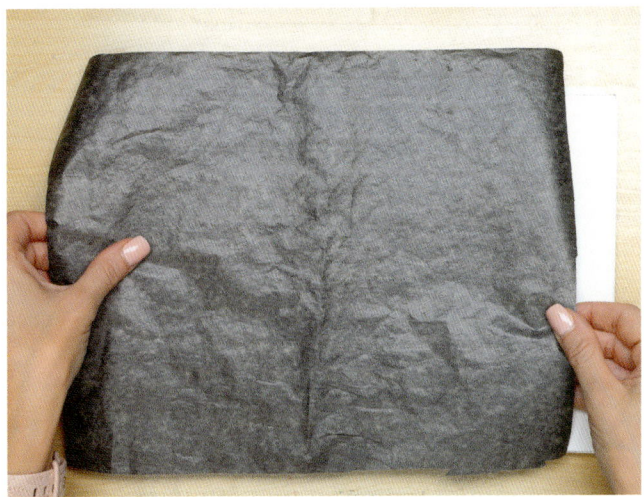

1. Print the image to match the exact size of your painting. Position the transfer paper, shiny side down, on your watercolor paper.

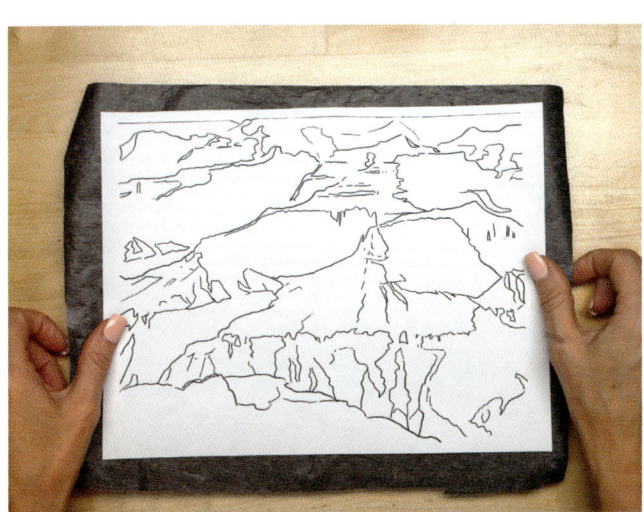

2. Place the line drawing or photo on top of the transfer paper.

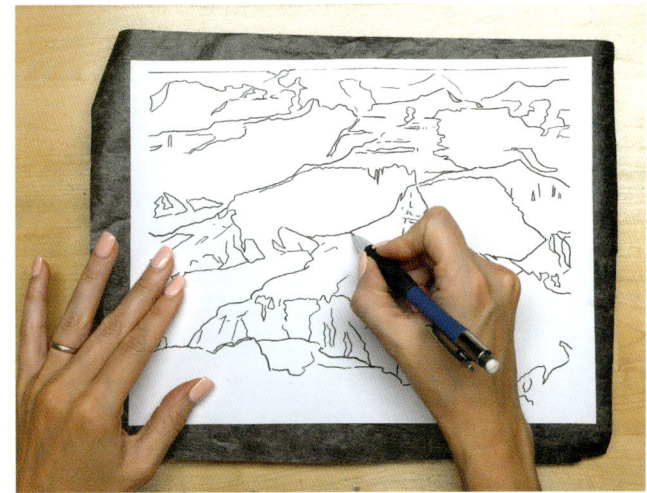

3. Trace over the lines with a pen or pencil.

A lightbox is another easy way to trace your image onto your watercolor paper. A lightbox illuminates an image from beneath, making it possible to see the lines and shapes through your paper. You can find a light box at almost any art supply store.

VALUE STUDIES

As a helpful warm-up before starting a full-size painting, try creating a small monochromatic value study. I use 4 x 4-inch (10 x 10 cm) paper. This simplifies the composition and will clarify the light and dark areas in the image.

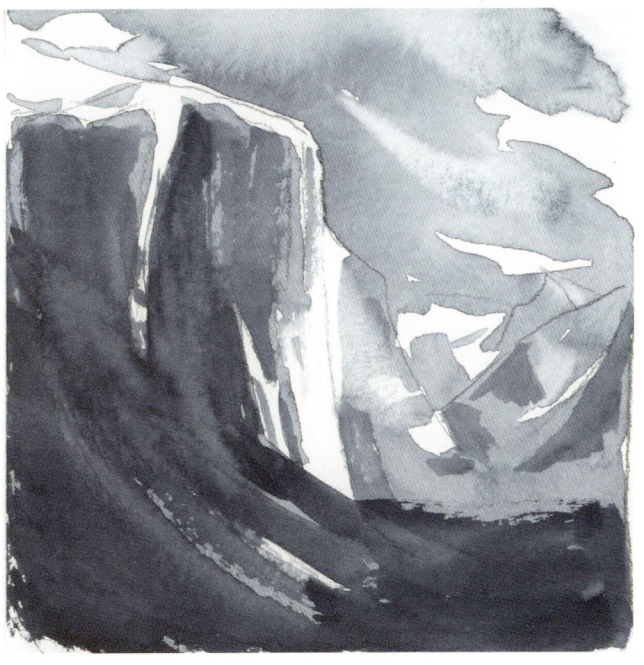

My value study for the Yosemite National Park painting.

Working FROM PHOTOS

When painting from photographs, several key factors
need to be considered to achieve the best results.

CHOOSE HIGH-QUALITY PHOTOGRAPHS

Set yourself up for success by working with images that
have good resolution, clear details, and strong lighting.
The best times to take photos are typically in the
morning or late afternoon when the sun's angled light
creates interesting scenarios with strong shadow shapes.

EDIT FOR COMPOSITION

While it might be tempting to simply replicate your
photograph, most images benefit from some cropping,
adjustments, and editing to enhance the composition.
I often use Photoshop to experiment with different
aspect ratios and tweak the contrast, brightness, or
saturation. There are also many excellent apps available
for editing photos on your smartphone.

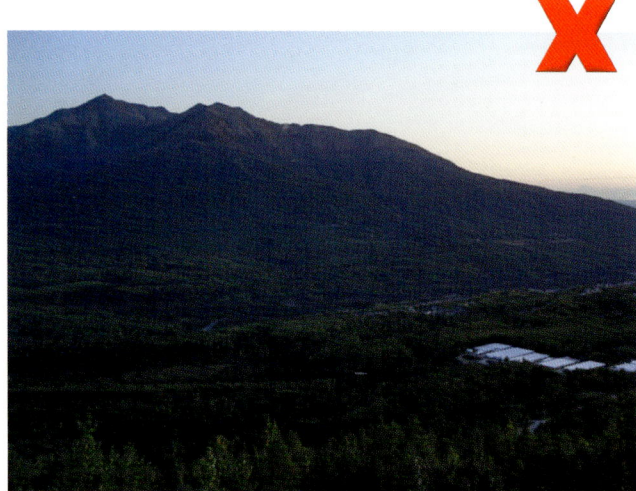

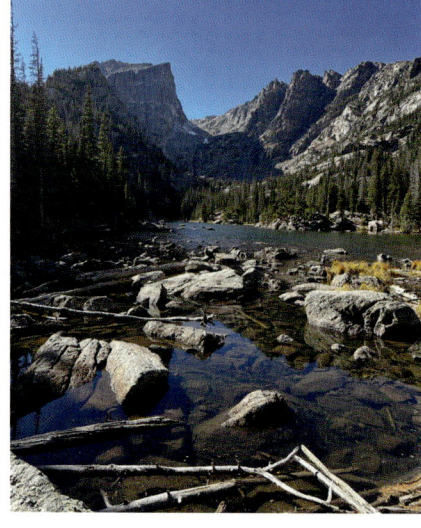

Original
photograph.

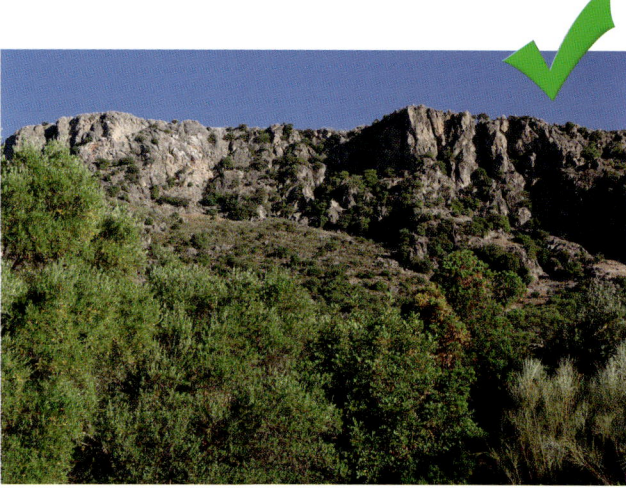

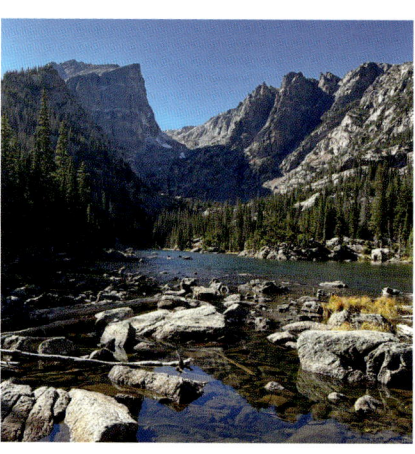

Edited
photograph.

AVOID PAINTING TOO MANY DETAILS

Photos capture *every* detail in a scene, but not all these elements need to be included in your painting. Simplify wherever you can, particularly in shadowed areas. Emphasize the major light and shadow shapes.

A helpful technique is to squint. This reveals the biggest details that need to be captured and shows what is less important.

CHANGE THINGS!

Don't be a slavish copyist of the photo. You can take artistic license and adjust, remove, add, exaggerate, or enhance any part of the photo that you wish!

USE MULTIPLE REFERENCES

Getting the "perfect" photo can be challenging, so it's often necessary to combine several images to create the painting you envision. For my painting of the Tetons, I'm working with old printed photos from the 1980s, with permission from my friend and fellow artist Mitch Castor. I love the composition with close-up trees silhouetted against the mountains, but I also want to include the pink lighting from a square image. I scanned the photos and used Photoshop to overlay one on top of the other. While it's not perfect, it helps me visualize the composition, allowing me to apply these elements to my final painting.

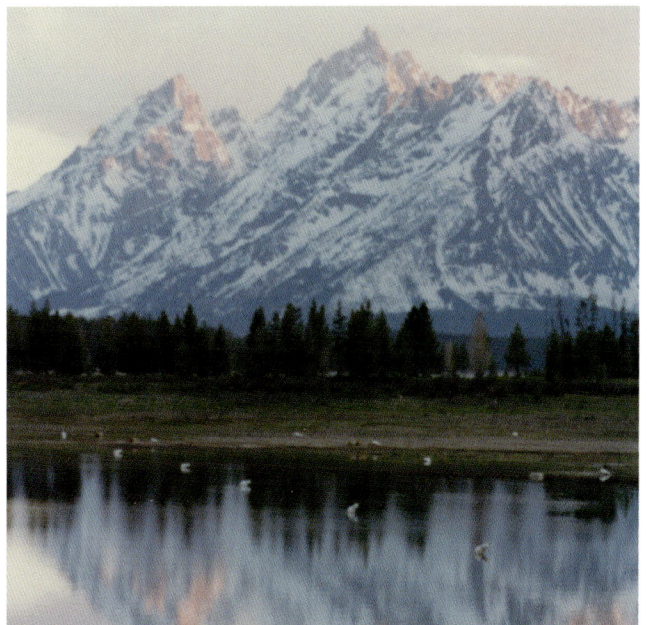

This image captures some pink lighting that I want to use.

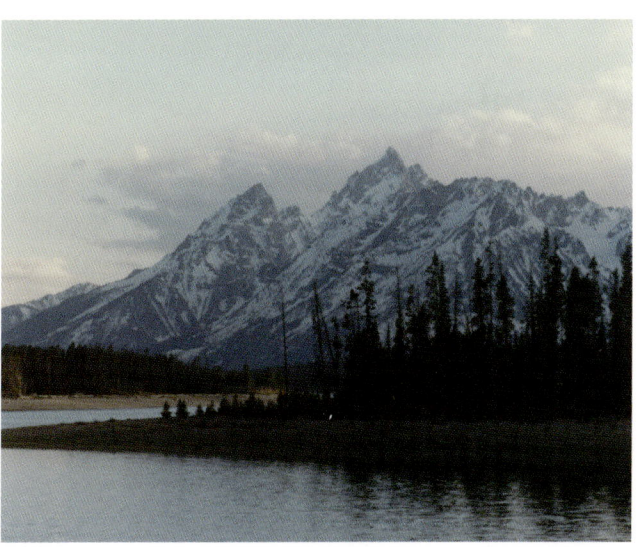

I like the close-up trees in this photo.

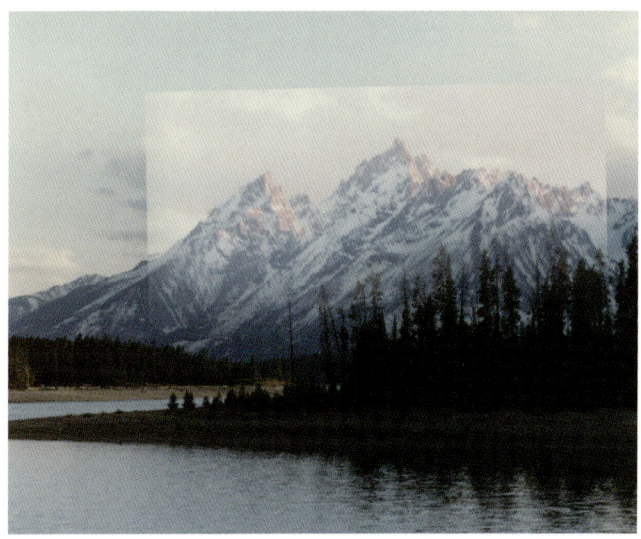

I combined two photos to create my reference for my painting of Grand Teton National Park.

Plein Air PAINTING

If you ever get the chance to paint from life, seize it! Some of my most cherished memories are of being surrounded by nature, observing its details closely, and forever capturing those moments in my artwork. Plein air painting can be challenging, but it's a valuable experience that will help you grow and improve as an artist. Here are my top tips for successfully painting with watercolors outdoors.

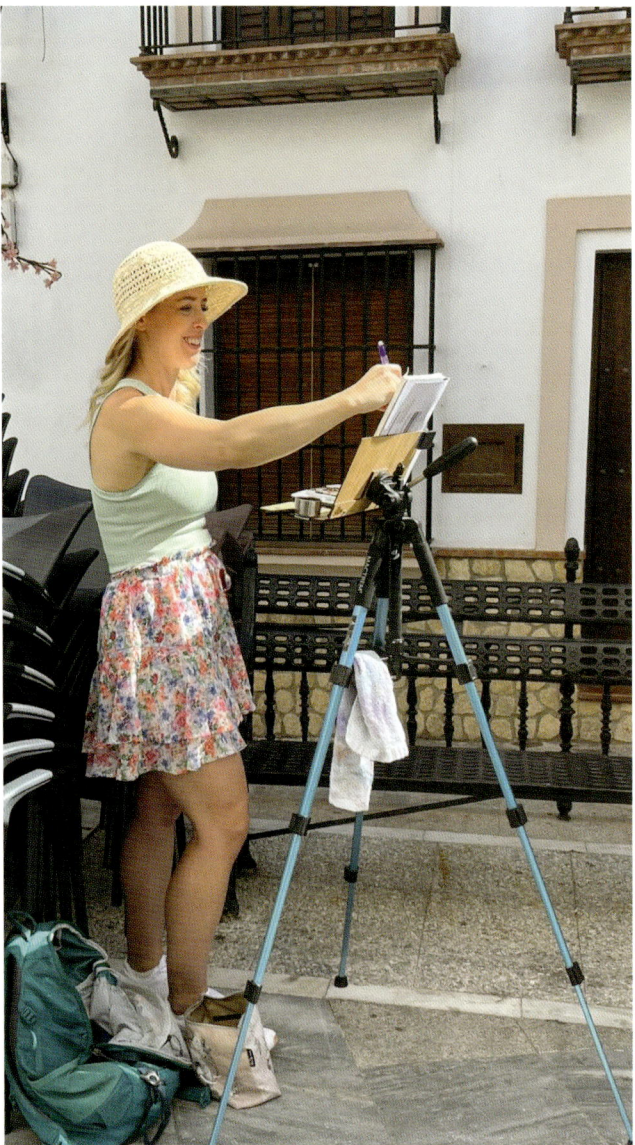

Plein air painting is something every artist should try.

SIMPLIFY YOUR GEAR

Make sure your setup is lightweight and portable! I like to be able to squeeze everything into my backpack. These are the items I typically bring on a plein air excursion:

- Lightweight tripod and easel
- Watercolor half-pan paints in a metal tin
- Small water jar and water bottle
- Rag or paper towel
- Travel brushes
- Watercolor paper block or journal
- Spray bottle
- Pencil and eraser

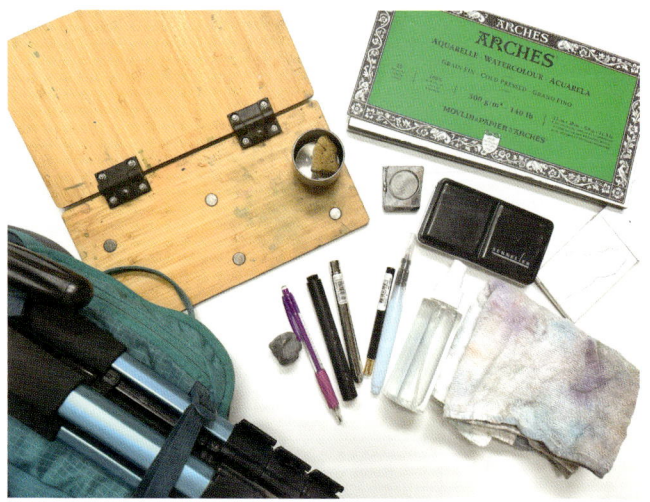

Here's what you'll need for plein air watercolor supplies.

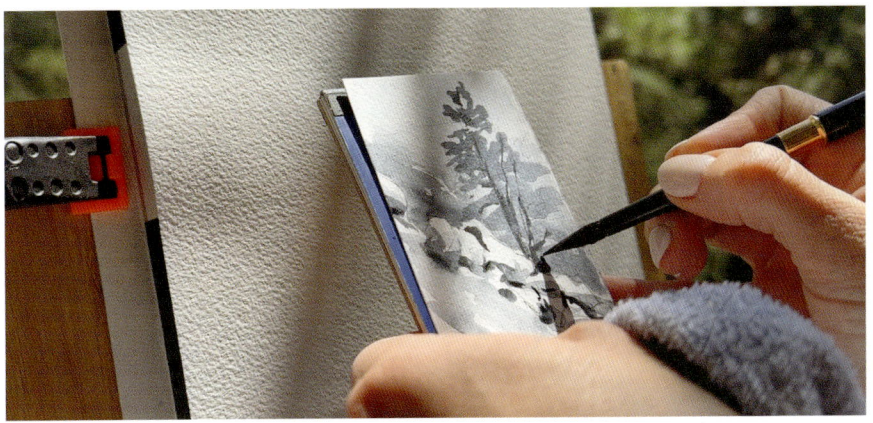

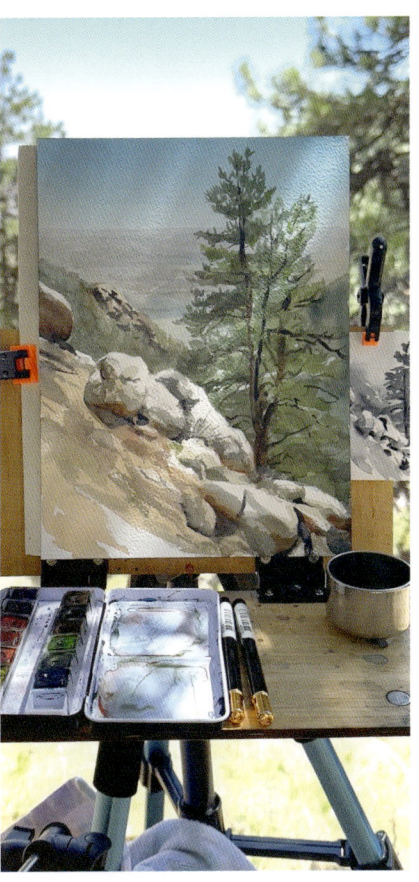

SELECT YOUR SUBJECT

Choose a simple scene and plan your composition. Take a photo of the scene to help you visualize it within the borders of a two-dimensional piece of paper. Do a couple of quick thumbnail sketches to plan your composition. Try to simplify it into just two or three values.

WORK QUICKLY

Outdoor lighting conditions shift quickly. Use large brushes and concentrate on the overall shapes instead of diving into details too early. Be deliberate in layering your colors, starting with light tones and gradually building up to darker ones.

USE A LIMITED PALETTE

Stick to colors you're familiar with, using a few primary hues (both warm and cool) along with versatile mixers like burnt sienna and Payne's gray. This limited palette can create a range of colors while ensuring cohesive harmony in your painting.

BE MINDFUL OF YOUR SURROUNDINGS

Dress according to the weather: I wear a wide-brimmed hat and sunscreen, and sometimes bug spray is essential. Stick to public areas and trails, and respect nature. Leave no trace by packing out all your supplies and any trash. Always inform someone of your whereabouts and carry a fully charged cell phone.

TAKE LOTS OF REFERENCE PHOTOS!

If you can't finish your painting on location, you can complete it in your studio. Take plenty of photos to document your experience and use them as references later.

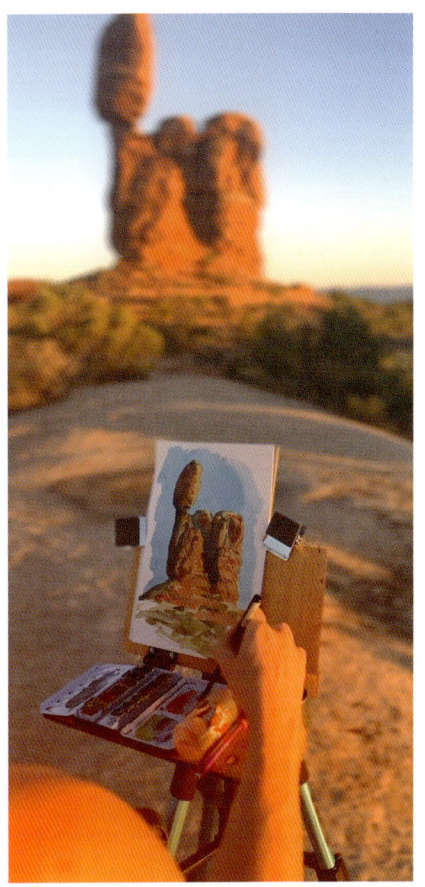

Basic Techniques

To successfully follow along and complete the projects in this book, it's important to understand some basic watercolor techniques.

TYPES OF WASHES

Watercolor washes can be painted on dry or wet paper. There are three essential types of washes.

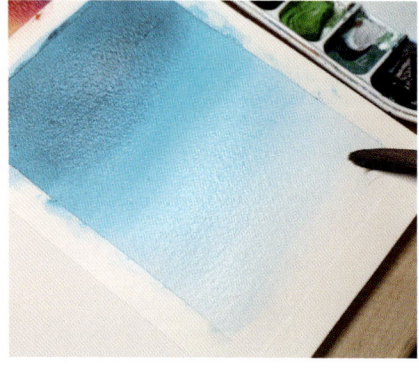

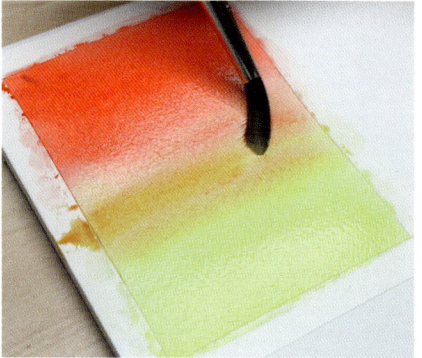

Flat Wash: This is a consistent, even layer of watercolor paint applied over an area. To paint a flat wash, load a brush with paint and spread it evenly to create a uniform color.

Graded Wash: This is a wash that gradually changes in value from dark to light or light to dark. This effect is achieved by diluting the paint with more water as you move across the paper.

Variegated Wash: This is a wash where two or more colors blend into each other on the paper, creating a soft transition. This is often used for skies.

Experiment with creating your own versions of each wash. Regular practice of these techniques will keep your skills sharp and eventually make them second nature.

Tip

Use a large brush if you need to cover a large surface area with your wash, and mix up plenty of paint on your palette before you begin.

WET AND DRY TECHNIQUES

There are a few basic watercolor techniques we'll go over here.

Wet-on-Wet

This technique involves applying wet paint to a wet surface and allowing the colors to spread and bleed into one another. Although it requires practice, mastering this method is rewarding, as it produces playful blends, soft edges, and atmospheric effects. Painting washes is a low-pressure way to practice these essential skills and to warm up before starting a painting session.

The wet-on-wet technique.

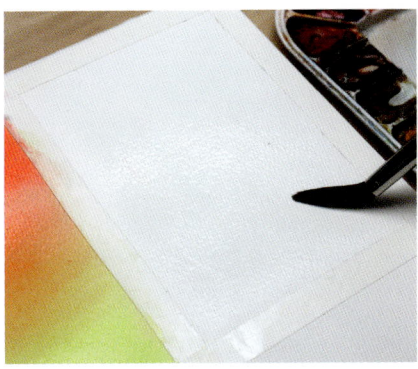

1. Use masking tape to outline a rectangle on your watercolor paper. Apply clear water within this area, ensuring the surface is glossy and evenly wet with no puddles.

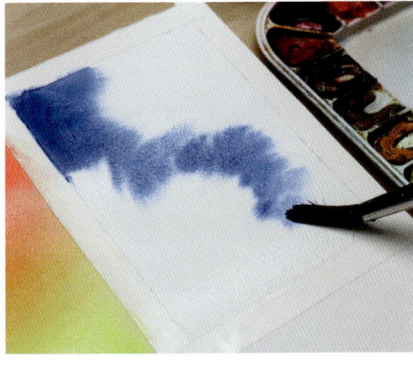

2. Load your brush with paint of a creamy or half-and-half consistency in any color of your choice. Then, paint a shape within the wet rectangle.

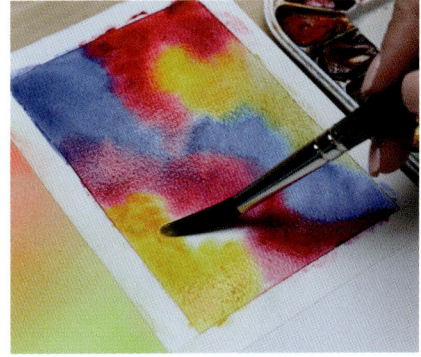

3. Rinse your brush before changing colors, then add one or two more colors, letting the edges blend naturally on the wet paper. Pay close attention to the amount of water in your brush. If the brush is too wet, it may cause backwash (also known as the "cauliflower effect") on your paper. If the brush is too dry, it might lift paint from the surface, making the wash appear blotchy. Aim to match the wetness of your brush to that of the paper.

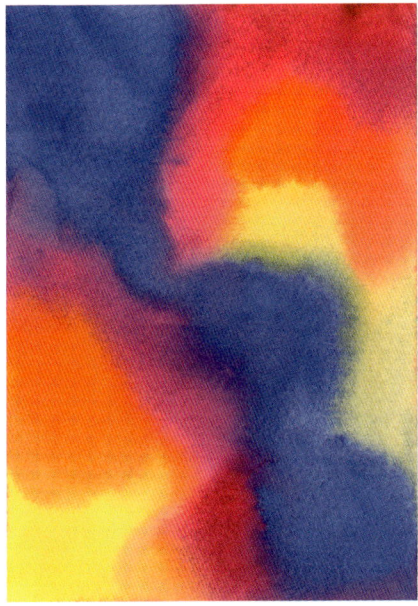

The finished
wet-on-wet wash.

Wet-on-Dry

This technique involves applying wet paint to dry paper, resulting in sharper, more defined edges. It provides excellent control over each brush stroke and is ideal for achieving fine details, sharp edges, and crisp features. Wet-on-dry is an ideal technique for small details and areas of the painting that require precision and control.

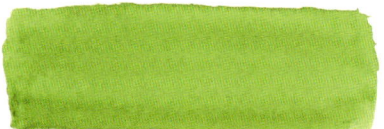

The wet-on-dry technique.

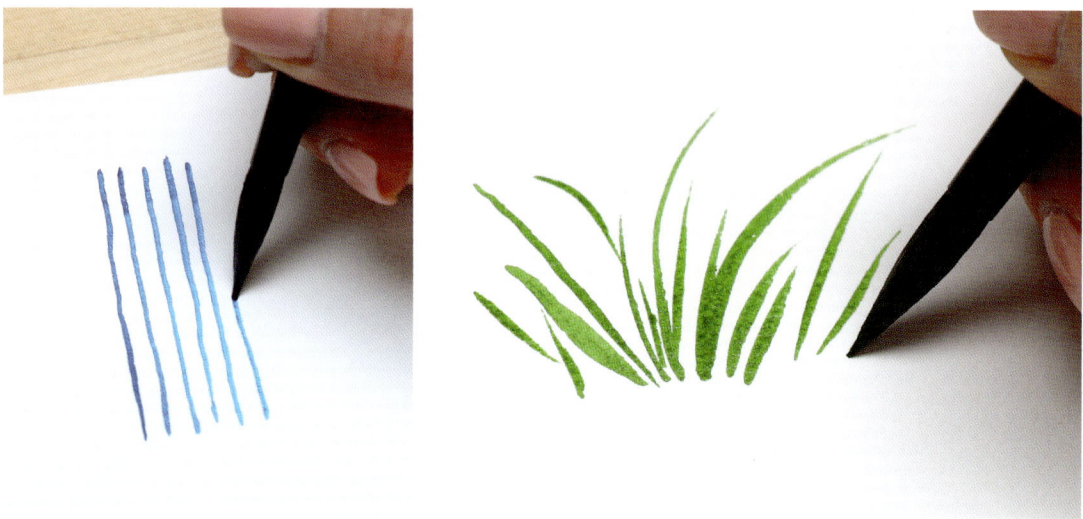

To practice wet-on-dry, experiment with different brush strokes. Use your round brush to create thin lines, thick lines, curved shapes, and flat washes.

You can soften the edges by gently swiping a clean, damp brush along the edge of your still-wet shape to blend and smooth.

Dry Brush

This technique involves using a relatively dry brush with minimal water, which allows the texture of the paper to show through. It produces a rough, textured effect, making it ideal for details such as tree bark, animal fur, or rough surfaces like rocks.

Examples of the dry-brush technique.

Glazing

Glazing is a technique that showcases the transparency of watercolor by applying a layer of color over a dry layer of paint. This method helps artists build color intensity, add depth, or adjust the tone without disrupting the underlying paint. It's important that your paper is completely dry before applying the glaze.

In this example, you can see the difference between wet-on-wet and glazing. The red circle was painted while the yellow shape was still wet, resulting in a soft blend between the two colors. In contrast, the blue circle was painted over the completely dry yellow shape, creating a clean, sharp edge.

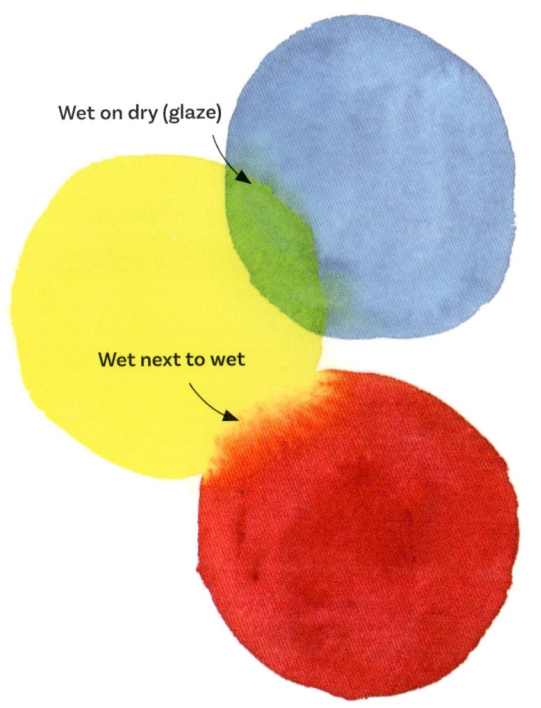

Wet on dry (glaze)

Wet next to wet

The blue circle was painted after the yellow circle was dry, whereas the red circle was painted while the yellow circle was still wet. You can see the glazing effect where the blue overlaps the yellow.

Basic Color Theory

Understanding basic color theory is crucial because it lays the groundwork for creating visually compelling and harmonious art. When you know which colors complement each other and why, you can make more informed decisions about your color choices in paintings. This knowledge also allows you to manipulate the perception of depth, light, and shadow, which is especially important for creating luminous landscapes.

Color has three distinct characteristics: hue, value, and intensity. In addition to their inherent characteristics, each color has a warm or cool bias. Cool colors tend to have a hint of blue, while warm colors lean slightly toward red. However, a color's temperature is not fixed—it shifts depending on the surrounding colors.

Hue refers to what we commonly think of as "color," such as the names of colors on the spectrum—red, yellow, blue, purple, green, and orange. These are pure hues with the most vibrant and intense color.

Value refers to the lightness or darkness of a color. In watercolor, the darkest values are achieved by using paint straight out of the tube. We can lighten the value of the color by adding water.

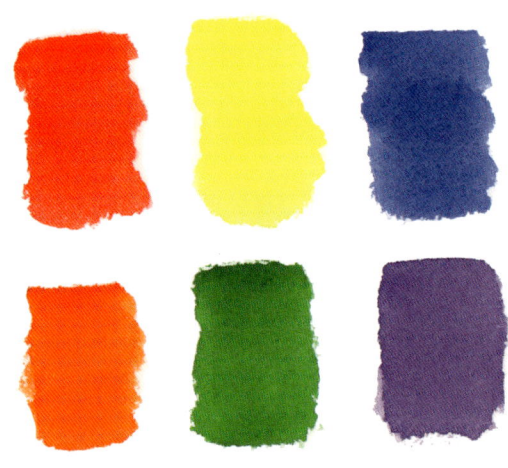

The six basic hues, or pure colors.

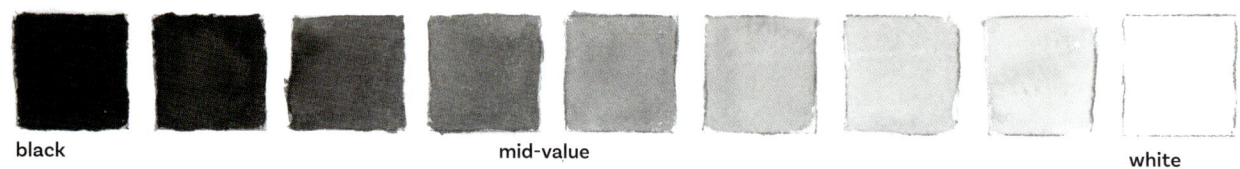

black   mid-value   white

Try making a value scale like this to see the range of values you can make with just one color.

Intensity, also known as *saturation,* describes how bright or dull a color is. A highly saturated color is very vibrant, while a less saturated color appears more muted. Unsaturated colors tend to look closer to black, gray, or white. You can adjust saturation by diluting the paint to let more of the paper's white show through, or by dulling a color by mixing it with its opposite on the color wheel.

Desaturation with water.

Desaturation with complementary color.

THE COLOR WHEEL

The color wheel is an invaluable tool for understanding how colors relate to one another. It organizes hues according to the colors of the light spectrum, like you see in a rainbow.

Colors are ordered into groups. The **primary colors**—red, yellow, and blue— serve as the foundation. Mixing two primary colors together creates a **secondary color,** such as violet, orange, or green. When you combine a primary color with a secondary color, you get a **tertiary color.** Colors that are close together on the color wheel are **analogous colors.**

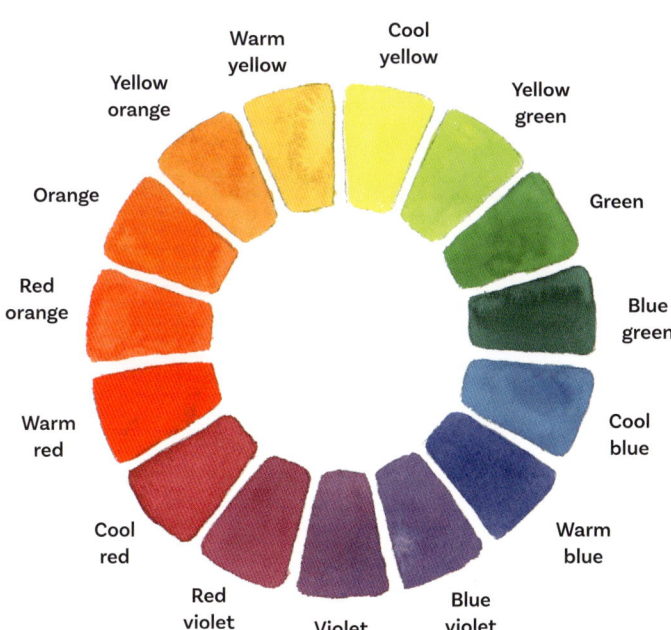

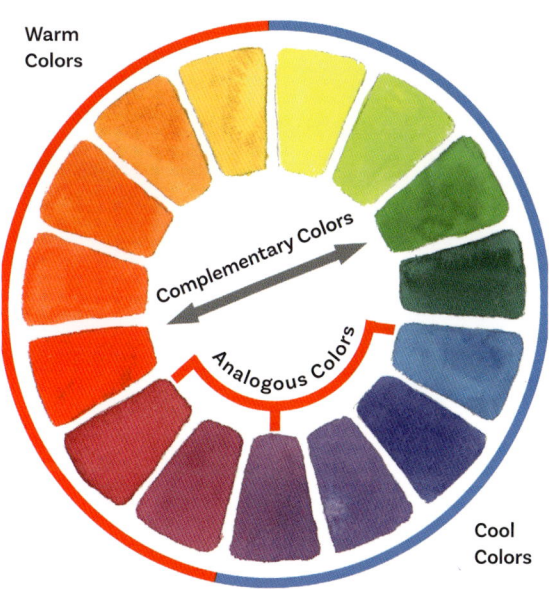

Most pigments lean toward either a warm or cool bias. Warm colors—such as yellows, oranges, and reds—are reminiscent of fire and deserts. Cool colors, like greens, blues, and violets, evoke the feeling of a dewy summer evening.

If you're new to watercolors, creating a color wheel is a great first step! A quality watercolor set will typically include two versions of each primary color—one warm and one cool. Use your own paints to recreate this color wheel as a starting point for your practice.

COLOR SCHEMES

You can design your painting based on any colors you choose—the reference image does not need to dictate your decisions!

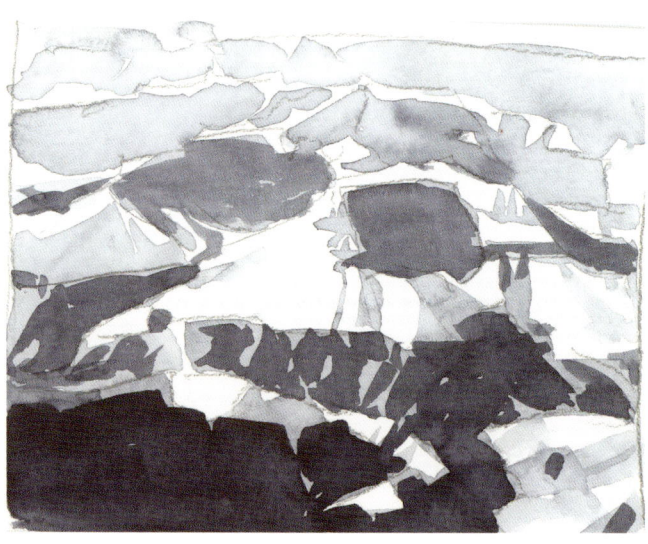

Monochrome

This color scheme uses just one color. I find mono-chrome particularly useful for creating thumbnail sketches and for grasping the value structure of a painting before introducing additional colors.

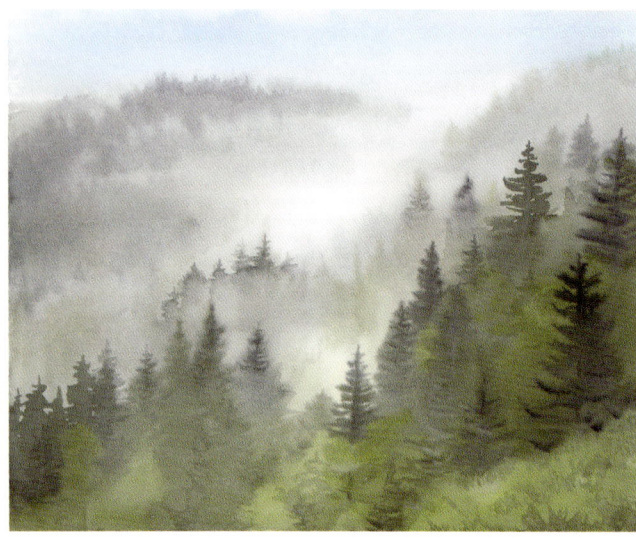

Analogous

Colors that are close together on the color wheel are considered analogous colors. My painting of the Great Smoky Mountains exemplifies an analogous color scheme with muted shades of blue, green, and yellow.

Complementary

Complementary colors are those directly opposite each other on the color wheel. Many paintings use this scheme because these pairs create a striking visual effect. Nature provides numerous examples—like purple and yellow flowers in a field or bright red and green autumn trees. In my painting of Delicate Arch, the vivid blue sky enhances the brilliant orange rocks, demonstrating the power of a complementary color scheme.

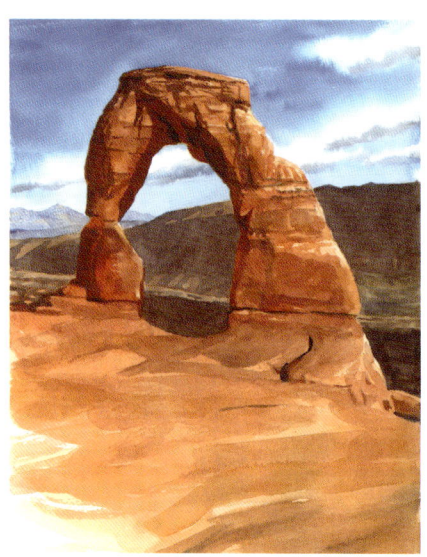

MIXING COLORS

Did you know that combining blue and red doesn't always result in violet—or at least not the shade you might expect? This is because different blues and reds interact differently. Some combinations produce a vibrant violet, while others create a "muddier" or "earthier" color.

To achieve the purest secondary colors, mix primary colors that are adjacent on the color wheel. For instance, ultramarine blue has a slightly warmer tone compared to phthalo blue.

Ultramarine blue.   **Phthalo blue.**

When placed side by side, phthalo blue shows a greenish tint, while ultramarine blue has a more violet hue. Similarly, scarlet lake is a warm red with an orange undertone, whereas quinacridone rose is a cool red with a violet undertone. For the most vibrant violet, combine a warmer blue with a cooler red. Mixing a cool blue with a warm red will still produce a shade of violet, but it will appear much duller and more earth toned.

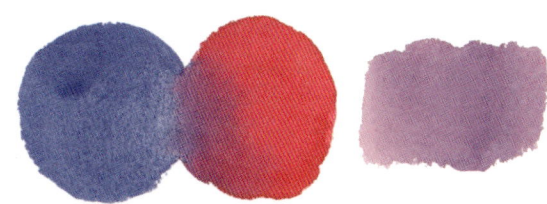

A warm blue and a cool red make a vibrant violet.

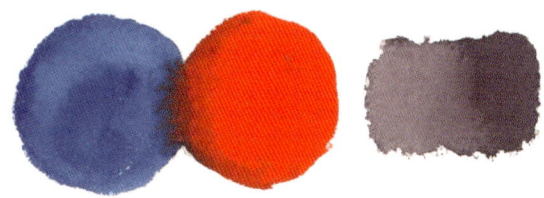

A cool blue and a warm red make a dull, earth-toned violet.

To truly understand your paints, try using a limited palette of no more than twelve colors and work with them consistently for at least a year. Experiment with different mixes using just two to three colors at a time and create swatches to practice adjusting each color's value. Over time, you'll instinctively reach for the right colors without needing to overthink it! Understanding the warm and cool biases in your paints is invaluable. This knowledge allows you to mix either vibrant or earthy tones, depending on your goals.

Tip

To add depth to a landscape painting, use cool colors in the background and warmer colors in the foreground. This color contrast helps the background recede and makes the foreground stand out.

Using White

There are several ways to "paint" white in watercolor.

NEGATIVE PAINTING

Planning for the white areas in your painting and deliberately avoiding them while applying paint is the most effective way to achieve luminous whites in watercolor. This technique is known as *negative painting*. Whenever possible, let the white of your paper shine through! In most cases, negative painting is the best way to utilize white in watercolor, and it's the technique you'll use most frequently.

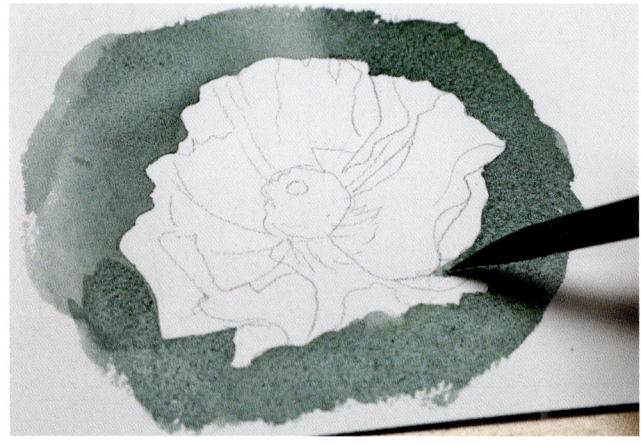

Carefully apply a green background around the edges of the white flower.

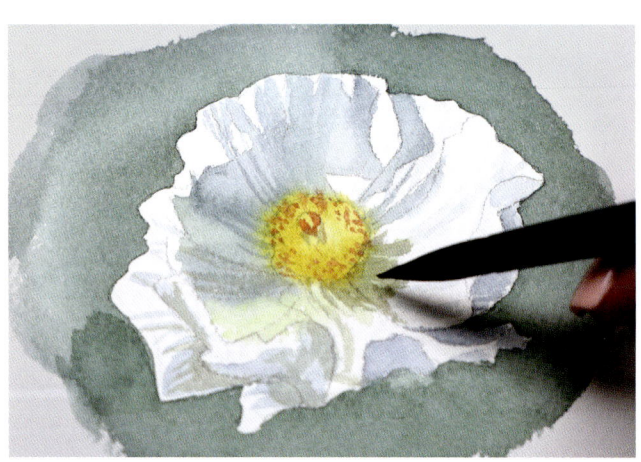

This example shows the effect of negative painting.

MASKING FLUID

When tiny white details appear in front of a larger dark shape, it can be challenging to paint around them without making the dark shape look patchy. To solve this, use masking fluid, also known as *liquid frisket*. Masking fluid is a liquid latex that can be painted on, enabling you to preserve the white of the paper while you paint freely all around or over it.

To apply masking fluid, use a small, inexpensive brush or a rubber brush. Wet the brush and swipe it on a bar of soap before dipping it into the masking fluid; this makes cleanup easier and protects the bristles. Be sure to wash the brush immediately after use.

Let the masking fluid dry completely before painting over the top. Never use a heat tool to speed up the drying process or the masking fluid will become permanently bonded to your paper. After your paint is dry, remove the masking fluid with clean dry fingers or by gently scrubbing with a paper towel or eraser.

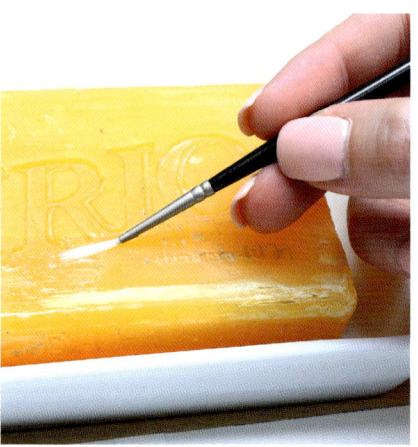

Wet the brush and swipe it on a bar of soap before dipping it in masking fluid.

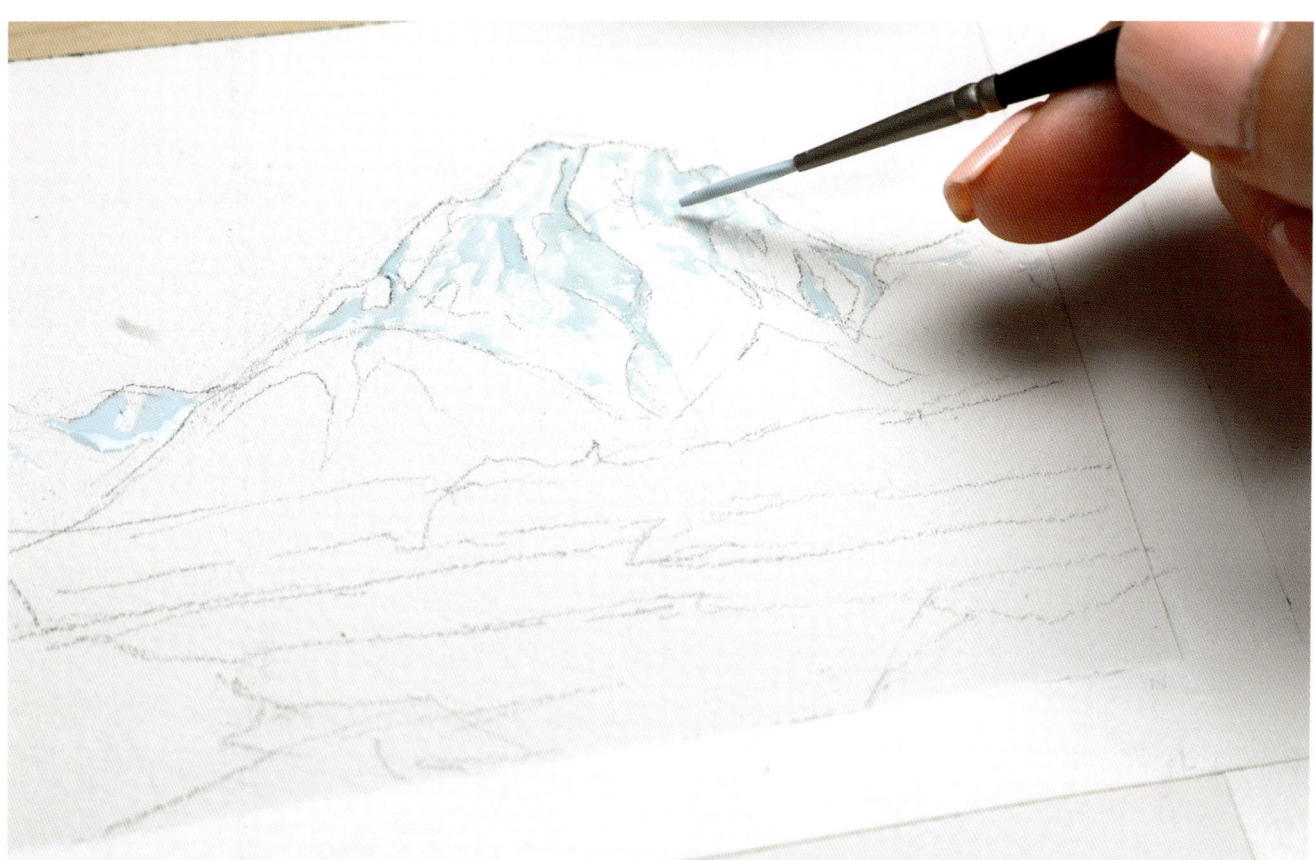

The blue-toned masking fluid is shielding the areas of the mountain that I want to stay white.

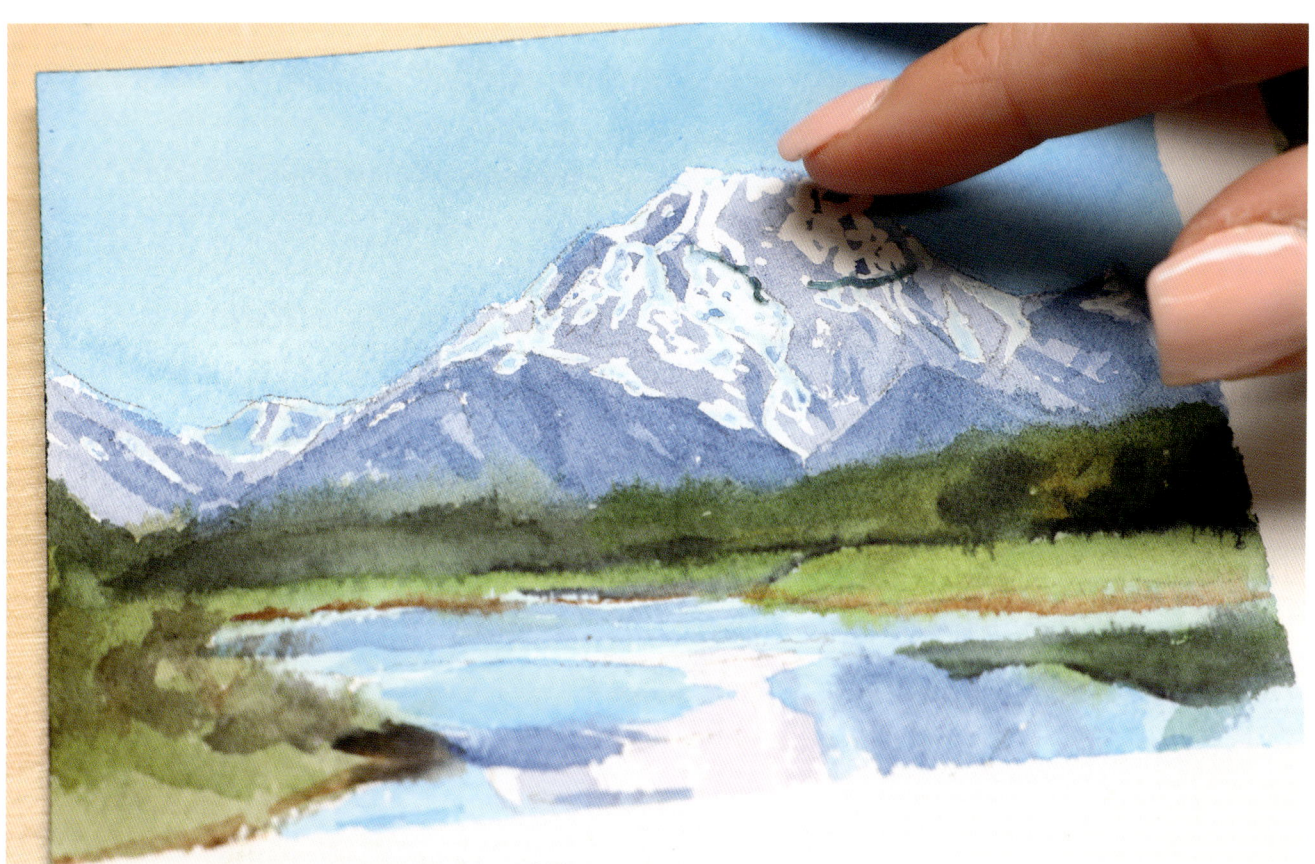

Remove the masking fluid by gently rubbing with your fingers.

LIFTING

Another way to restore the white of the paper is to use a lifting technique. This is often used to make corrections but can also be effective for creating soft white shapes, like fuzzy clouds in a blue sky.

You can lift paint with a clean damp brush while the paint is still wet. Use a bold stroke with heavy pressure. Your brush will soak up the paint. Remove the paint onto your paper towel and repeat as much as is necessary to create the white shape you want. You can also lift paint with a sponge or paper towel.

Lifting can be done once the paint is dry, too—but you will need to rewet the area to reactivate the paint before gently scrubbing or blotting with your brush, tissue, or sponge. Be careful not to scrub too much or you can damage the surface of the paper. If it begins to pill, you've scrubbed too hard.

Keep in mind that some colors lift easier than others. Staining paints are harder to lift than nonstaining pigments.

The lifted paint creates a fluffy cloud shape.

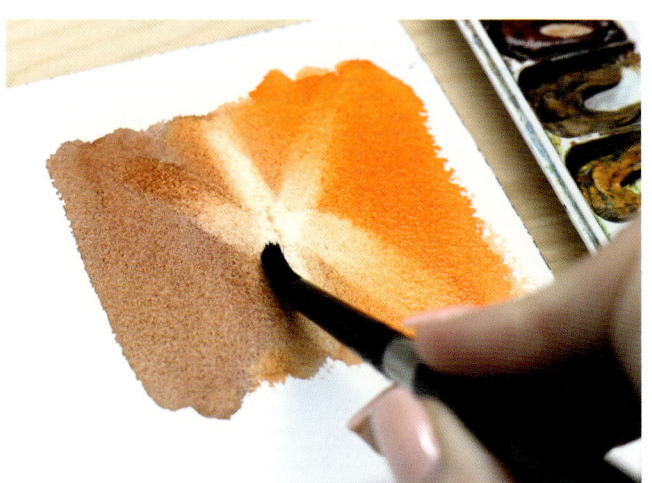

The lifted paint creates sunbeams.

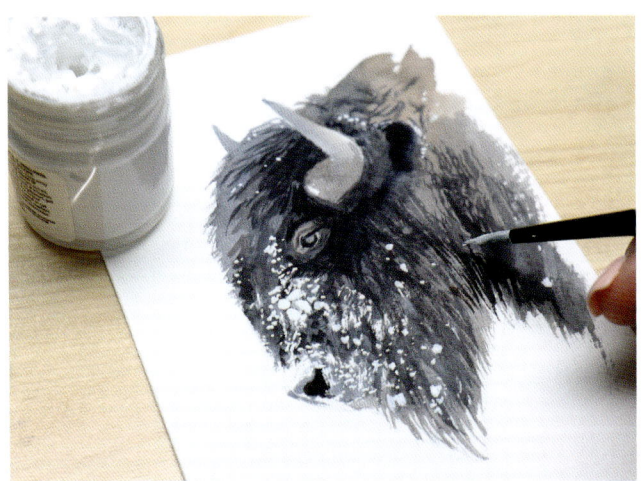

I used opaque white paint to add patches of sticky snow to the bison's shaggy hair.

WHITE OPAQUE PAINT

The easiest method for painting white in watercolor is to use an opaque (nontransparent) white paint. Opaque white is a fantastic solution for painting stars in a night sky, little white flowers in a field, or whiskers on an animal.

As you practice these techniques, you'll discover your favorites and become more skilled at analyzing reference photos. This will help you select the best methods for preserving whites in each new painting.

Water Control

Controlling the amount of water used at any given moment is essential for creating beautiful watercolor paintings. To master this skill, you must understand two key factors: (1) the consistency of your paint and (2) the wetness of your paper.

PAINT CONSISTENCIES AND ADJUSTING VALUES

One of the biggest challenges for beginner watercolor artists is learning to adjust paint values to achieve a range of lights and darks while managing the water content in the paint.

The number one mistake beginners make is just using too much water! The water-to-paint ratio is confusing for many people, so in this section of the book, we'll discuss the different paint consistencies, how to create them, and what they're used for.

As you already know, watercolor values, which are your lights and darks, are adjusted by adding water to the paint. For dark values, we use thicker paint *with less water*, and for light values, we add water.

For very light washes, and pastel tones, use a watery consistency.

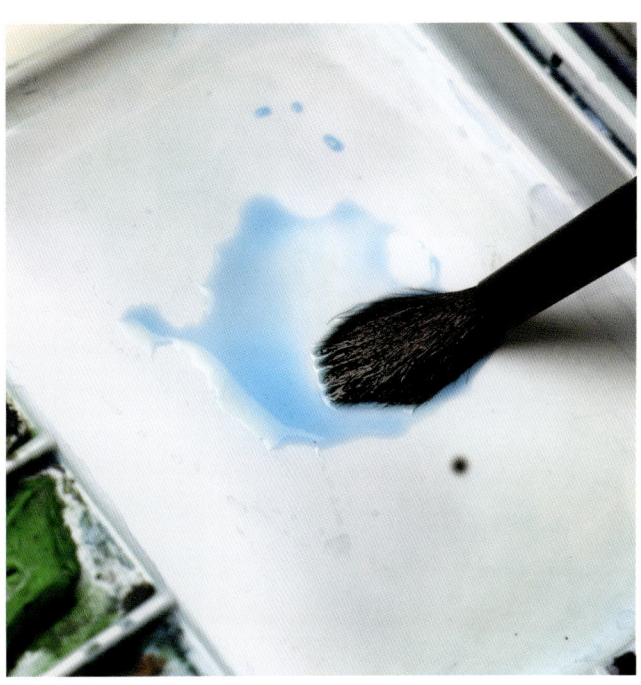

Watery paint consistency.

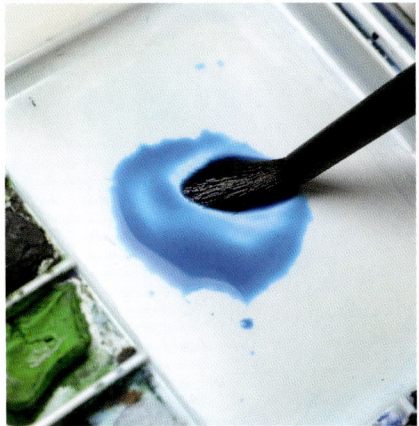

Milky paint consistency.

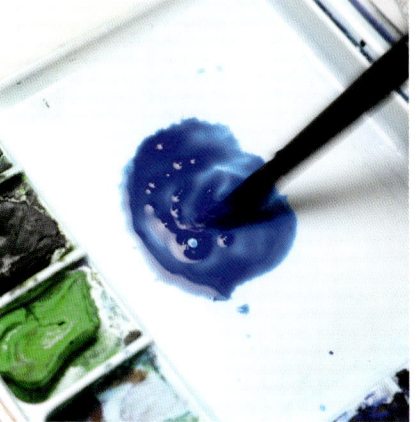

Half-and-half paint consistency.

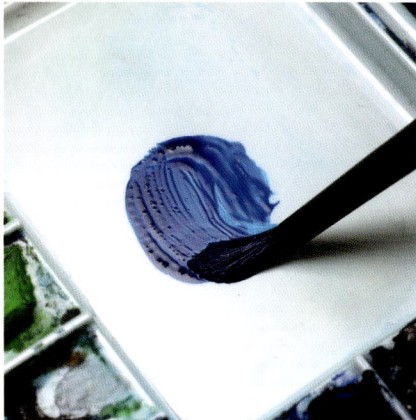

Heavy cream paint consistency.

For slightly darker midrange tones, use a milky consistency. For medium to dark values, use a half-and-half–like ratio. For the darkest values, use thick paint, which is more like heavy cream.

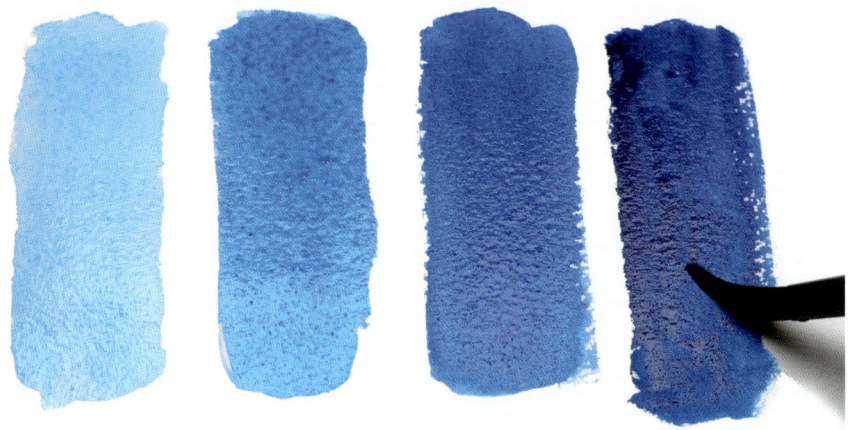

The four consistencies of watercolor paint.

From left to right: watery, milky, half-and-half, and heavy cream paint consistencies. These four consistencies are crucial not only for painting a range of values, but also for effectively applying different watercolor washes, like wet-on-wet and wet-on-dry.

PAPER WETNESS

Understanding the varying wetness levels of your paper is just as important as mastering different paint consistencies. If there's too much water on the paper, causing it to pool or puddle, the paint will just sit in the water, leaving you with little control (see photo at right). When your paper is glossy or satiny, with the water evenly dispersed and soaked into it, you'll have much more control when applying paint. This is the ideal paper wetness for most wet-on-wet techniques.

These three examples at right show wet phthalo blue brush strokes applied to different paper wetness levels that are tinted with quinacridone rose. On the left, I tried adding watery paint to a puddle. The paint is impossible to control and just sits there where the water is pooling.

In the middle example, I used a half-and-half paint consistency on a glossy or satin paper surface. The result is a perfectly soft, slightly "fuzzed out" shape.

On the right, I applied wet paint to an already dry surface. The paint does not move at all.

It's a great idea to play around with the four different paint consistencies and try them on varying paper wetness levels to see what happens. You will quickly discover that some paint consistencies work best on dry paper, and some work best on wet paper.

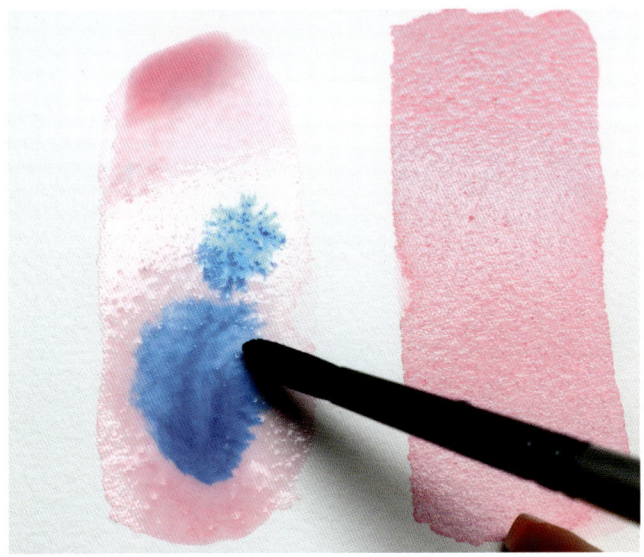

Too much water leads to little control (left); paper that is glossy with water provides much more control (right).

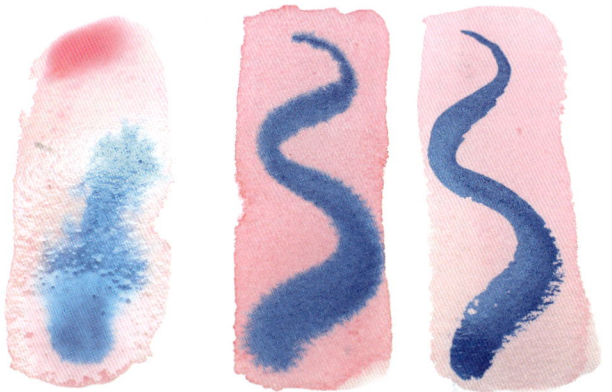

Paint applied to a too-wet background is hard to control (left); half-and-half paint on a glossy paper surface makes a soft stroke (middle); and wet paint on a dry surface does not move at all.

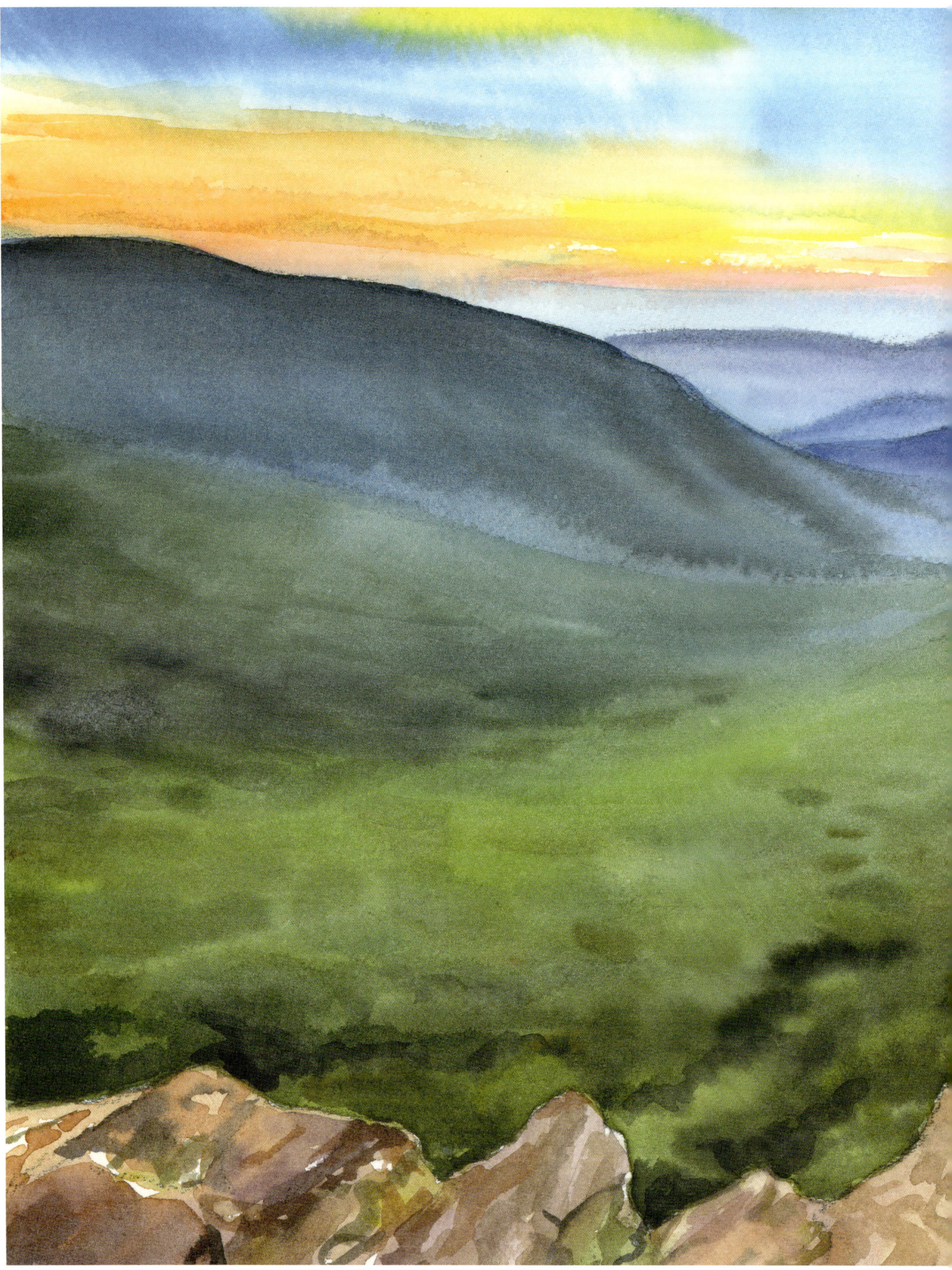

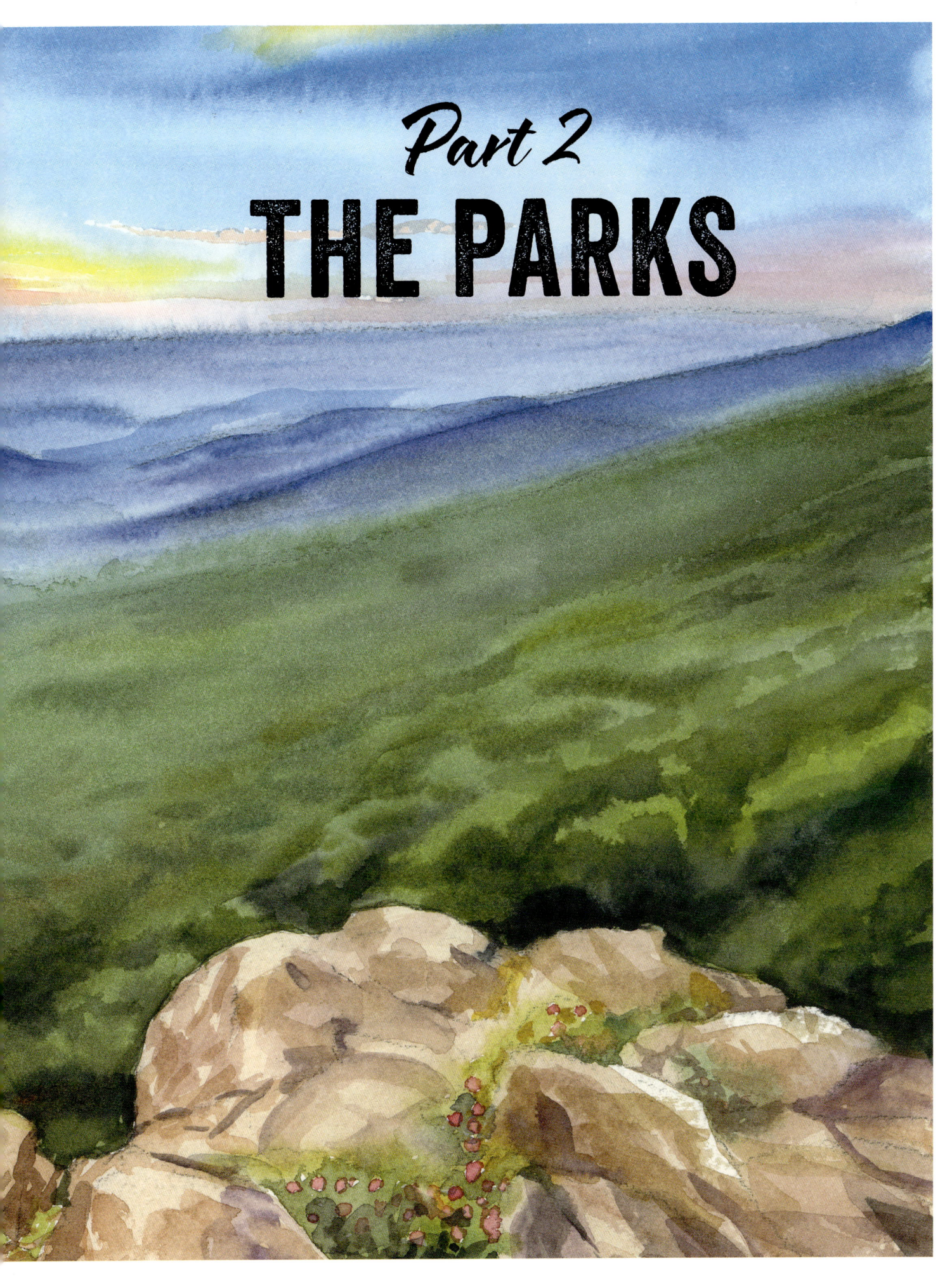

Part 2
THE PARKS

OLYMPIC NATIONAL PARK
Washington

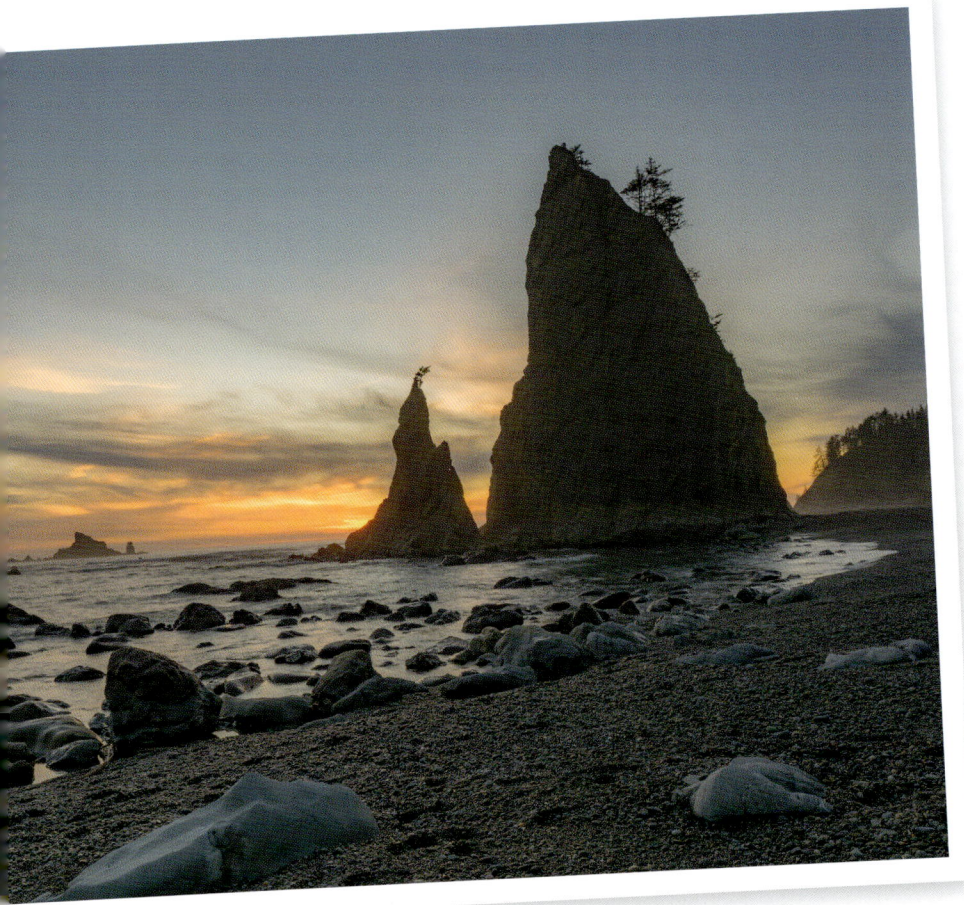

Reference photo

Olympic National Park is a remarkable fusion of three distinct ecosystems: glacier-capped mountains, rocky Pacific coastline, and ancient temperate rainforest. Located in Washington state and spanning nearly a million acres, the park offers abundant artistic opportunities and endless exploration!

This sunset scene features Split Rock at Rialto Beach, a stunning example of the coastal forests and sea stacks that are iconic to Olympic National Park.

Download template and reference photo.

Brushes

Round, sizes 6 and 10

Paper

Fabriano Artistico 140-pound (300 gsm), cotton, cold-pressed block, 9" x 12" (23 x 30.5 cm)

Color Palette

Gamboge Nova

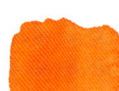

Transparent Orange

Quinacridone Rose

Marine Blue

Ultramarine Blue

Burnt Sienna

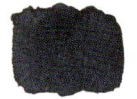

Indigo

1. Draw the sea stacks and rocks. It's easy to get lost in the details, but remember, it's okay if the rock shapes are not perfect!

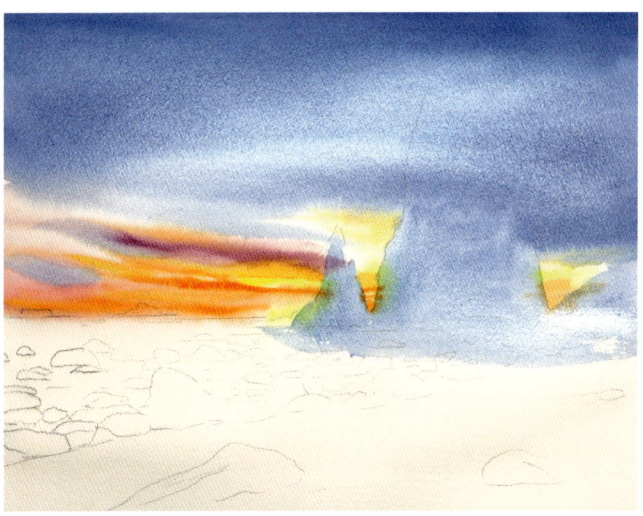

2. Wet your paper using a spray bottle or large clean brush. Paint the sky using your biggest brush. Start with horizontal strokes of gamboge nova, then transparent orange, followed by quinacridone rose, and finally marine blue. Apply ultramarine blue from the top, letting it meet the sunset colors in the middle without blending them. Paint the rock formations with the first wash of ultramarine.

Scan to watch a video.

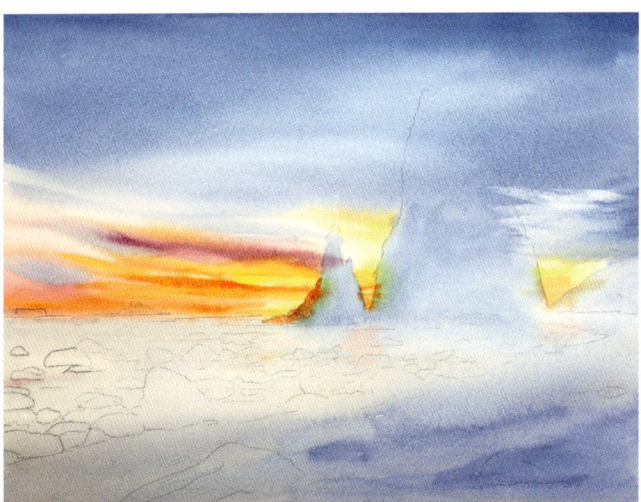

3. Paint some transparent orange along the edge of the smaller rock formation where the sun's glow creates a halo effect. For the ocean, apply a first wash using a tinted mix of ultramarine blue. Add subtle hints of quinacridone rose where the sunset colors reflect on the water. Paint the shore with a first wash of ultramarine blue mixed with burnt sienna to create a grayed-down tone.

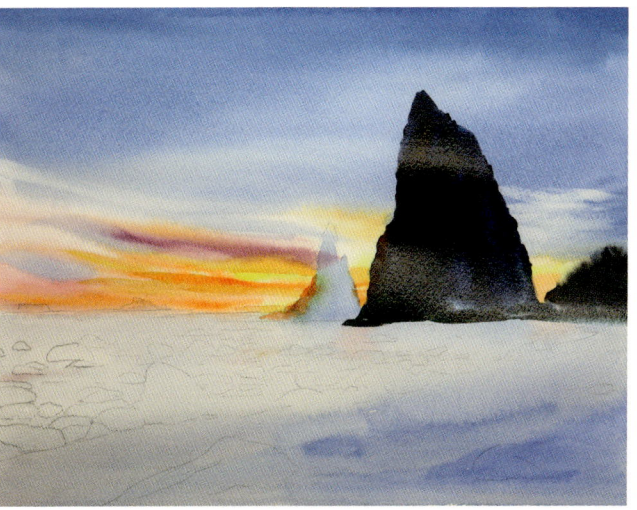

4. "Paint" the large rock shapes with clear water, staying within your pencil lines. For the distant tree-covered hill, extend the water slightly above the lines. Drop in indigo in a thick, creamy consistency. While still wet, add burnt sienna in the same consistency to neutralize the blue and darken the rocks. Apply this same combination to the distant landscape on the right side of the composition. Prewetting the sky helps your paint "fuzz out," creating the illusion of forest trees.

Scan to watch a video.

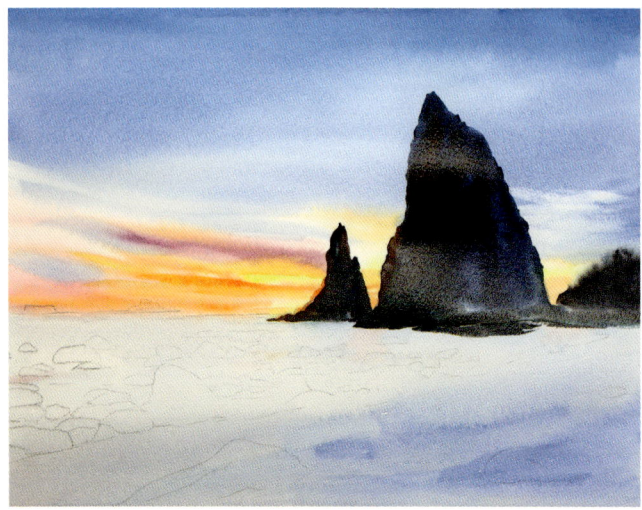

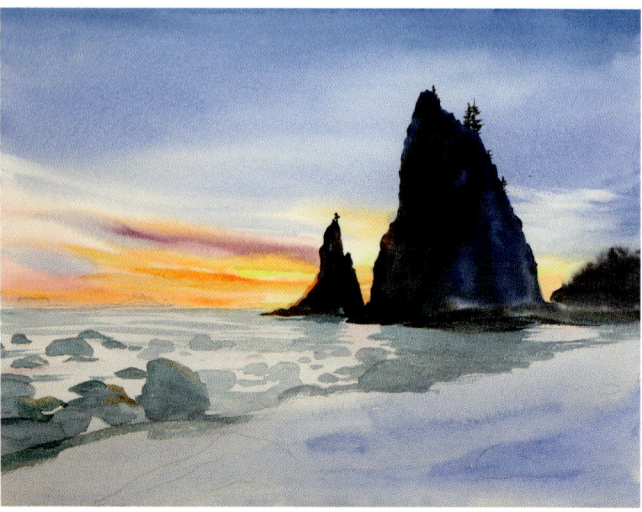

5. Paint the smaller sea stack with indigo and burnt sienna, just avoiding the orange sunlit edge.

6. Add tiny trees to your rock formations. Dilute marine blue with a little water on your palette and use your small round brush to paint the first layer on all the ocean rocks and the shadows of the sea stacks on the water.

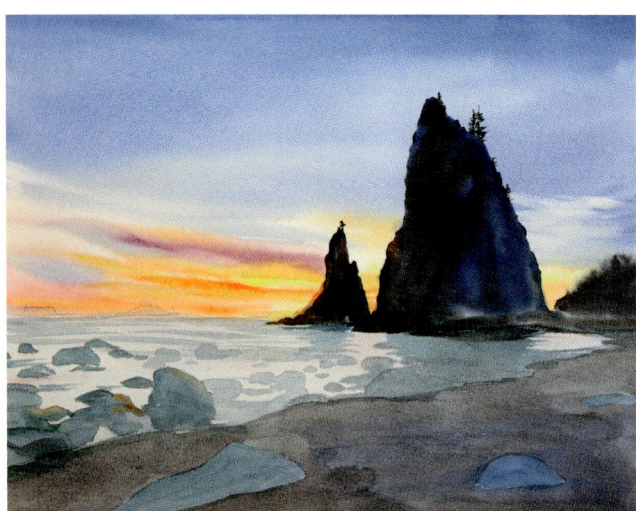

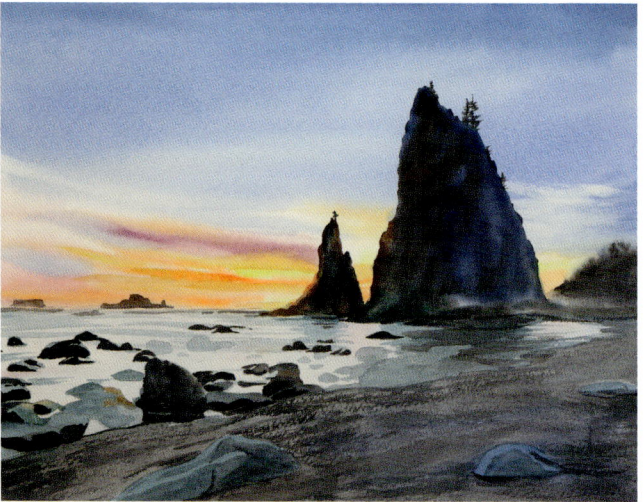

7. Mix a milky, neutral blend of ultramarine blue and burnt sienna to paint the sandy shoreline. Fill the large rock shapes with your diluted marine blue.

8. Mix several puddles of ultramarine blue, burnt sienna, and indigo on your palette. Begin painting the rocks using all three colors with your small round brush. To create a dry-brush texture that mimics pebbles, gently scrape your brush at an angle along the shoreline.

Scan to watch a video.

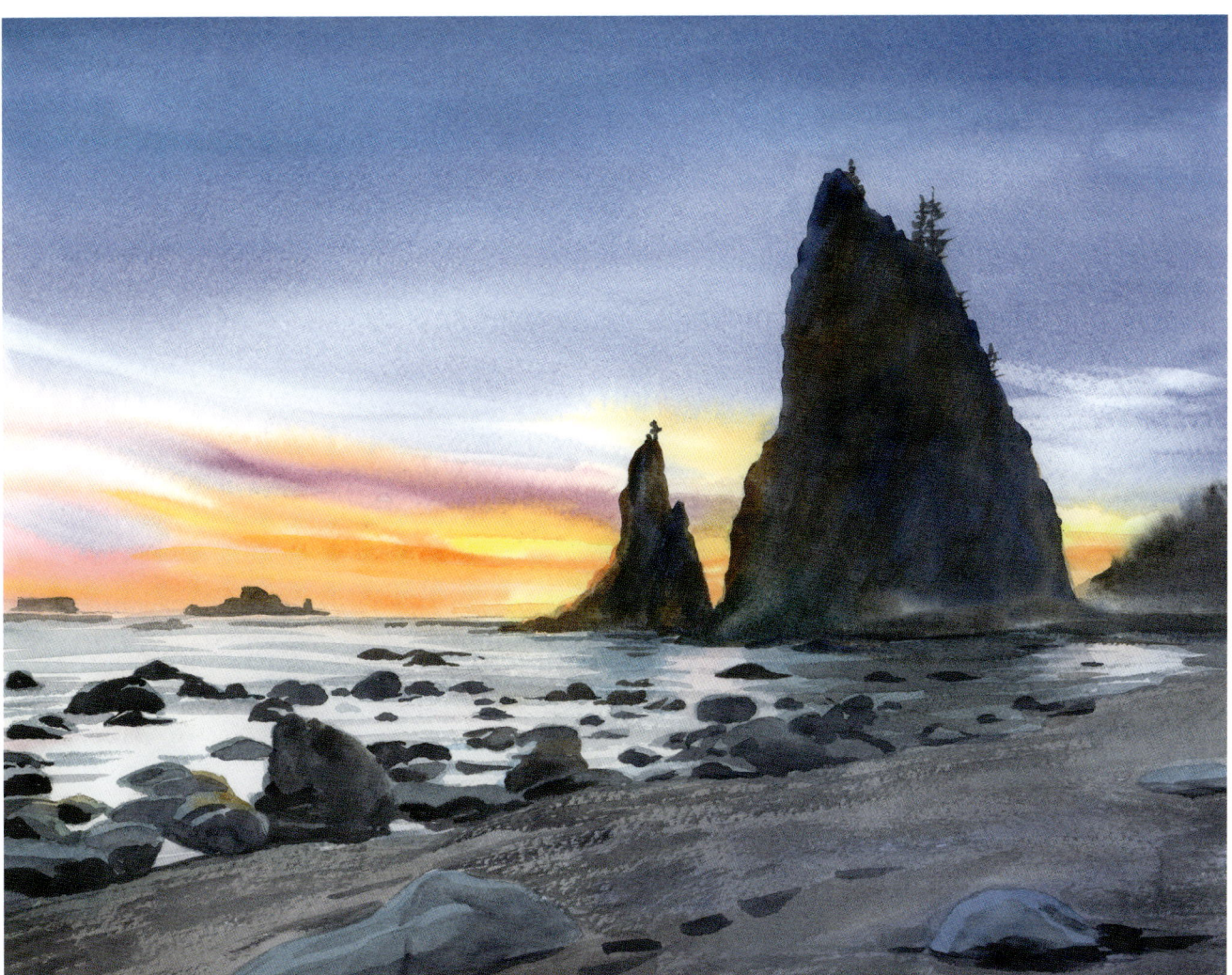

9. Complete your painting by adding shadows to the rocks. If your sea stacks appear too blue, you can tone down any overly bright colors by glazing with their complementary color on the color wheel. For example, I applied a thin wash of burnt sienna over the rocks to adjust the color. I also added a glaze of marine blue to the upper part of the sky to create a smooth gradient from dark to light.

Mossy Tree

Olympic National Park protects several lush temperate rainforests, which are found in only a few isolated spots around the world. Due to the region's annual rainfall of 14 to 23 feet (4 to 7 m), these moss-covered trees are best painted from photos!

Brush

Round, size 6

Download template and reference photo.

Color Palette

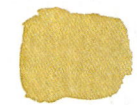 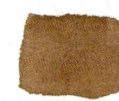   

Yellow Ochre   Sap Green   Burnt Sienna   Hansa Yellow Light   Marine Blue   Indigo

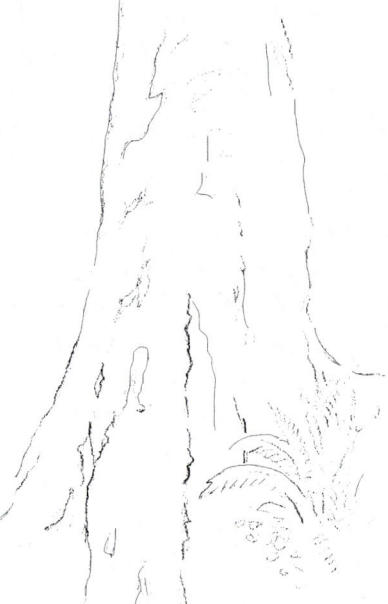

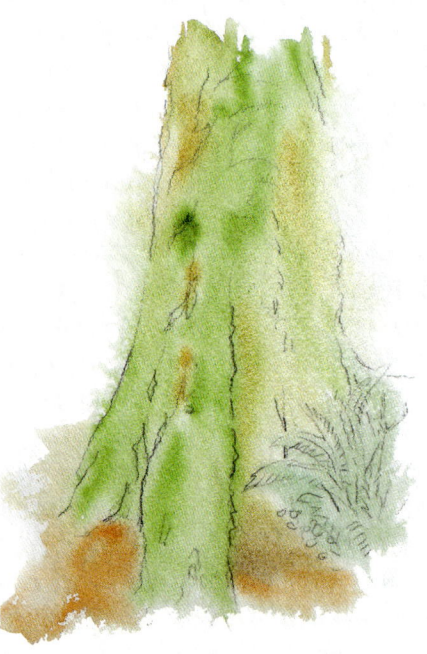

1. Sketch the shape of the tree, marking any unique shapes in the roots. Include a fern plant at the base of the tree.

2. Use a spray bottle to lightly mist your paper, letting some water splash outside the pencil lines. Apply your first wet-on-wet wash using yellow ochre, sap green, and burnt sienna. Some of the paint will spread beyond the tree, creating a foggy, damp atmosphere.

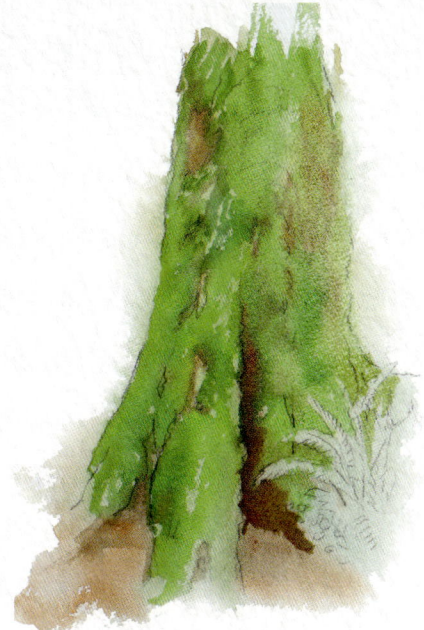

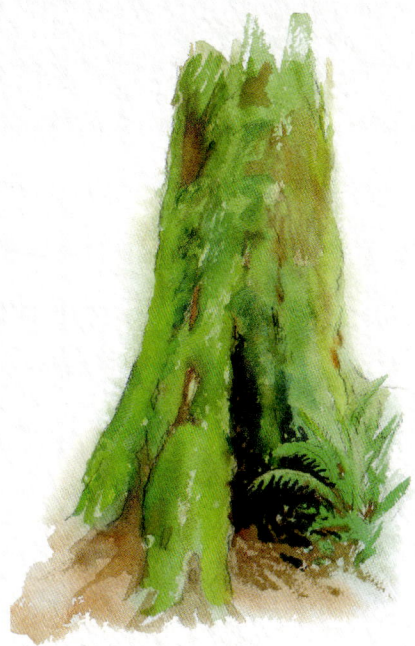

3. Continue building up your colors, using thicker paint to darken the values. Combine hansa yellow light and marine blue to create a bright jungle green for the soft moss. This mix also works beautifully for the fern leaves.

Scan to watch a video.

4. Introduce indigo into the darkest cracks between the tree roots and behind the fern. Use negative painting around the leaf shapes to help them stand out.

Scan to watch a video.

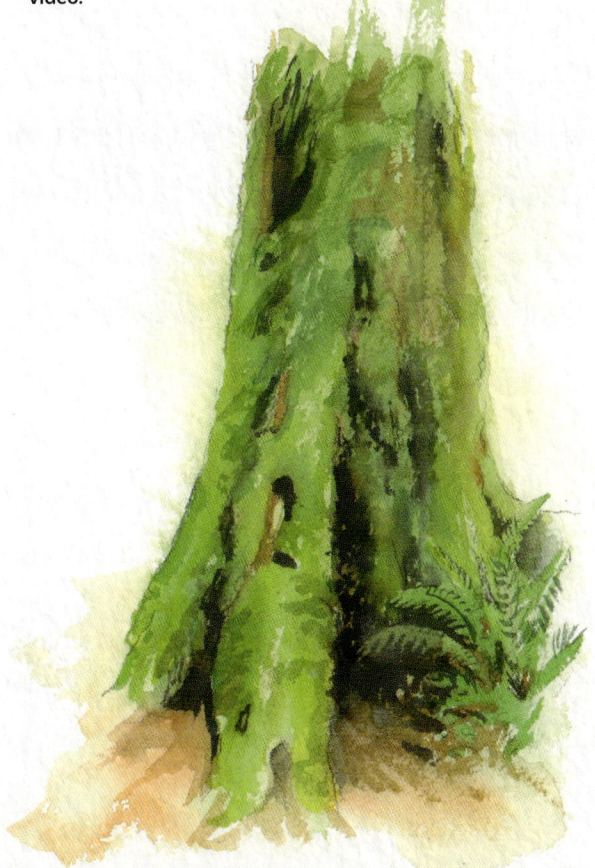

5. As the painting dries, use dry-brush techniques to add color and texture to the tree—no smooth washes here! Add as much or as little detail as you like.

REDWOODS NATIONAL PARK
California

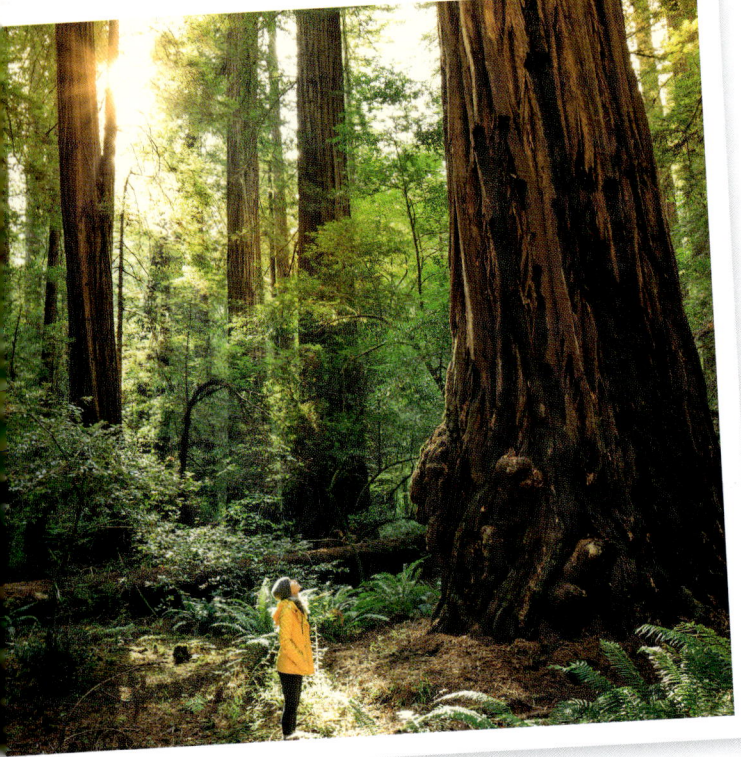

Redwoods National Park is home to the tallest trees in the world, some of which are more than 1,000 years old! Most of the redwoods were logged during the nineteenth and twentieth centuries, decimating a forest that once covered 2 million acres (8,094 square km). Thanks to the National Park System, the remaining trees still stand, and efforts are being made to protect, rebuild, and replant the forest.

Reference photo

Brushes

Round, sizes 6 and 8

Paper

Arches 140-pound (300 gsm), cotton, cold-pressed block, 7.9" x 7.9" (20 x 20 cm)

Download template and reference photo.

Color Palette

Hansa Yellow Light

Gamboge Nova

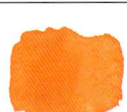

Transparent Orange

Marine Blue

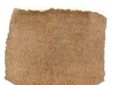

Burnt Sienna

Ultramarine Blue

Indigo

The first time I saw the majestic redwoods, I felt compelled to whisper—almost like I was stepping into an ancient cathedral. The magnificent trees fill you with a sense of reverent awe and gratitude for being allowed to take up some small space on this earth among these giants. I perched on a massive fallen log and did a small painting from life, trying to catch the glow of light between the trees. Capturing the immense scale was utterly impossible, so I zeroed in on a small snapshot of the forest.

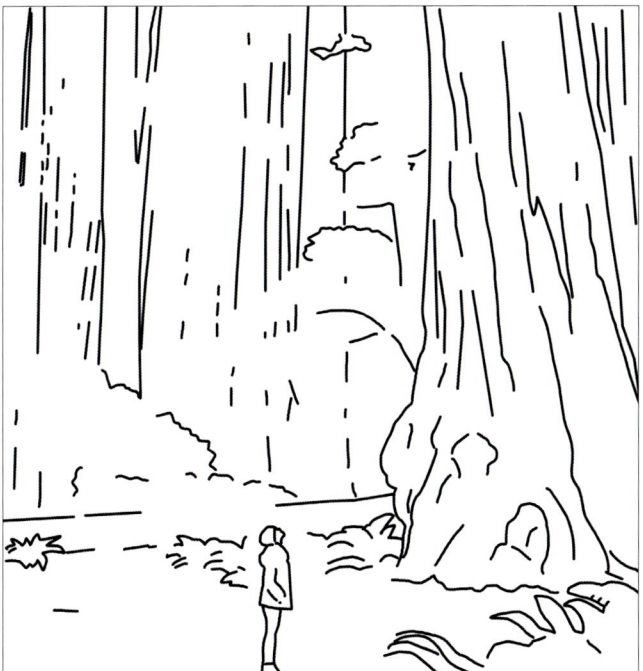

1. Sketch the scene, either by tracing or freehand.

2. Wet the paper with clean water. You want the surface to have a glossy sheen, but no puddles. Load up your size 8 round brush with hansa yellow light and begin painting everywhere you see yellows and greens in the forest. Avoid areas where the sky is visible through the trees. Use your warm yellow (gamboge nova) to paint around the sun flare on the top left tree.

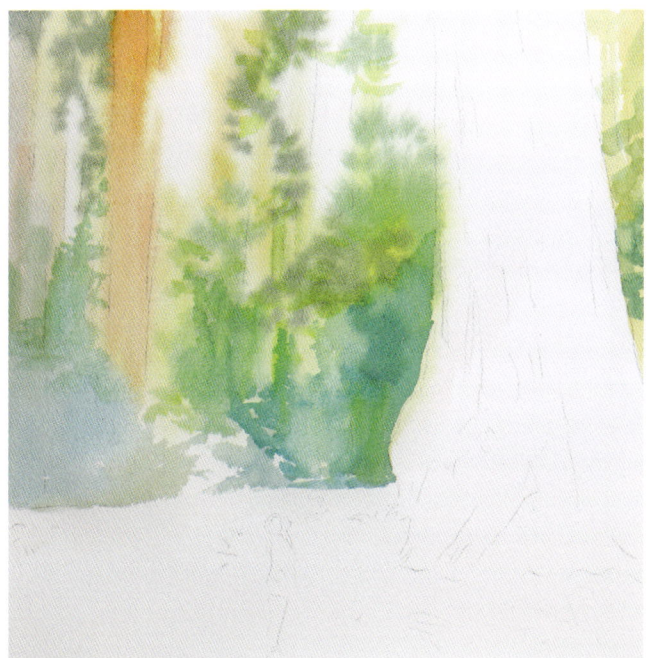

3. Use some slightly diluted transparent orange to begin painting the slender tree shapes.

You can mix marine blue and hansa yellow light to create a beautiful vibrant green, perfect for the lush foliage. Have fun blobbing in paint, alternating between warm and cool greens. Concentrate your golden greens closer to the light sky areas and reserve your more bluish greens for the dense forest areas closer to the ground.

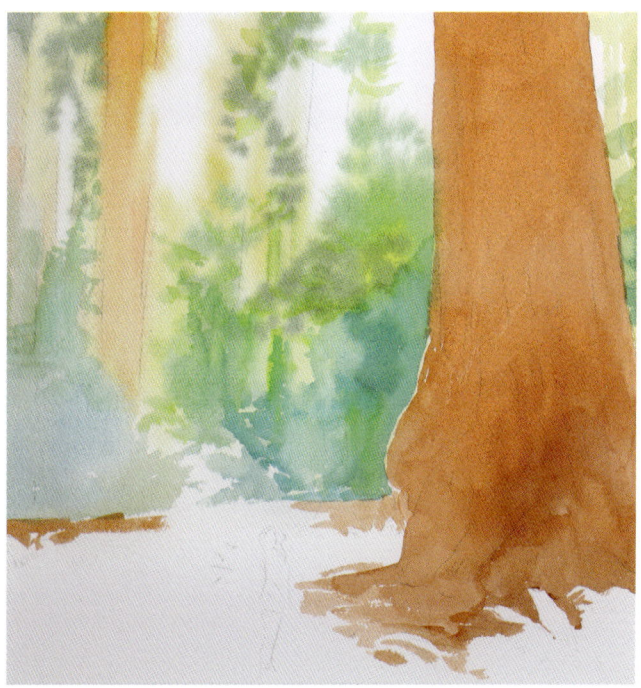

4. Use a medium wash of burnt sienna to paint the first layer of the largest redwood tree. Be careful to paint around the fern shapes in the foreground.

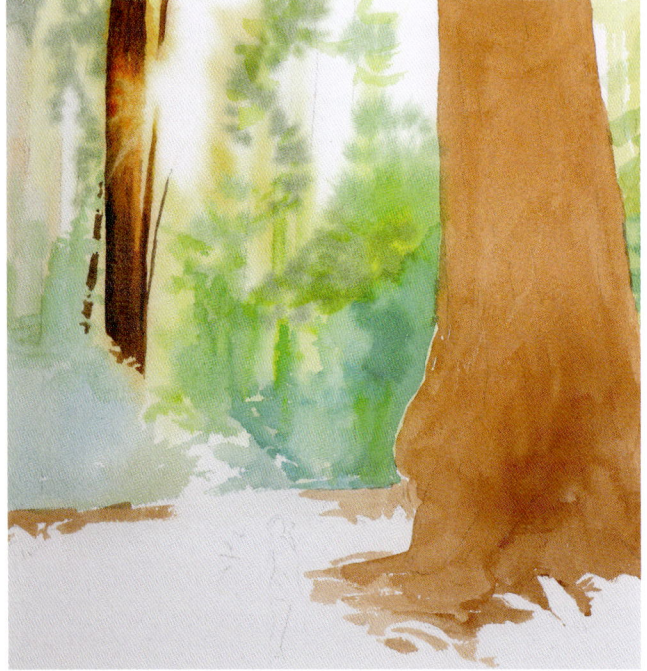

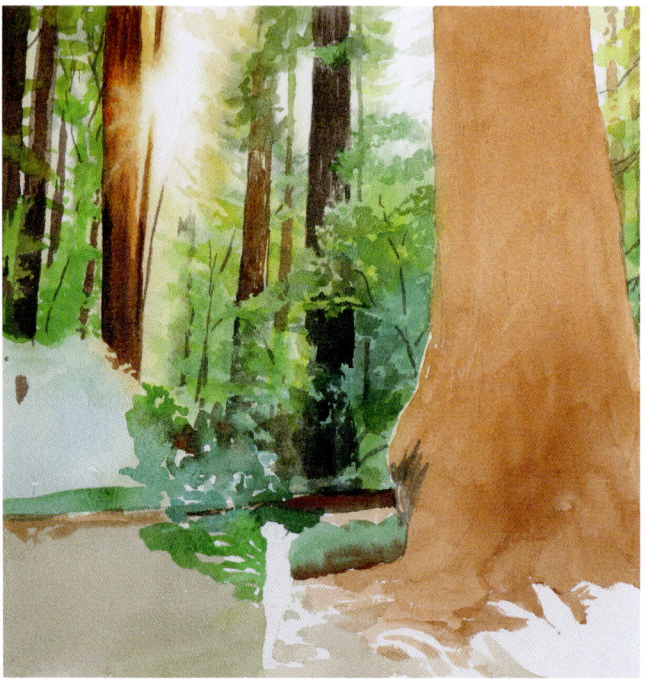

5. To paint the sun flare on the tree, load up your size 6 round brush with burnt sienna and paint around the light. Rinse and remove, then use transparent orange to paint right next to the darker brown. The goal is to use brighter and lighter colors and values gradually as you approach the bright sun spot raking across the tree. You can then use a clean, thirsty brush to lift out paint in the shape of sun rays.

6. Begin filling in the rest of the trees and foliage. Mix burnt sienna and ultramarine blue to create a darker brown for the tree trunks. Use a loose, dabbing motion of the brush to paint the leaves over and around the trees. Add slender branches using the pointed tip of your small round brush.

Scan to watch a video.

Scan to watch a video.

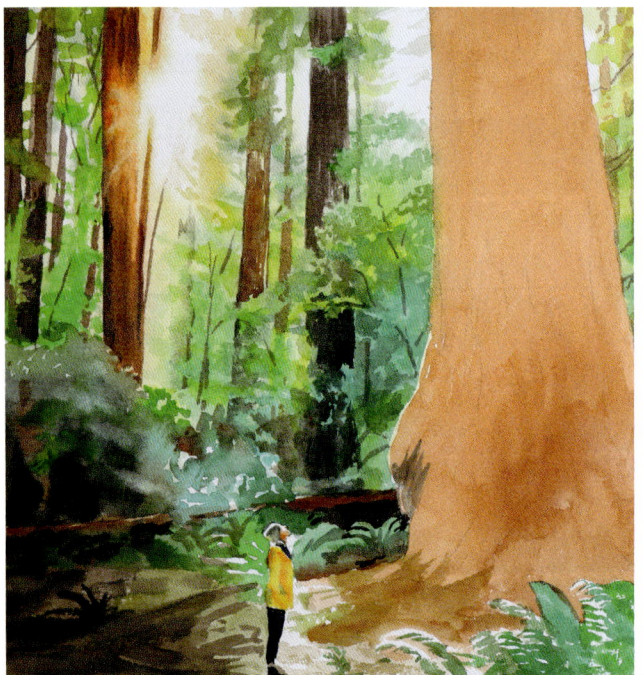

7. Paint in the bushes and ground using muted earthy colors. Paint the ferns with your mix of marine blue and hansa yellow light. Make sure to leave some of the white of the paper to capture the look of sunlight shining through the leaves. Paint the hiker's jacket with hansa yellow light and transparent orange and leave a rim of white around the top of her head. Try not to fixate on too many details—squint at the reference and try to include only the most necessary shapes and values.

Scan to watch a video.

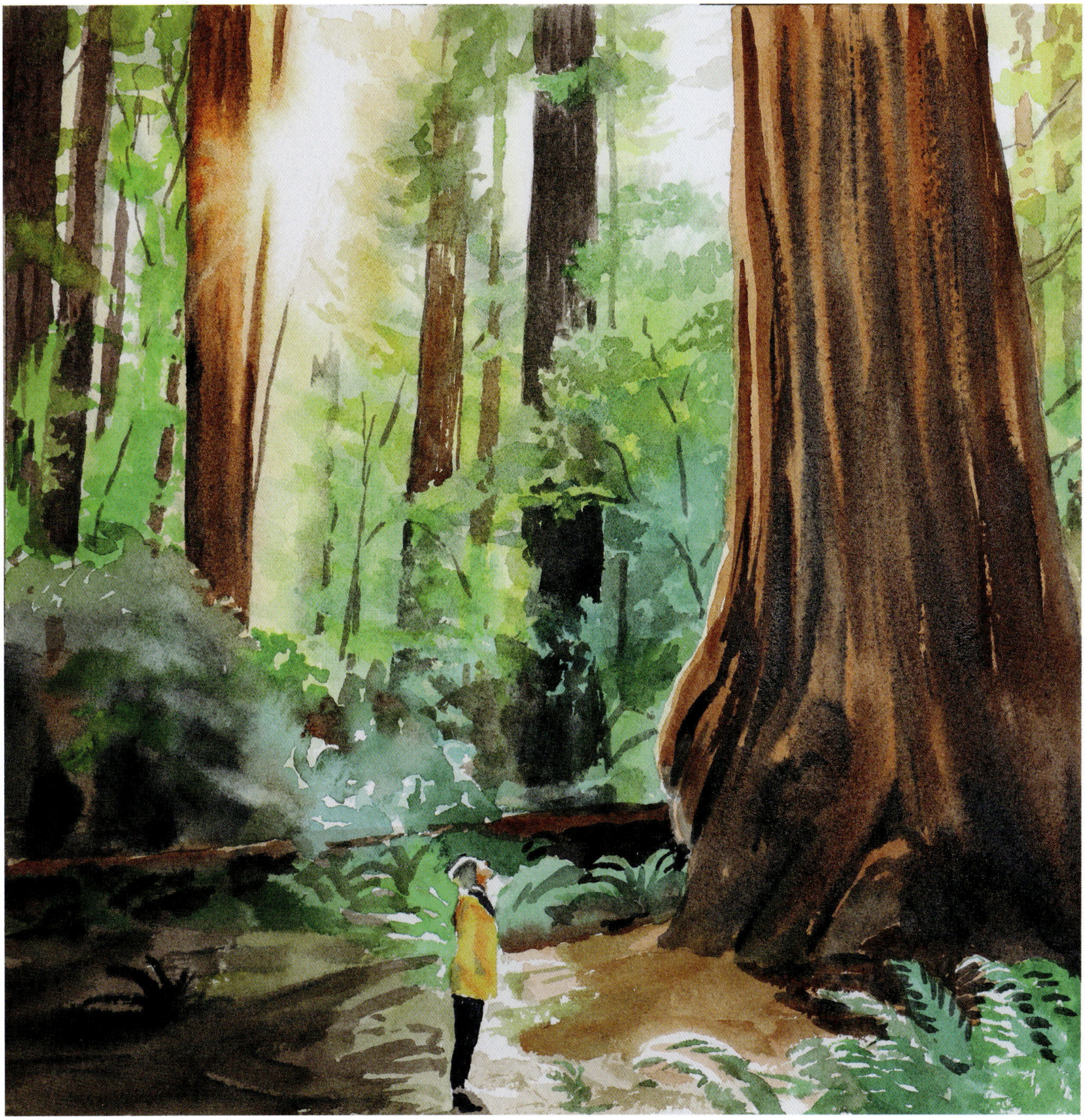

8. Finish the largest redwood with streaks of burnt sienna, using ultramarine and indigo for the darkest brown and black ridges in the bark. Include the lovely curling shapes at the base of the trunk and concentrate your darkest values at the bottom of the tree. Add a shadow beneath the tree and the hiker to indicate the sun shining behind them. Add any final details like twigs and dark marks separating the fern leaves.

Scan to
watch a
video.

YOSEMITE NATIONAL PARK
California

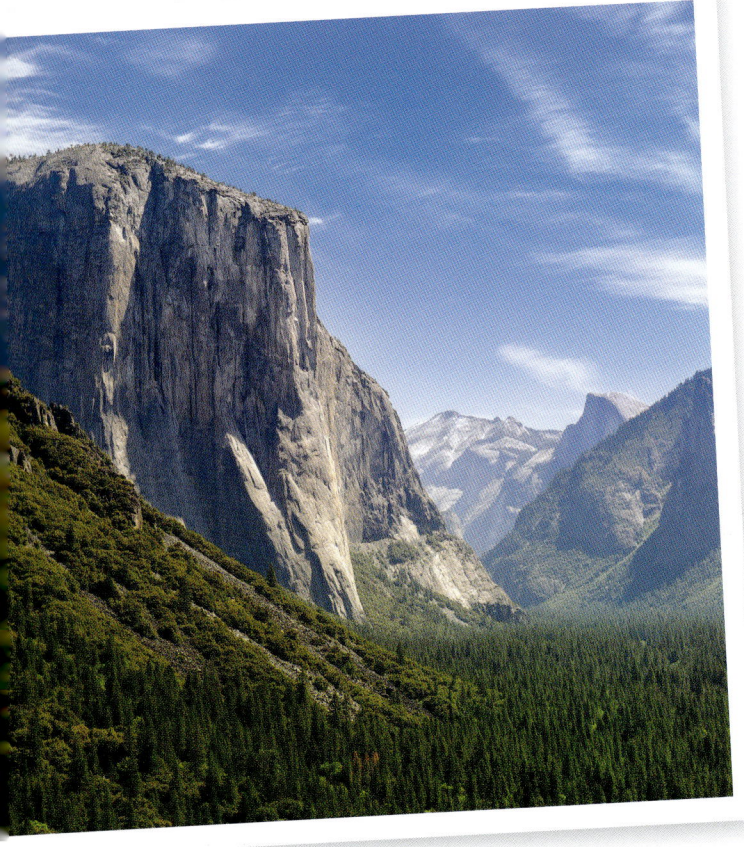

Yosemite was one of the first established national parks, designated in 1890. The 7 square mile (18 square km) valley is the picturesque home of Yosemite Falls, North America's tallest waterfall, which cascades 2,425 feet (739 m) to the valley floor far below. The sheer granite faces of El Capitan and Half Dome (both pictured in this composition) are natural canvases for the spectacular light shows of sunrise and sunset—it's a place unlike anywhere else in the world.

In this painting, we'll get to practice a soft wet-on-wet sky and build up layers gradually to carve out the dramatic shadowed rocky cliff faces of El Capitan.

Download template and reference photo.

Reference photo

Brushes

Round, sizes 6 and 10

Paper

Arches 140-pound (300 gsm), cotton, cold-pressed block, 7.9" x 7.9" (20 x 20 cm)

Color Palette

Phthalo Blue (GS)

Burnt Sienna

Ultramarine Blue

Permanent Alizarin Crimson

Indigo

Gamboge Nova

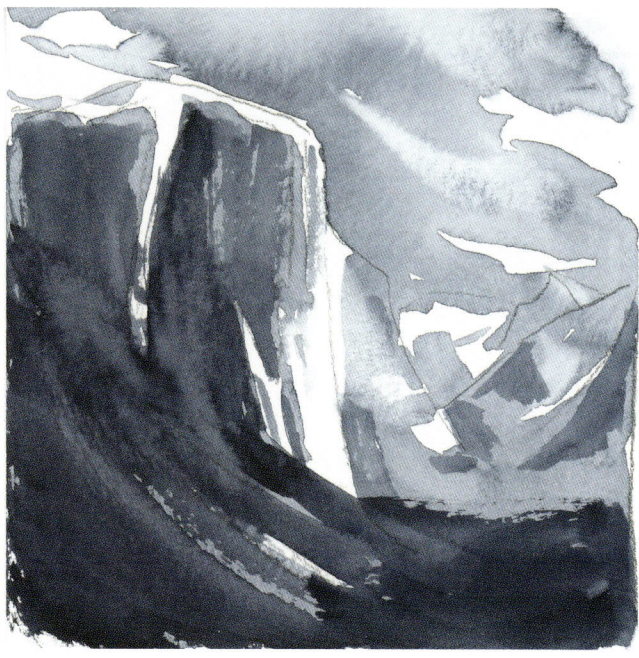

Here is my 4 x 4-inch (10 x 10 cm) value study, quickly painted in a single color (indigo) to break the composition down into roughly three values. The clouds and sunlit rock faces are the lightest values, the sky and furthest mountains are in the midtone range, and the darkest shadows and foreground represent my darkest values.

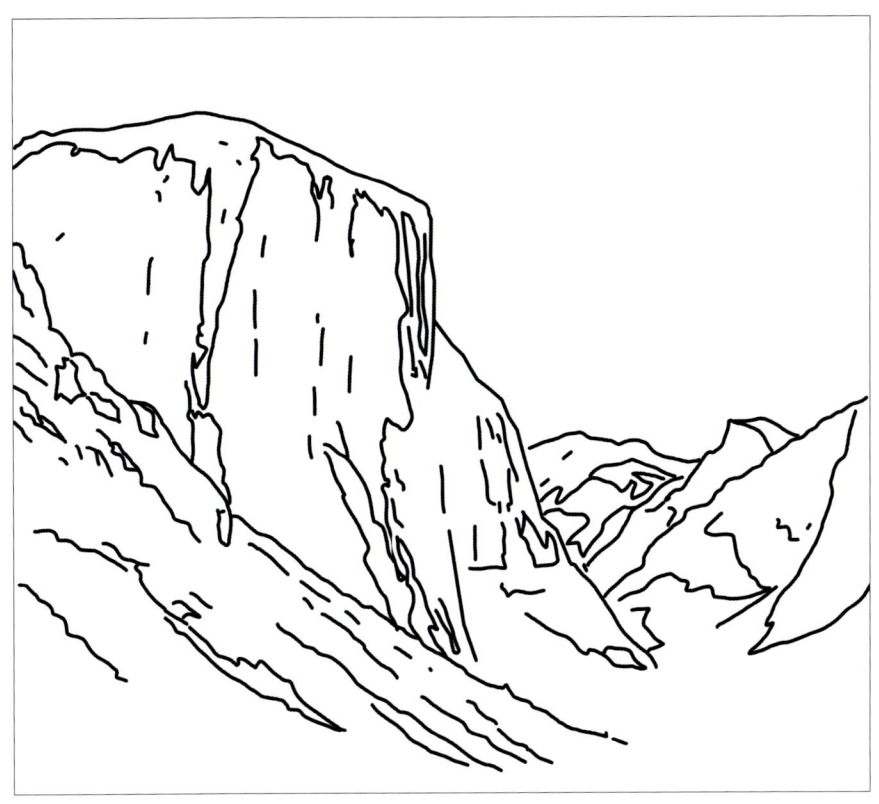

1. I use a square watercolor block, but you could also use tape to frame your composition on your watercolor paper. Sketch or trace the image, especially noting the large blue shadow shapes on the rock faces. Resist the urge to draw every crack and detail in the rocks and foreground. You only need to sketch enough information so that you can confidently begin painting.

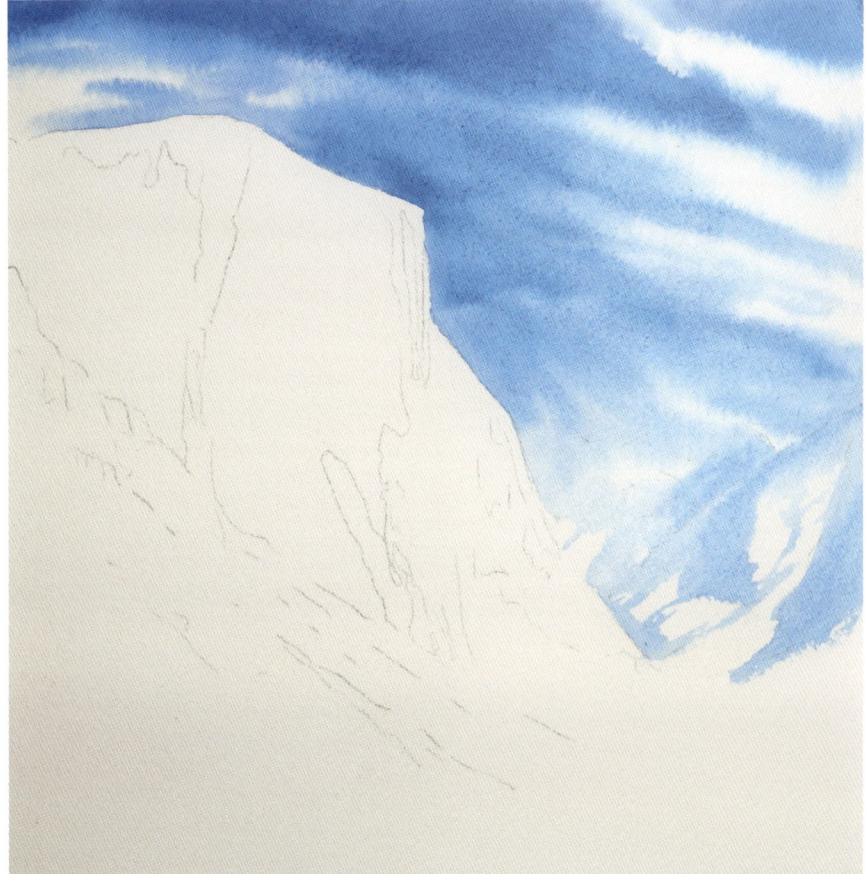

2. On your palette, mix up some phthalo blue in a milky-to-creamy consistency. You will need enough paint to cover the sky and part of the distant mountains. Using your largest brush, paint clear water onto the sky and background mountains, keeping your water contained to that area. The surface of the paper should be glossy, with the water evenly dispersed—no puddles! Load up your brush with creamy phthalo blue paint and start to drop color into the sky, painting around any areas where you wish to leave white cloud shapes. As you work your way down toward the distant mountains, gradually remove paint from your brush by dipping it in water and dabbing on your paper towel to remove the excess. The goal is to lighten your values as the sky dips down beyond the horizon.

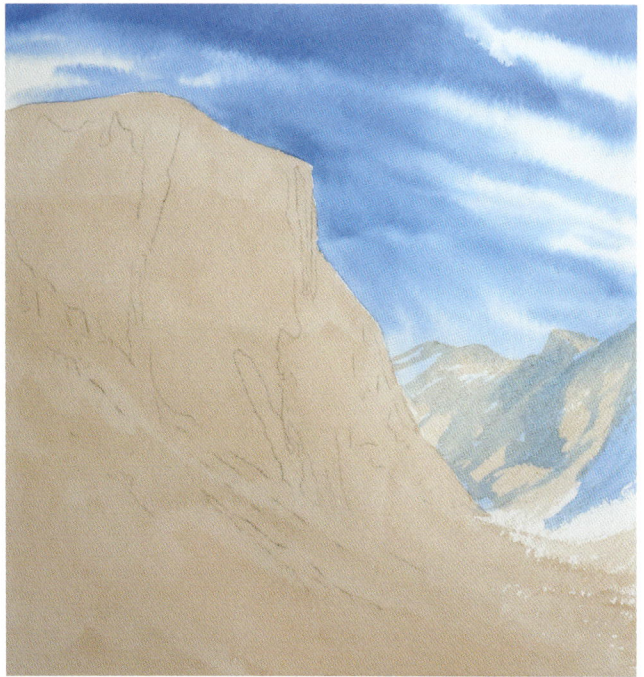

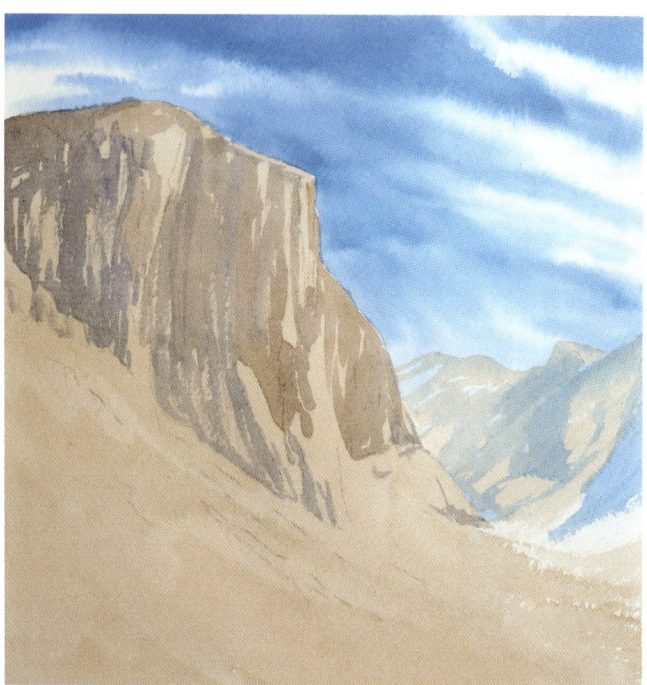

3. Mix up a large puddle of watery burnt sienna. This will be our first layer for the foreground. Make sure your sky is completely dry before using your large round brush to paint all the rock faces and foreground with a soft wash of burnt sienna, directly onto the dry paper. For the distant mountains, paint *around* the blue shadow shapes you created with your phthalo blue.

4. It's time to add more detailed layers to El Capitan. Mix up a light wash of burnt sienna and a separate puddle of watery ultramarine blue. Using upstrokes and downstrokes, loosely paint the vertical lines you see in the rock face, still negative-painting around the brightest sunlit areas. Let this layer dry.

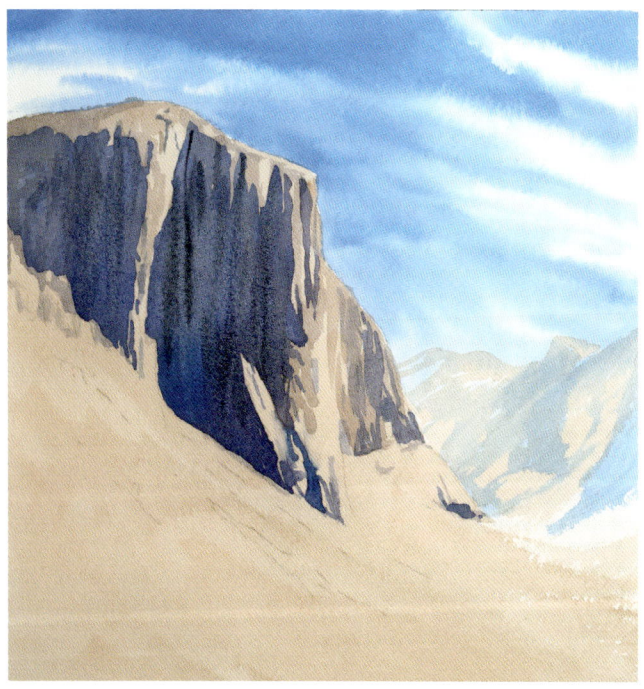

5. Mix up a medium dark, bluish-purple puddle of ultramarine blue with a hint of permanent alizarin crimson, and create a second puddle of phthalo blue in a milky consistency. Working quickly, paint a flat wash of this dark blue to create the two large shadow shapes on the rock face of El Capitan. Phthalo blue can be painted toward the bottom, where some of the warmth of the ground is reflected upward.

Scan to watch a video.

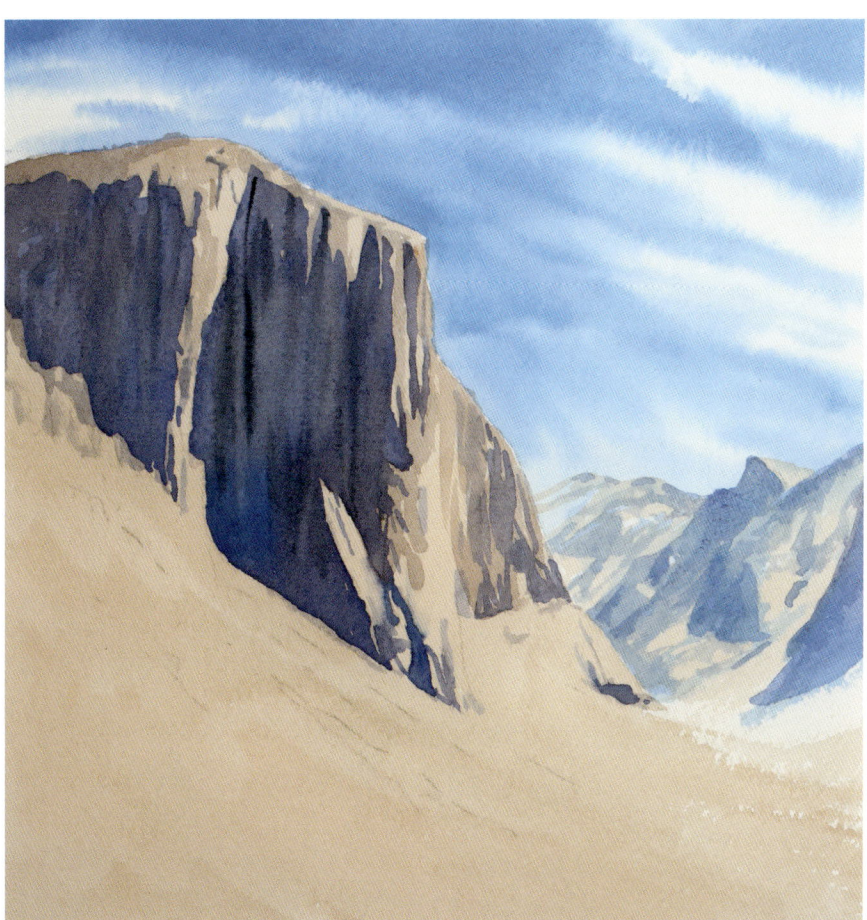

6. Water your ultramarine blue mix down slightly, dabbing your brush on your paper towel, and use some dry brushing to paint the same color over the less intense shadows on the rocks. Use some watered down phthalo blue to slightly darken the shadows on Half Dome and the farthest mountains. While your shadows are still damp, use your smaller brush to add streaks of dark indigo to create the deep cracks in the rocks.

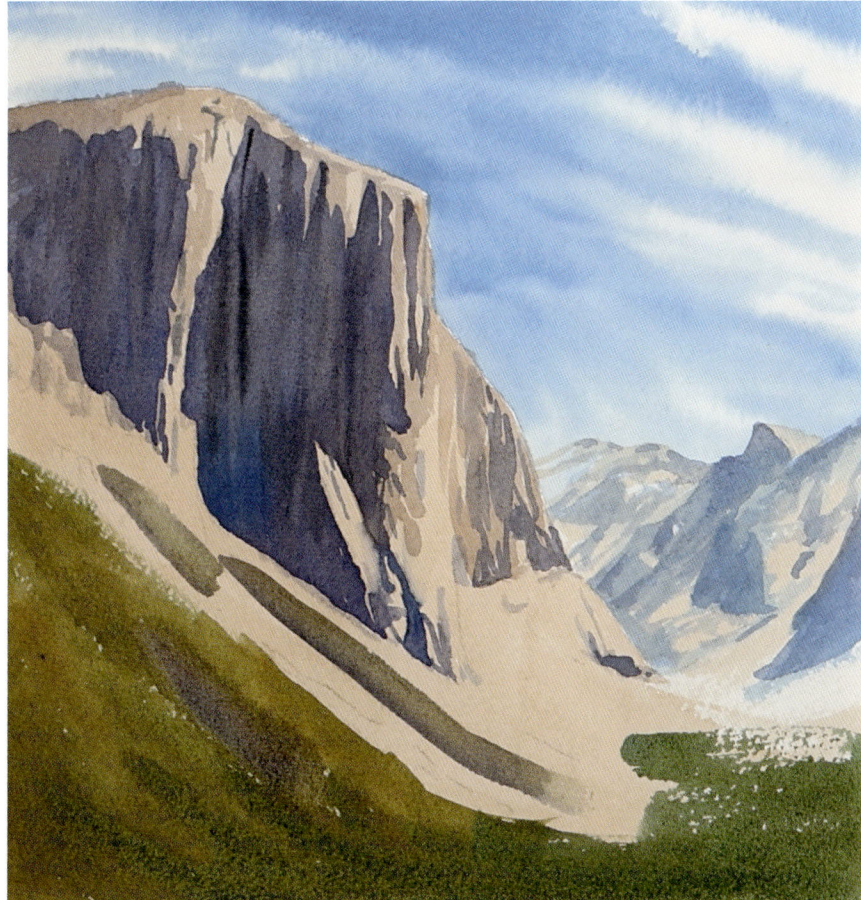

7. For the foreground, mix up an earthy green using ultramarine and gamboge nova. Where the trees and ground are more verdant in the valley, use a mix of phthalo blue and gamboge nova.

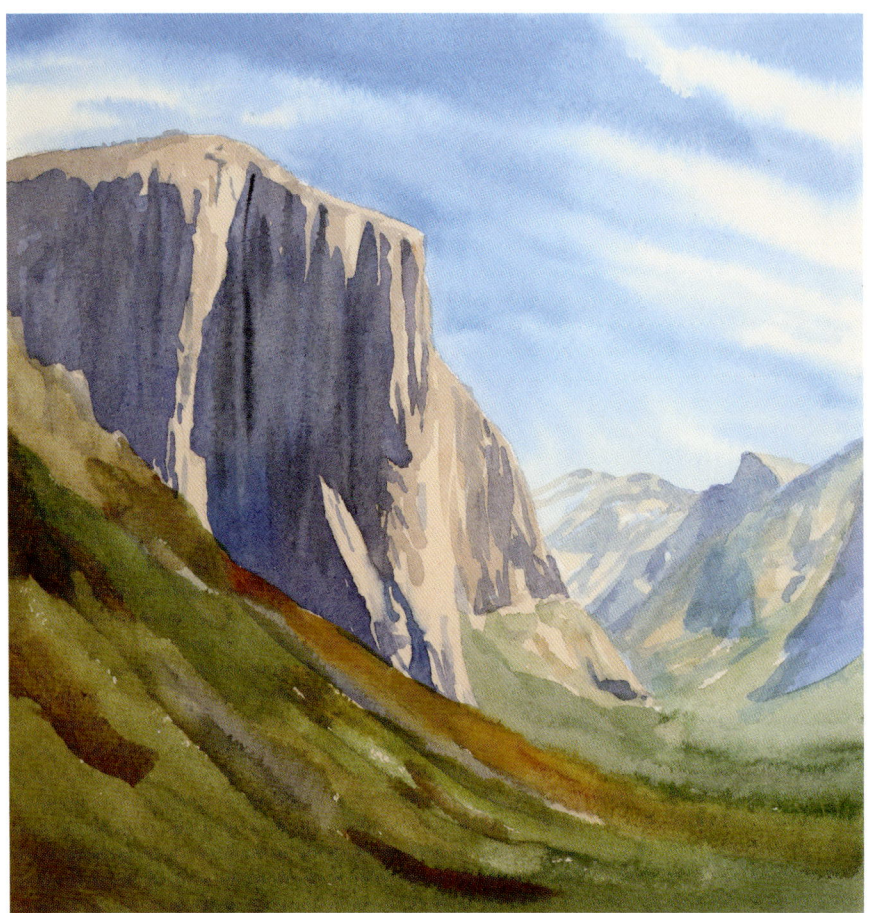

8. Working quickly, paint streaks of medium to dark color side by side, using your large round brush. Have fun alternating between your greens, allowing the colors to blend next to each other, with splashes of burnt sienna adding a hint of warmth. Move your brush in the direction of the curved slope. Use a watered-down version of your phthalo blue and gamboge nova mix to paint a soft, seafoam green into the ground where the valley is fading into the distance. These lighter values in the scene help create a convincing sense of atmospheric perspective.

Scan to
watch a
video.

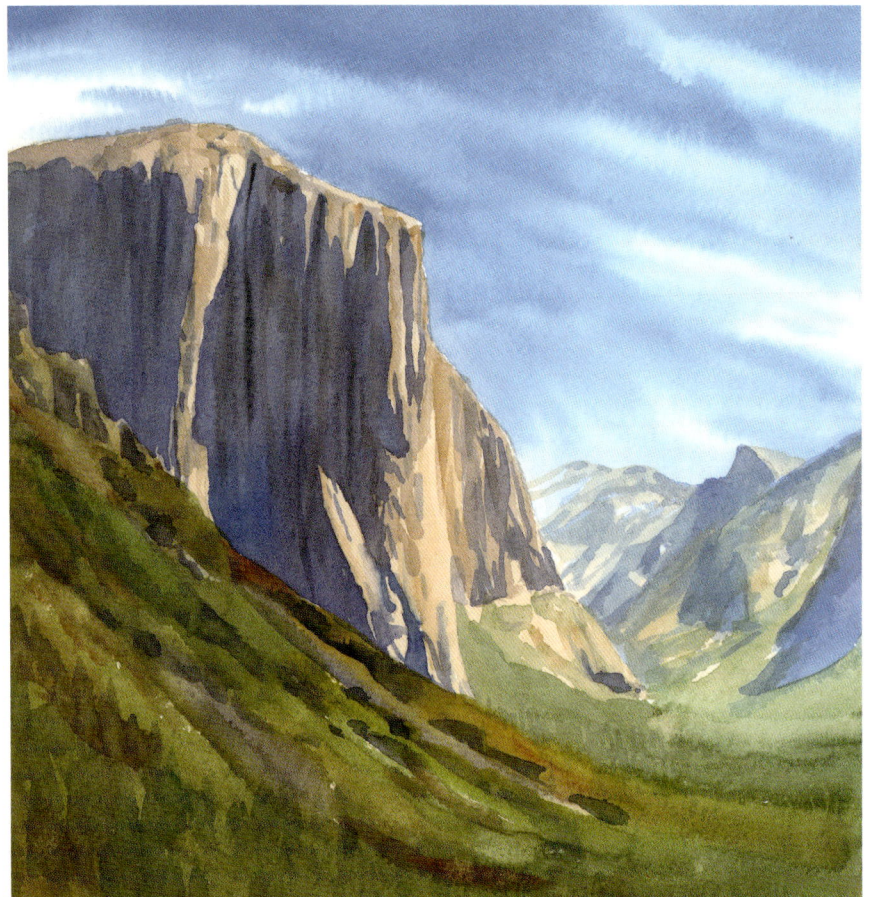

9. Load up your brush with more earthy green. Holding it with the tip pointed toward the top of your composition, use the round brush's natural shape to blot trees into the foreground, especially in the lower left corner. Don't make them too patterned or symmetrical! Add dark shadow shapes in the slope to hint at patches of trees and shadows on the rocks.

Scan to
watch a
video.

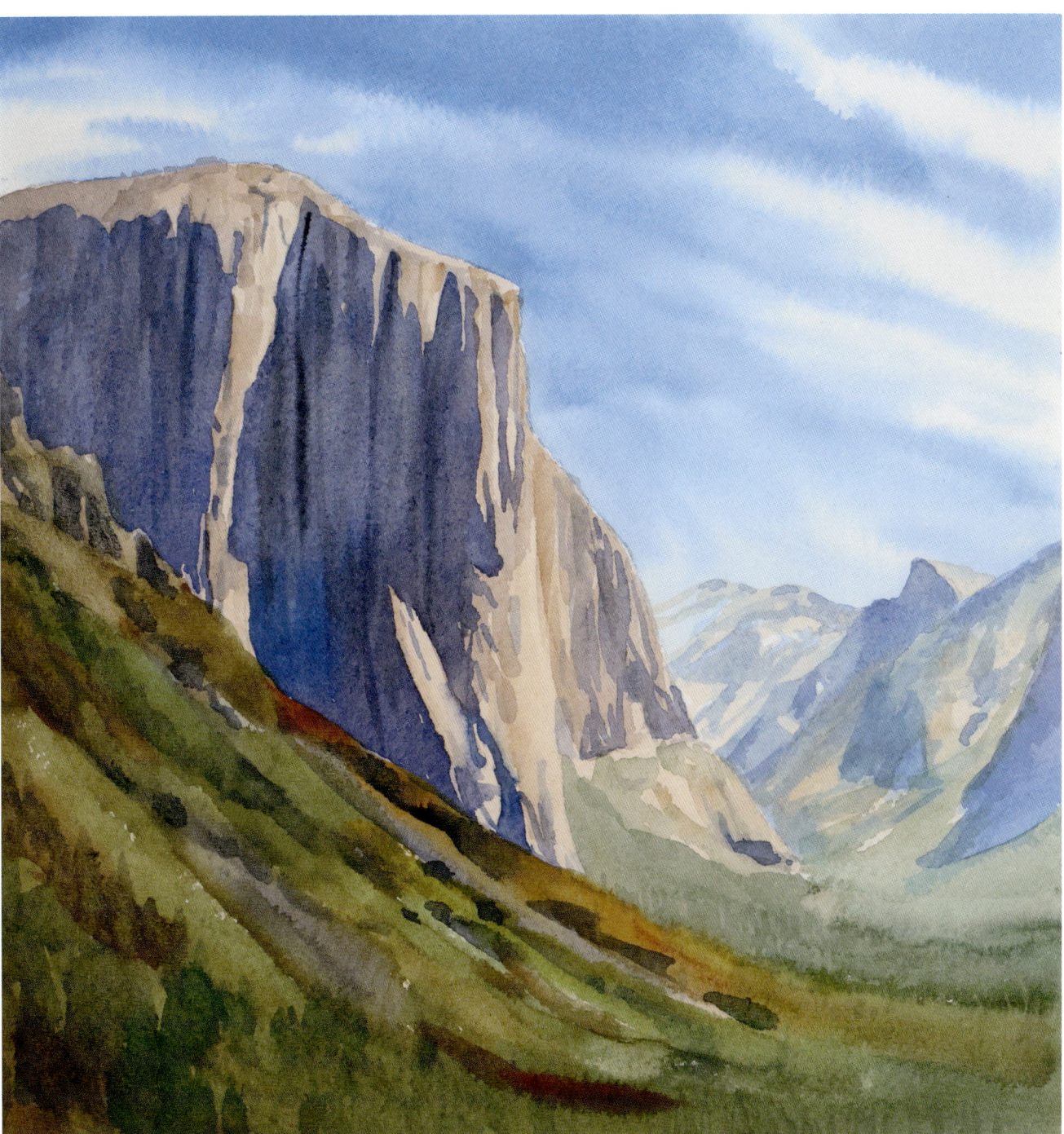

10. Add any finishing details. If there is anything in the painting that bothers you, make some adjustments! You can always rewet an area and gently scrub to smooth and soften. I decided the clouds in my sky looked too even, almost like three fingers, so I used clear water to again wet the sky, then dropped in some more phthalo blue, mostly in the top right corner, to make the clouds more hazy and less prominent.

Steller's Blue Jay

Steller's blue jays are common in Yosemite and many other western national parks. Attend to your picnic items, or else you may spy one of these bold little birds swooping in for a snack!

Download template and reference photo.

Brush

Round, size 6

Color Palette

Phthalo Blue (GS)   Ultramarine Blue   Burnt Sienna

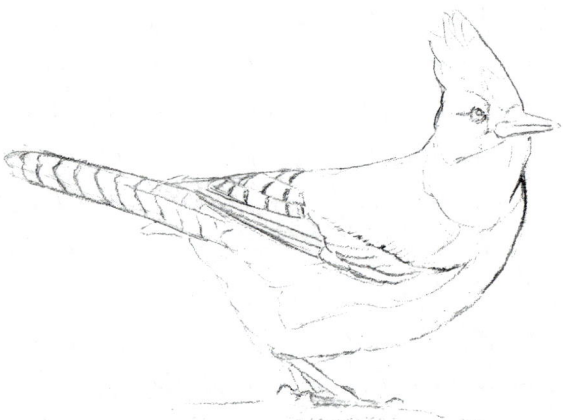

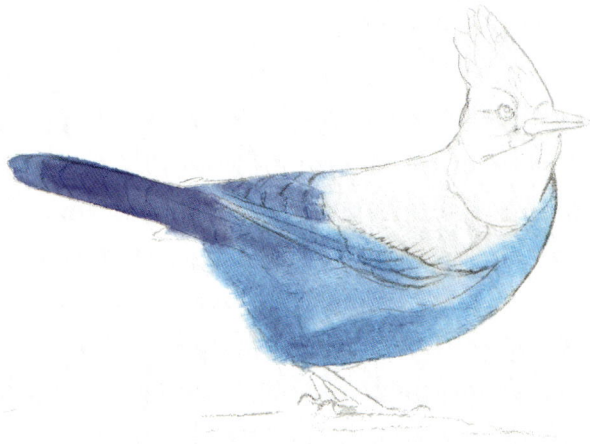

1. Sketch or trace the bird, using a kneaded eraser to lighten the lines.

2. Start by painting clear water inside of your pencil lines everywhere you wish to paint blue. Extend your water a finger's width beyond the pencil line in the area under the tail. We want this to be a soft, "fuzzed-out," wet-on-wet edge. Take some creamy phthalo blue and paint in the shadowed cool blue areas on the belly, using a lighter version of the blue where the feathers are in the sunlight. Note how the blue softens and spreads a little where you wet the paper beyond your pencil marks. Switch to ultramarine blue on the tail feathers.

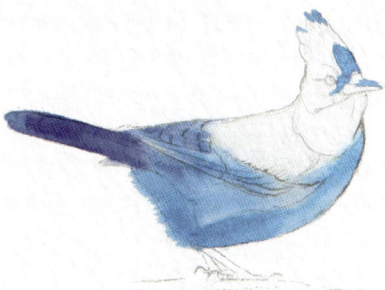
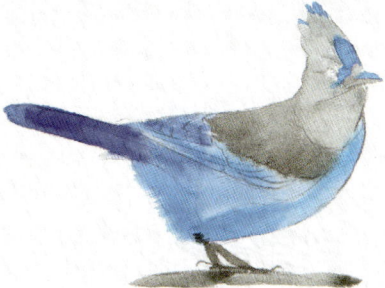
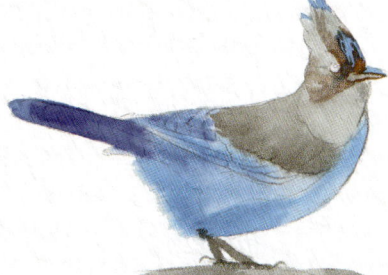

3. Use phthalo blue on the blue areas of the head.

4. For the cool grey color on the jay, mix a watery combination of phthalo blue, burnt sienna, and a hint of ultramarine blue.

5. Use burnt sienna to darken areas of the head and add a rich chocolate brown circling the neck and beak.

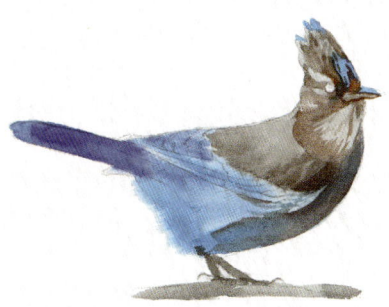

6. Use a slightly cooler (blue) version of your watered-down ultramarine blue and burnt sienna mix for the shadows on the breast and belly, adding soft dry-brush texture to create the look of downy feathers.

Scan to watch a video.

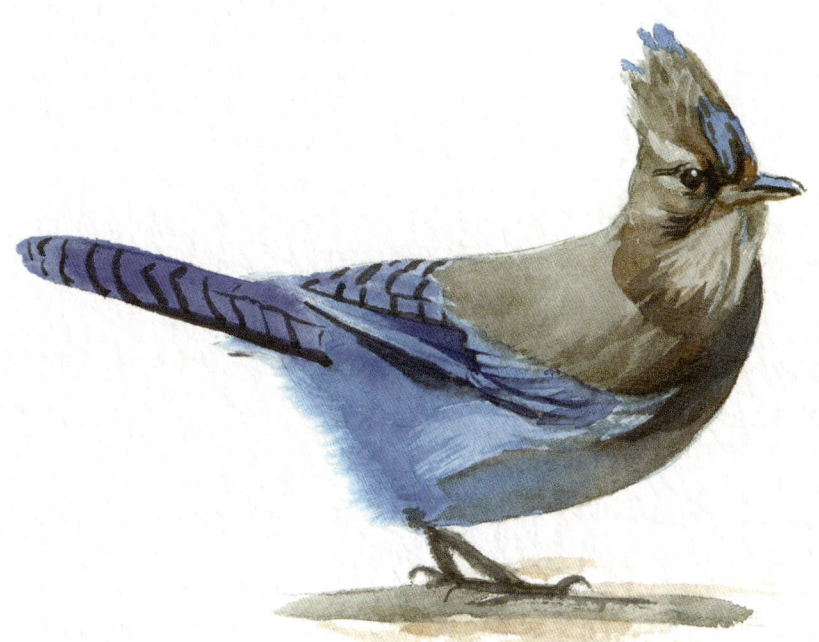

7. To create black, mix a creamier combination of ultramarine blue and burnt sienna. Use this to paint the striped pattern on the feathers, the shadows under the wing, and the rounded eye. Make sure to negative-paint around the tiny white highlight inside of the eye. Final details should always be painted wet-on-dry. You can use dry-brush techniques and delicate brush strokes to create subtle feather shapes on the crested head. Use careful, curved strokes to separate the feathers on the wing. Paint some texture on the ground beneath the bird using watered-down burnt sienna.

GLACIER NATIONAL PARK
Montana

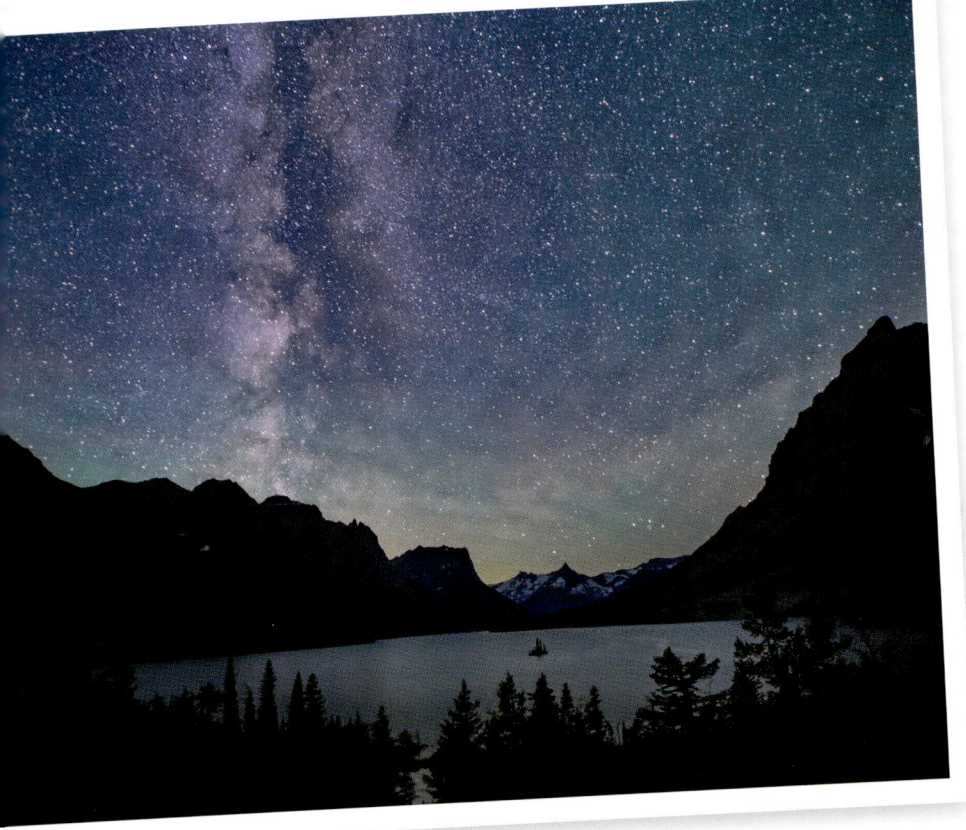

Glacier National Park in Montana, established as the tenth national park in 1910, is an artist's paradise, featuring sprawling glaciers, lakes, mountains, diverse wildlife, and a rich cultural history. Evidence of human presence in the area dates back more than 10,000 years.

This image depicts St. Mary Lake, a popular hiking destination on the east side of the park. If you are fortunate enough to witness the aurora borealis during your visit, it will be an unforgettable experience. For this painting, we'll use the wet-on-wet technique to capture the vibrant night sky.

Download template and reference photo.

Reference photo

Brushes

Round, sizes 8 and 10

Paper

Fabriano Artistico 140-pound (300 gsm), cotton, cold-pressed block, 9" x 12" (23 x 30.5 cm)

Color Palette

Ultramarine Blue

Marine Blue

Hansa Yellow Light

Quinacridone Rose

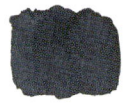

Indigo

Burnt Sienna

Opaque white

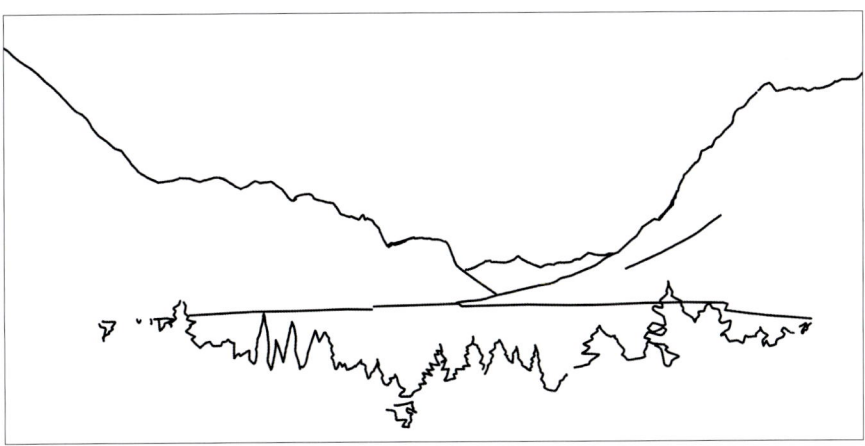

1. Sketch only the contour of the mountain slopes, lake, and tree line. The sky will be created entirely with paint.

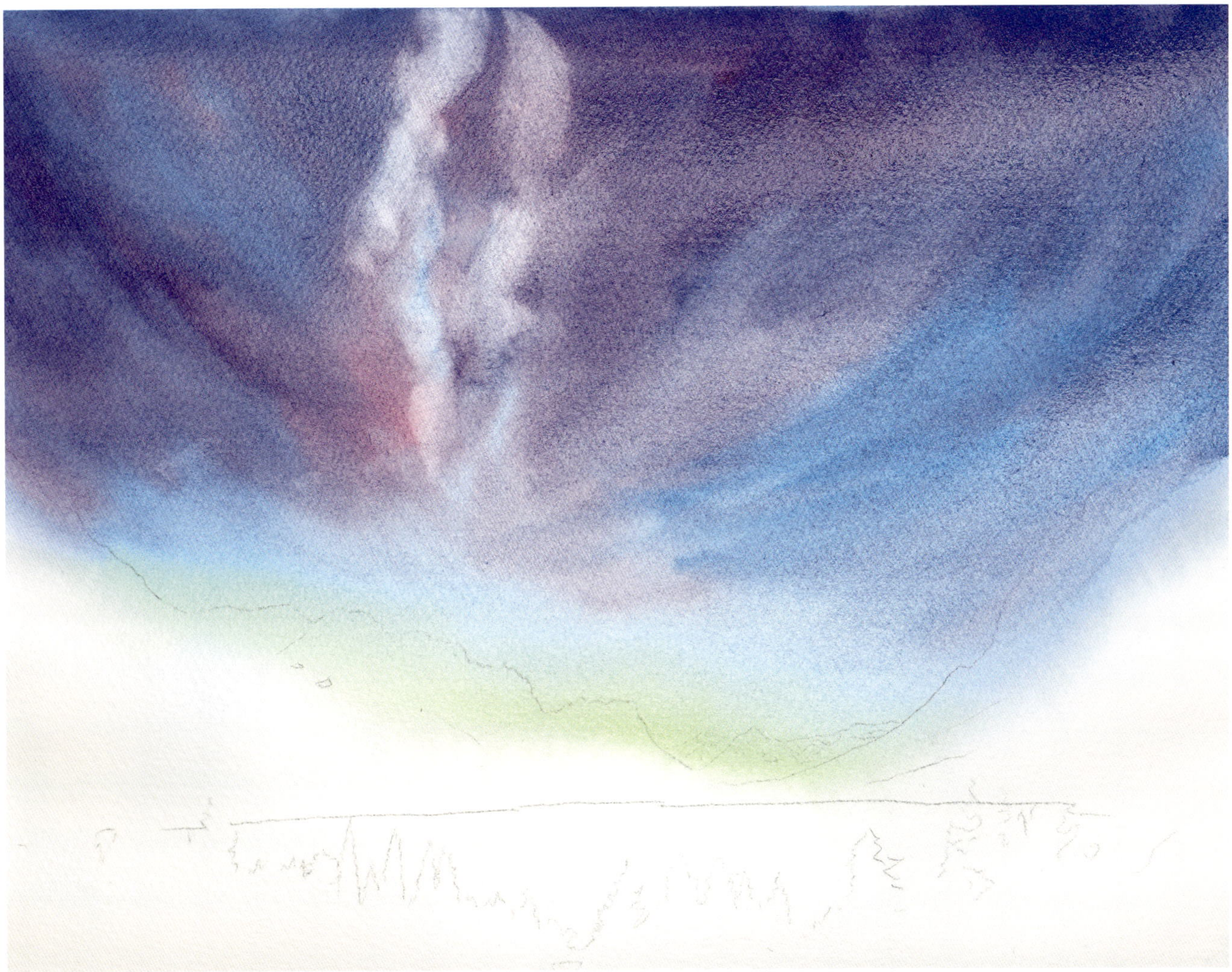

2. Soak your paper with clear water using a spray bottle and spread the water evenly with a large round brush. The surface should be glossy wet but without puddles. Begin by applying creamy ultramarine at the top, brushing it evenly toward the center. As you approach the horizon, blend in marine blue, and then add hansa yellow light near the mountains. It's okay if this color spreads beyond the sky.

Next, apply quinacridone rose into the sky to create purple tones, focusing on the center.

Use a clean, damp brush to lift some color, creating the effect of cloudy northern lights.

Allow this layer to dry completely before proceeding.

Scan to watch a video.

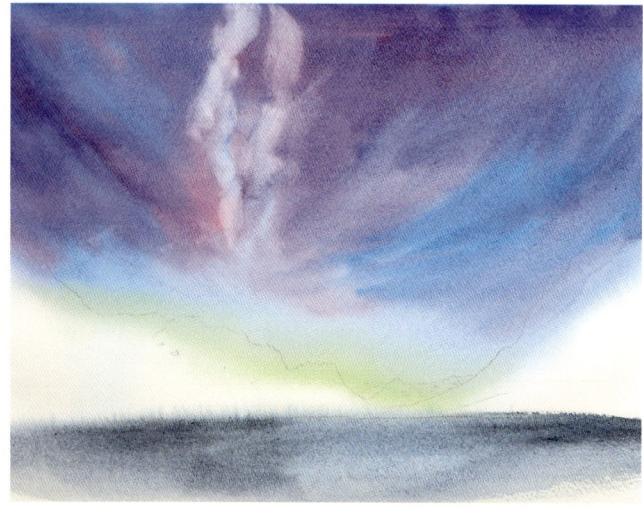

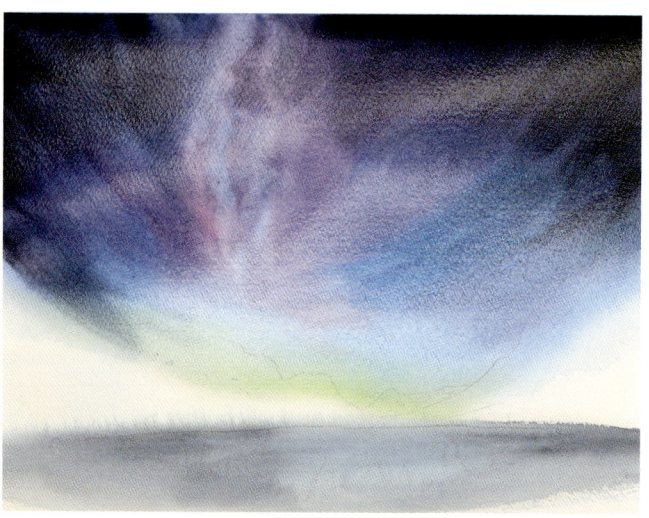

3. Paint the lake using the wet-on-wet technique with ultramarine and indigo. Darken the values where the mountains cast subtle shadows on the water.

4. Rewet the entire sky and darken with a wet-on-wet layer of indigo using your largest brush. Focus on the top and corners to create a vignette effect. Allow this to dry completely.

Scan to
watch a
video.

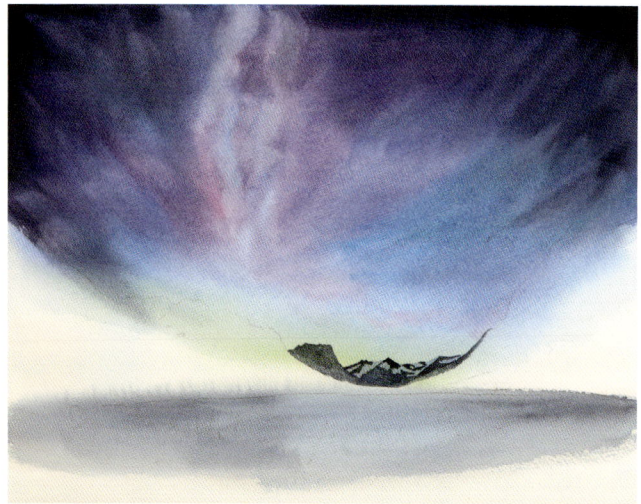

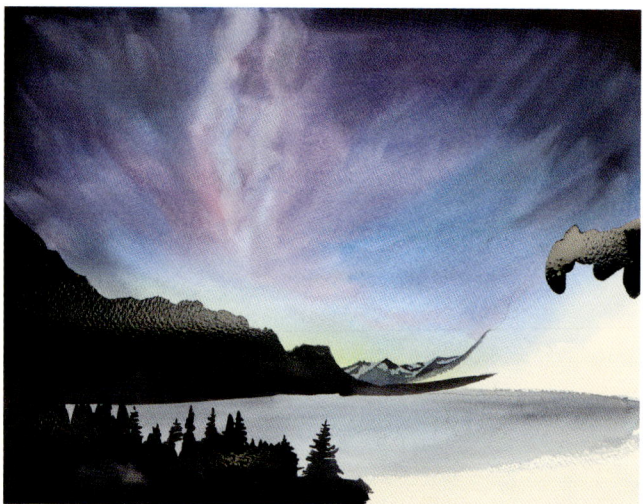

5. Apply a medium wash of ultramarine blue over the most distant mountains. Once dry, use a small brush to apply a thin layer of indigo, carefully painting around the tiny snow-covered areas on the peaks.

6. Prepare a generous, creamy puddle of black paint. I prefer to mix black using mostly indigo with some burnt sienna. Load your brush and start painting the silhouettes of the mountains and trees.

Scan to
watch a
video.

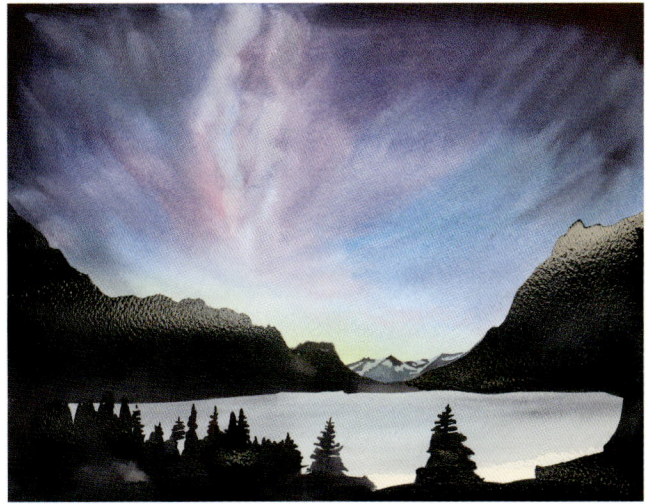

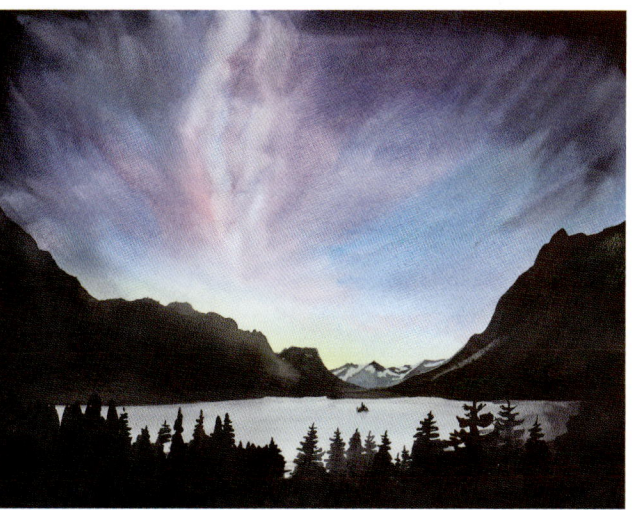

7. Switch to a smaller brush for the trees. Paint a quick vertical line, then use a side-to-side squiggly motion to create the branches. Work quickly, and don't worry about making the trees "perfect."

8. Complete the trees by connecting the dark shapes to form a "frame" around the body of water. Add the small tree-covered island in the lake. Use a clean, damp brush to lift some paint from the mountain on the right, giving it the appearance of being illuminated by the northern lights.

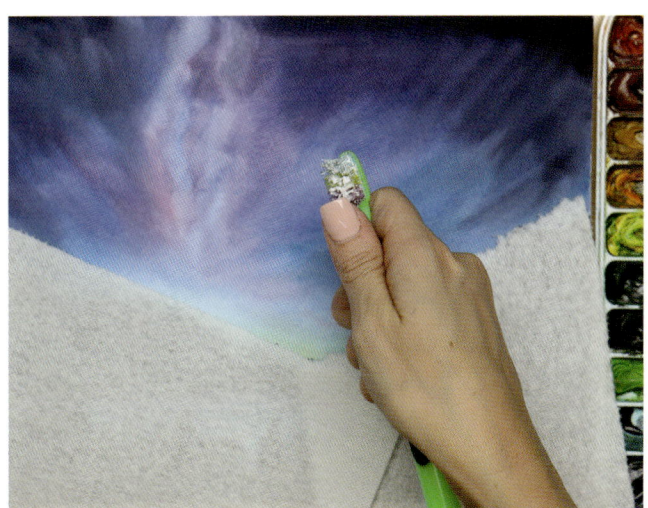

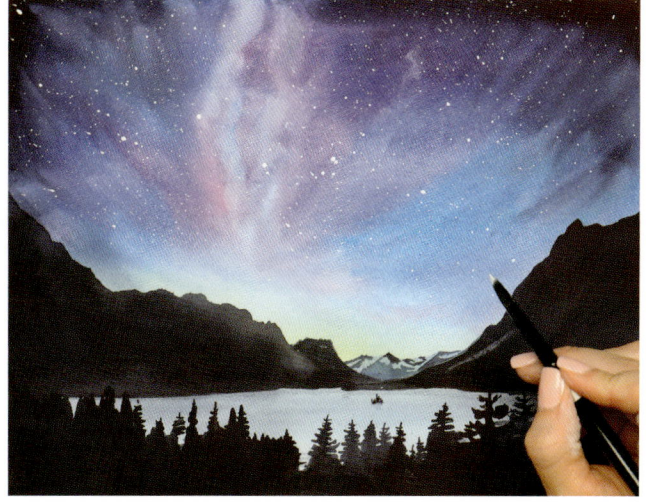

9. To paint stars, use an opaque white paint like gouache, acrylic, or bleedproof white. Protect the mountains with paper towels. Load an old toothbrush with the white paint and gently drag your thumb across the bristles to scatter tiny droplets of white across the surface.

10. Remove the paper towel and use a small round brush to add the finishing touches to your painting by dotting in a few final stars.

Scan to watch a video.

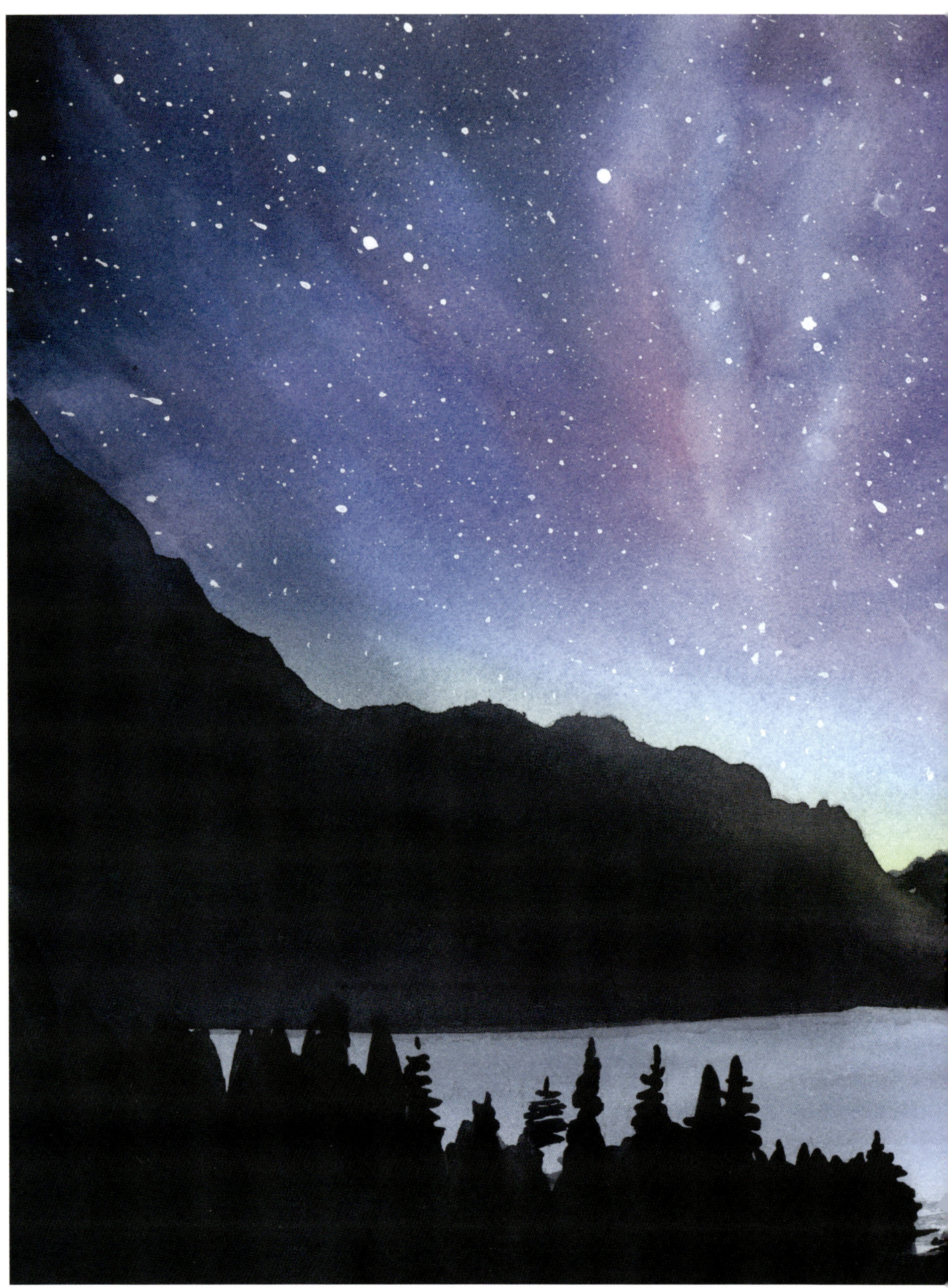

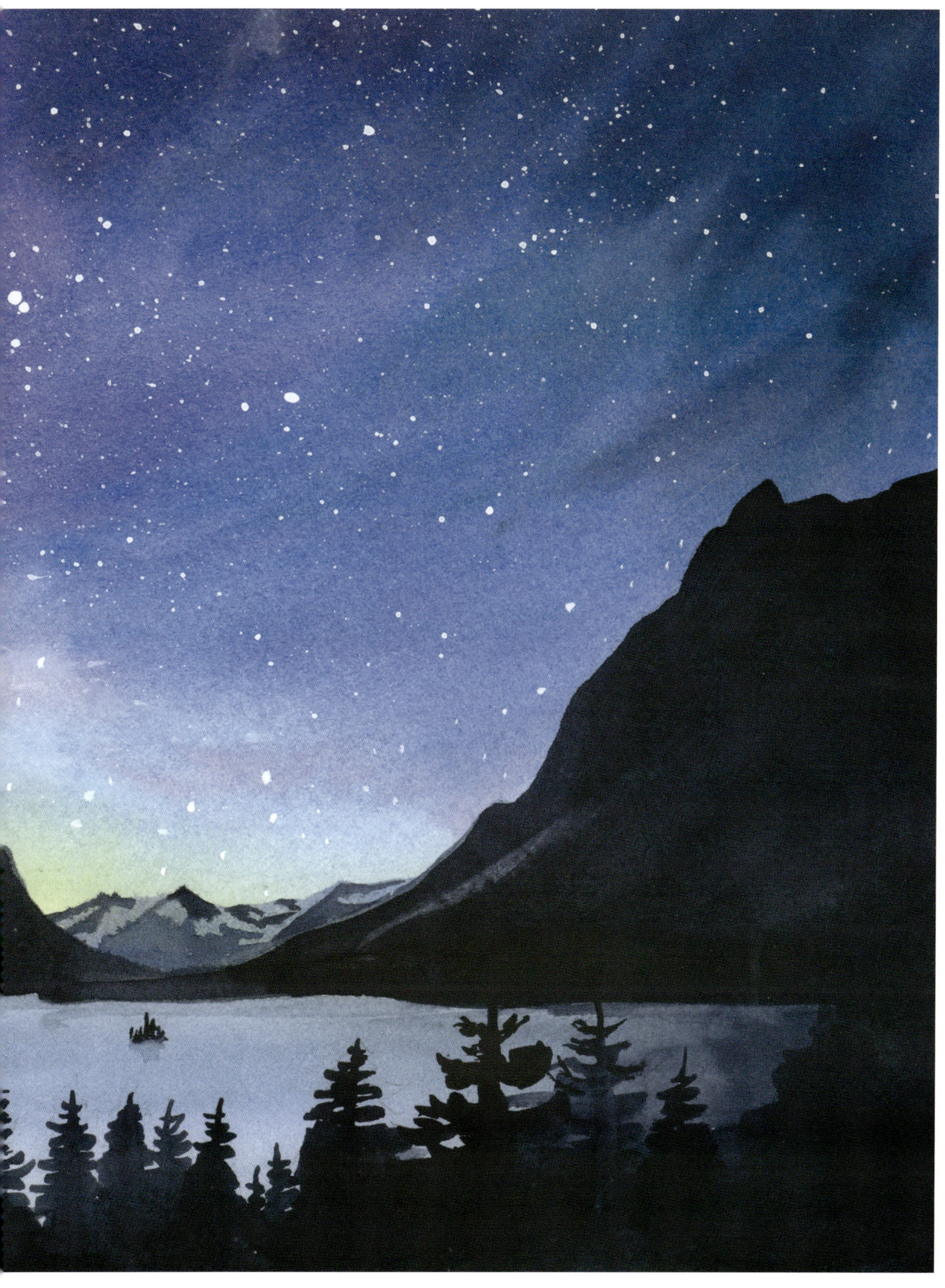

Bighorn Sheep

Glacier National Park is known for its impressive wildlife, including grizzly bears, elk, moose, and, of course, bighorn sheep!

Brush

Round, size 6

Color Palette

 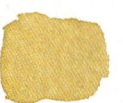 

Ultramarine Blue · Yellow Ochre · Burnt Sienna

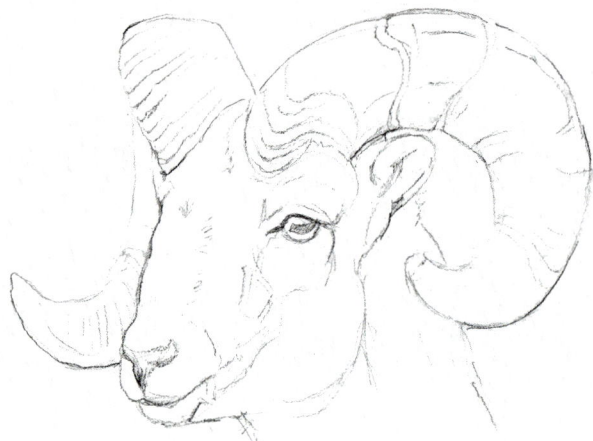

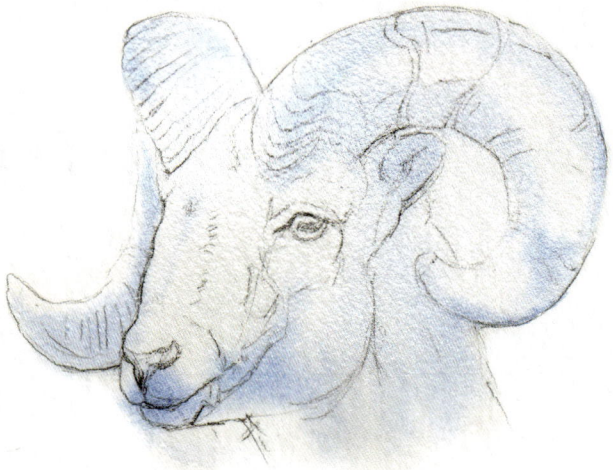

1. Sketch the contours of the head, leaving some "lost edges" along the highlighted curve of the horns.

2. Wet the entire paper with clean water, then apply ultramarine blue in a milky consistency to the areas that will be in shadow.

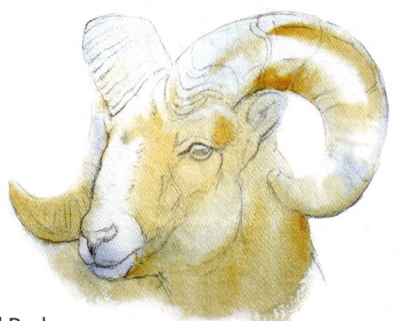

3. While the blue layer is still damp, apply a layer of yellow ochre using thicker paint. Be sure to avoid areas of white, such as the muzzle and the tops of the horns.

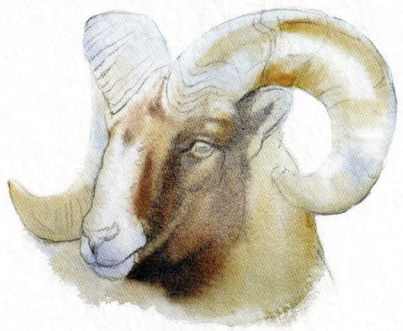
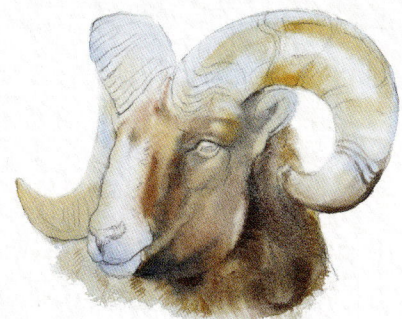
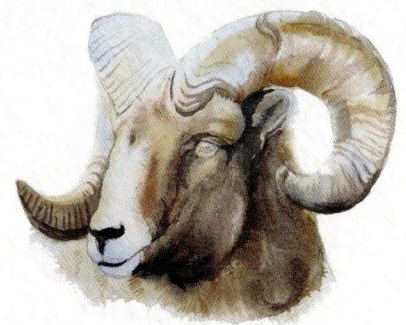

4. If the paper has started to dry, allow it to dry completely before applying more color. Once dry, rewet the shadow areas and add burnt sienna. Use ultramarine blue and burnt sienna for the darkest shadow areas. With the tip of your round brush, begin to suggest fur texture on the neck. This can be accomplished with short, quick, parallel brush strokes. Move your brush in the direction the fur is growing.

Scan to watch a video.

5. Mix burnt sienna and ultramarine blue to create a dark chocolate brown and use it to paint the neck. Begin adding the delicate curved rings on the horns.

6. Create black paint by mixing your darkest combination of ultramarine blue and burnt sienna. Use a small round brush to apply this dark color to the nose, mouth, and the shadows of the ears, lower jaw, and horns.

Scan to watch a video.

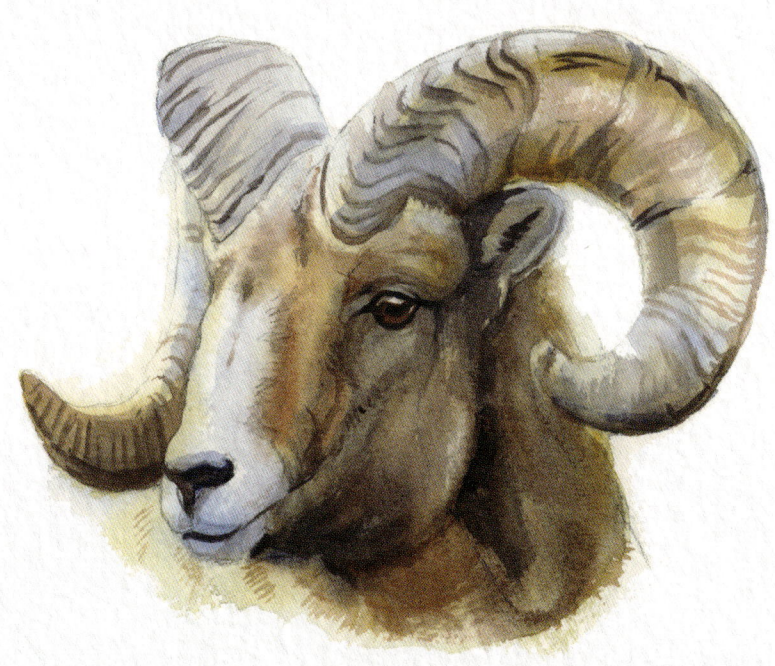

7. Add the final details. Paint the eye using burnt sienna and ultramarine blue, carefully negative-painting around the highlight. Add subtle fur texture using the wet-on-dry technique and include a few more curved rings on the horns. Finish with a few splashes of diluted ultramarine blue for a painterly touch!

Scan to watch a video.

GRAND TETON NATIONAL PARK
Wyoming

If your ideal excursion involves stunning mountain peaks, alpine lakes, and majestic vistas, Grand Teton National Park in northwest Wyoming is a must-visit. This image captures Jackson Lake, the largest glacial lake in the park and one of the best spots to catch the sunrise!

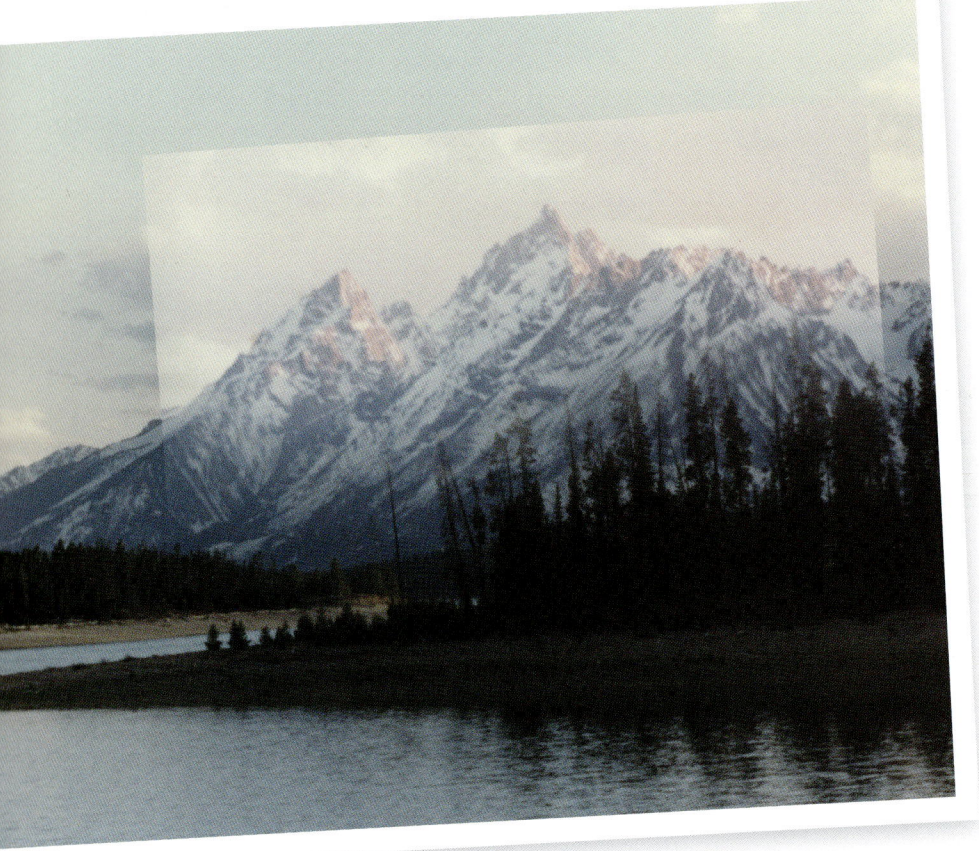

Reference photo

Download template and reference photo.

Brushes

Round, sizes 6 and 10

Paper

Fabriano Artistico 140-pound (300 gsm), cotton, cold-pressed block, 9" x 12" (23 x 30.5 cm); taped to resize down to 8" x 10" (20.5 x 25.5 cm)

Color Palette

  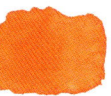 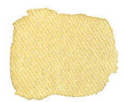   

| Phthalo Blue (GS) | Ultramarine Blue | Transparent Orange | Yellow Ochre | Burnt Sienna | Quinacridone Rose | Indigo |

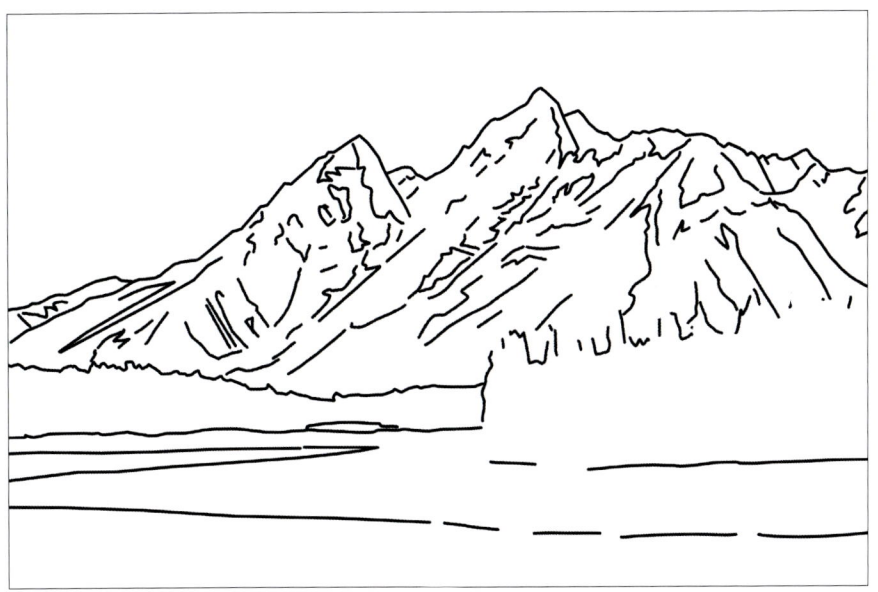

1. Sketch or trace the image onto your watercolor paper. You do not need to sketch any tree details—clouds, tree shapes, and reflections can be drawn with paint.

Note

....

See pages 20-21 in Part 1 for more details on working from multiple photos. On page 66 is my rough mockup combining two images using photo-editing software.

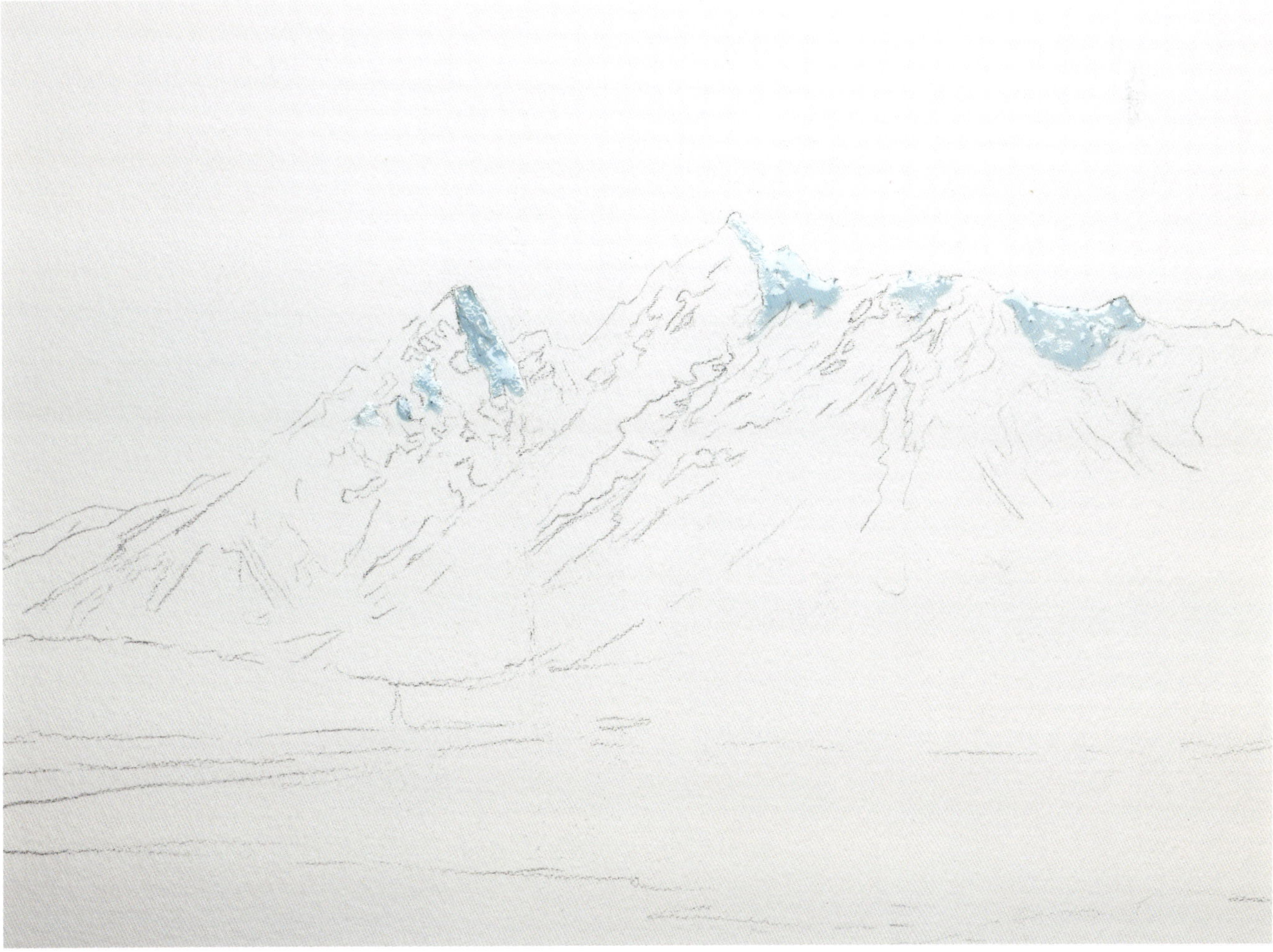

2. Use masking fluid to protect the sunlit pink areas on the mountaintops. This step is optional—you can always paint around these areas. I like to use masking fluid when I want to apply a quick wash to a large section while protecting the white of the paper in small, isolated spots. Allow the masking fluid to dry for at least 10 minutes.

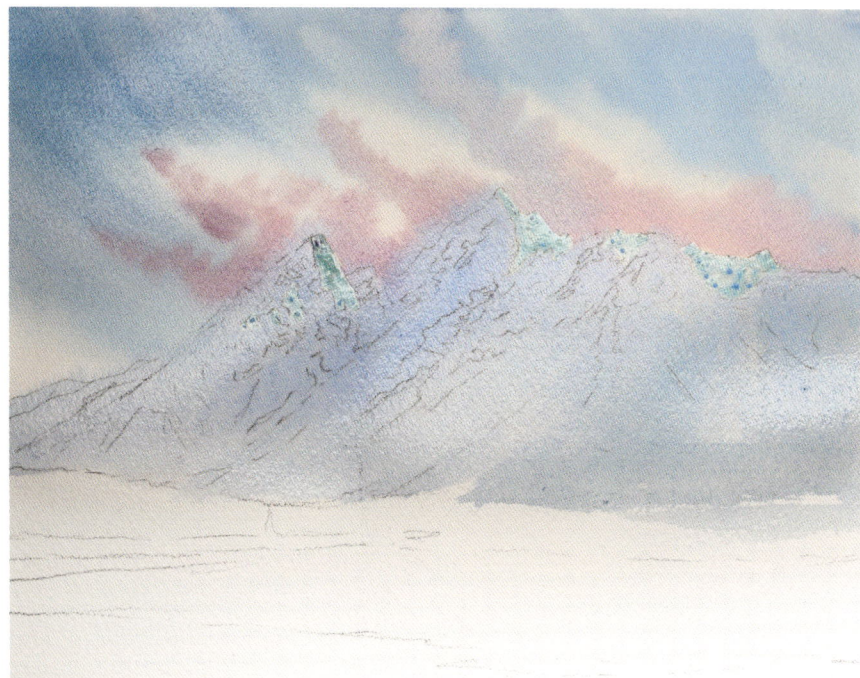

3. With a spray bottle and large brush, wet the top two-thirds of your paper. Prepare a tinted wash of ultramarine blue and phthalo blue. With your largest brush, quickly paint the blue sky, leaving out some puffy white clouds in any shape you like. Apply the same blue wash over the entire mountain range. Add soft pink cloud shadows with quinacridone rose. Let it dry completely.

Scan to
watch a
video.

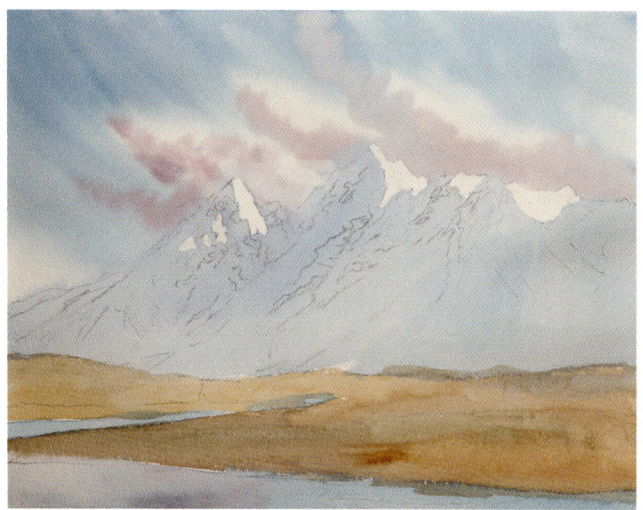

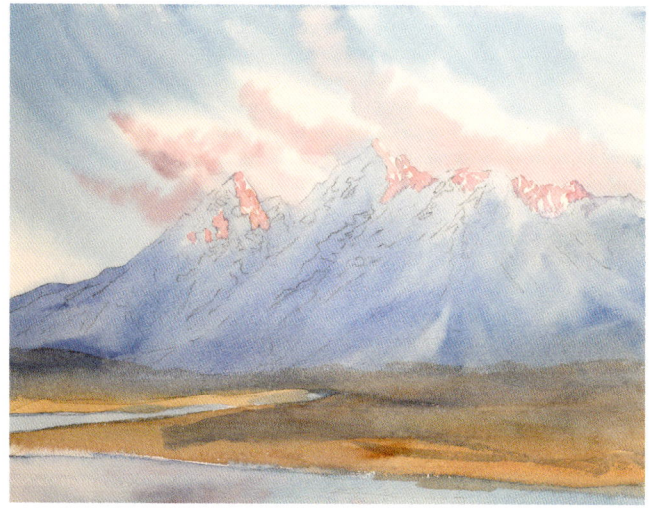

4. Apply a base layer of yellow ochre and burnt sienna to the ground. For the lake, use a light wash of ultramarine blue and phthalo blue. While the paint is still wet, add quinacridone rose to loosely reflect the colors of the sky. When the mountains and sky are dry, remove the masking fluid.

5. Load your small brush with a milky, slightly diluted quinacridone rose and paint the pink-tinted sunlit mountain peaks, leaving tiny white gaps to suggest snow highlights. Then, use a watery ultramarine blue to apply a second wash over the mountains.

Scan to
watch a
video.

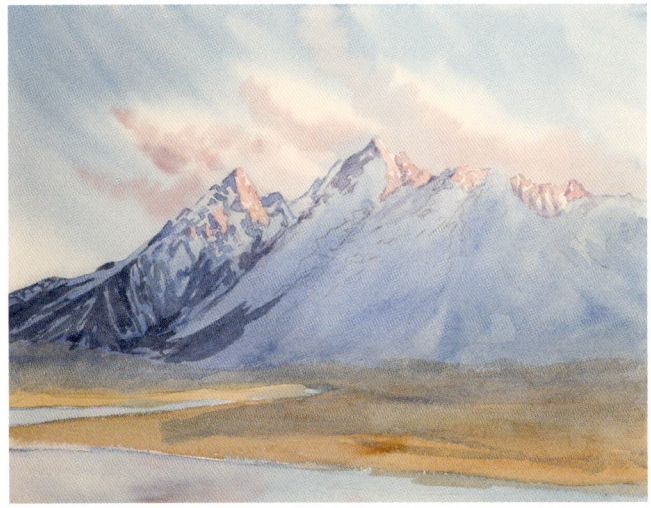

6. Begin painting the intricate valley shapes in the mountain side. For this, I use my size 6 round brush and a milky mix of indigo and ultramarine blue.

Scan to watch a video.

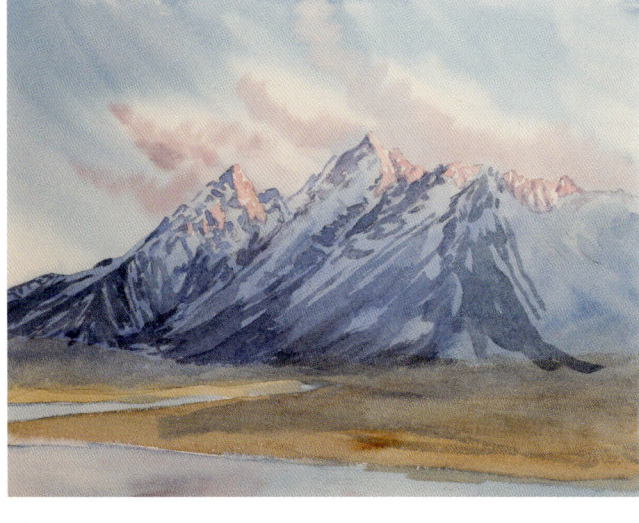

7. Keep painting the slender valley shapes, intentionally leaving small gaps as you go. Extend these shapes all the way down to the ground mass.

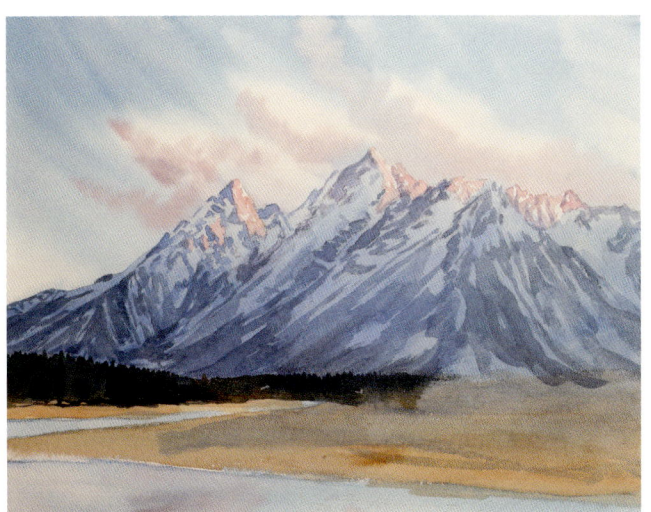

8. When painting the trees, visualize them as a single, unified shape rather than separate individual trees. Use a mix of indigo and yellow ochre to create a deep, earthy green for the forest.

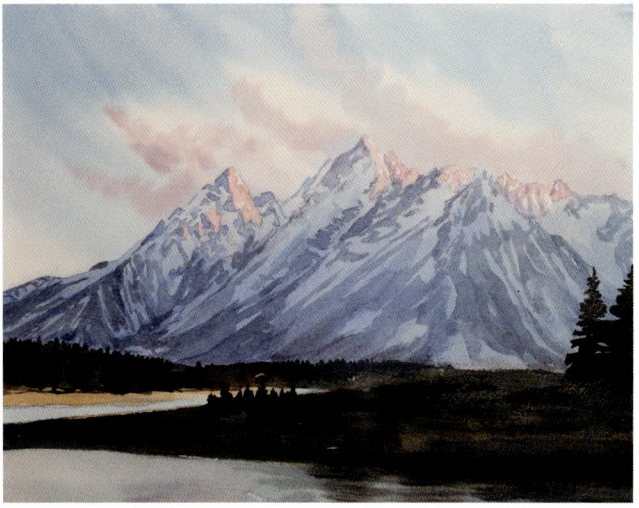

9. Darken the ground using the same mix of mostly indigo and yellow ochre. Use a larger brush to work quickly. Apply side-to-side squiggly strokes to paint the taller trees along the shore, and gentle horizontal strokes to create reflections on the water.

Scan to watch a video.

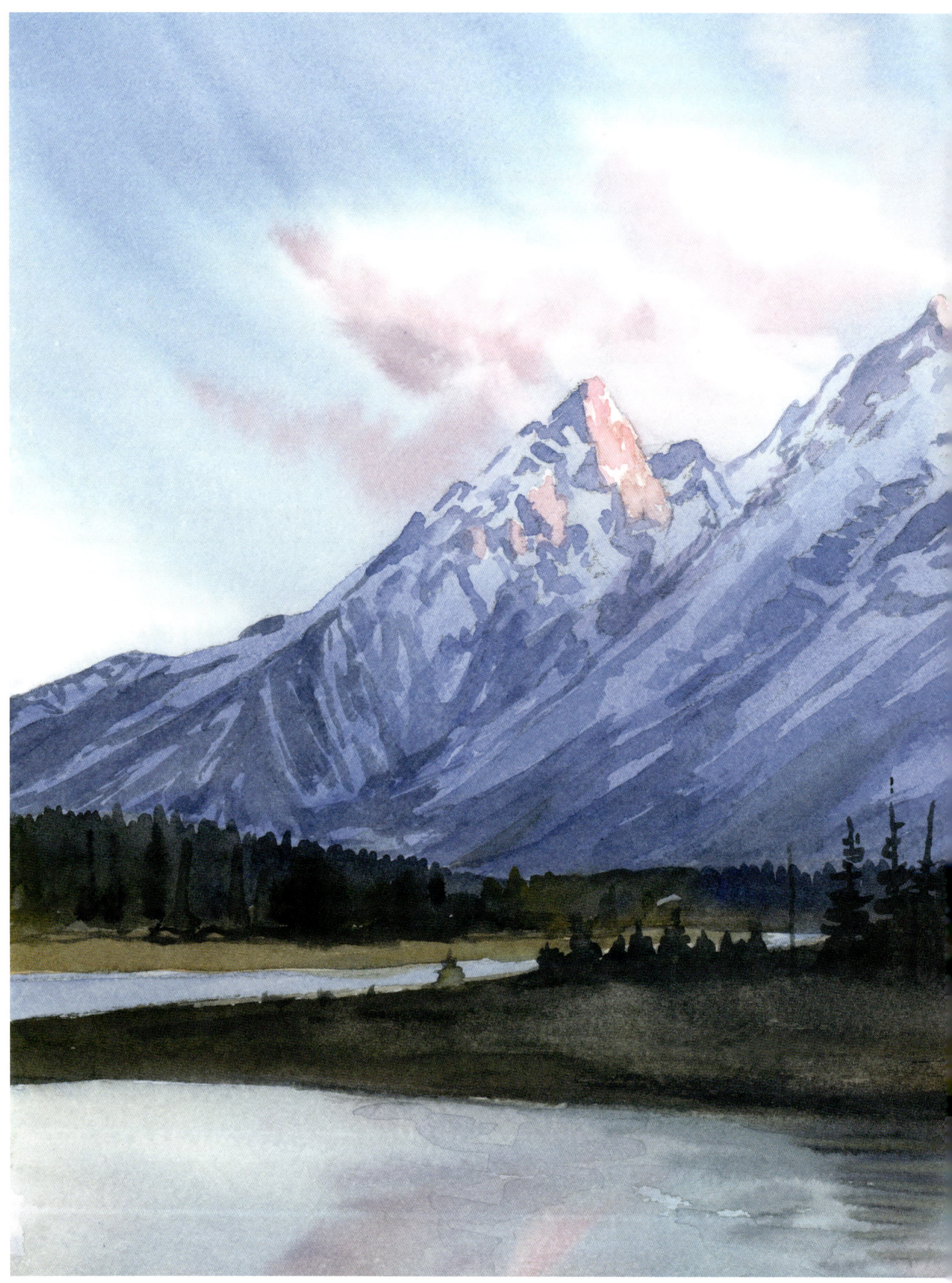

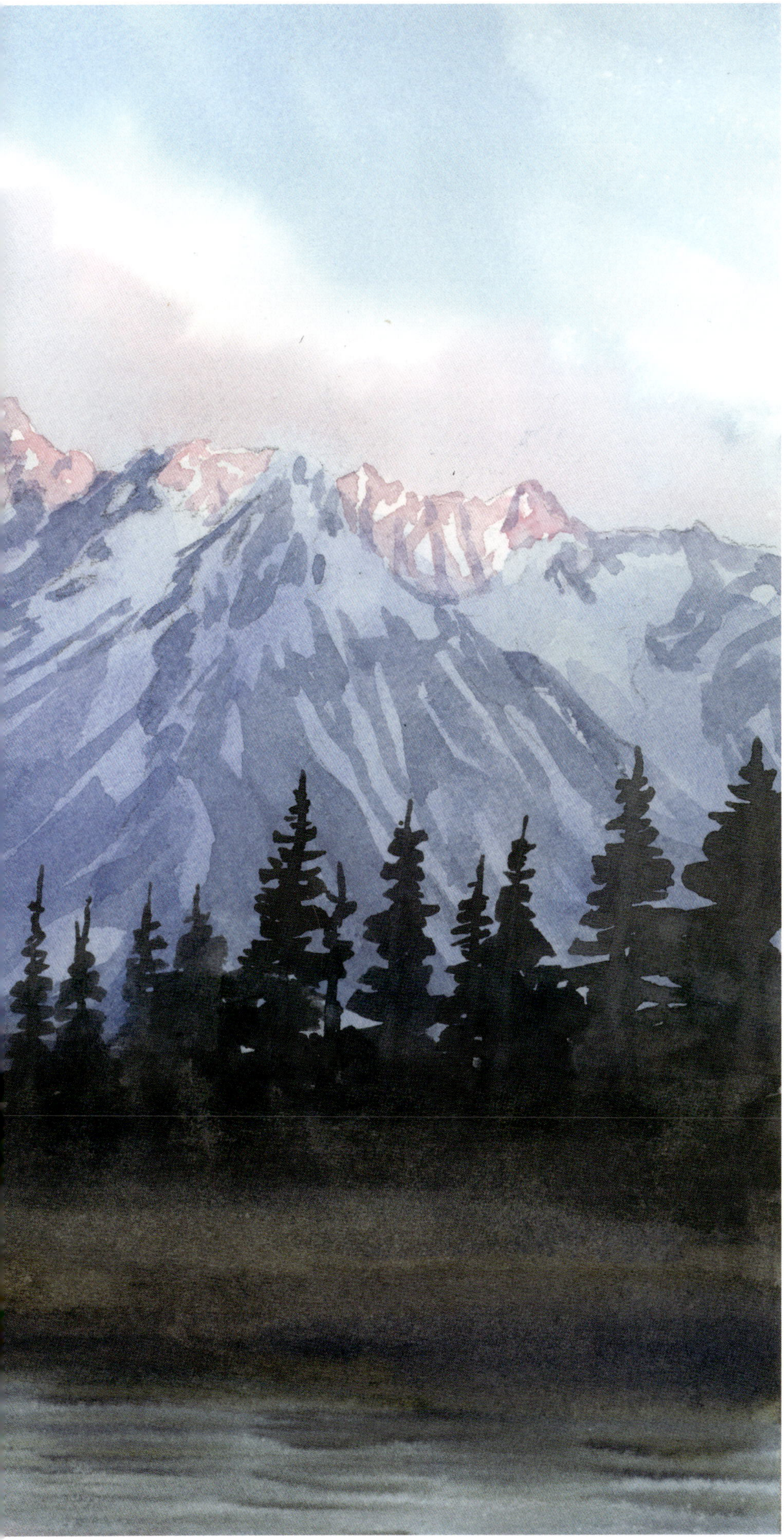

Scan to watch a video.

10. Complete the trees by making the tree line asymmetrical. Work quickly to ensure the colors blend smoothly, wet next to wet.

Grizzly Cub

Grizzly bears are a frequent sight in the Tetons. Wyoming's most famous bear, known as Grizzly 399, drew the attention of dozens of wildlife photographers and was renowned for raising at least twenty-two cubs before she was sadly killed by a vehicle as I was writing this book. In this grizzly cub painting, I simplified the palette to just two colors. You can use various techniques, like wet-on-wet and dry brush, to create textures for the fur and bark.

Download template and reference photo.

Brushes

Round, sizes 6 and 10

Color Palette

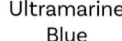

Ultramarine Blue   Burnt Sienna

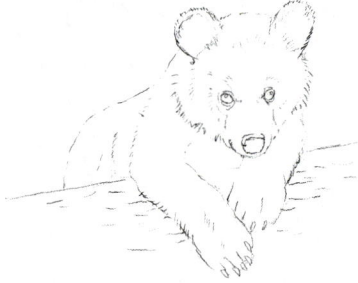

1. Sketch or trace the bear.

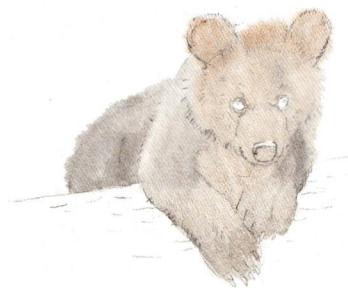

2. Begin by wetting the paper within the lines and extending at least a finger's width beyond the bear's head and back. While the paper is still glossy, drop in a milky mix of ultramarine blue and burnt sienna. The paint will naturally "fuzz out," giving the fur a soft, fluffy appearance.

Scan to watch a video.

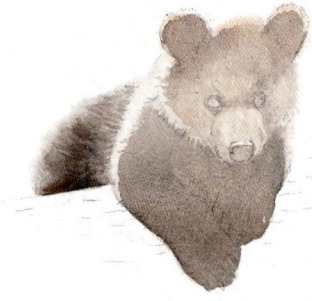

3. Start layering more color, adjusting the brown by varying the ratios of ultramarine blue and burnt sienna. For highlights on the bear's fur, be mindful not to cover the entire cub with dark brown. Let some of the lighter first wash show through. You can splay the bristles of your brush and use short, quick brush strokes to paint layers of textured fur.

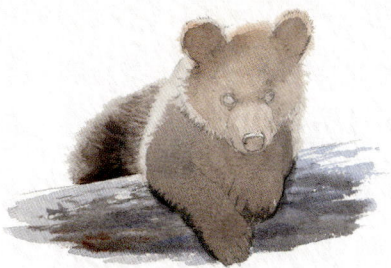

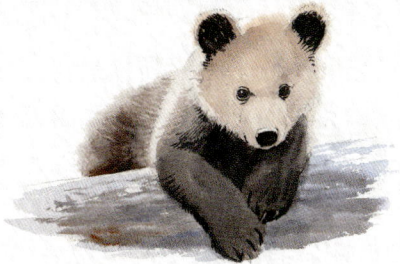

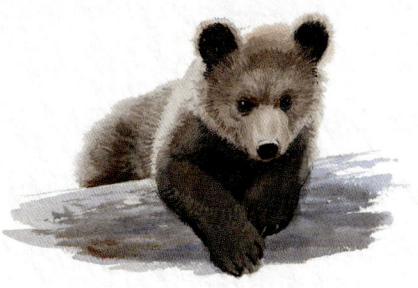

4. Apply a light wash of ultramarine blue as a base layer on the log. Then, add texture by using scrubby brush strokes and dry-brush techniques.

5. To create black, mix equal parts of ultramarine blue and burnt sienna to a creamy consistency, adding just enough water for smooth flow. Use a small brush to paint the cub's inner ears and eyes, and the shadows on its chest and paws.

Scan to watch a video.

6. Keep layering fur texture with your mix of ultramarine blue and burnt sienna. Move your brush strokes in the direction the fur grows, radiating out like sunbeams from the center of the face.

Scan to watch a video.

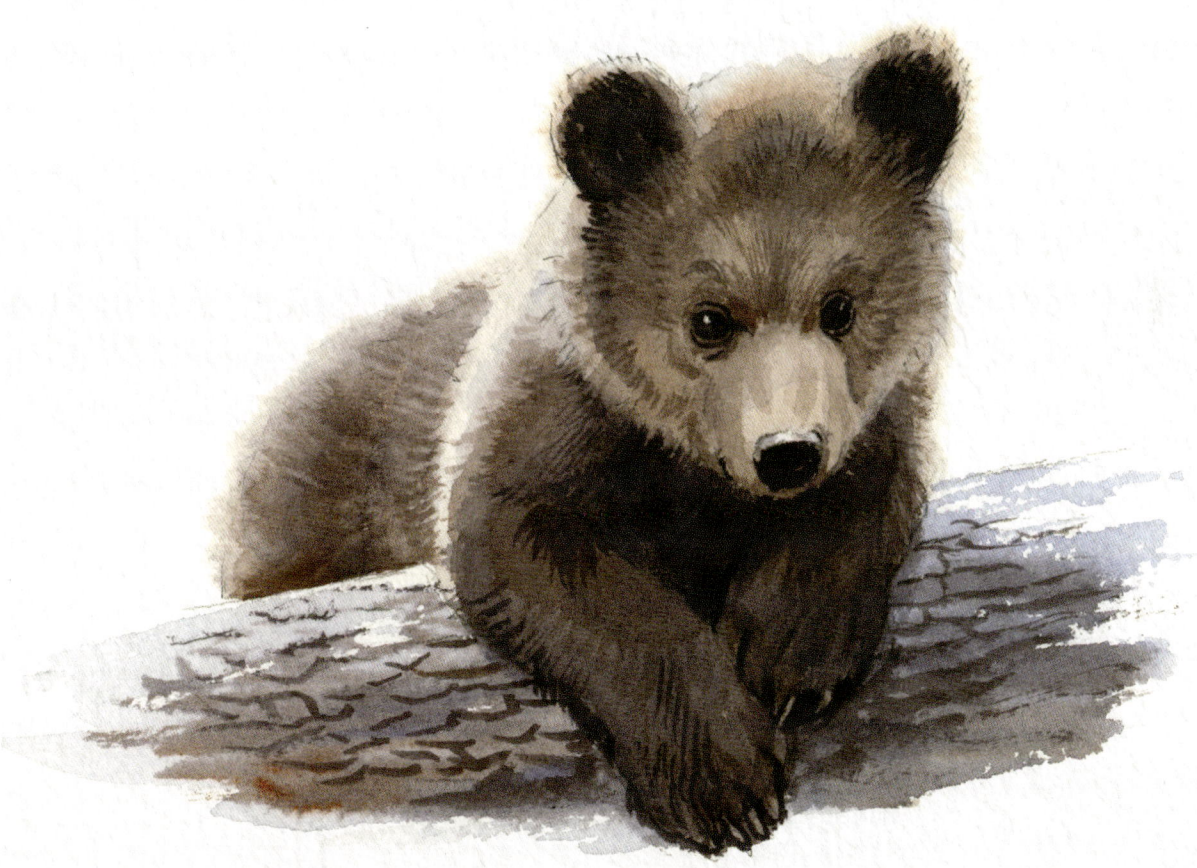

7. Add the finishing touches by painting a few final strokes to suggest fur on the legs. Use your darkest mix of ultramarine blue and burnt sienna to carve out the shapes of the bark.

YELLOWSTONE NATIONAL PARK
Wyoming/Montana/Idaho

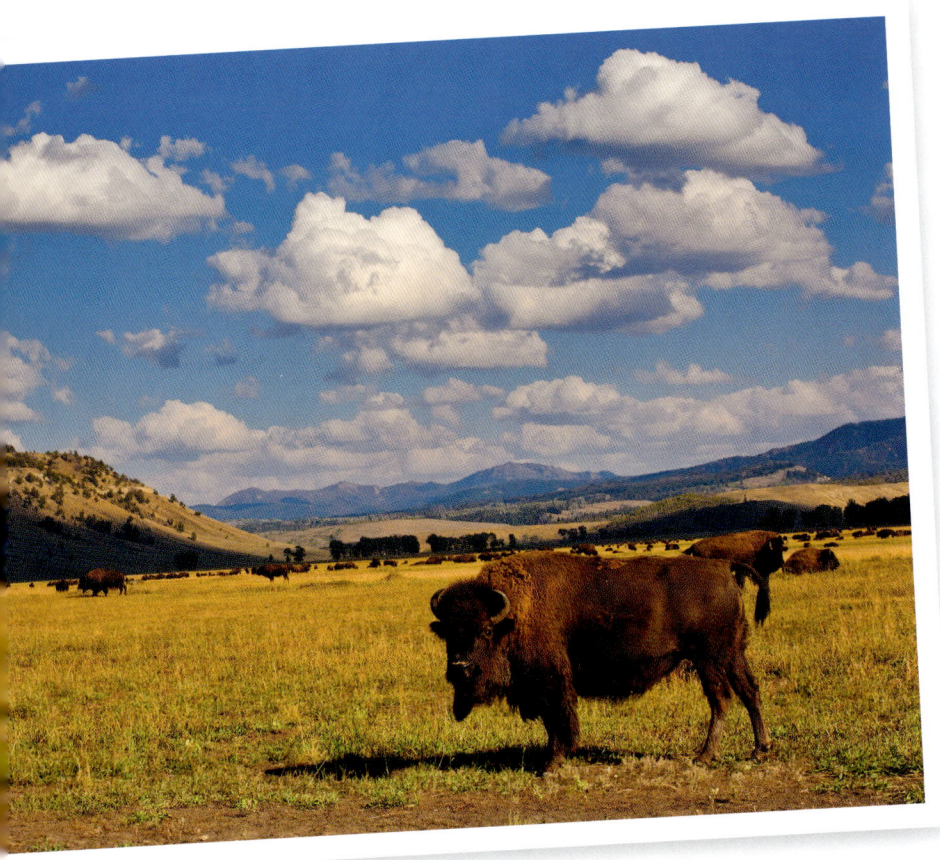

Reference photo

Yellowstone National Park was the *first* national park established in the United States, protected through an Act of Congress signed by President Ulysses S. Grant in 1872. Although this massive park, which extends into three different states (Wyoming, Montana, and Idaho) is most known for its geysers, I wanted to create a painting that represented the park's wildlife. Every year, thousands of visitors marvel at the Yellowstone Park bison herd, which is the oldest and largest public bison herd in the United States, numbering nearly 5,000. It's difficult to imagine that there were once millions of bison roaming the plains, but by the late 1880s, they were hunted nearly to extinction. Thankfully, like with the great redwood forests, the government intervened just in time to protect and allow repopulation.

Download template and reference photo.

Brushes

Round, sizes 6 and 10

Paper

Fabriano Artistico 140-pound (300 gsm), cotton, cold-pressed block, 9" x 12" (23 x 30.5 cm); taped to resize down to 8" x 10" (20.5 x 25.5 cm)

Color Palette

Phthalo Blue (GS)

Permanent Violet

Ultramarine Blue

Gamboge Nova

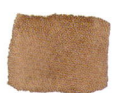

Burnt Sienna

Indigo

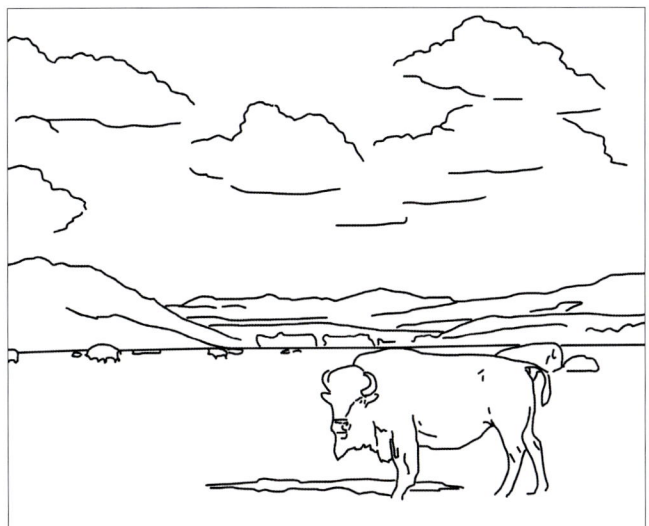

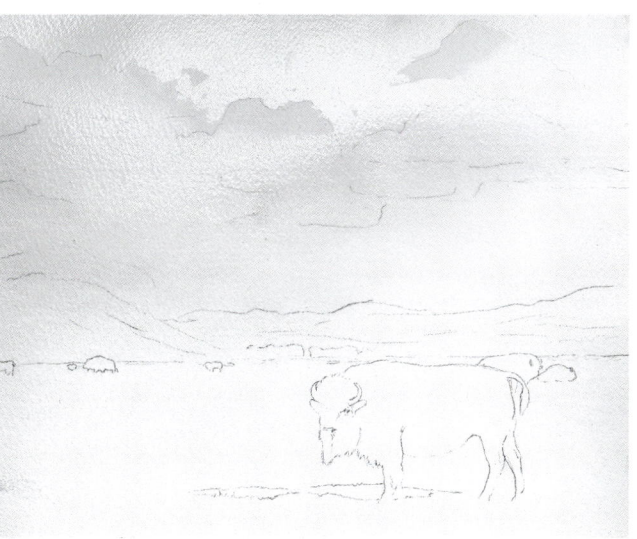

1. For this image, it is a good idea to lightly sketch the largest clouds, just so that you can be confident in their placement and overall design. Draw the shadow shapes on the distant hills and bison.

2. With your largest round brush, paint clear water into the sky area, avoiding the bright white clouds.

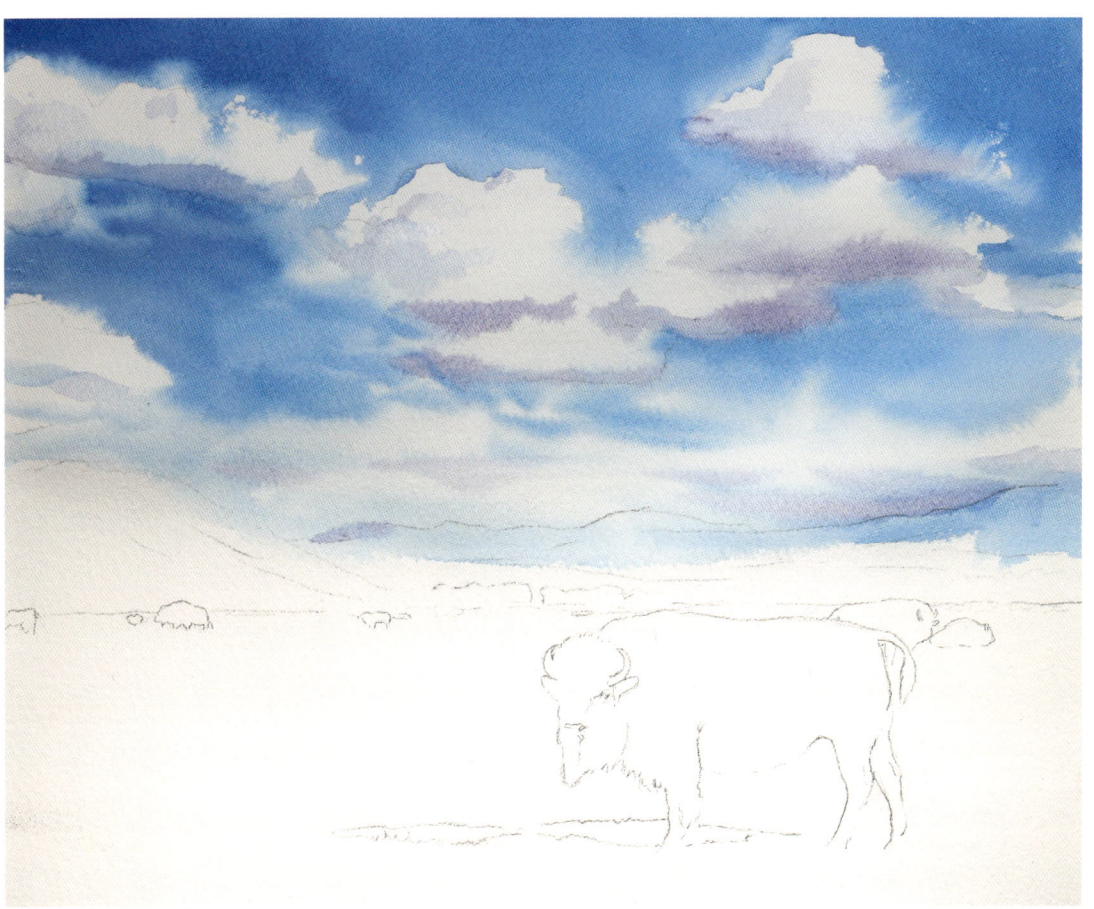

3. Load up your brush with phthalo blue, painting in the blue sky as quickly as possible. This is a great exercise in negative painting, working your way around those white cloud shapes. Add some permanent violet beneath the clouds for shadows.

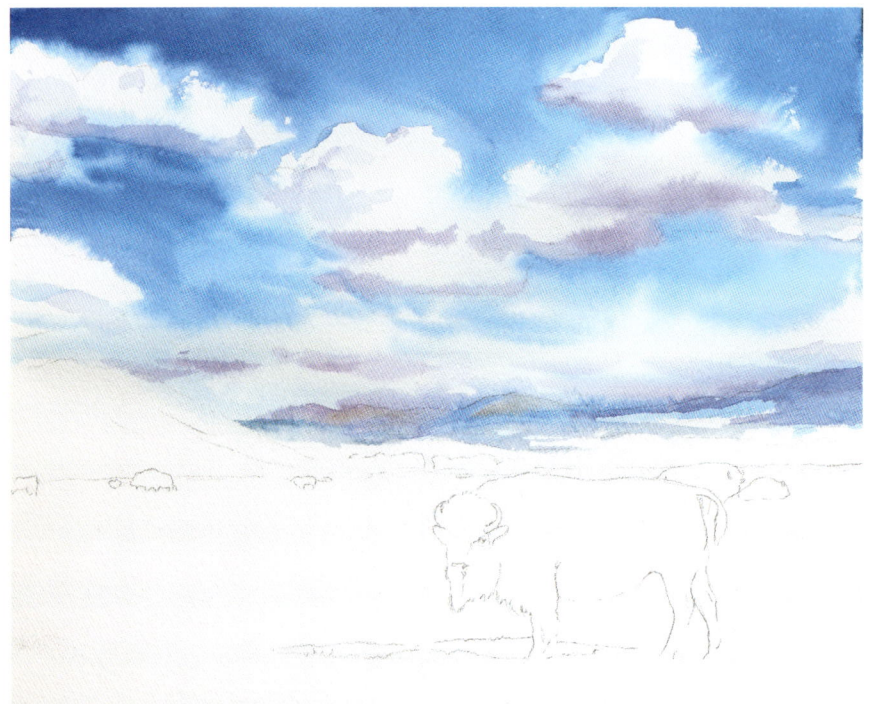

4. Working with light values, use your smaller brush to begin painting the distant line of mountains. Alternate between violet and ultramarine blue for some lovely color variety. These blues and violets help create atmospheric perspective. If your cloudy sky is still damp, this will allow the mountain edge to soften wet-on-wet, creating the illusion of distance.

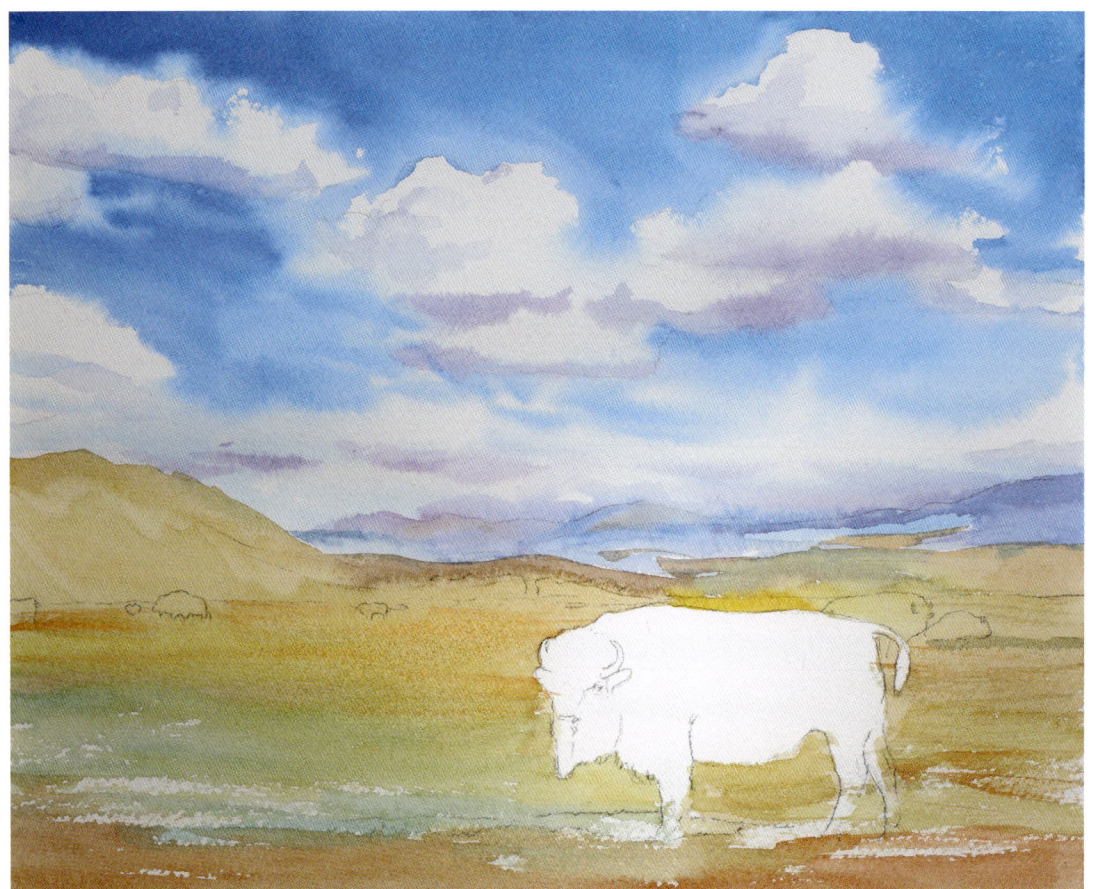

Scan to watch a video.

5. Begin painting the grassy plains using gamboge nova, light hints of phthalo blue, and burnt sienna. You can paint right over the distant bison herd, but negative-paint around the foreground bison.

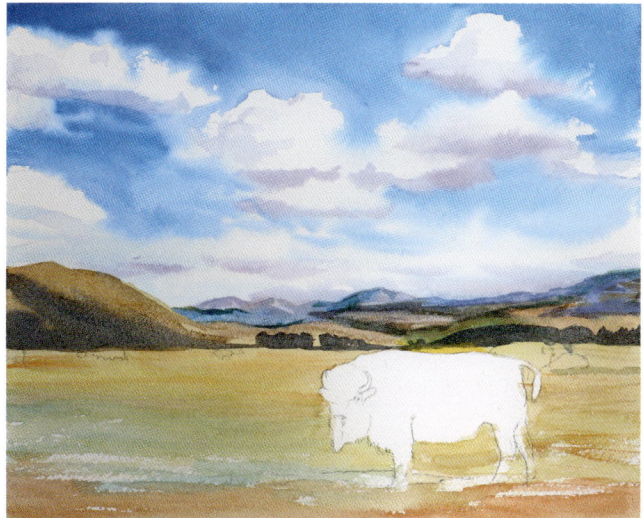

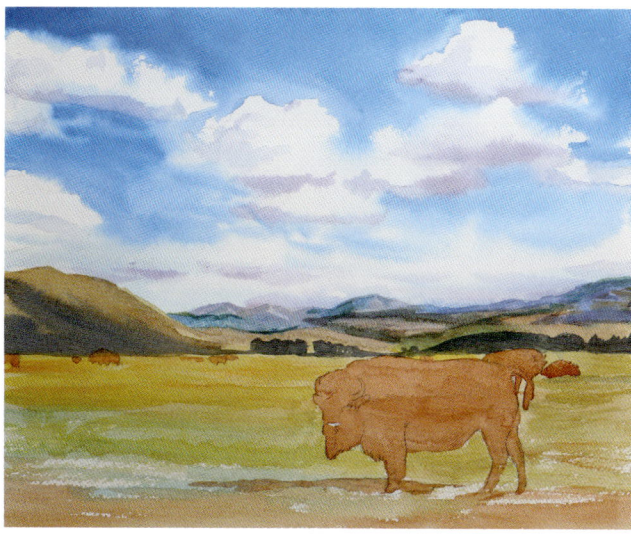

6. While your first wash of gamboge nova is still damp, drop in the cloud shadows on the hills using ultramarine blue. Use your smaller round brush to paint tree clusters and more dark shadows across the mountains.

Scan to watch a video.

7. For a first layer of color on the animals, use a watery wash in a medium value of burnt sienna, carefully painting the solid shapes of each bison.

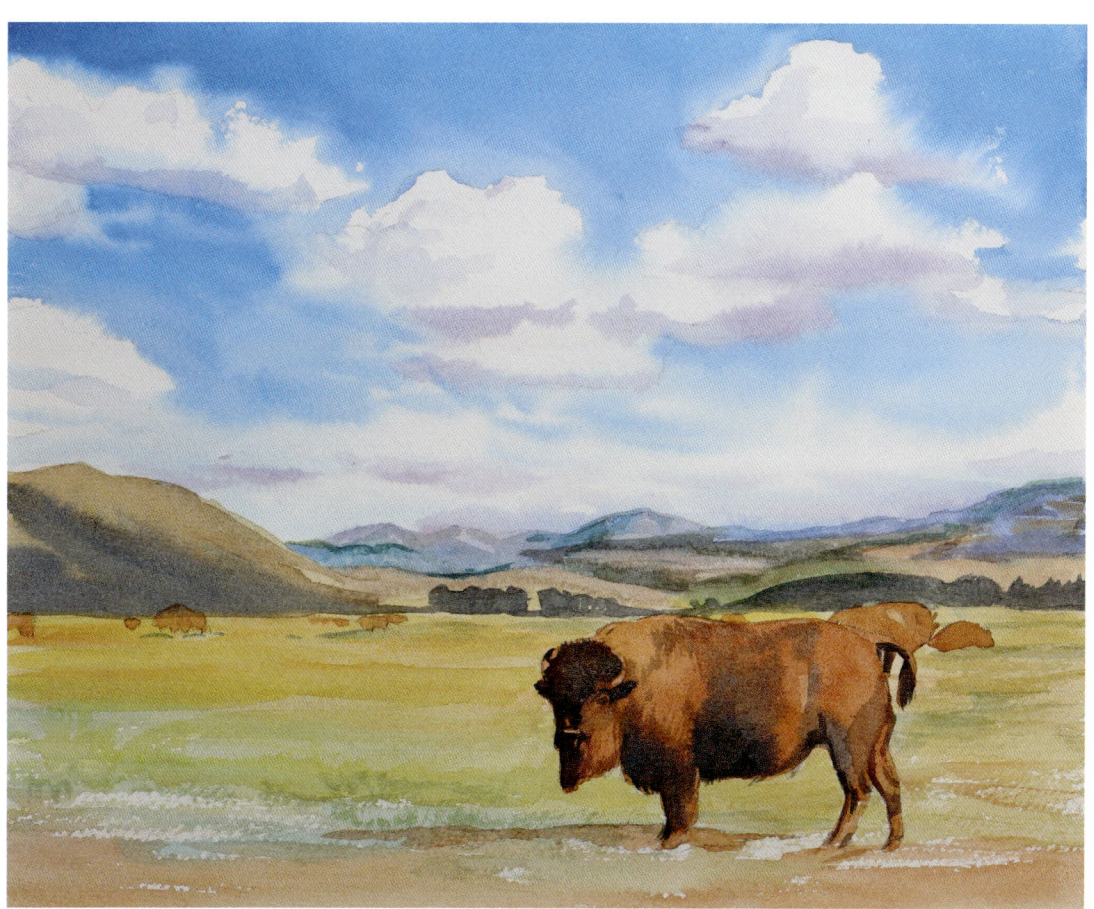

8. Mix your ultramarine blue and burnt sienna to create darker browns for the thick fur on the bison's head and belly. Gradually add layers of color for the shadows, leaving the areas in sunlight lighter in value. Use indigo for the darkest darks on the ears, nose, tail, and underbelly.

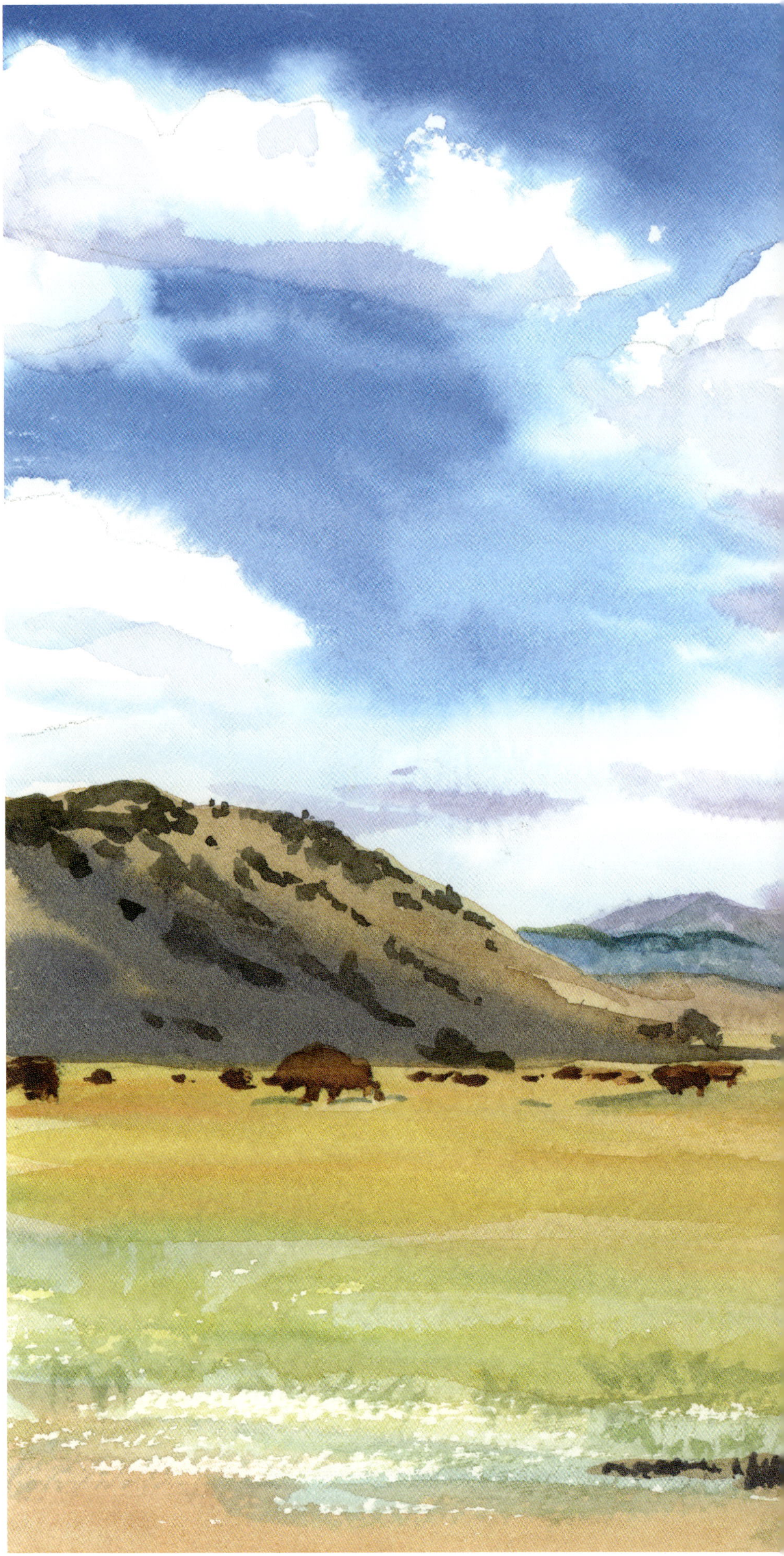

Scan to watch a video.

9. Add final details like scrubby trees on the hillside, shadows on the distant bison shapes, and a long skinny shadow beneath the foreground bison. You can use the dry-brush technique to add grassy texture to the plains. Don't add too much detail—step back from your work and squint often to ensure you are focusing on the most important things.

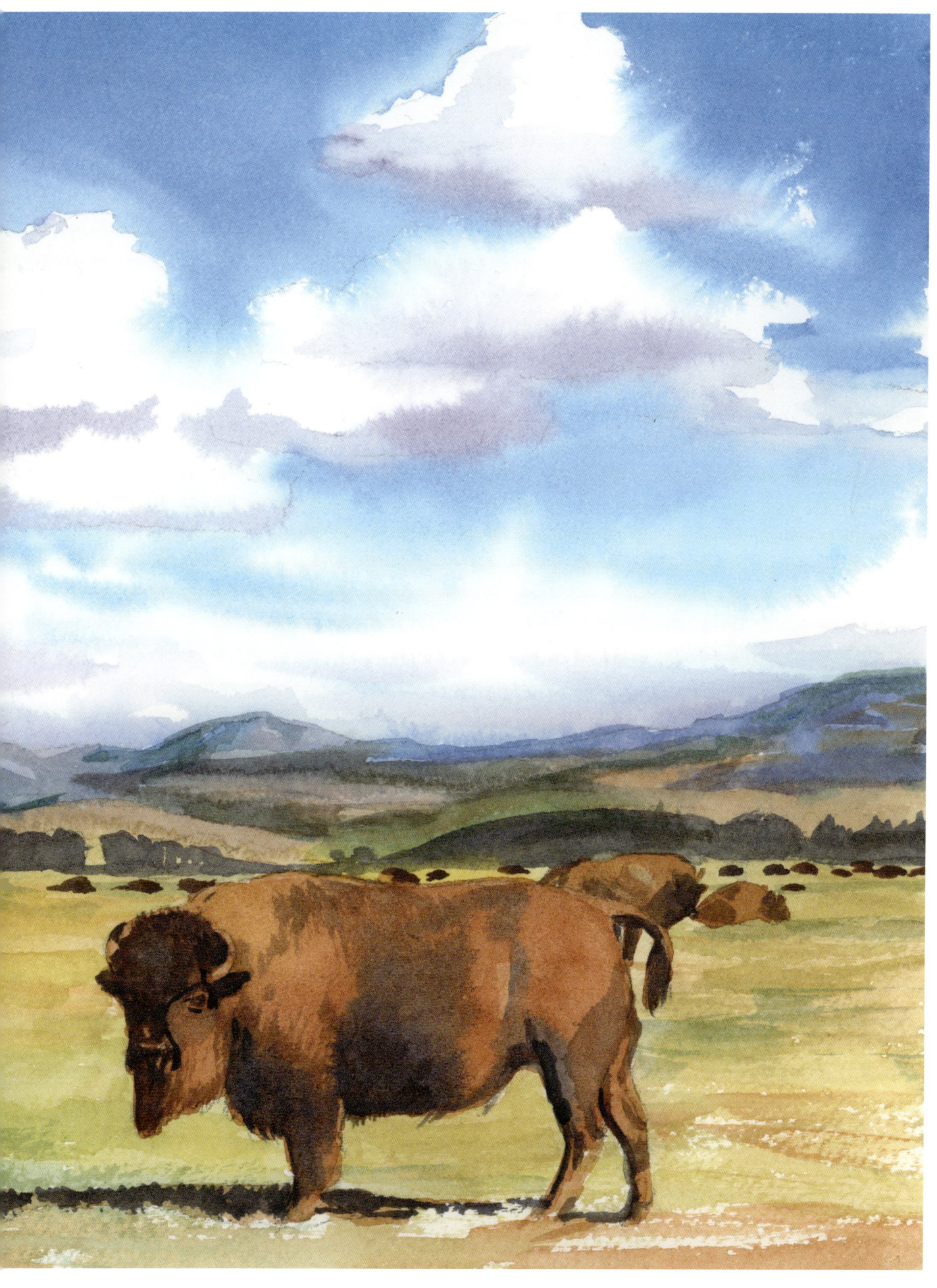

Red Fox

Red foxes are the smallest canids in Yellowstone, but they are numerous!
If you are lucky enough to spot one, you will immediately recognize it
by its bushy tail, reddish color, and black "socks."

Download template and reference photo.

Brush

Round, size 8

Color Palette

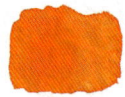   

| Transparent Orange | Hansa Yellow Light | Burnt Sienna | Ultramarine Blue | Indigo |

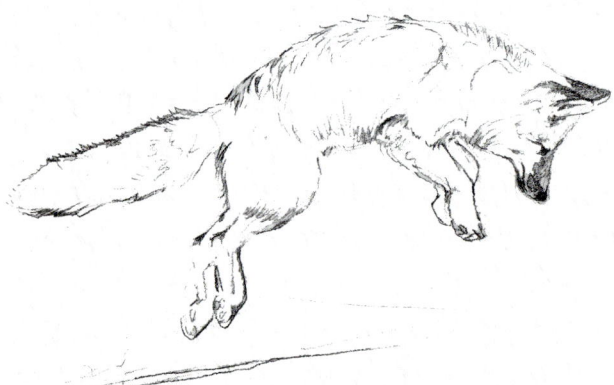 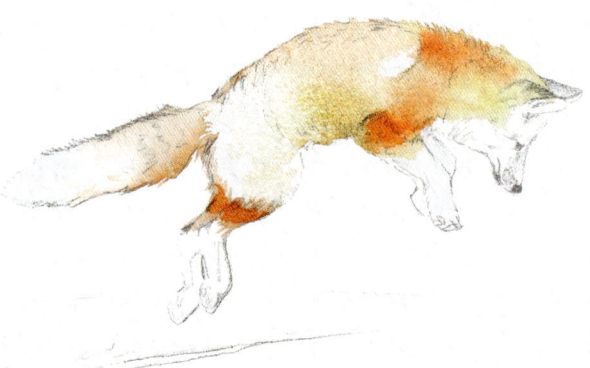

1. Sketch the fox. You can use bolder lines on the feet and ears where the coloring is darker, and plan for some lost edges in areas where the fur is white, such as on the tip of the tail, back of the feet, and the forehead.

2. Mix some transparent orange with water on your palette and paint this diluted orange into the areas of the fox where you see any orange, light or dark. Add some touches of hansa yellow light to the belly and neck for pops of warmth. While your light wash of transparent orange is still wet, drop in a creamy, darker version of your transparent orange at the tops of the legs and neck.

Scan to watch a video.

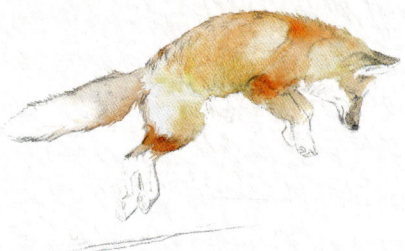 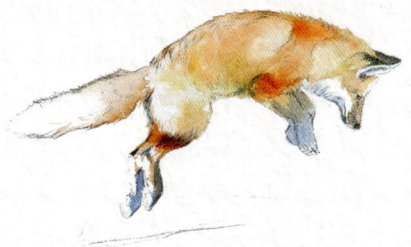 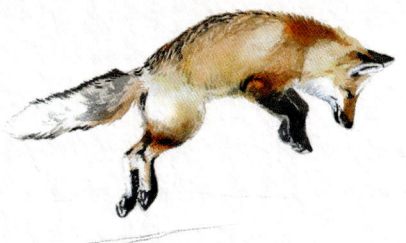

3. Continue layering light washes of transparent orange and burnt sienna. Be conservative here and don't jump into the details too soon. It's important to create a foundation of color before adding any darks.

4. Use a light wash of ultramarine blue on the fronts of the feet and as a shadow tone on the white neck fur.

Scan to watch a video.

5. Now it's time to add black and grey details. Use indigo mixed with a little burnt sienna to paint the black feet, nose, eye, ear tips, and soft fur on the tail and back. You can use a lighter version of your black mix to add fur details to the middle of the tail. For a lost edge, avoid using any paint on the tip of the tail.

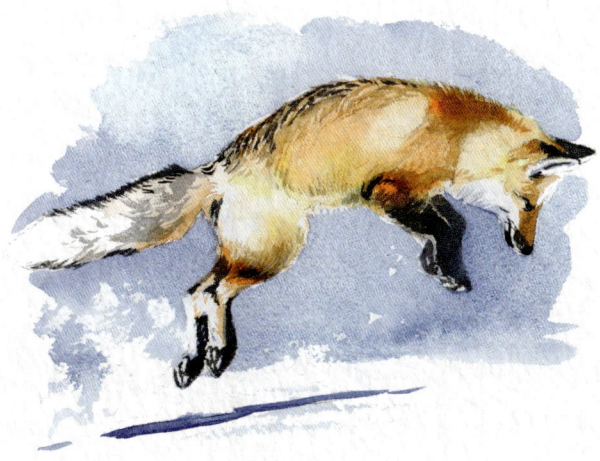

6. Paint a loose and splashy background and dark shadow under the fox with ultramarine blue. Leave little dots of the paper untouched and dry, especially behind the back legs. This suggests the motion of snow flying up as the fox leaps forward.

7. Finish with some blooms. Timing is important for this technique! Your background should still be damp. Take a brush loaded with clean water and gently touch the tip of the brush to the paper. The water on your brush will immediately push aside the drying paint, creating little "explosions" in the background. I love using this technique for snow!

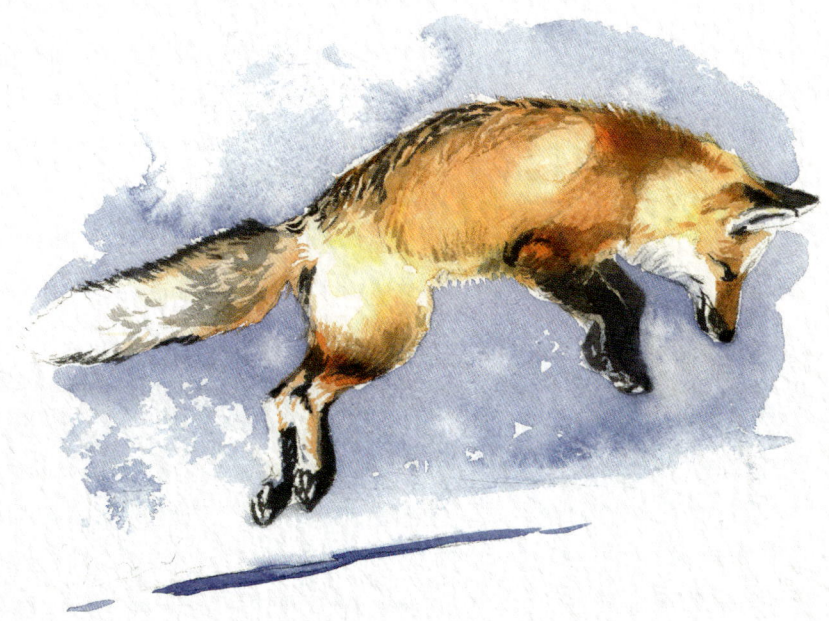

BRYCE CANYON NATIONAL PARK
Utah

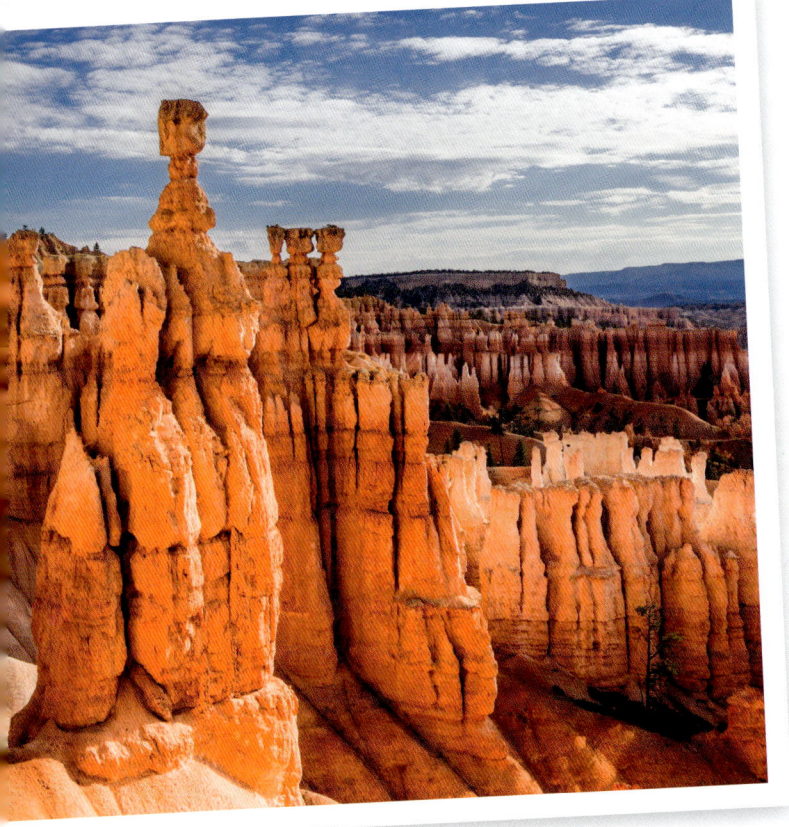

Reference photo

Bryce Canyon National Park was established in 1923. It is known for its unique geological formations including the world's largest concentration of hoodoos (rock columns) and series of natural amphitheaters created by erosion and frost. In this painting, we will get to use our brightest oranges and reds to paint this stunning, rocky wonderland!

Download template and reference photo.

Brushes

Round, sizes 6 and 8

Paper

Arches 140-pound (300 gsm), cotton, cold-pressed block, 7.9" x 7.9" (20 x 20 cm)

Color Palette

Ultramarine Blue

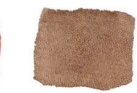

Transparent Orange

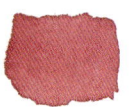

Burnt Sienna

Permanent Alizarin Crimson

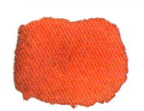

Indigo

Scarlet Lake

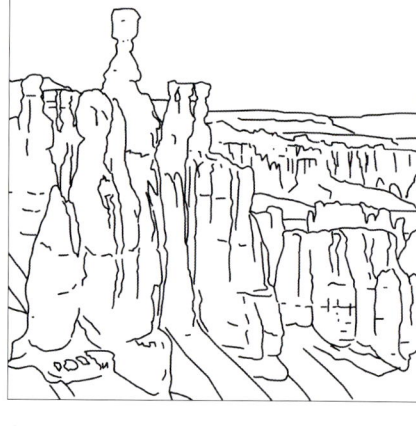

1. Sketch or trace the image, including important vertical lines separating the irregular rock columns. Be sure to indicate light shapes so that you can negative-paint around those sunlit spots.

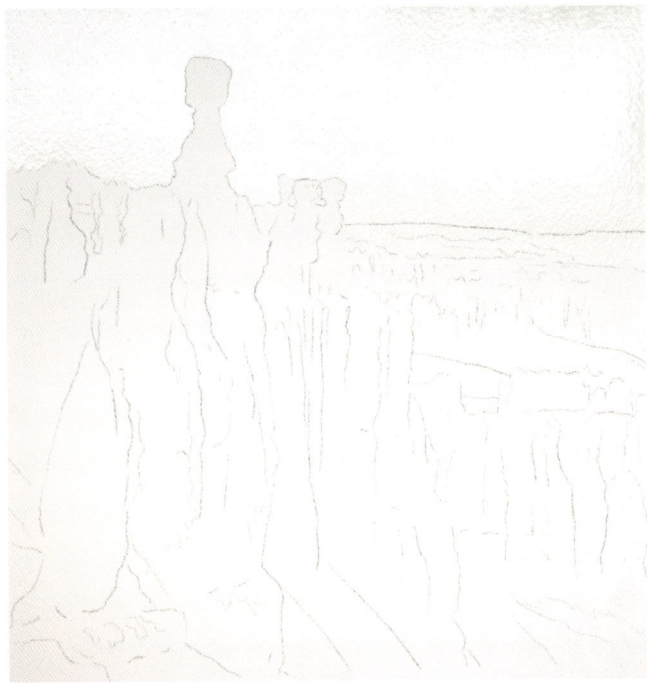

2. With your largest round brush, paint clear water into the sky, avoiding the rock formations. You can paint a little bit into the distant landscape, but do not cover up the orange rocks with water. We want those edges to remain crisp and clear. You may need to wet the paper twice to ensure an even, glossy wetness level.

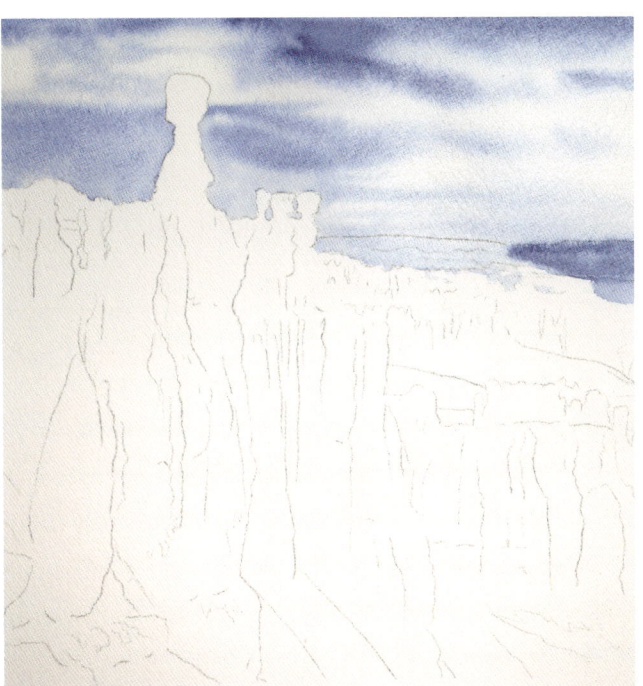

3. Load up your brush with ultramarine blue and begin painting in the streaks of blue sky, leaving some of the white of the paper untouched. Paint over the most distant horizon with darker blue and use a lighter value for the nearer canyon. Allow the sky to dry completely before painting the next wash.

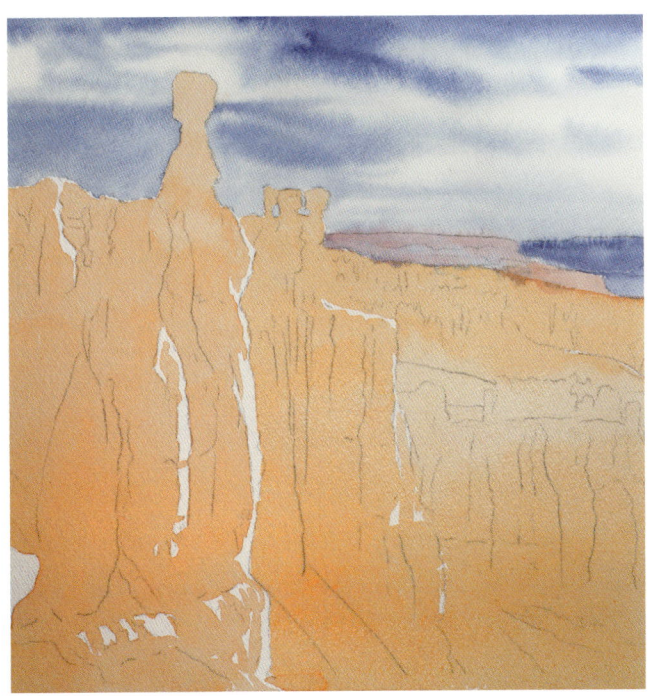

4. On your palette, pour a small puddle of water and mix in some creamy transparent orange. You can also add in some burnt sienna to make it a little less brilliant in chroma. Tilting your board at a slight upright angle, paint a flat wash over the entire rocky foreground, negative-painting around the sunlit edges on the right side of the columns. Paint some watered-down permanent alizarin crimson over the far canyon wall. Let it dry completely.

Scan to watch a video.

Tip

....

Make sure you have a large puddle of watery paint to use for this first rock layer. You do not want to stop in the middle of the wash to mix more!

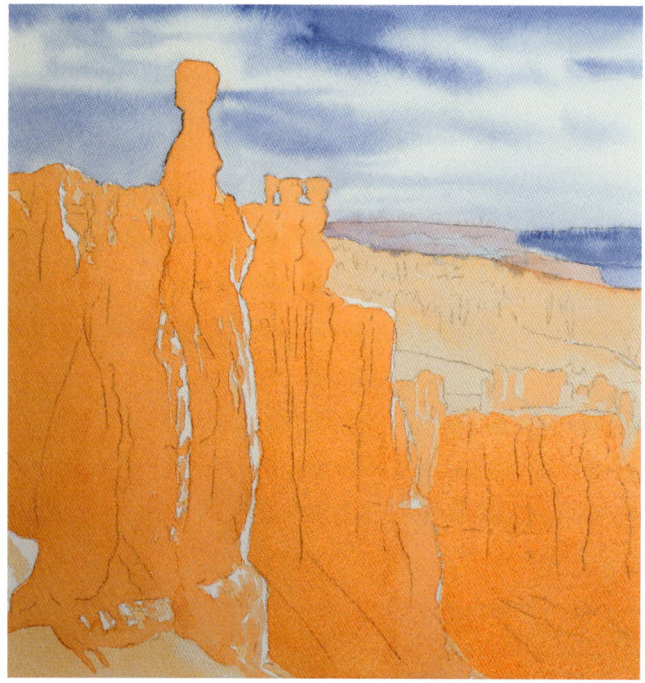

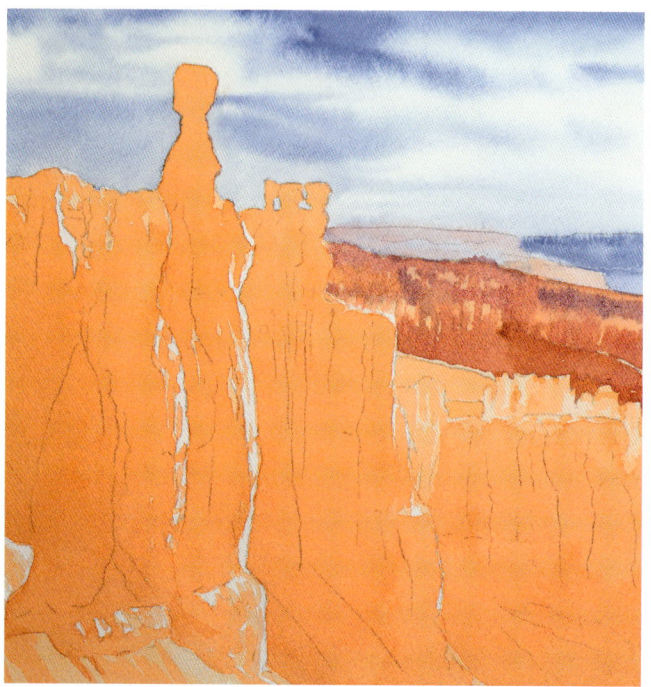

5. If you still have some paint left over from your first wash, now mix in some more pigment—transparent orange and burnt sienna—to create a darker version of the same mix. Paint a second glazed wash over the rocks, again avoiding the sunspots, and the more distant canyon. Be sure to work carefully, especially on the rock tower intersecting the sky—if your orange covers the blue sky, it will create a transparent dark brown edge that won't look clean.

6. Begin painting the details in the background canyon. Start with a layer of permanent alizarin crimson, leaving some of the light orange showing in between brush strokes.

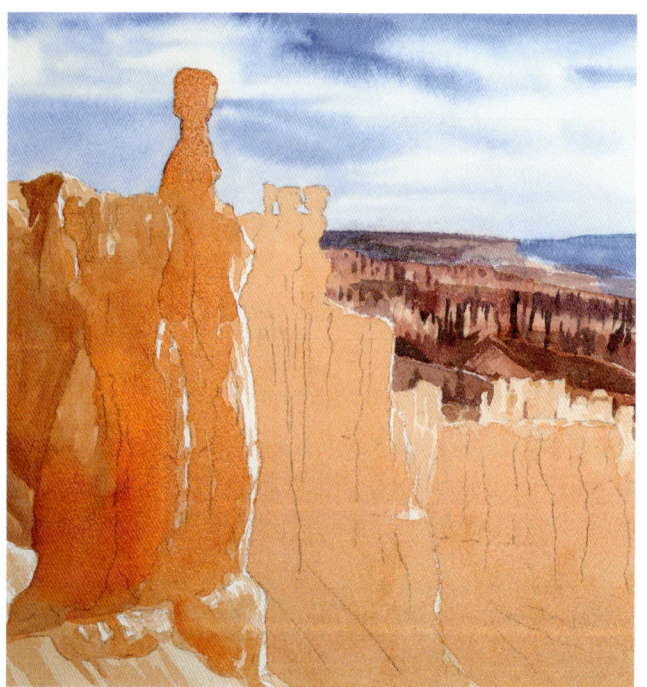

7. Use indigo and burnt sienna to paint the dark shadows separating the distant hoodoos. Mix up some ultramarine blue and permanent alizarin crimson to paint the purple rock layers. Work with loose, vertical brush strokes. Begin painting a third layer over the foreground. We can now use more concentrated pigment to begin adding darker values to the rocks. Introduce some scarlet lake to add pops of red in the shadows.

Scan to watch a video.

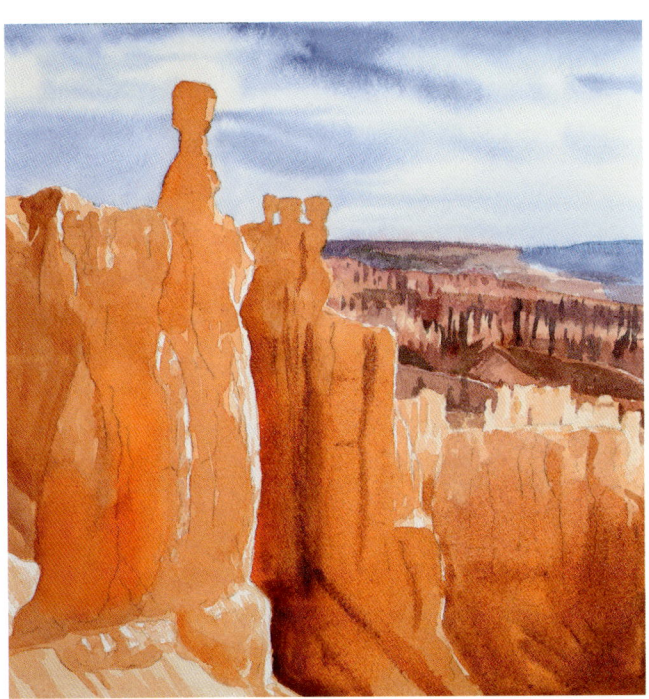

8. Continue painting the foreground with your biggest brush and a generous amount of milky paint, alternating between transparent orange, scarlet lake, and some burnt sienna. Use more pigment and less water where you want to create darker values in the cracks and shadows.

9. Load up your small brush with indigo to paint the vertical separations between the columns and horizontal rock layers. Add any final touches. These dark details are the icing on the cake!

Scan to watch a video.

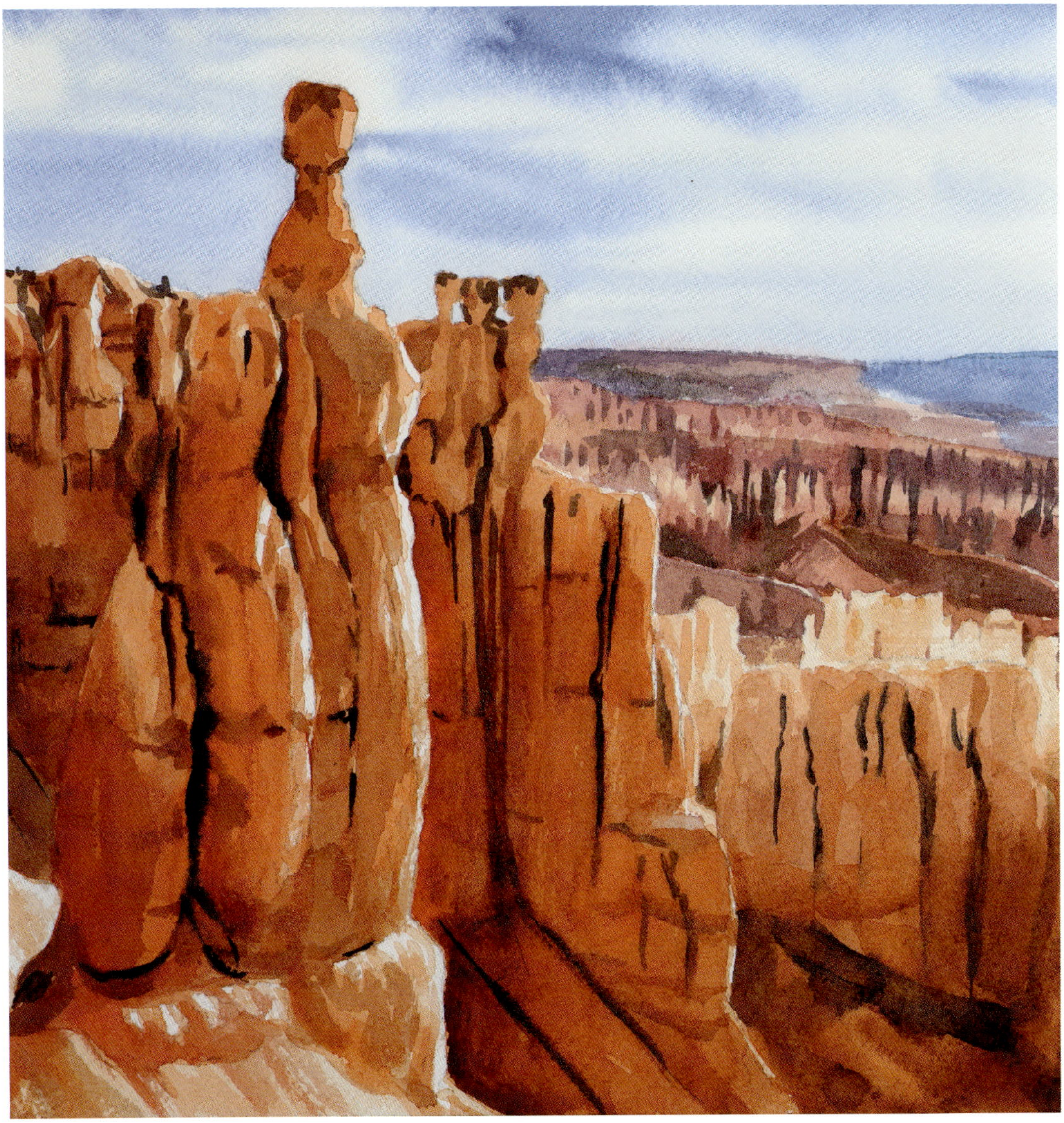

ZION NATIONAL PARK
Utah

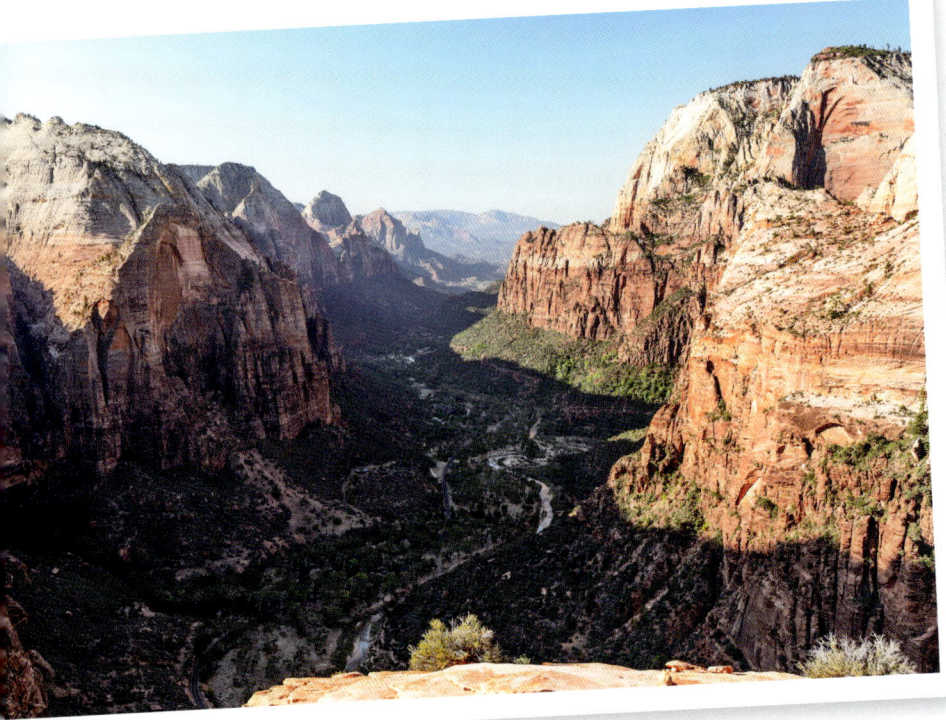

Zion National Park in southwestern Utah is renowned for its vast canyon, which averages 2,000 feet (610 m) in depth. The park features a variety of terrains, providing some of the most breathtaking views imaginable. This extraordinary scene is from the iconic Angel's Landing—definitely a bucket-list hike if you're not too afraid of heights! This painting utilizes a lot of colors, so to help simplify it down to its essence, a value study is very helpful. Note that the entire valley, with its canyon walls and winding river, can be grouped into one big shape inside the shadow.

Reference photo

Download template and reference photo.

Brushes

Round, sizes 8 and 10

Paper

Fabriano Artistico 140-pound (300 gsm), cotton, cold-pressed block, 9" x 12" (23 x 30.5 cm); taped to resize down to 8" x 10" (20.5 x 25.5 cm)

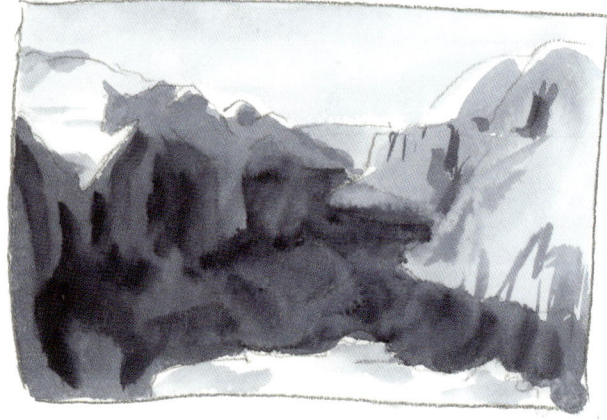

Value study.

Color Palette

Phthalo Blue (GS)

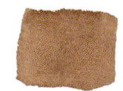
Burnt Sienna

Ultramarine Blue

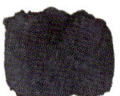
Indigo

Gamboge Nova

Yellow Ochre

Hansa Yellow Light

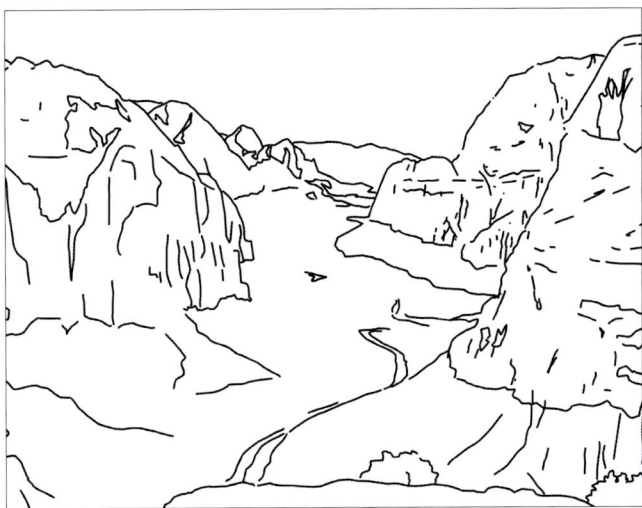

1. Sketch or trace your outline.

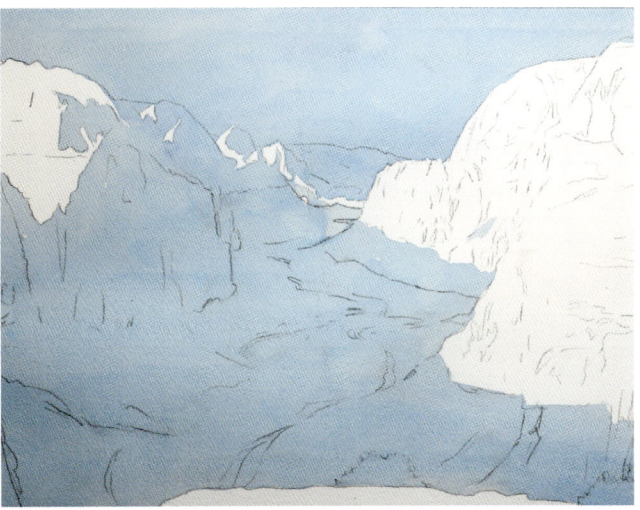

2. Mix a generous amount of watery phthalo blue. Using your largest round brush, apply a flat wash over the entire sky and shadowed areas, avoiding only the sunlit rocky sections. Tilting your board at a slightly upright angle allows gravity to assist with your wash.

Scan to watch a video.

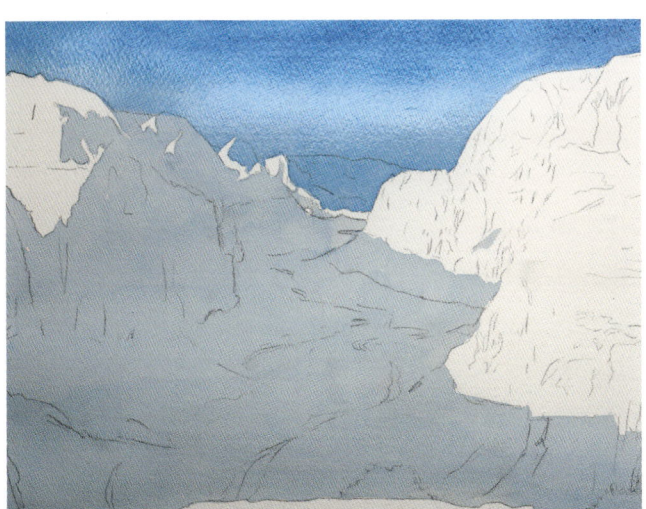

3. When your first wash is fully dry, you can apply a second wash to the sky. Prewet the paper for this layer to help the phthalo blue spread and soften evenly. Use slightly thicker paint at the top to create a vignette effect.

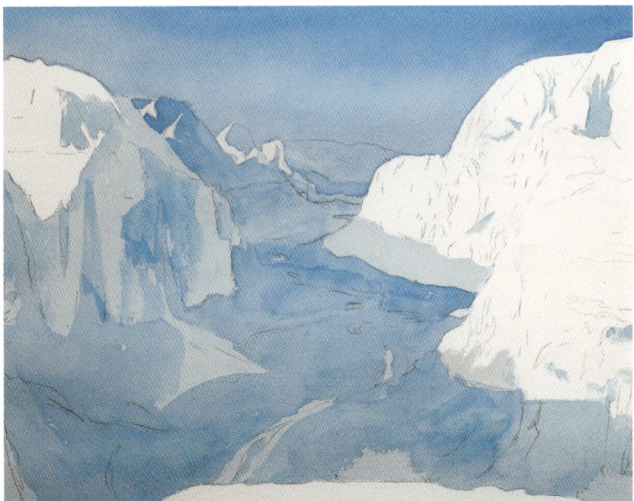

4. Add another layer of phthalo blue to the valley, focusing the color only on the areas that will be the darkest.

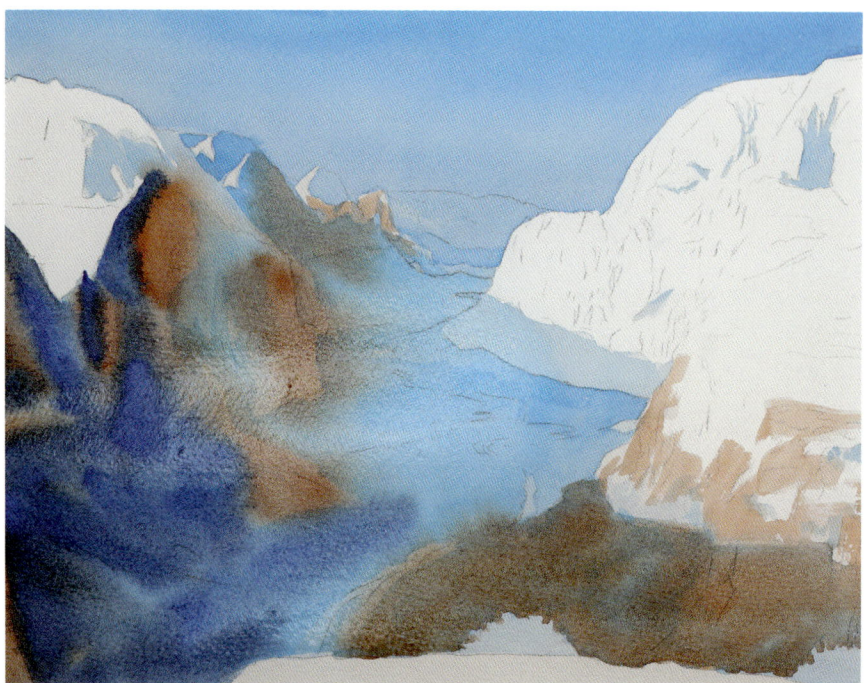

5. Start painting the dark shapes in the valley using the wet-on-wet technique. Prewet the surface with clear water, keeping within your shadow shape. Then, drop in creamy burnt sienna and ultramarine blue, looking at the reference photo for guidance. Apply burnt sienna where you see red rock walls and use ultramarine blue for the darkest shadows and green foliage.

Scan to watch a video.

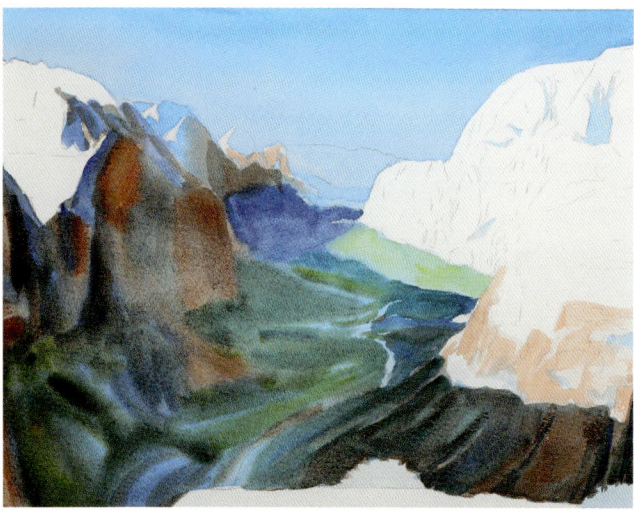

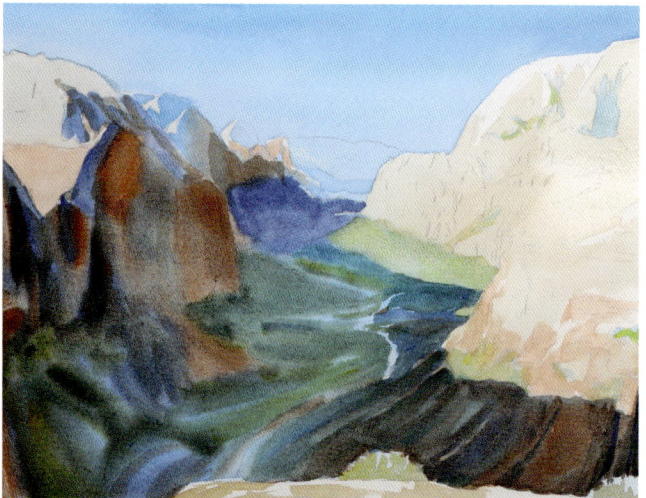

6. To paint the green valley, use gamboge nova. When applied over your blues, it creates a beautiful earthy green. Negative-paint around the winding river. Work quickly while the surface is still wet—this is the ideal time to drop in as much dark color as possible before it dries. It may look a bit "blobby" and undefined but move your brush strokes in the direction of the sloping rocks to start hinting at the terrain. Use indigo for the dark crevices in the rocks.

7. Apply a thin wash of yellow ochre to the sunlit rocks. Then, mix in some burnt sienna to add subtle rock texture on the flat, sunlit foreground. For the plants in the foreground, use a mix of gamboge nova and ultramarine blue as the first layer of color. Paint over the sunlit phthalo blue areas with hansa yellow light to create a more vibrant spring green.

Scan to watch a video.

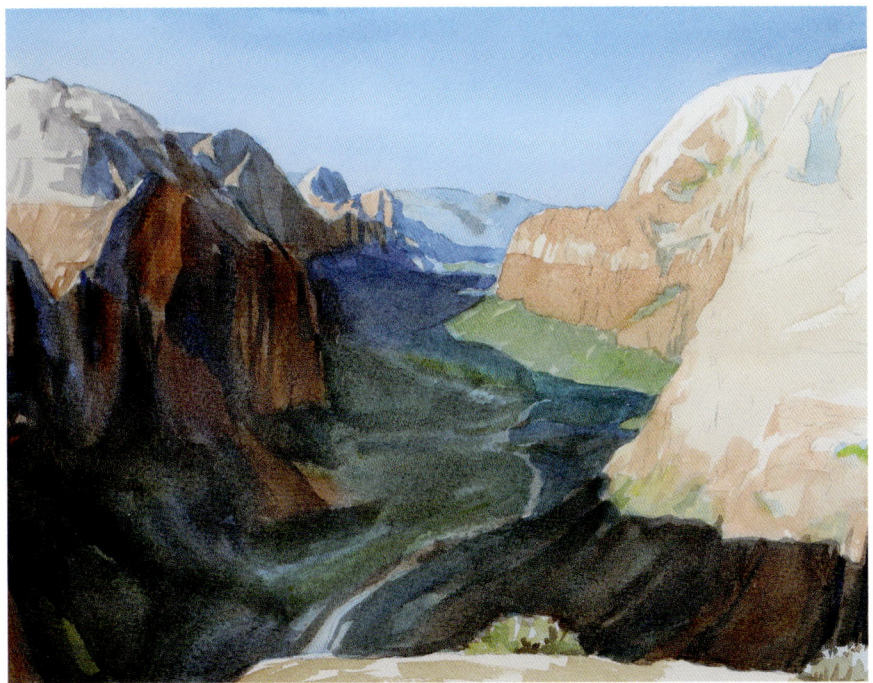

8. Now it's time to start adding details! Apply a watery wash of burnt sienna to the sunlit rocks to suggest the reddish striations on the mountainside. Use a creamy mix of ultramarine blue and burnt sienna to paint the dark shapes on the cliff sides. To distinguish the distant mountain from the sky, add a light ultramarine blue wash.

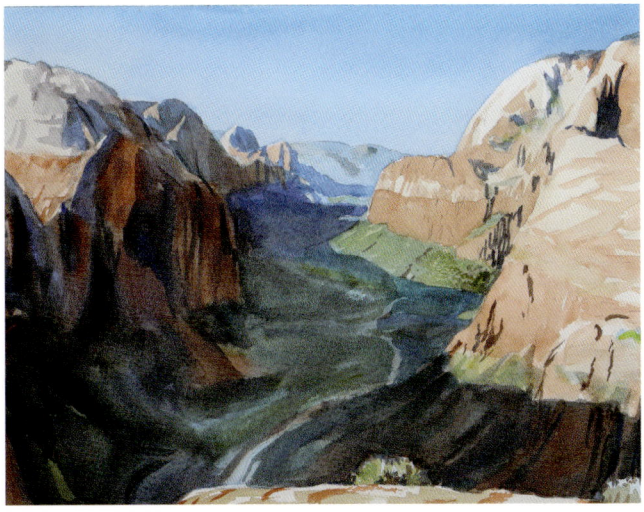

9. Use subtle brushstrokes with burnt sienna to add texture and detail to the mountains. With your smaller round brush, apply a mix of ultramarine blue and burnt sienna to enhance the shadows and cracks on the mountainside. Add more detail to the foreground landing and bushes as well.

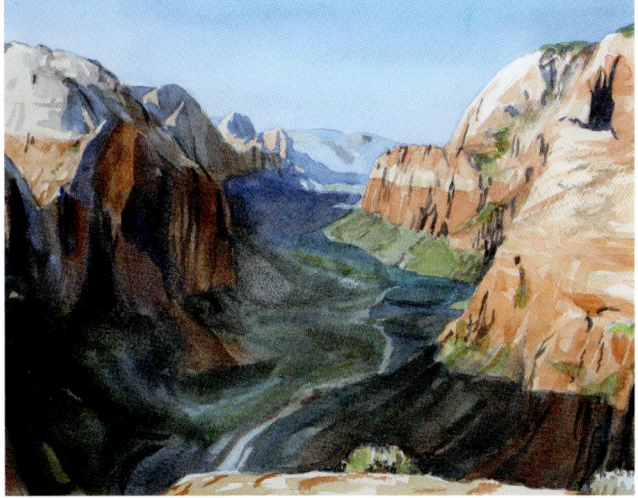

10. Start painting the green plants on the mountains. Apply another layer of burnt sienna to the sunlit rocks, and continue adding small, dark brushstrokes to represent crevices and shadow shapes. Use quick, loose strokes, and don't worry about being exact.

Scan to watch a video.

Scan to watch a video.

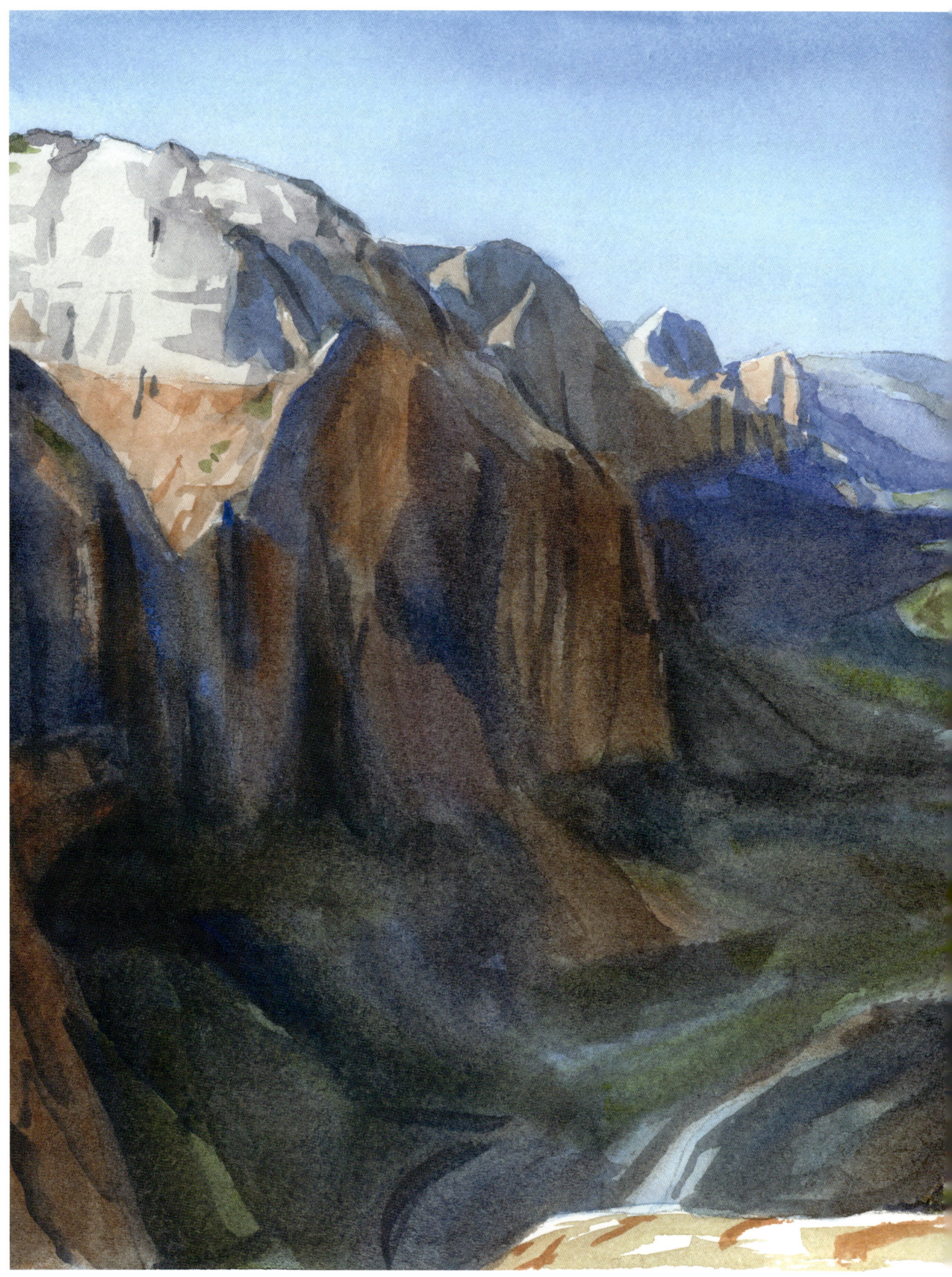

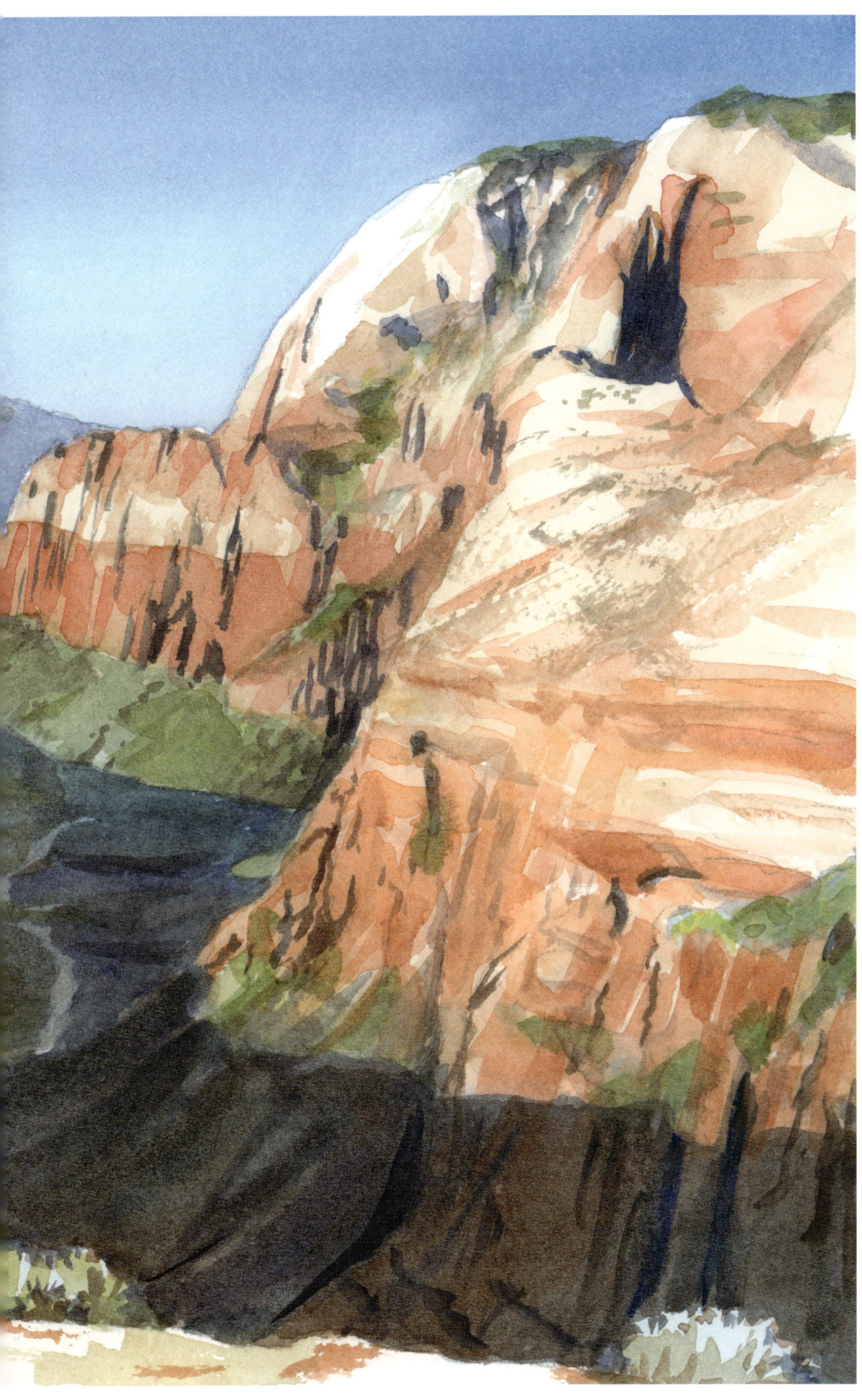

11. Add a dry-brush texture to the right side of your painting and include any additional details you'd like.

ARCHES NATIONAL PARK
Utah

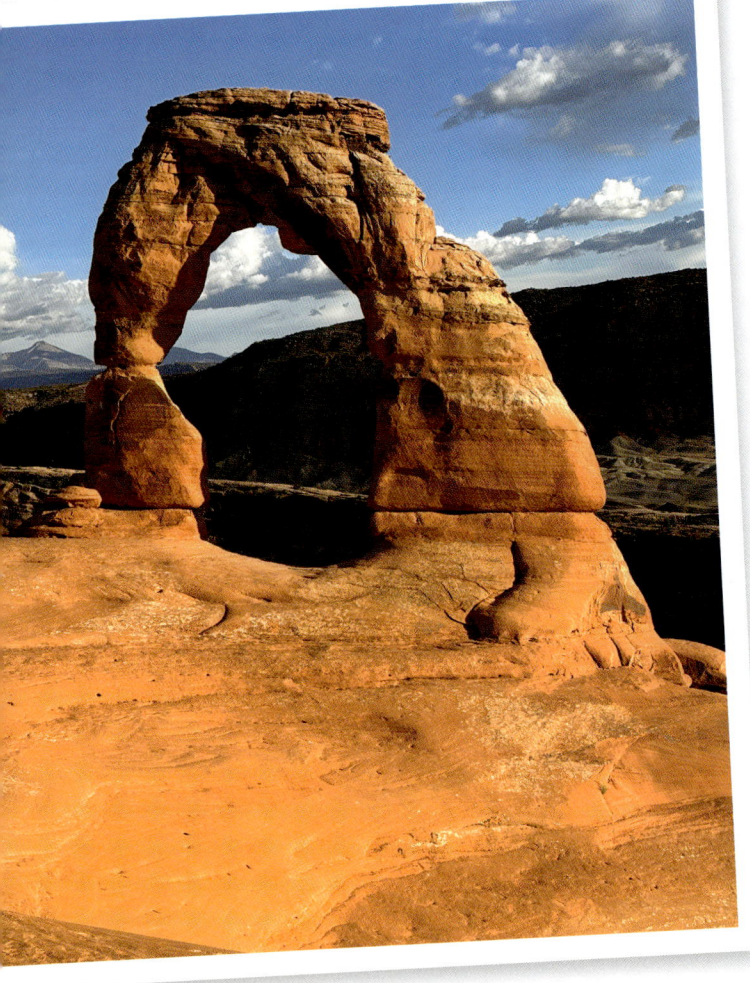

Reference photo

Arches National Park has more than 2,000 natural stone arches, including Delicate Arch, which we'll paint here. It is the world's most famous arch, proudly displayed on Utah state license plates. I visited the park in 2023 with my sisters, who are also artists, and we enjoyed a weekend of plein air painting and hiking. We marveled at the unearthly rock formations and the constant shifts of light and color as late afternoon sank into twilight. It truly is a magical place!

Download template and reference photo.

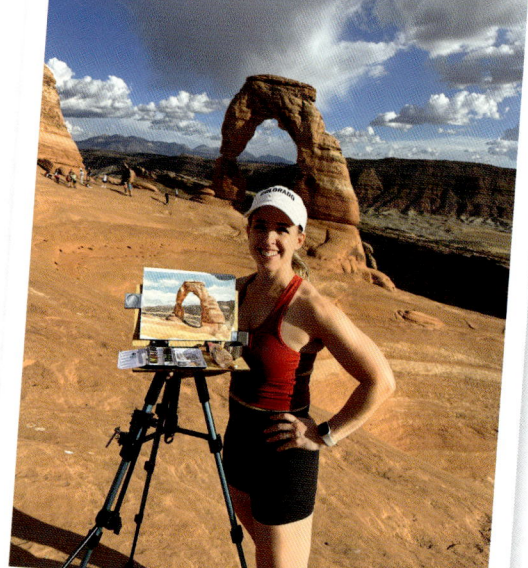

Hiking and painting at Delicate Arch.

Brushes

Round, sizes 8 and 10

Paper

Fabriano Artistico 140-pound (300 gsm), cotton, cold-pressed block, 9" x 12" (23 x 30.5 cm); taped to resize down to 8" x 10" (20.5 x 25.5 cm)

Color Palette

Phthalo Blue (GS)

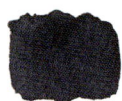

Indigo

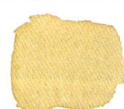

Yellow Ochre

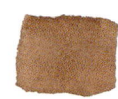

Burnt Sienna

Ultramarine blue

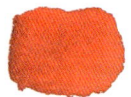

Scarlet Lake

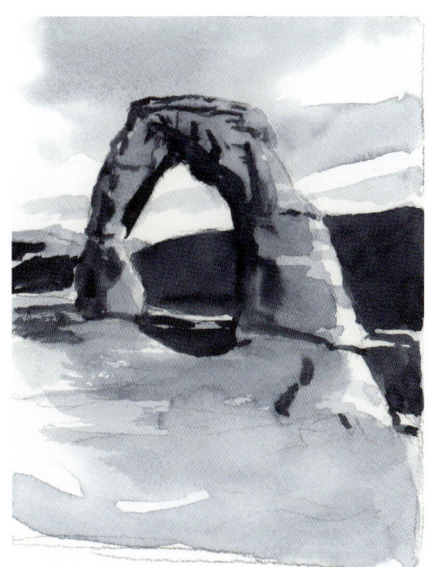

It's helpful to start with a monochromatic study to get a good idea of where your lightest lights and darkest darks will go. This is also a great opportunity to explore any changes from the reference photo that you'd like to make. I decided to change the shapes of the clouds a little, and to create a washy foreground, leaving some of the white of the paper untouched.

Value study.

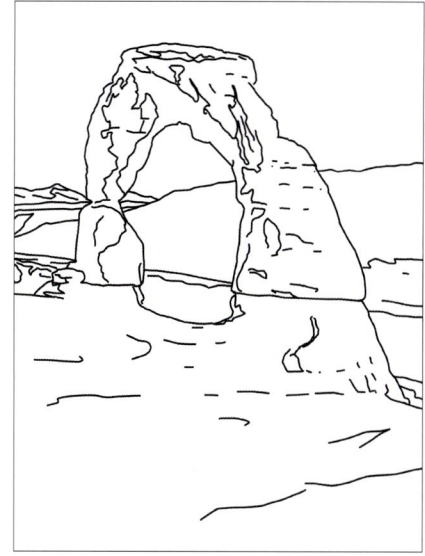

1. Sketch or trace your drawing onto your watercolor paper. Be sure to draw the shapes created by the shadows inside of the arch. Don't sketch the clouds—we'll create the clouds using just paint.

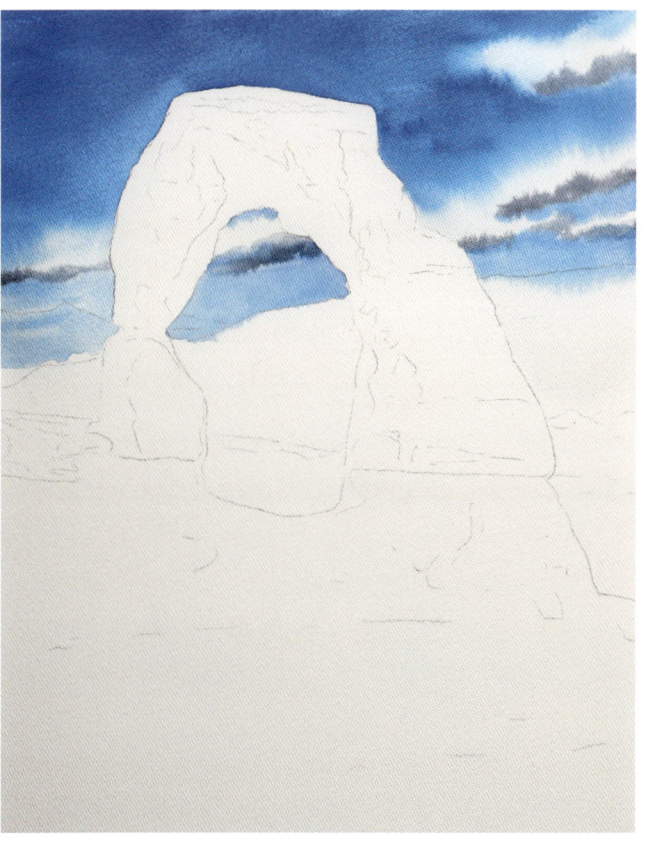

Scan to watch a video.

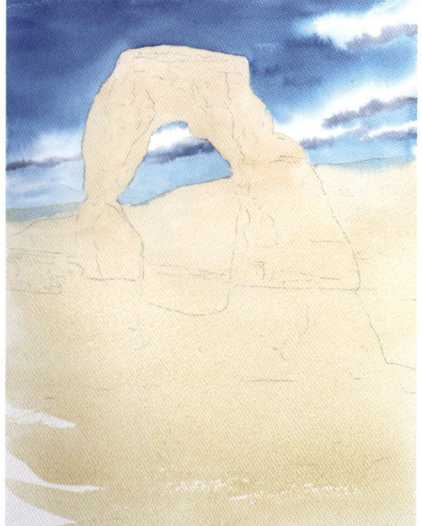

2. Start painting the sky using the wet-on-wet technique. On your palette, premix a generous amount of phthalo blue in a milky-to-creamy paint consistency. Use a clean brush loaded up with clear water to "paint" the sky, avoiding the arch. You want your sky to be evenly wet with a glossy sheen, no puddles. Making sure your brush is just damp (not wet), drop in your phthalo blue, painting around where you want your clouds to be. Add some dabs of indigo on the underside of each cloud to create the heavy cloud shadows.

3. Let your sky dry completely to avoid it bleeding into your arch. Mix up a large puddle of watery yellow ochre with a hint of burnt sienna. Use your large brush to paint a wet-on-dry flat wash across the entire arch and landscape with broad and loose brush strokes at the bottom.

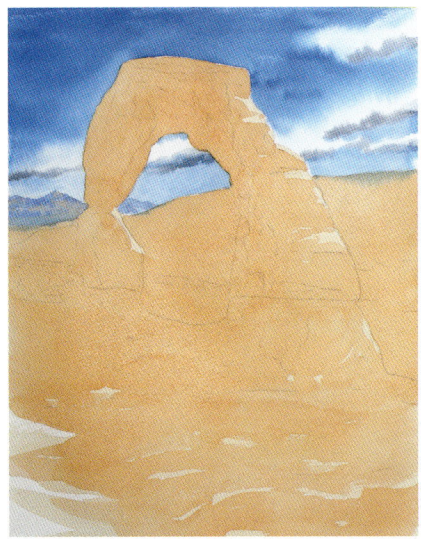 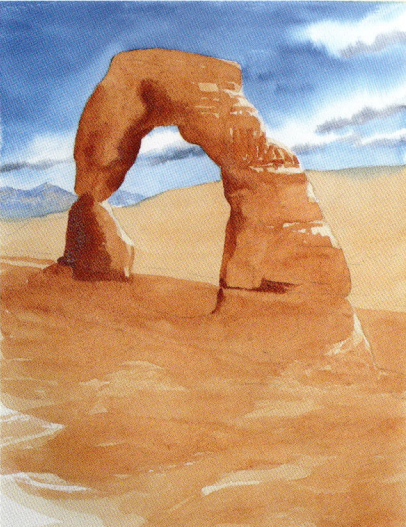 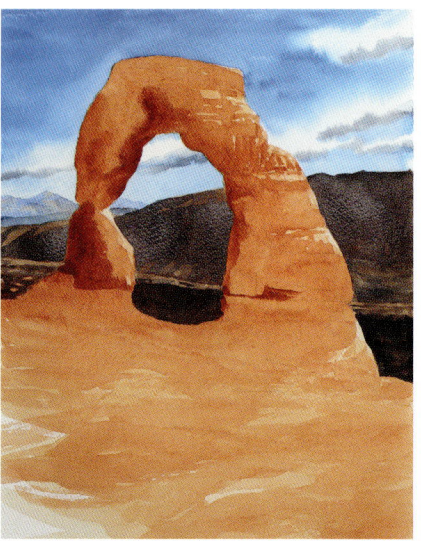

4. Once the first wash is dry, mix up a darker (medium value) wash of yellow ochre and burnt sienna. Paint a second flat wash across the landscape, this time leaving some little gaps on the right side of the arch to show sunlit rock edges.

Scan to watch a video.

5. Mix up a medium-value puddle of burnt sienna in a milky paint consistency to begin darkening the isolated arch and foreground. Take your time with this step, beginning to note some of the shadow and crack shapes on the arch.

6. Paint the background landscape. Use a light tint of ultramarine for the distant peaks. Mix burnt sienna and ultramarine blue to create a rich chocolate brown for the mountain just behind the arch. Negative-paint around the sunlit ridges, but if they are too bright and are competing with the arch, darken them up a little. Resist the temptation to paint any details in the background. Everything behind the arch should serve to support the "star of the show" rather than distract from it.

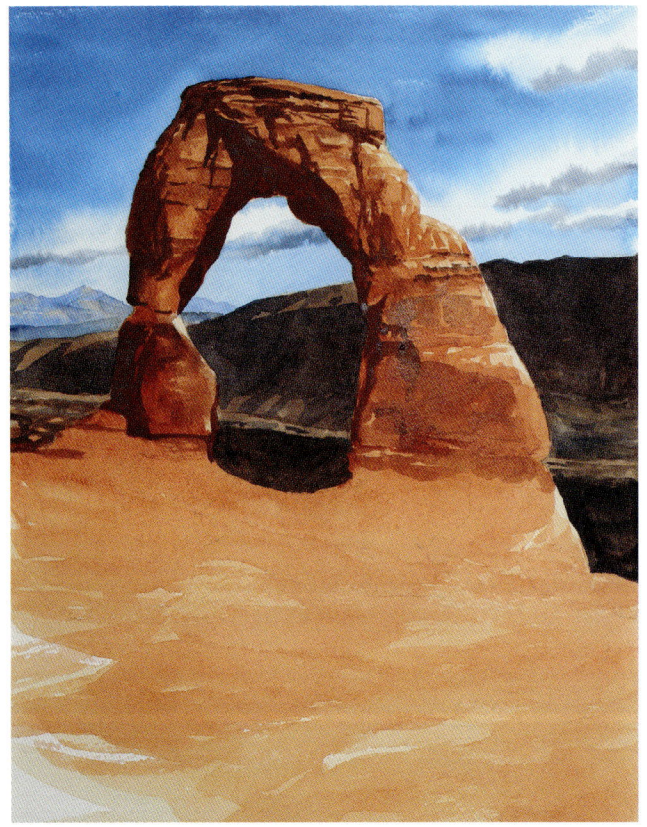

7. Add the darkest shadows and details to the arch. Mix up more of your dark ultramarine blue and burnt sienna combo. Use this to paint all the crisp shadows on the arch, connecting your shapes wherever possible. Use more burnt sienna with some scarlet lake mixed in for the rich reddish tones on the flat portions of the arch.

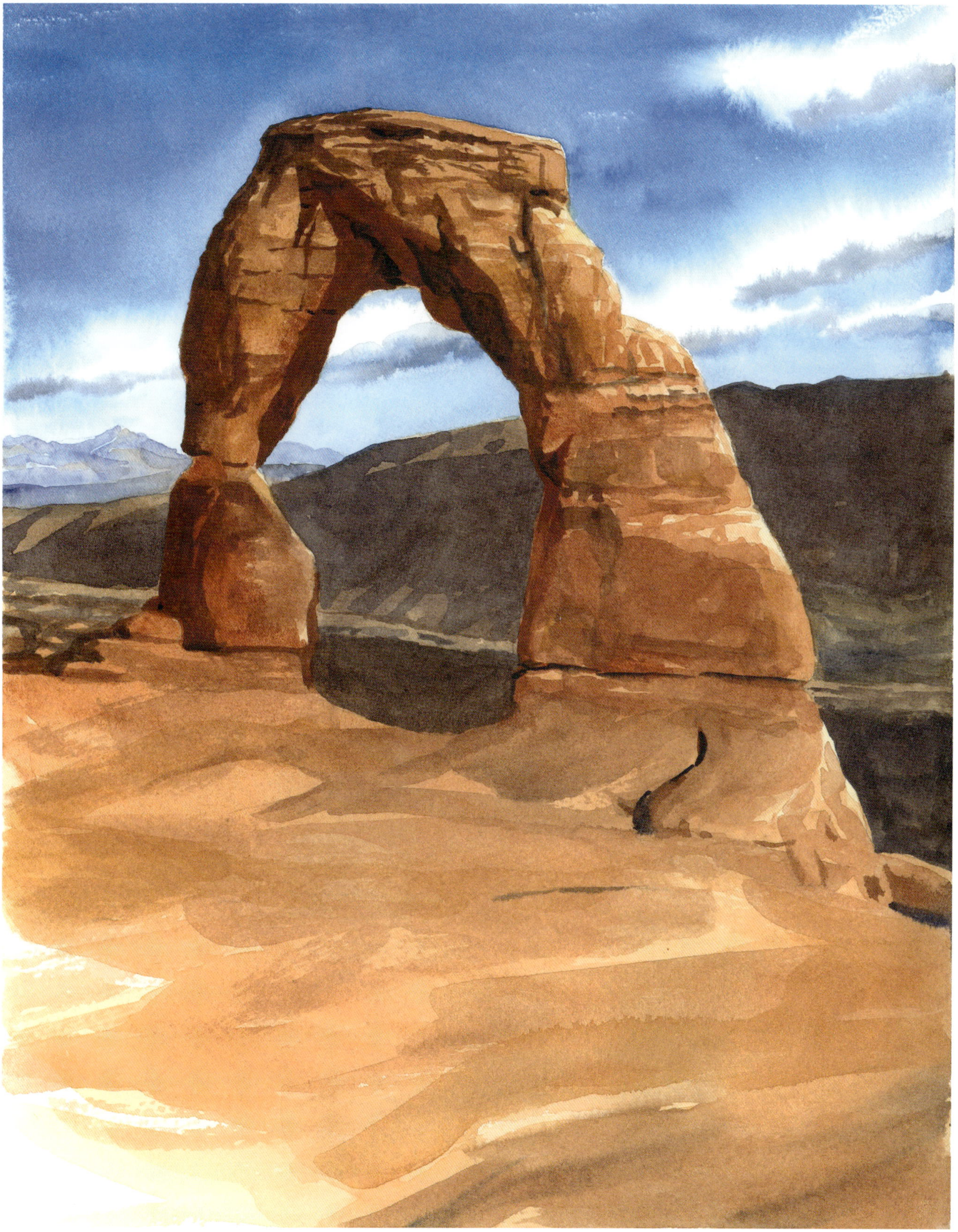

8. Add your final details. Use your largest brush with some subtle tinted washes of burnt sienna and yellow ochre to create the look of swirling stone at the base of the arch. Use your darkest mix of ultramarine blue and burnt sienna with your smaller round brush to paint the creases and shadows in the rocks.

Scan to
watch a
video.

GRAND CANYON NATIONAL PARK
Arizona

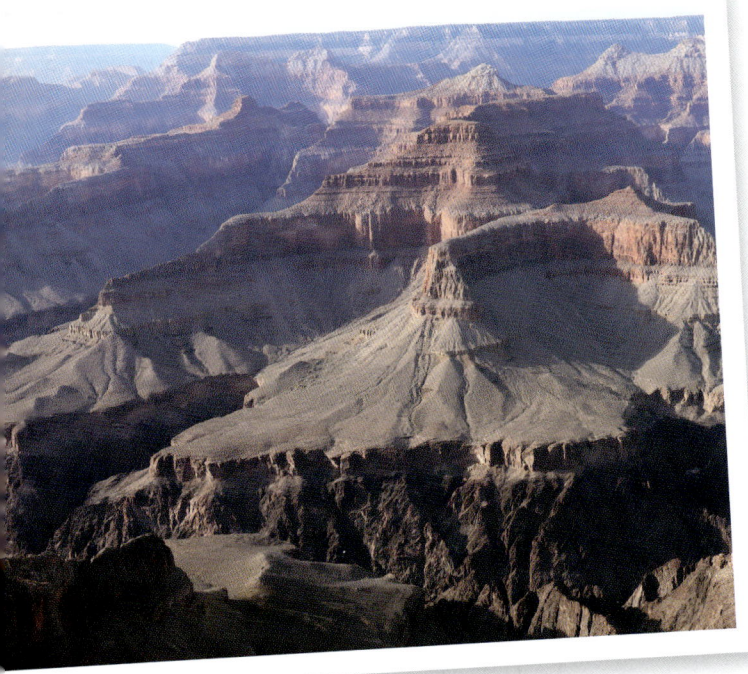

The Grand Canyon draws millions of visitors every year from across the globe and has been a source of inspiration for many generations of painters. I had the privilege of visiting the Grand Canyon in 2021. My attempts at painting the canyon en plein air felt painfully inadequate in the presence of such magnificence, but I was able to gather some wonderful photo references (including the one we're painting here!) that will forever remind me of the grandeur and wonder of this special place. In this painting, we'll play with a unique "wet next to wet" approach to painting each of the light and shadow shapes. Using just one large round brush to avoid picking at the details, we'll paint bright colors side by side, creating a washy blend that captures the many colorful rock layers present in the canyon.

Reference photo

Download template and reference photo.

Brush

Round, size 10

Paper

Fabriano Artistico 140-pound (300 gsm), cotton, cold-pressed block, 9" x 12" (23 x 30.5 cm); taped to resize down to 8" x 10" (20.5 x 25.5 cm)

Color Palette

Phthalo Blue (GS)

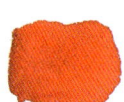

Scarlet Lake

Ultramarine Blue

Yellow Ochre

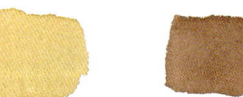

Burnt Sienna

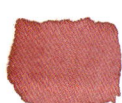

Permanent Alizarin Crimson

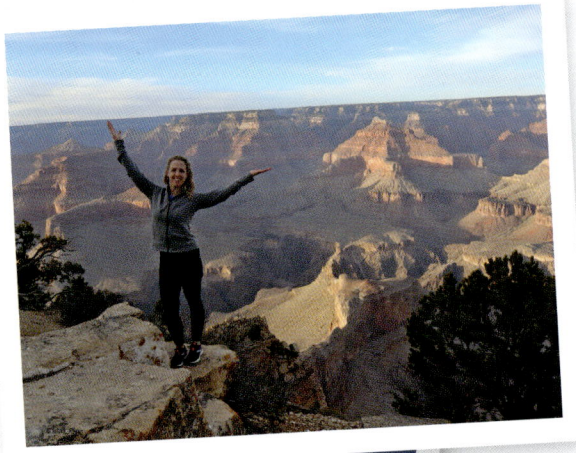

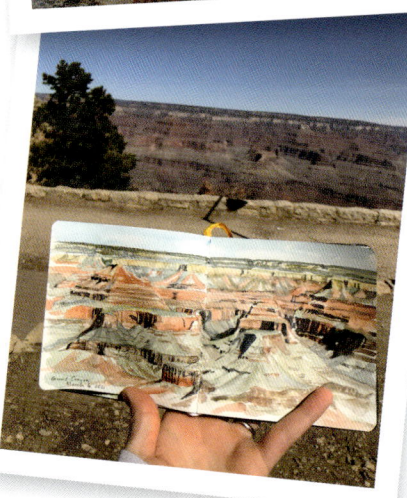

Hiking and painting at the Grand Canyon.

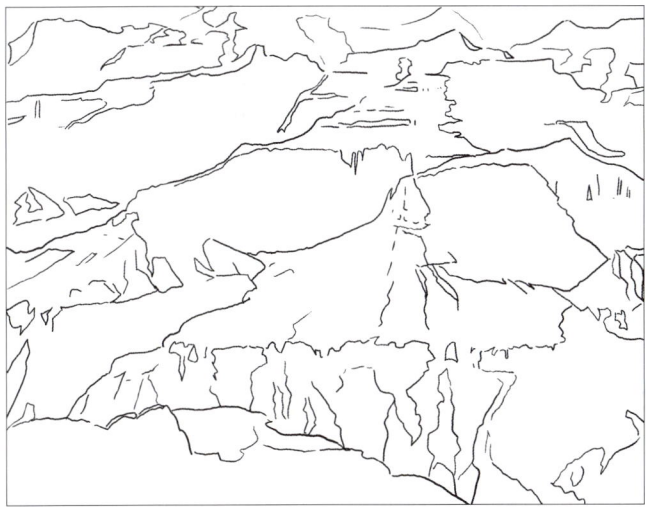

1. Trace the outline onto your watercolor paper.

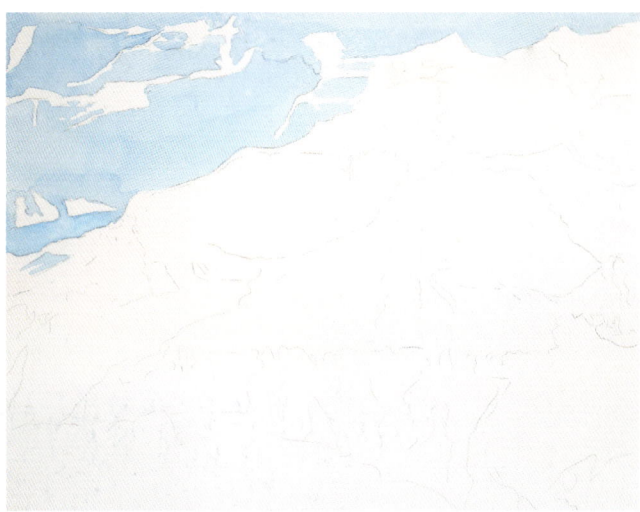

2. Mix up a large puddle of watery phthalo blue. Beginning at the top, paint in the faint shadow shapes in the distant canyon. Be sure to avoid any areas where the sunlight is hitting, since these will be a warmer, more reddish color. Notice how the shadows appear darker and more detailed the closer they are to the viewer.

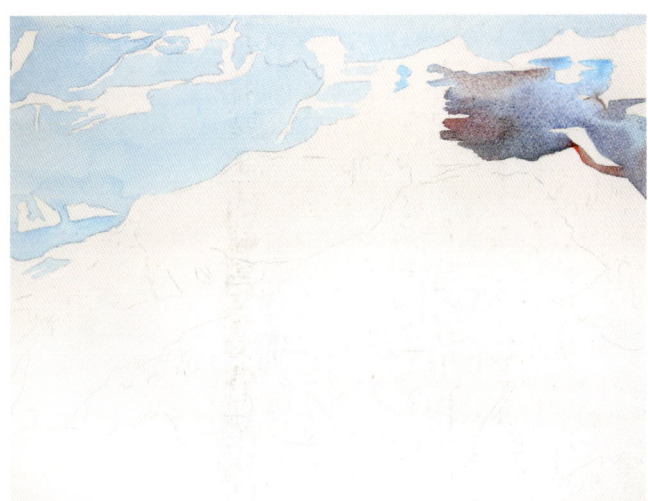

3. We can now begin to use a method I like to call "wet next to wet" to put down dark colors inside the shadow shapes. Mix up several separate puddles of color in a medium to dark value using scarlet lake, phthalo blue, and ultramarine blue, and some combinations of all three. The goal is to create each shadow shape quickly like a flat wash, but we will dip our brush into multiple colors.

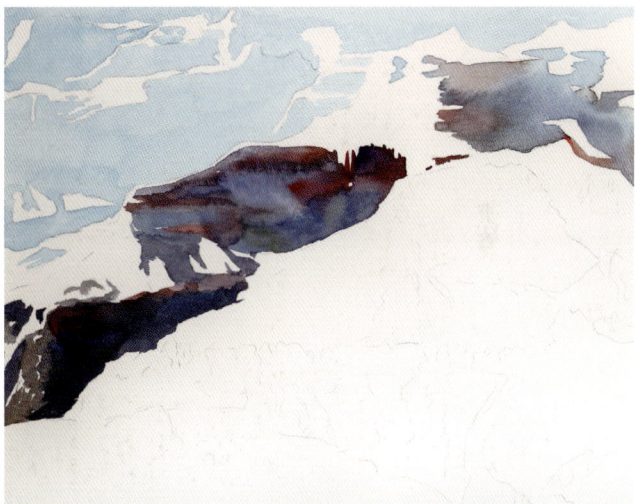

4. Put down side-by-side, wet-on-dry brushstrokes to create the solid shape. Where you see red layers of rock in the shadow, especially at the top of the canyon, use scarlet lake and muddy purples. As the shadows move downward, switch to more blues on your brush. Tilting your board at a slight (15–30 degree) angle will allow gravity to work in your favor.

Scan to watch a video.

Tip

You might see some blooms forming, especially if your paint and brush are very wet. Embrace these and have fun seeing how they dry! Avoid the urge to over-blend on the paper.

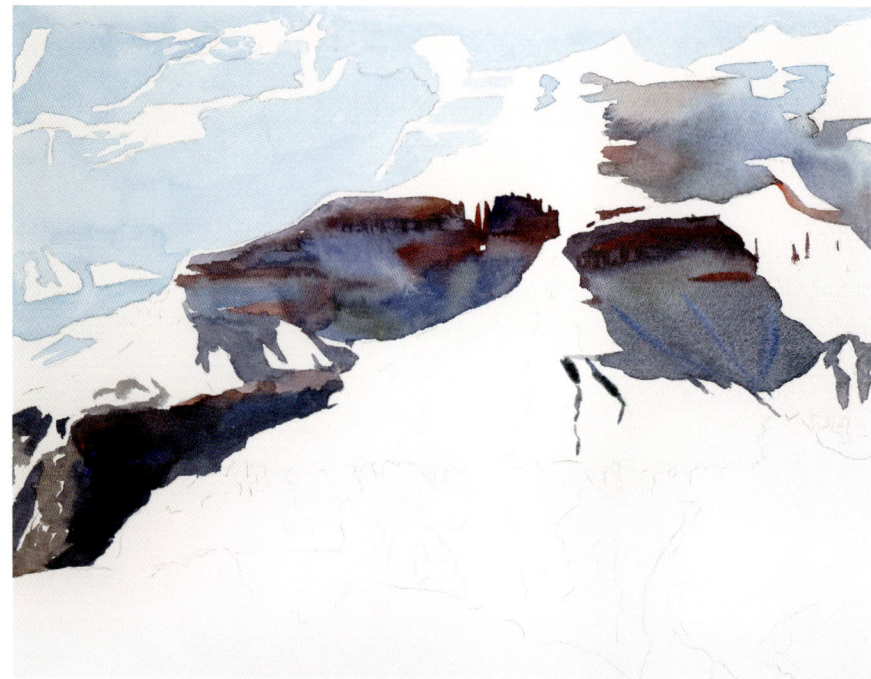

5. Paint the next shadow section the same way. Don't overthink your colors or try to make them exactly like the photo—squint at the reference and look for where the colors are generally more red or more blue, and paint the shapes in as quickly as you can. The faster you paint, the fresher your watercolors will look!

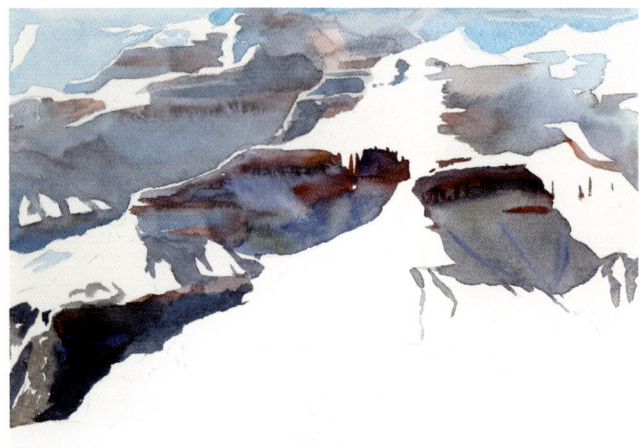

6. It's time to add more paint to the distant canyons. Mix up a very light wash of phthalo blue and another puddle of watered-down scarlet lake. Be careful to keep your values light here! Loosely paint in each shadow shape with this second layer, avoiding the sky. We use lighter washes for the canyons that are farthest away and darker layers for the areas that are closer to us.

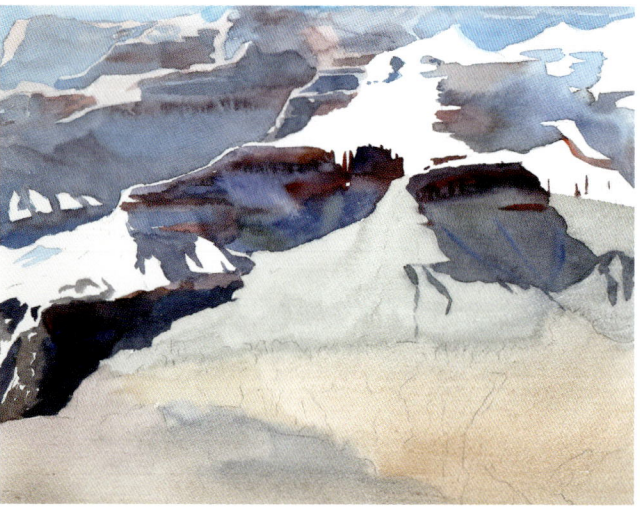

7. Mix up a generous amount of watery ultramarine blue and yellow ochre to create a cool gray. Mix a second puddle with this same color but add in some burnt sienna and a little more yellow ochre for a slightly warmer wash. Quickly paint a flat wash across the foreground, switching to your warmer mix to paint a first layer on the reddish-brown cliffs toward the bottom of the composition.

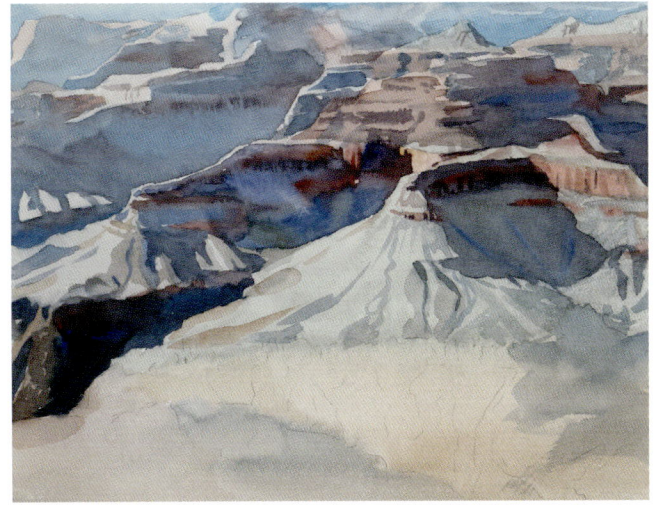

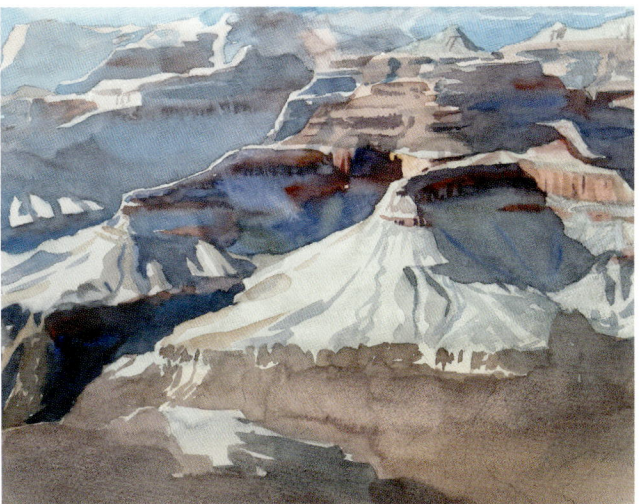

8. While this is drying, paint a light wash of scarlet lake over the areas of the scene where the sunlit rock is more reddish. You can also begin to add some details, like gulleys and cliff lines.

9. Now, let's add a second layer to the foreground. Mix a generous amount of a medium-value chocolate-brown color using burnt sienna, permanent alizarin crimson, and a bit of ultramarine blue. Paint this over the entire shadow in the foreground, again trying to connect the entire shape and avoiding the areas in light.

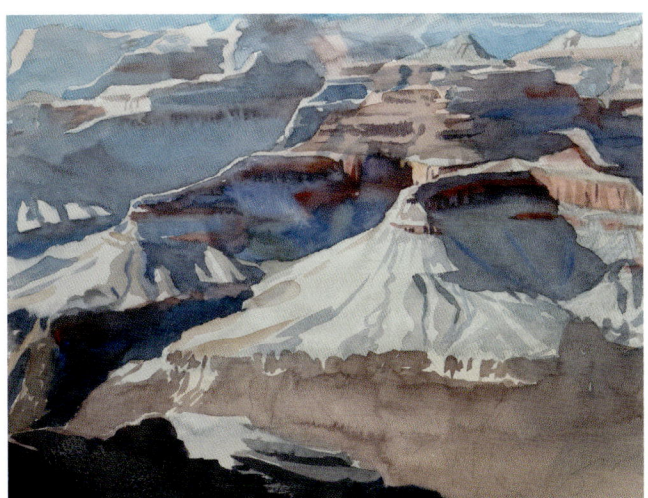

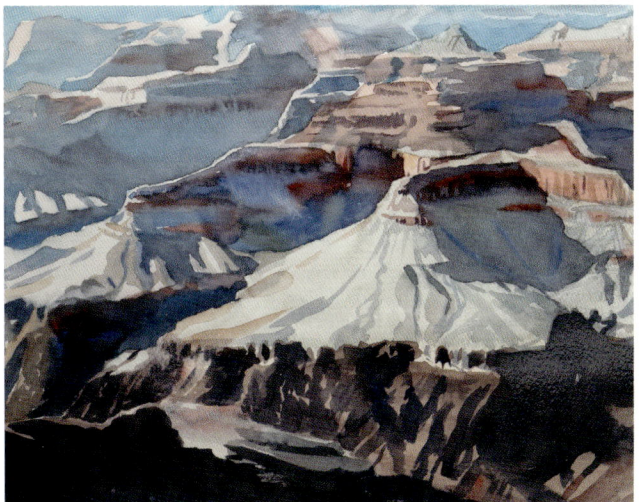

10. While this is drying, mix up your darkest darks using a creamy combo of burnt sienna and ultramarine blue. Aim for color variety again, so make two different puddles of dark paint, one leaning more blue, and one leaning more red.

11. Paint your darkest shadow shape. Have fun letting your brush dance and splash! Just paint around the sunlit ridges and plateaus. To create more texture, you can use the dry-brush technique to scrape your brush along the surface of the paper.

Scan to watch a video.

Tip

···

Mix up lots of paint! You want to avoid having to stop and mix more halfway through your wash.

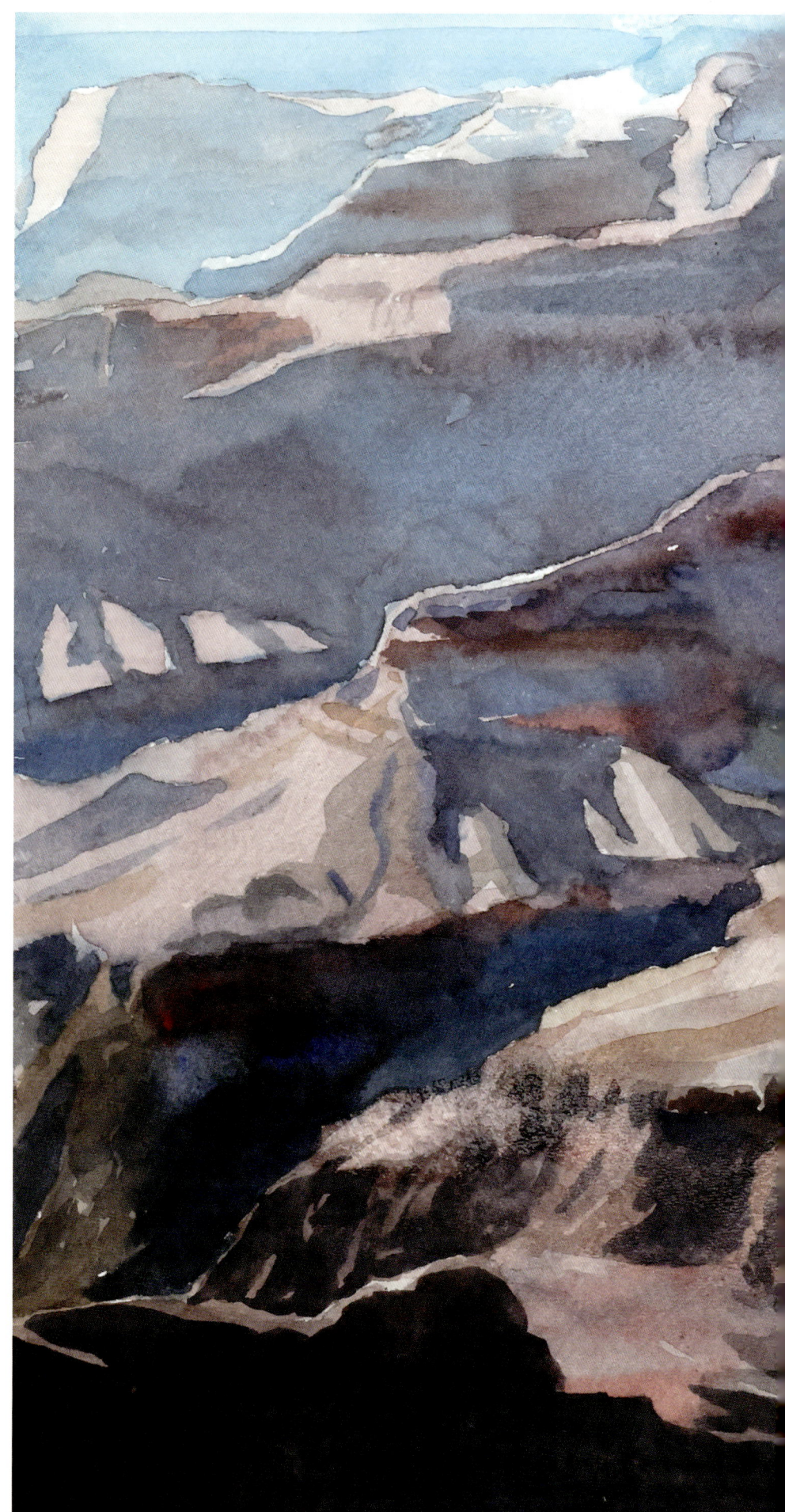

12. When your painting is completely dry, make color adjustments if needed. Here, I mixed up some watery permanent alizarin crimson and painted it over all the areas that needed more red. Finally, add any finishing details or shadows that will give texture and movement to the painting.

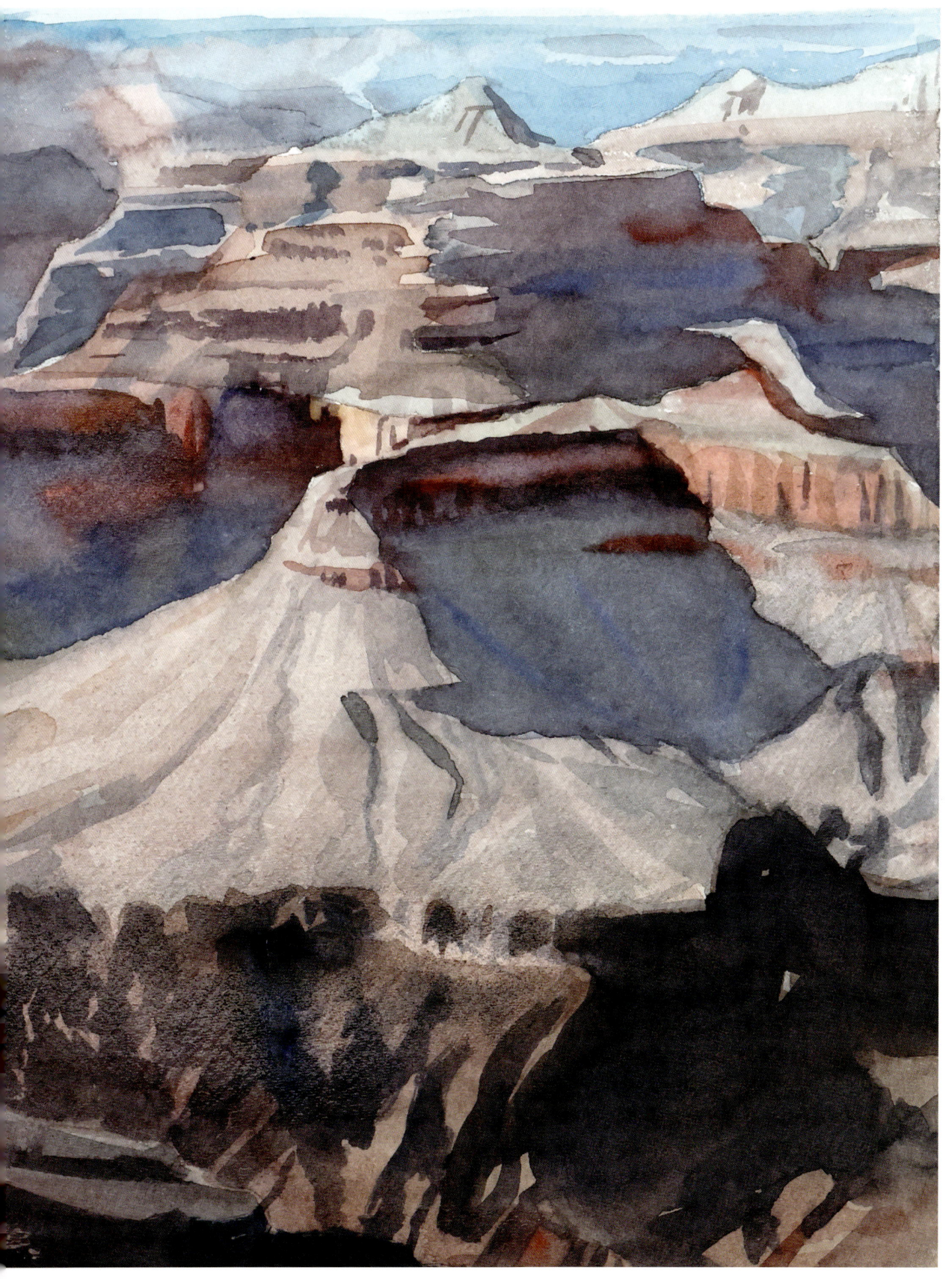

Juniper Tree

These twisted juniper trees can be seen across the south rim of the Grand Canyon. I am fascinated by the shapes and expressions that are created by these hardy trees! Despite growing in some of the most inhospitable locations where wind and heat would destroy most plants, junipers can live up to 650 years!

Download template and reference photo.

Brush(es)

Round, size 6

Color Palette

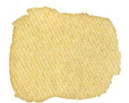   

Yellow Ochre   Burnt Sienna   Ultramarine Blue   Hansa Yellow Light

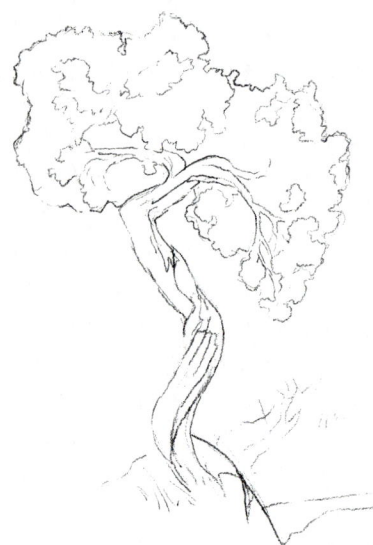

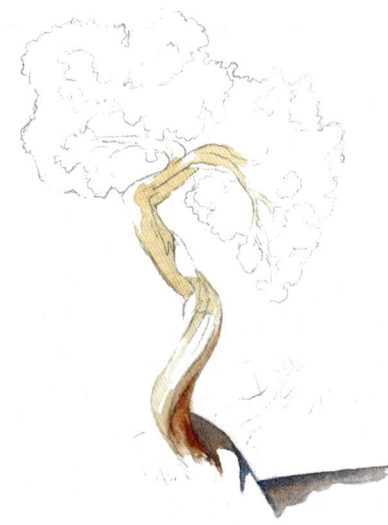

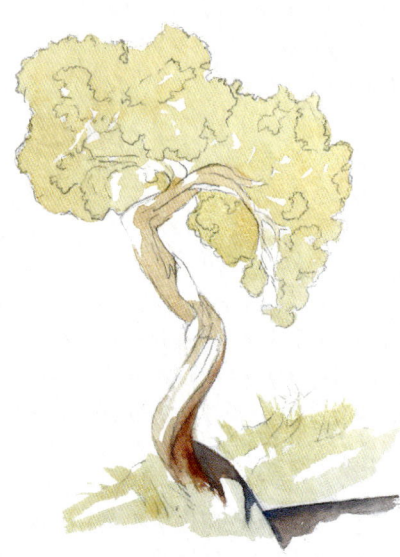

1. Trace or sketch the tree.

2. Begin with a wash of yellow ochre over any areas of the trunk that are in shadow. You can paint the midtone areas, too, but make sure to leave some bright highlights on the trunk where the white of the paper shines through.

3. Paint in the foliage and ground with watery yellow ochre, wet-on-dry, leaving some light spots or little gaps within the mostly solid mass of greenery.

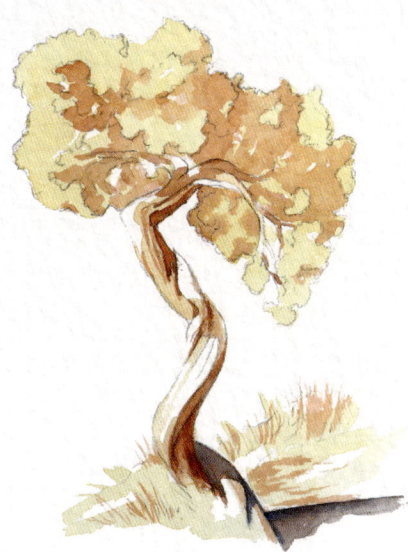

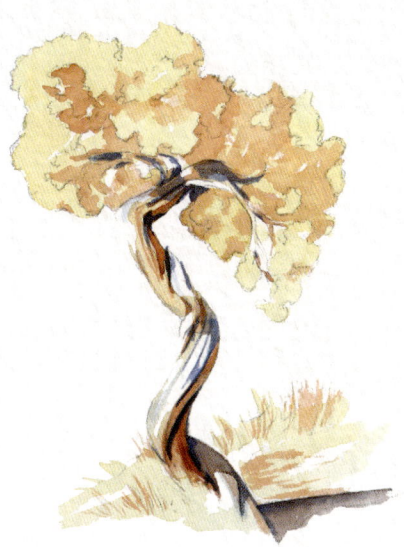

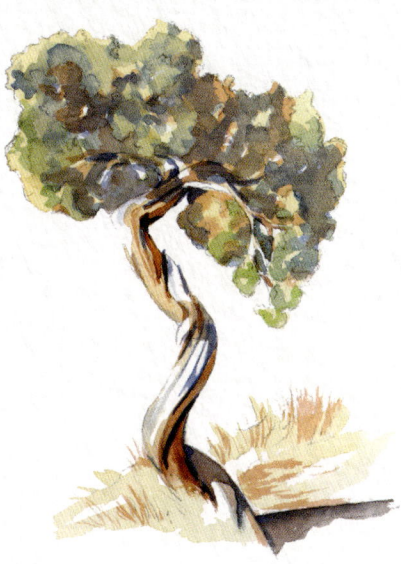

4. Add a second layer using burnt sienna to begin carving out the shadow shapes in the trunk and foliage.

5. Use ultramarine blue to darken the shadows and creases of the trunk.

6. Use a combination of hansa yellow light and ultramarine blue to darken the foliage and begin coloring it green. Use a blobbing motion of the brush—don't try to paint too detailed!

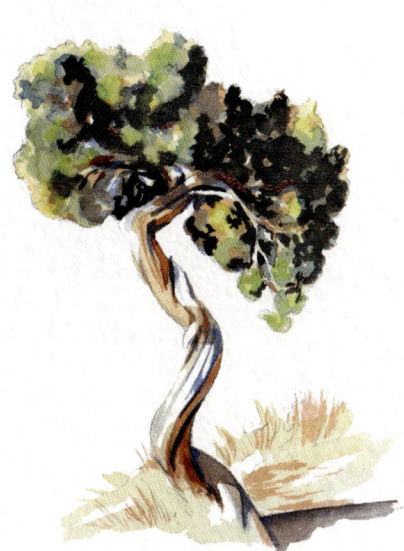

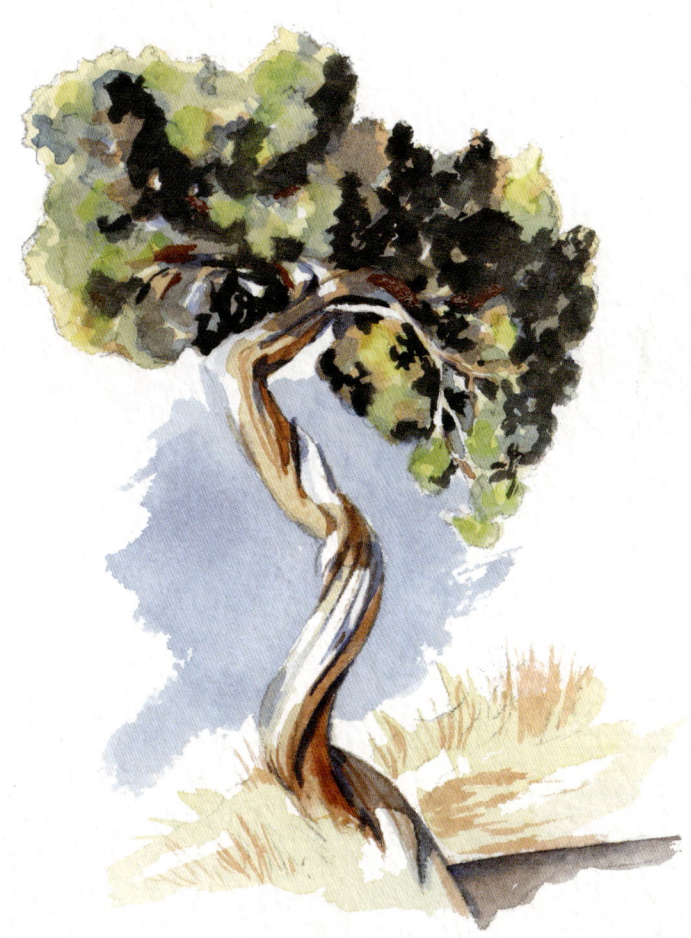

7. Mix a very dark combination of yellow ochre, ultramarine blue, and burnt sienna to create a rich greenish black. Use this to paint your darkest darks. This should be your final layer on the tree.

8. If you want to hint at the distant canyon behind the juniper tree, you can add a quick wet-on-dry background wash of ultramarine blue.

SAGUARO NATIONAL PARK
Arizona

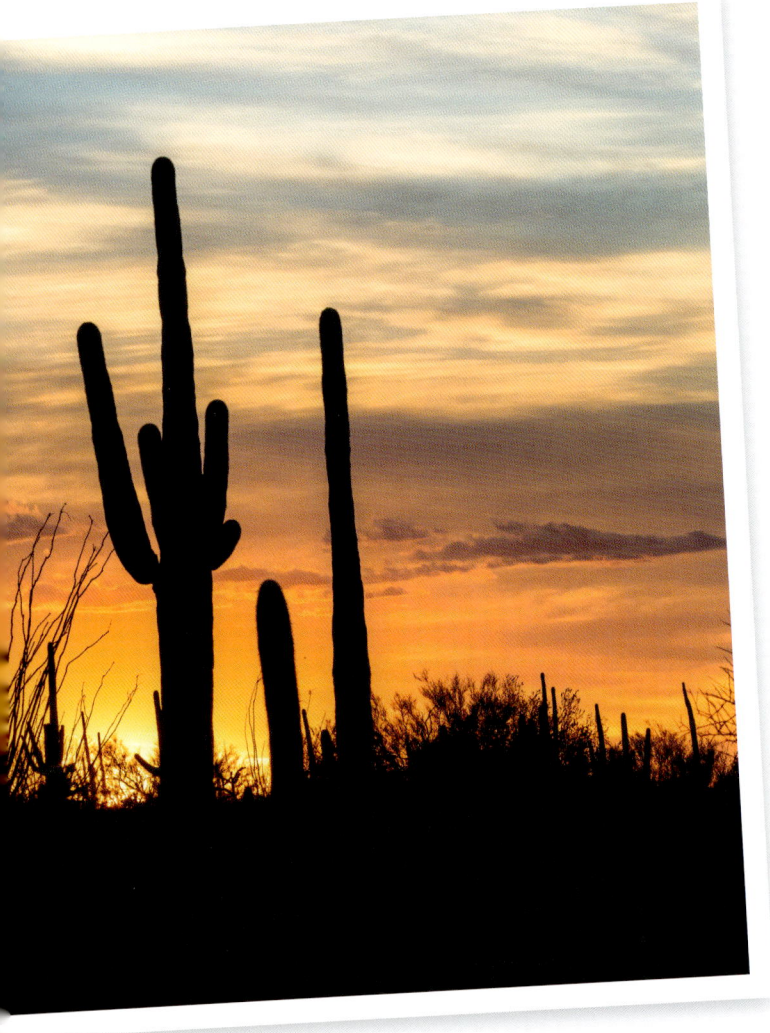

Reference photo

Saguaro National Park was established in 1994 to protect the flora and fauna of the southern part of Arizona. The park is home to the saguaro, the country's largest cacti species, which are a symbol of the American West and are found exclusively in the Sonoran Desert. An exemplary saguaro can grow up to 40 feet (12 m) tall and live for more than 150 years. These treelike cacti are slow growers; their arms do not begin to grow until they are between 50 and 70 years old, and a full-grown cactus can weigh up to a ton! I chose this sunset scene in Saguaro National Park to capture the vibrant blend of colors and to show off the noble silhouettes of these famous desert icons.

Download template and reference photo.

Brushes

Round, sizes 6 and 10

Paper

Fabriano Artistico 140-pound (300 gsm), cotton, cold-pressed block, 9" x 12" (23 x 30.5 cm); taped to resize down to 8" x 10" (20.5 x 25.5 cm)

Color Palette

Hansa Yellow Light

Gamboge Nova

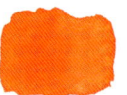

Transparent Orange

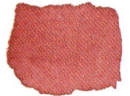

Permanent Alizarin Crimson

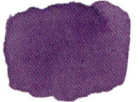

Permanent Violet

Phthalo Blue (GS)

Indigo

1. Sketch the silhouette of the cacti. You can use multiple reference images or even just make up your own! Cactus plants are simple to sketch and an easy subject on which to improvise.

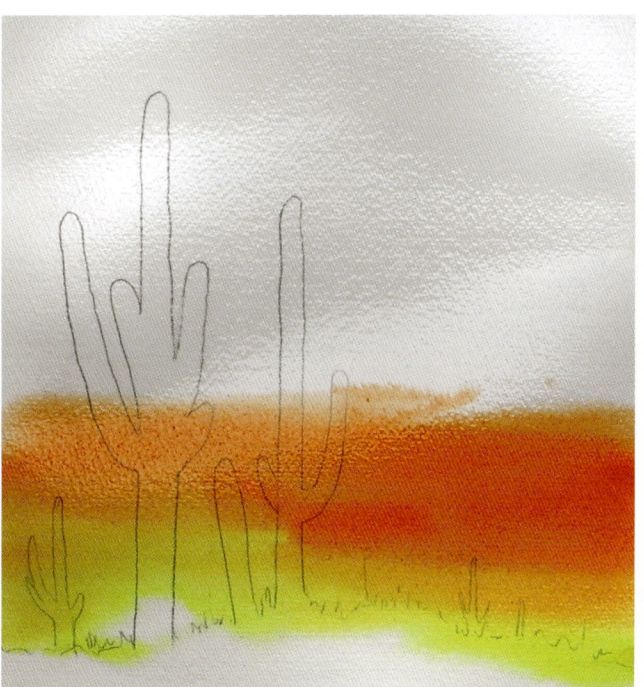

2. Use a spray bottle or large brush to soak your paper. No need to "paint around" anything—just wet the entire surface, aiming for a glossy, even sheen. The sky must be painted quickly, while the paper is still wet. Load your brush with creamy hansa yellow light and start at the bottom of the sky. Use smooth, horizontal brush strokes, but paint around a half-moon shape near the bottom left. This represents your bright setting sun!

Scan to watch a video.

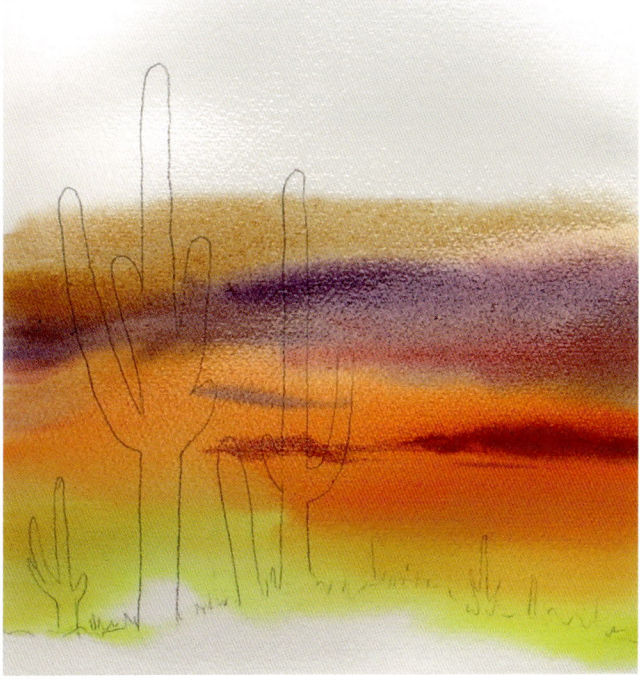

3. As you work your way up, change up your colors, rinsing in between to keep the colors fresh. Use gamboge nova, transparent orange, permanent alizarin crimson, and permanent violet.

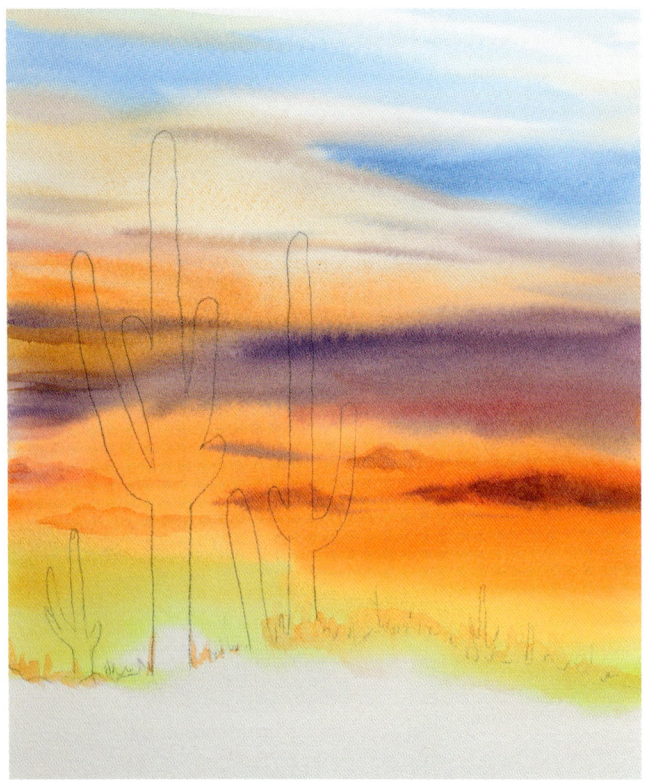

4. At the top of the sky, add some phthalo blue, leaving streaks in between untouched with paint. With gamboge nova in a milky paint consistency, use your smaller round brush to paint an orange glow along the hill. Begin to suggest the shape of tall grass and foliage here.

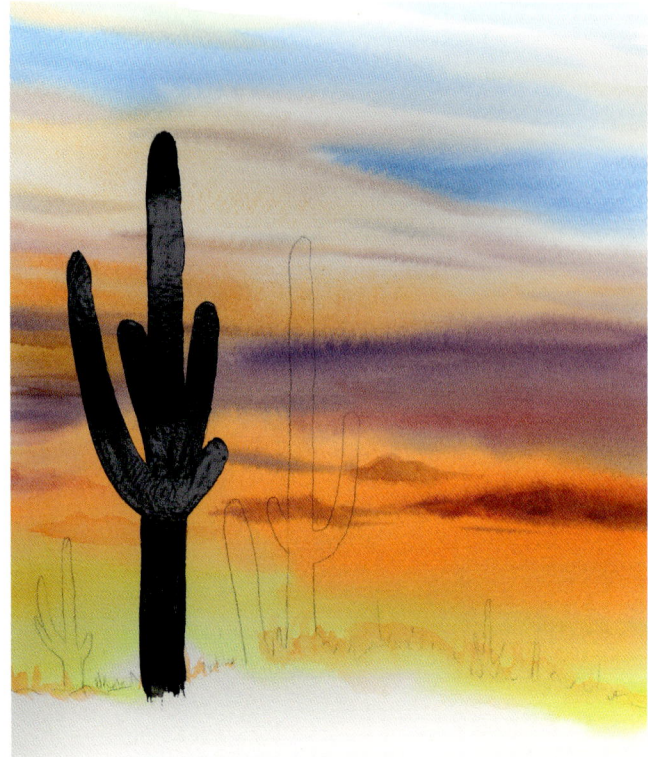

5. Let your sky dry completely. For the cactus silhouettes, mix up a generous amount of creamy black, or use indigo mixed with a little burnt sienna. You want to have a large enough puddle of paint to cover the entire foreground without having to stop and mix more.

Scan to watch a video.

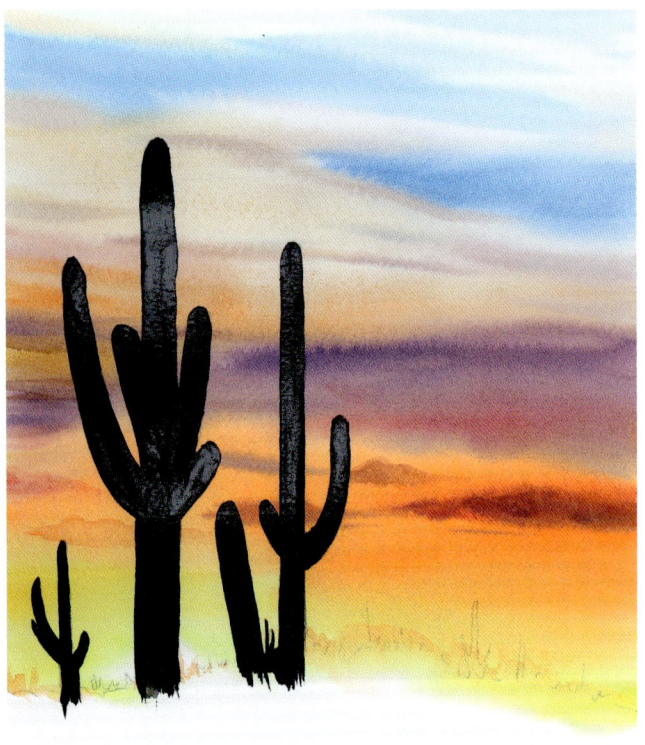

6. Finish the cacti first, using a small brush loaded with paint. If you wish to alter your drawing, you can use your black paint to adjust the shapes. They do not have to be perfect!

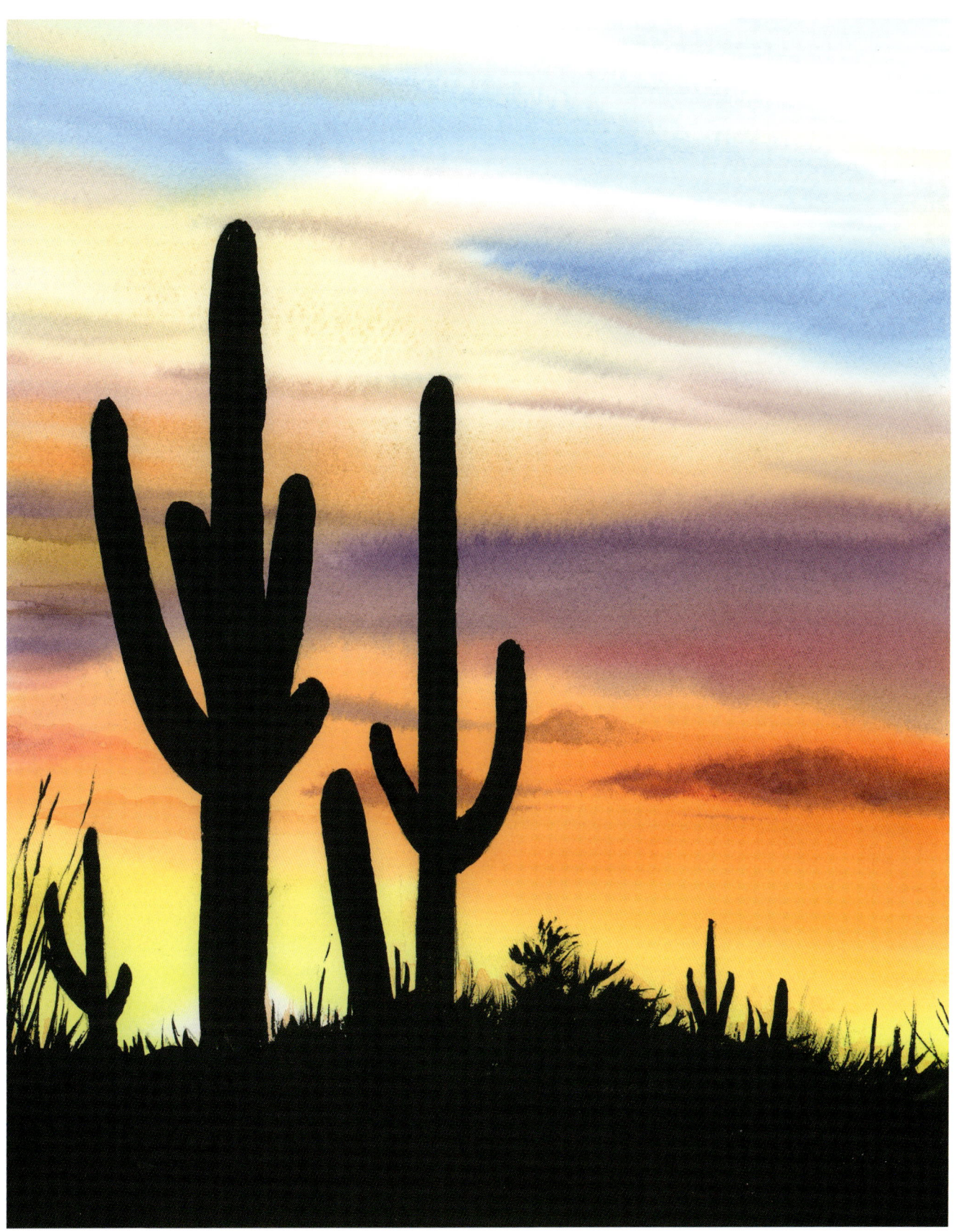

7. Finish the foreground with your larger brush and lots of black paint. I like to work left to right to prevent dragging my hand through wet paint. Add finishing details like tiny distant saguaro silhouettes and tall blades of grass.

MESA VERDE NATIONAL PARK
Colorado

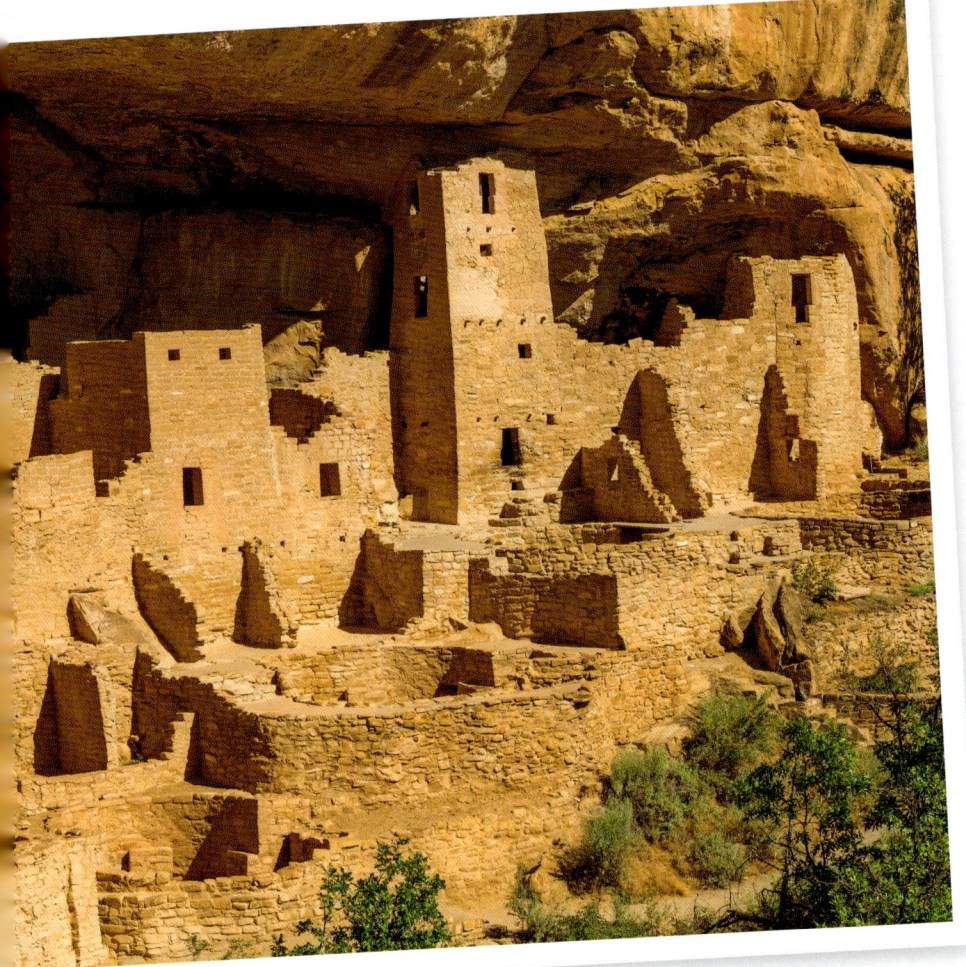

Reference photo

The ancestral Pueblo people built a thriving community with cliff dwellings in southwestern Colorado, where they lived for more than 700 years. Around 1300 AD, they mysteriously disappeared. Established in 1906, Mesa Verde National Park was created to protect this sacred piece of history.

Download template and reference photo.

Brushes

Round, sizes 4 and 8

Paper

Arches 140-pound (300 gsm), cotton, cold-pressed block, 7.9" x 7.9" (20 x 20 cm)

Color Palette

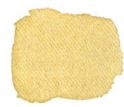

Yellow Ochre   Ultramarine Blue   Phthalo Blue (GS)   Burnt Sienna

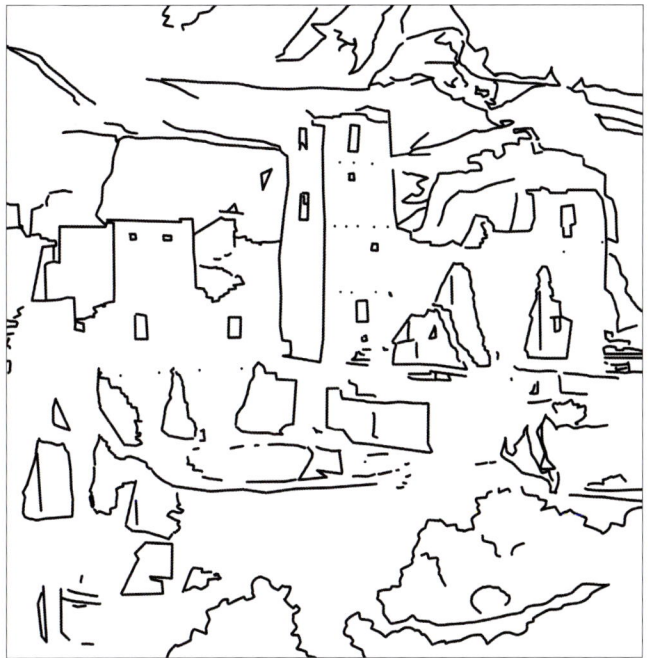

1. Trace the drawing.

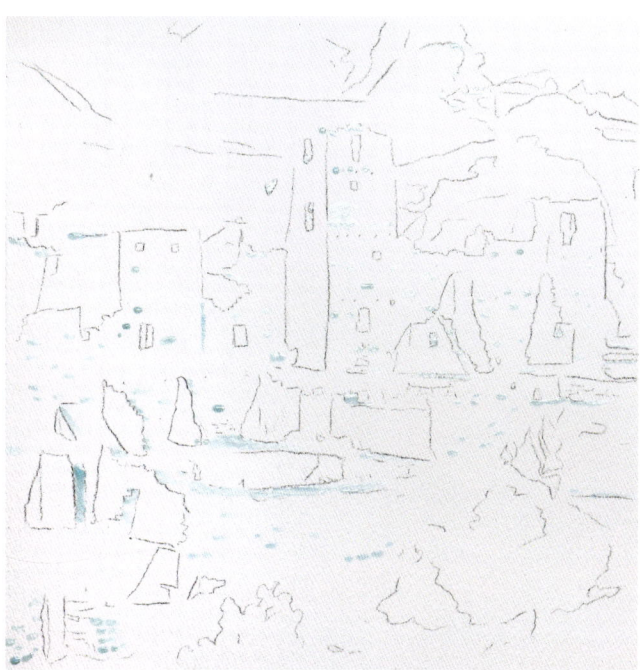

2. Sketch the shadow shapes of the dwellings, taking note of any hard edges and highlighted areas. Load up a rubber brush or small paint brush with masking fluid and apply it to small areas with bright highlights such as bricks and sunlit sills. Allow this to dry.

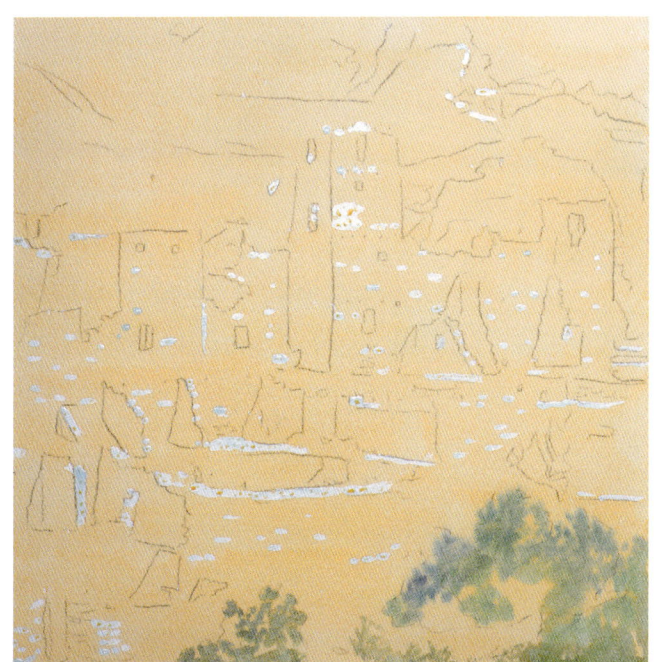

3. Paint the first wash wet-on-dry using a watery yellow ochre. While the wash is still damp, drop in some ultramarine blue and phthalo blue to paint some soft suggestions of foliage. Let it dry.

Scan to watch a video.

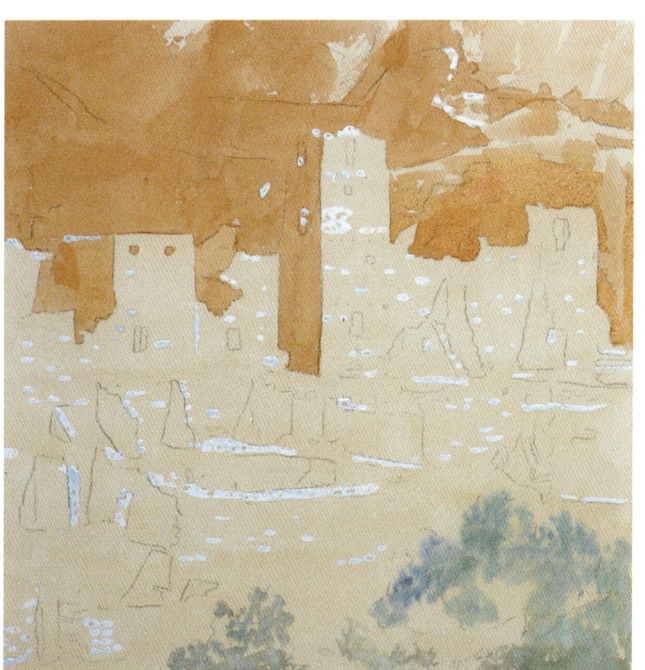

4. Use a milky consistency of yellow ochre mixed with a generous amount of burnt sienna to begin painting the shadow shapes. Lighten your values where the rocks are emerging into the light to create a subtle transition from dark to light.

Scan to watch a video.

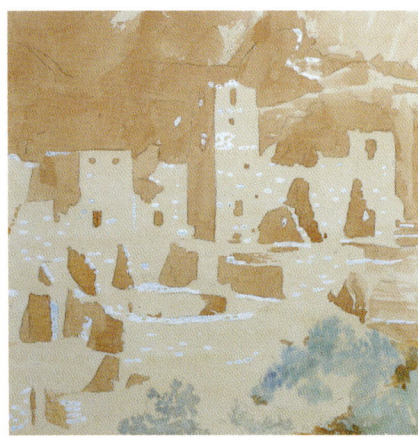

5. Use this same mix to paint in all of the little shadow shapes created by the strong sunlight.

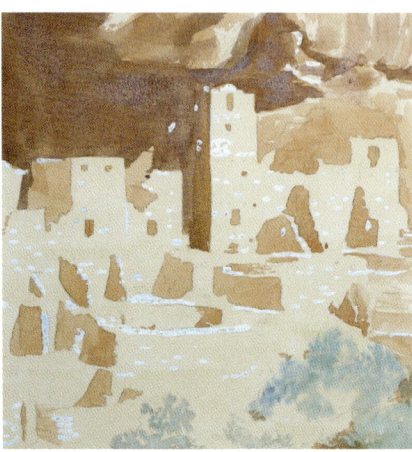

6. Create a large, milky puddle of chocolate brown by mixing burnt sienna with ultramarine blue. Use this to intensify the shadows.

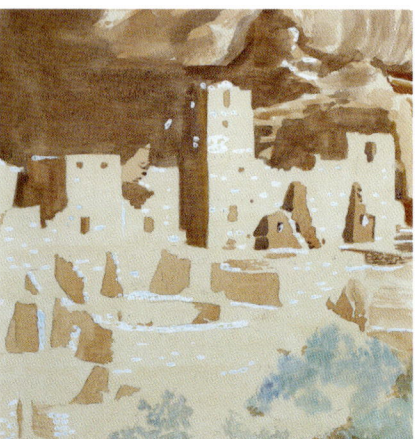

7. Apply a second layer of chocolate brown over the shadows of the structures. Observe how there's a "shadow within the shadow."

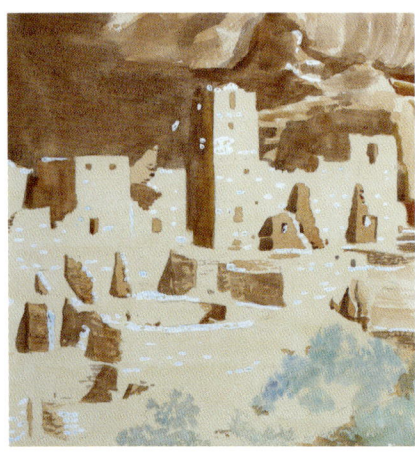

8. Use your small brush to suggest bricks within some of the shadows by leaving small gaps where the original wash shows through.

Scan to watch a video.

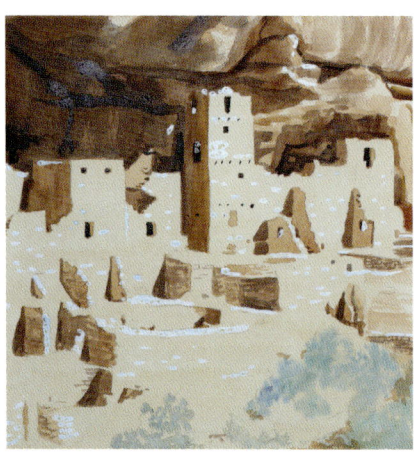

9. Mix a thick, nearly black blend of ultramarine blue and burnt sienna. Use this to paint the deepest cracks in the rocks and the shadows within the windows.

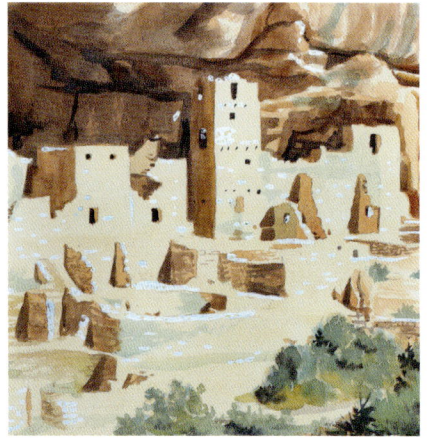

10. For the foliage, mix a green using yellow ochre and phthalo blue. Paint the bushes with loose, blobby brush strokes. Then, use a watery version of this green to add light strokes to the rocks and buildings, creating color harmony. To add depth, apply shadows to the bushes using your nearly black mix of ultramarine blue and burnt sienna.

Scan to watch a video.

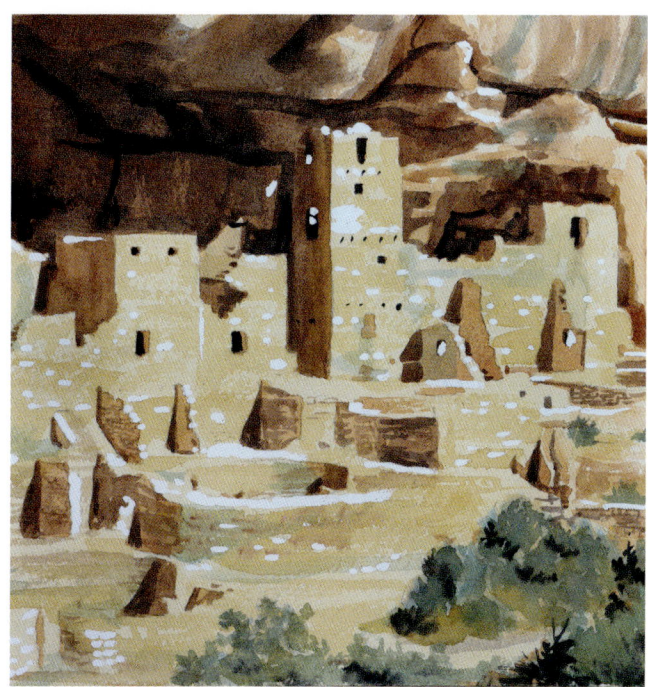

11. Apply another wash of yellow ochre to the structures by holding your brush at a sideways angle and scraping it across the surface. This dry-brush technique will easily create texture.

Scan to watch a video.

12. Make sure your surface is completely dry before carefully removing the masking fluid with clean, dry fingers or an eraser. Finish your artwork by refining the masked areas, as the shapes often need to be sharpened. Apply a light wash of yellow ochre to some highlights and use your smallest brush to add any final brick details.

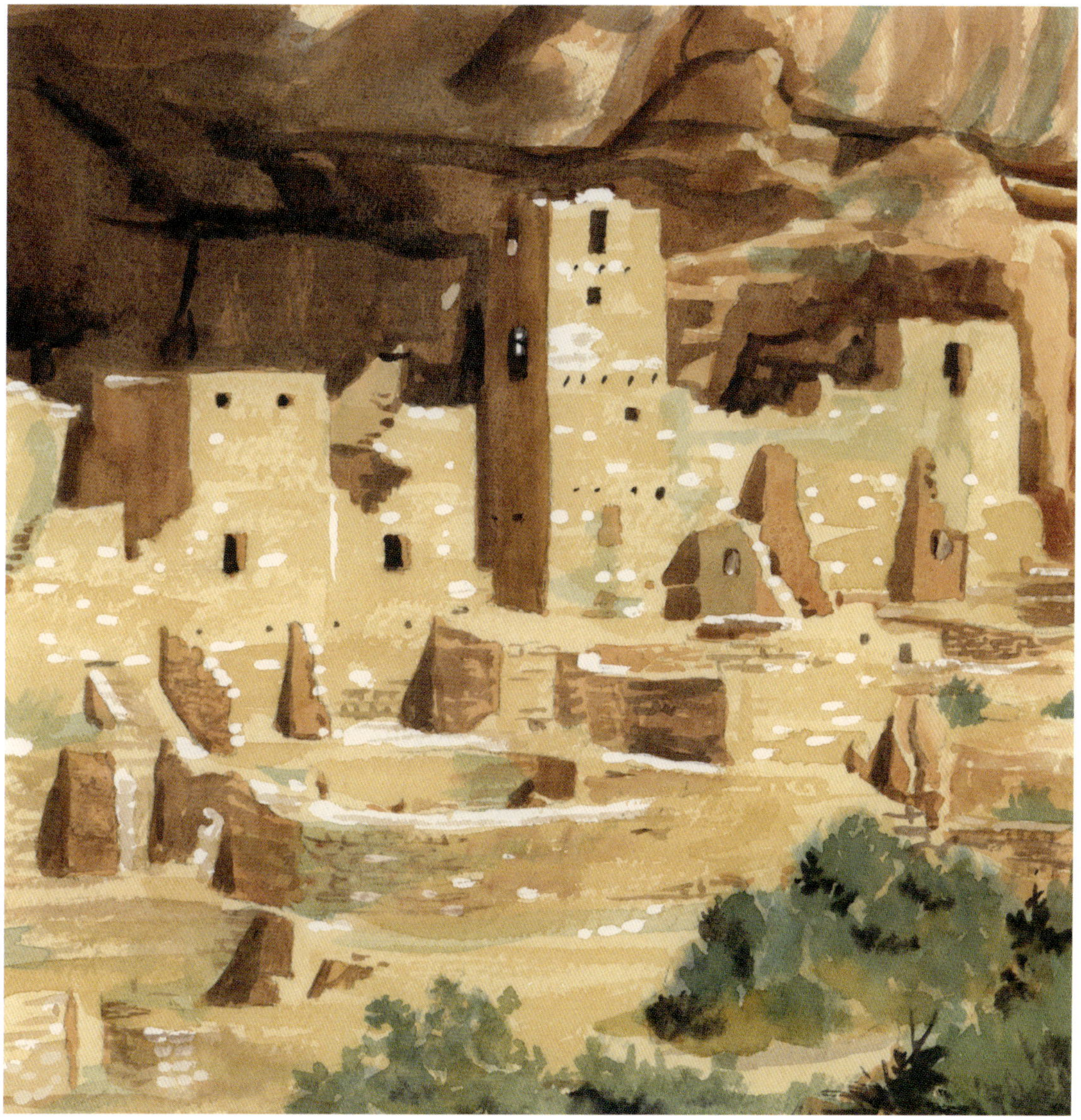

ROCKY MOUNTAIN NATIONAL PARK

Colorado

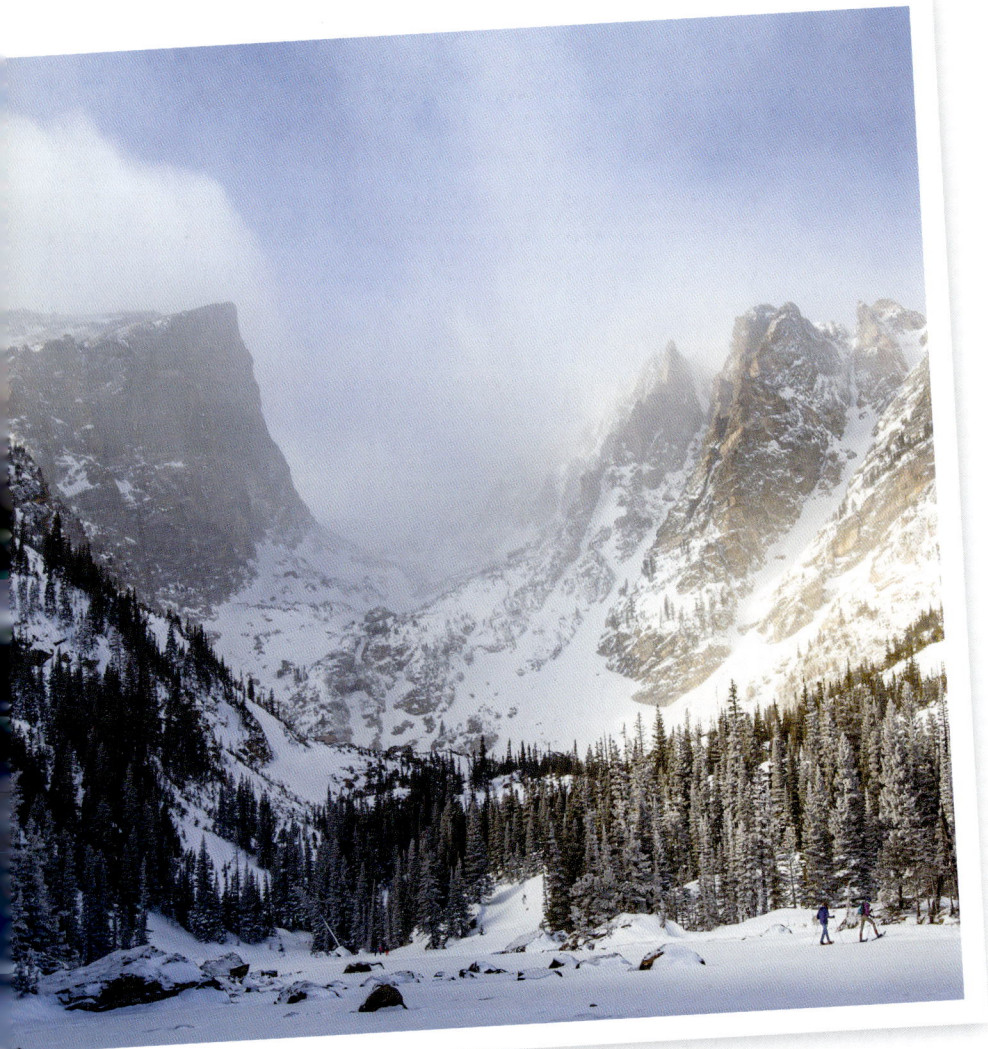

Reference photo

Rocky Mountain National Park in Colorado, located just a short drive west of the city of Denver, is one of the most popular national parks in the United States. With more than 350 miles (563 km) of hiking trails, the park offers a chance to fully immerse yourself in nature, with opportunities to see abundant wildlife, waterfalls, glacial lakes, and stunning mountain peaks. The park boasts more than 60 peaks that rise above 12,000 feet (3.6 km). This winter scene captures the enchanting Dream Lake, which can be reached via the popular Emerald Lake hiking trail. For this artwork, we will use a *very* limited palette of just two colors. I love the variety of hues I can achieve with this combination of ultramarine blue and burnt sienna.

Download template and reference photo.

Brushes

Round, sizes 6 and 10

Paper

Arches 140-pound (300 gsm), cotton, cold-pressed block, 7.9" x 7.9" (20 x 20 cm)

Color Palette

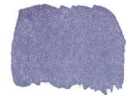

Ultramarine Blue

Burnt Sienna

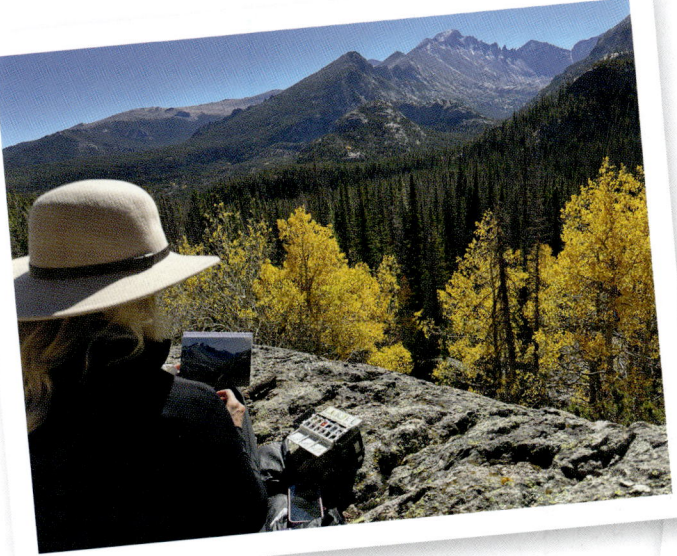

I have visited Rocky Mountain National Park many times, and on several occasions, I've had the opportunity to paint en plein air. On this beautiful autumn morning, I painted Longs Peak, at 14,259 feet (4.3 km), it is the tallest mountain in the park and can be seen from many miles away.

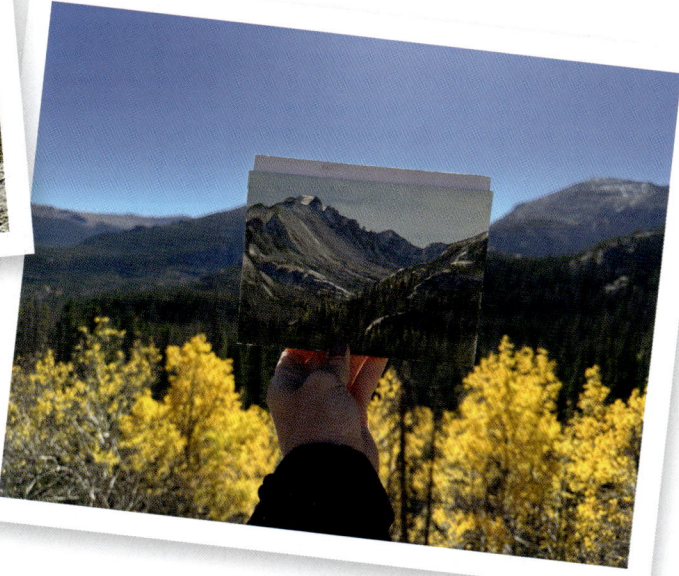

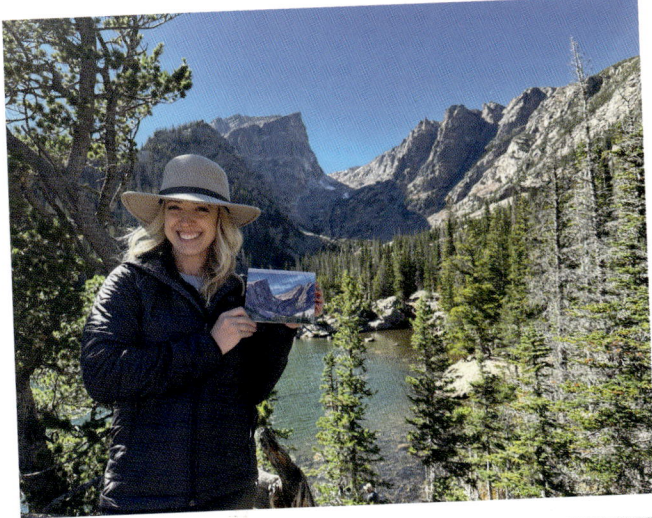

Here, I painted Dream Lake under very different lighting conditions compared to our winter scene. The October afternoon sun created beautiful and dramatic light and shadow shapes on Flattop Mountain.

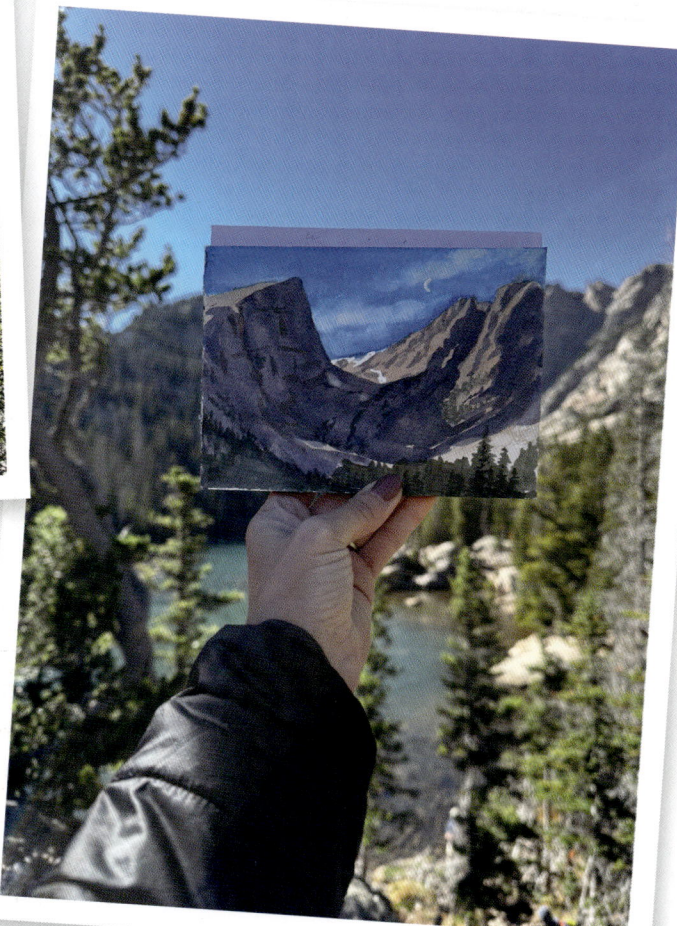

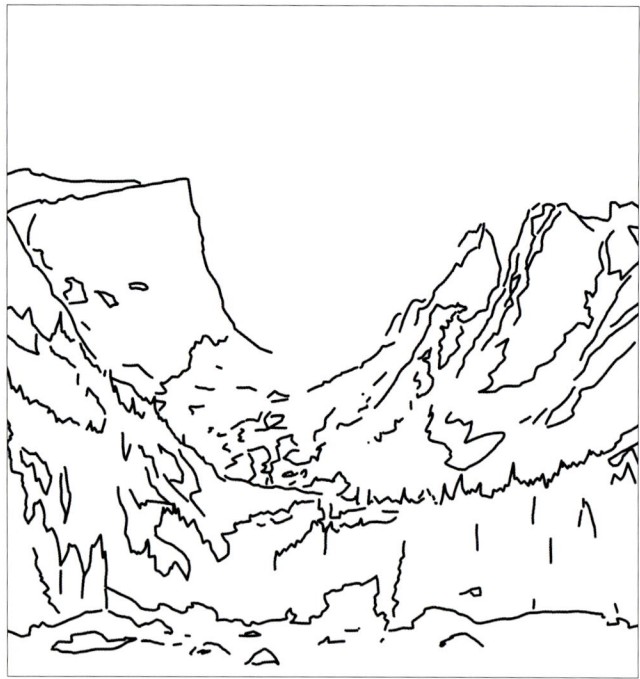

1. Lightly sketch or trace the scene onto your watercolor paper. Avoid pressing too hard with your pencil and be sure to leave "lost edges" where the fog obscures the slopes, creating soft, undefined areas without lines.

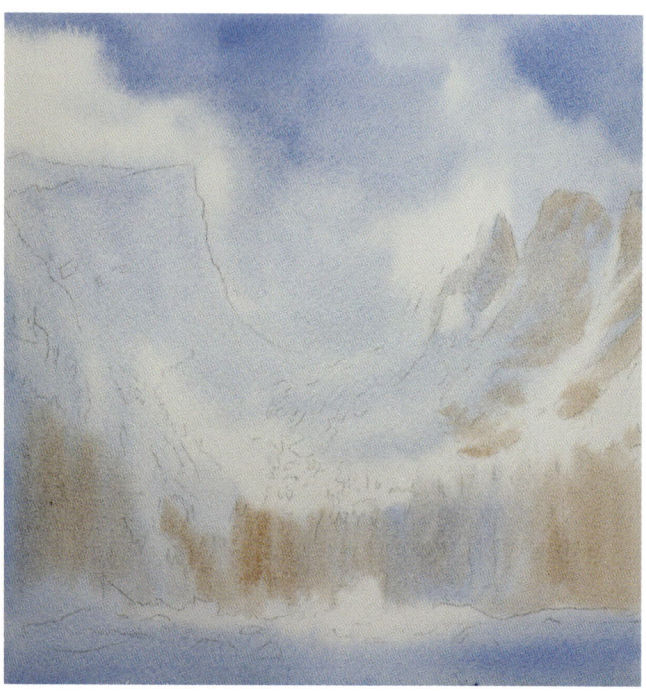

2. Begin with the wet-on-wet technique. Lightly spray or brush clear water over the entire surface of your paper, allowing it to soak evenly until it has a glossy sheen. Load a large round brush with ultramarine blue mixed to a milky or creamy consistency and paint the sky and foreground. Using a more diluted blue, paint in the mountains. While the paper is still damp, drop in some burnt sienna for the trees and slopes on the right, ensuring your brush isn't holding excess water.

Scan to watch a video.

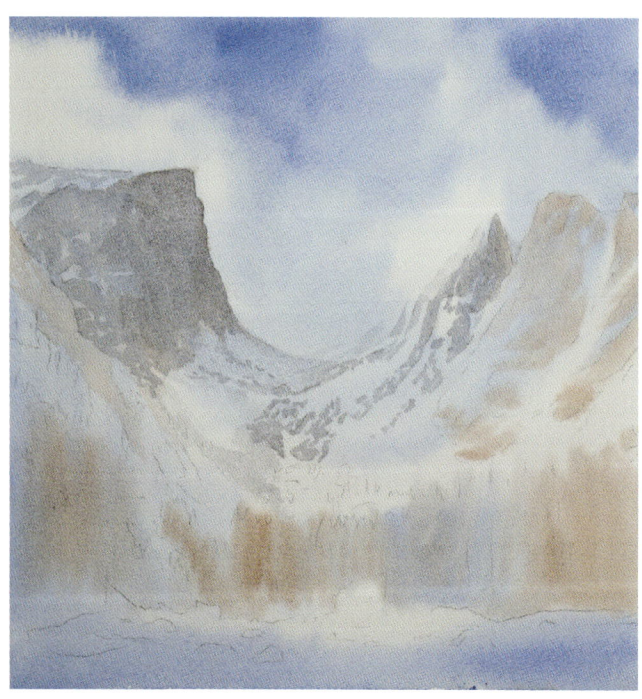

3. Mix equal parts of ultramarine blue and burnt sienna to create a soft, neutral gray. Switch to a smaller brush and use this color to paint the mountain rock, carefully avoiding the lighter areas that represent snow.

4. Add more burnt sienna to your mix for the rocks on the right but keep the values light. To create atmospheric perspective, make the most distant shapes lighter in value. Use ultramarine blue in areas that need a cooler color temperature.

Scan to watch a video.

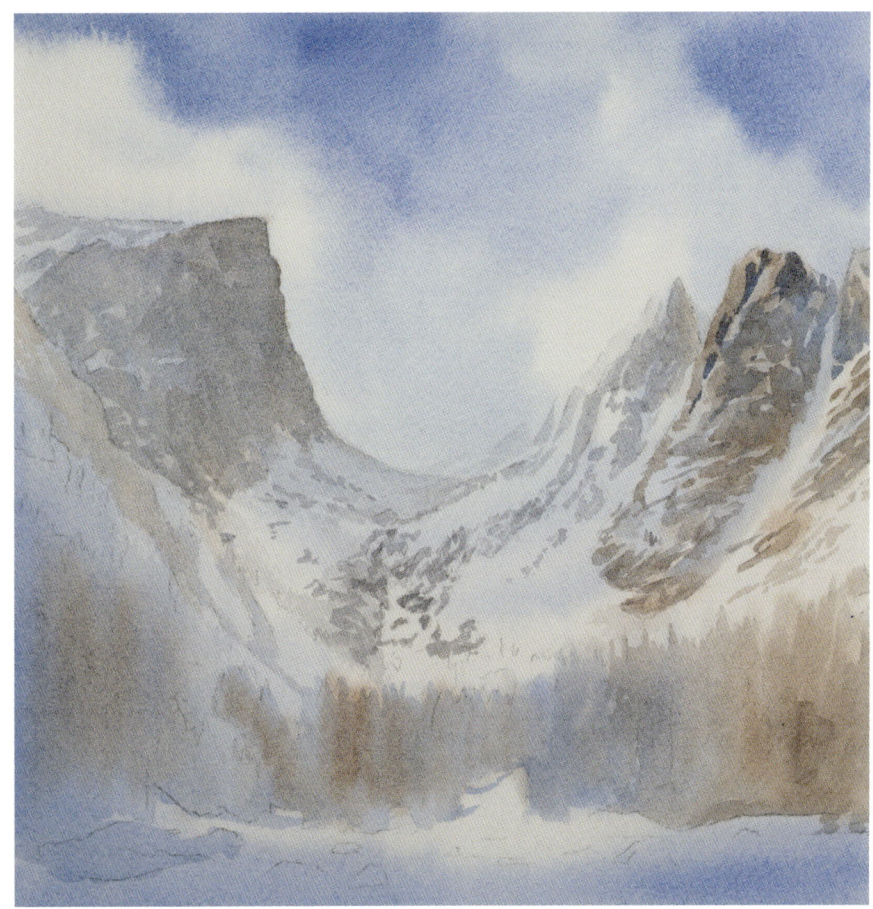

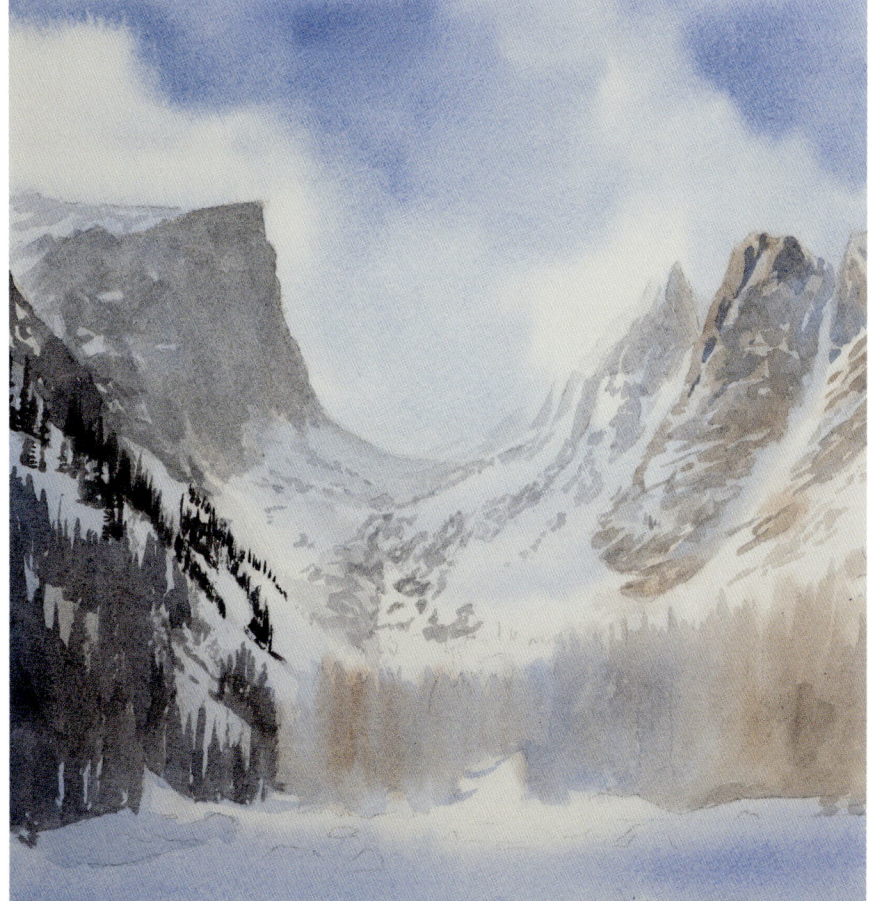

5. For the trees, mix a very dark combination of ultramarine blue and burnt sienna. Use quick, side-by-side upstrokes to paint the pointed evergreens. Water down the paint for the trees in the foreground, creating an underpainting for darker details. We will add these in the next layer.

Scan to watch a video.

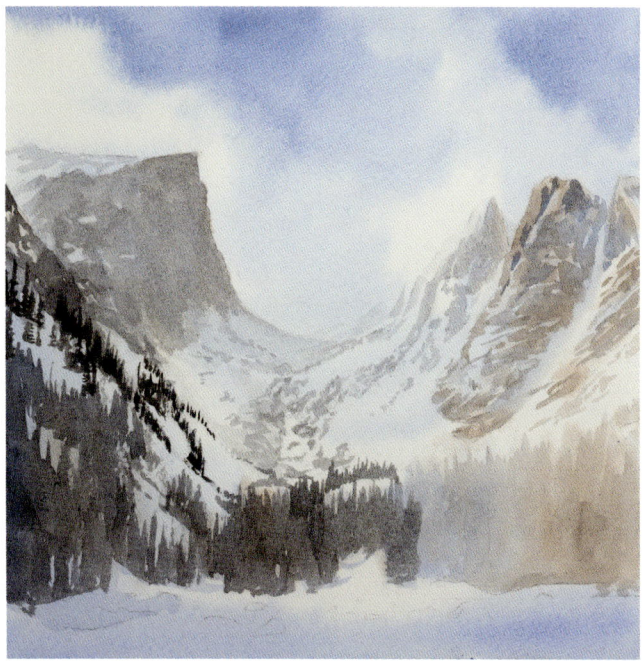

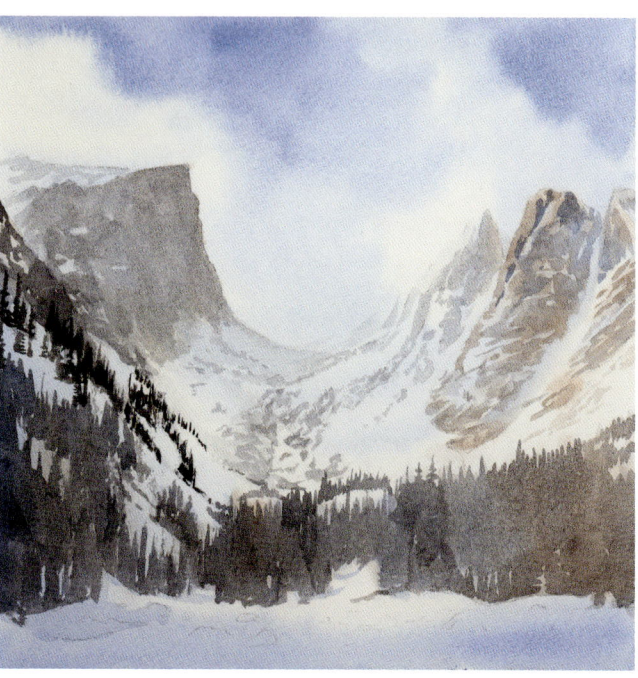

Scan to watch a video.

6. Continue painting a medium gray underpainting with watery upstrokes and downstrokes to outline the tree clusters. Remember to leave gaps where the snowy ground shows through between the trees.

7. Alternate between warm and cooler versions of your gray mix to add variety and interest to the wash.

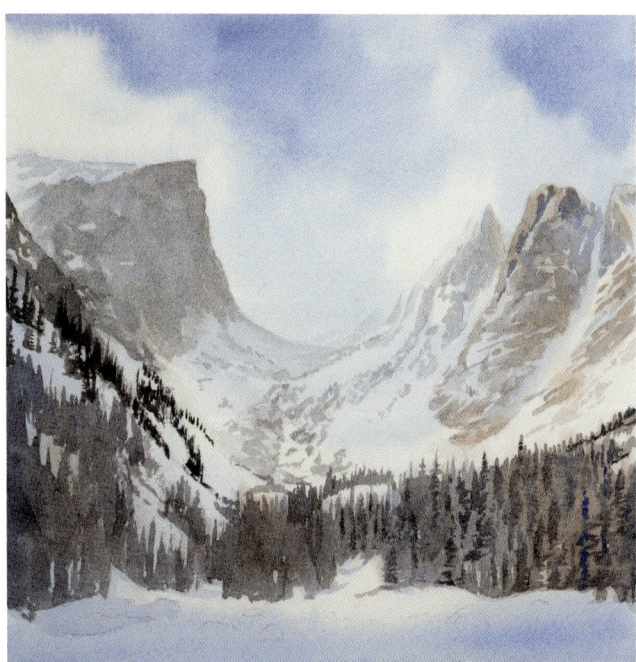

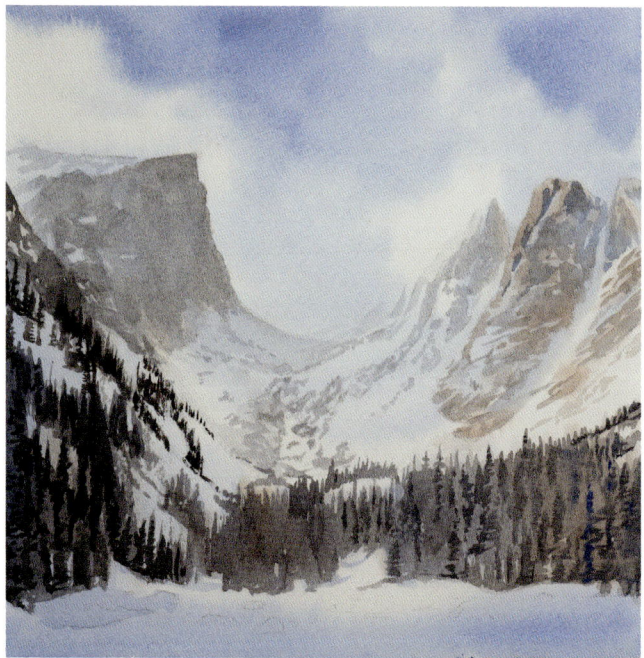

8. As the gray wash starts to dry, begin adding darker shadows between the trees. Use a side-to-side motion with a small round brush to hint at the texture of frosty branches.

9. Mix a creamy, nearly black blend of ultramarine blue and burnt sienna. Use this mixture to complete the trees and add rocks to the frozen lake.

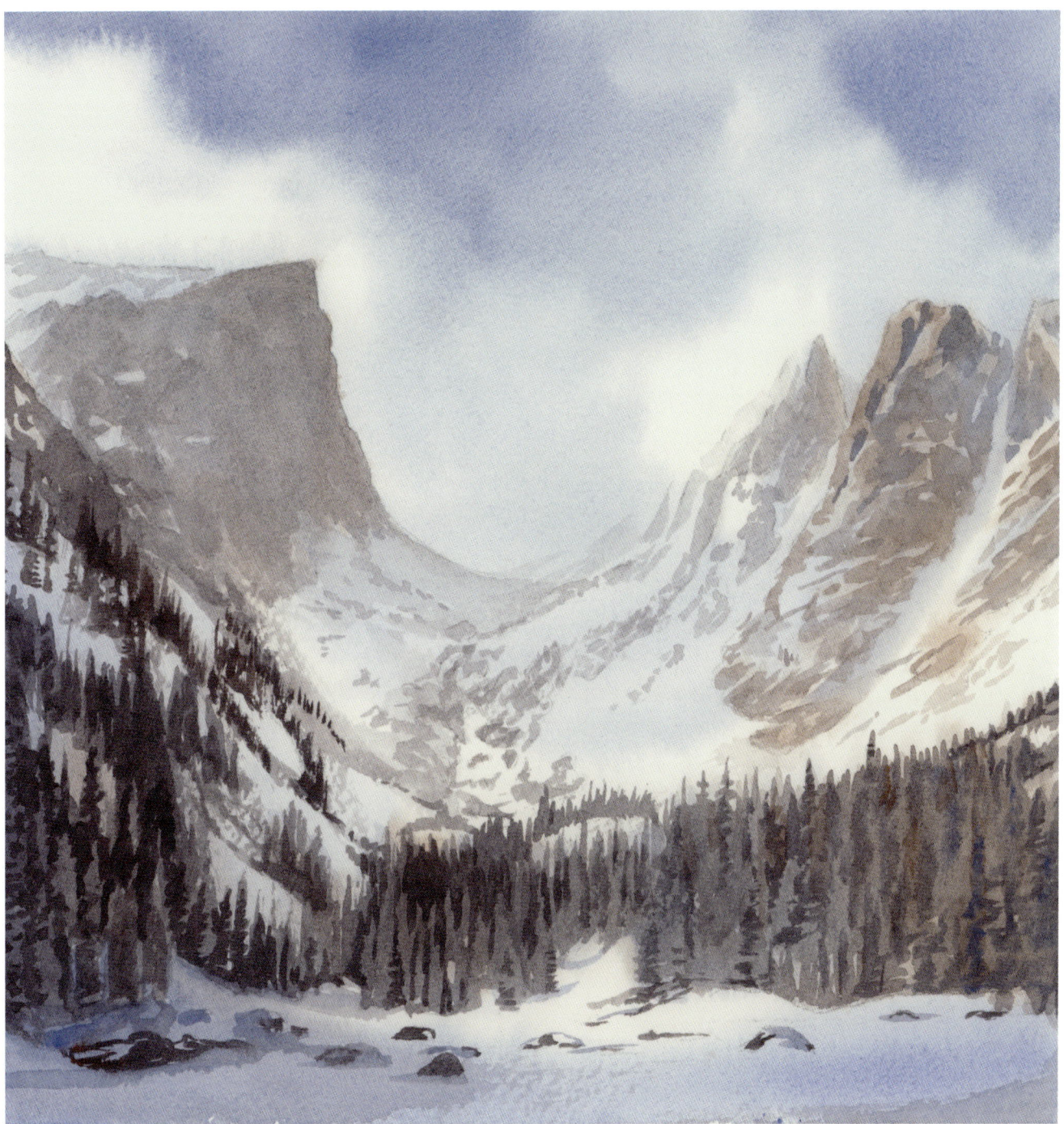

10. Add final details like touches of pure ultramarine blue or burnt sienna in the trees, dry-brush texture, and blue shadows on the snowy sides of the rocks. Avoid overworking it; subtlety is key to preserving the soft, hazy feel of winter snow and fog.

BIG BEND NATIONAL PARK
Texas

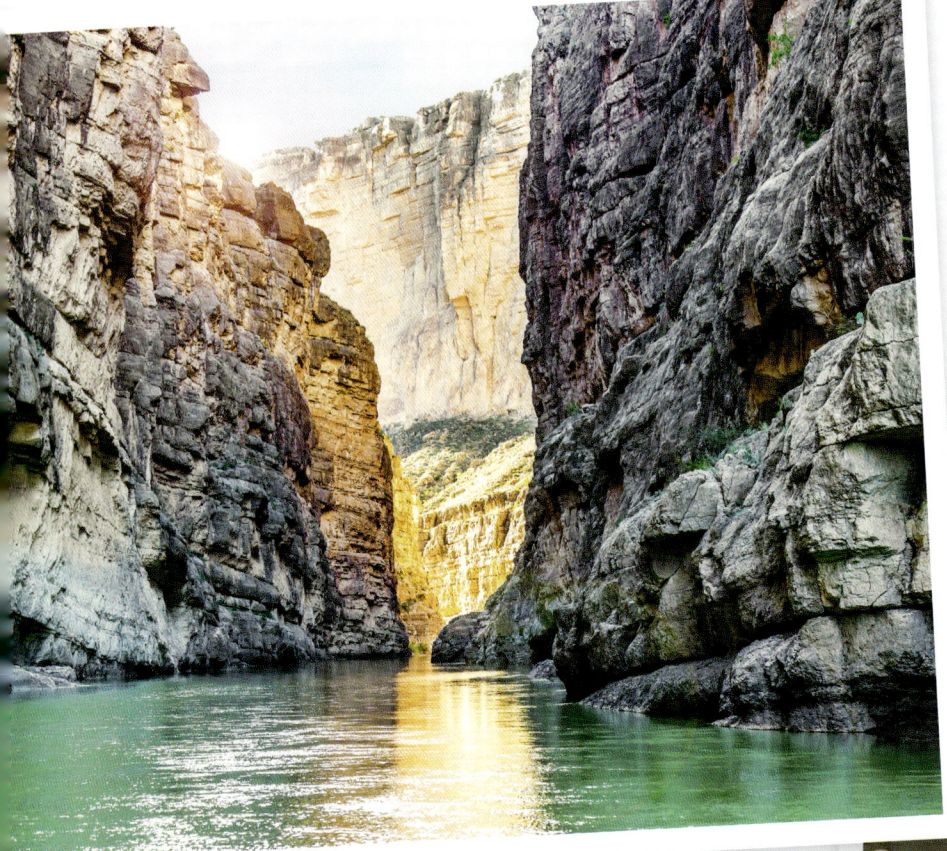

Big Bend National Park is one of the most unforgettable places I have ever visited! The park is a sprawling 1,262 square miles (3,269 square km) and contains a fascinating blend of ecosystems, from the Chihuahuan Desert to the Rio Grande River to the Chisos Mountains. My favorite location in the park is Santa Elena Canyon, the subject of this painting.

Download template and reference photo.

Reference photo

Brushes

Round, sizes 8 and 10

Paper

Fabriano Artistico 140-pound (300 gsm), cotton, cold-pressed block, 9" x 12" (23 x 30.5 cm); taped to resize down to 8" x 10" (20.5 x 25.5 cm)

Color Palette

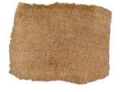
Burnt Sienna

Gamboge Nova

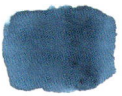
Marine Blue

Hansa Yellow Light

Indigo

Permanent Alizarin Crimson

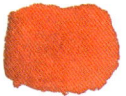
Scarlet Lake

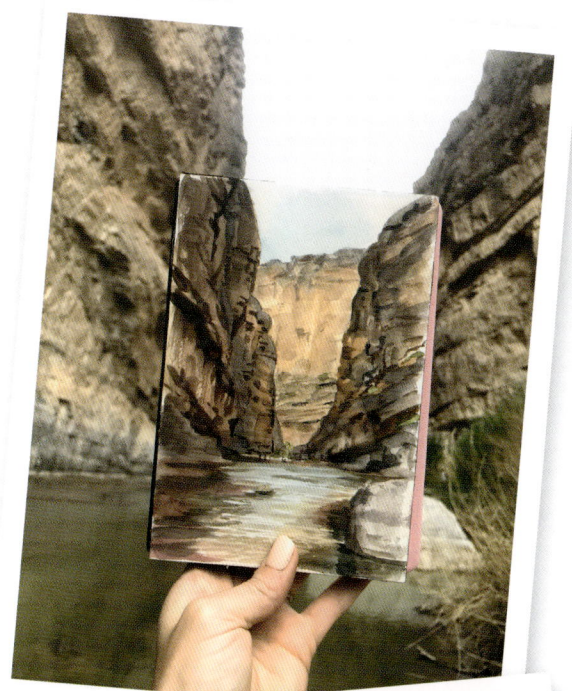

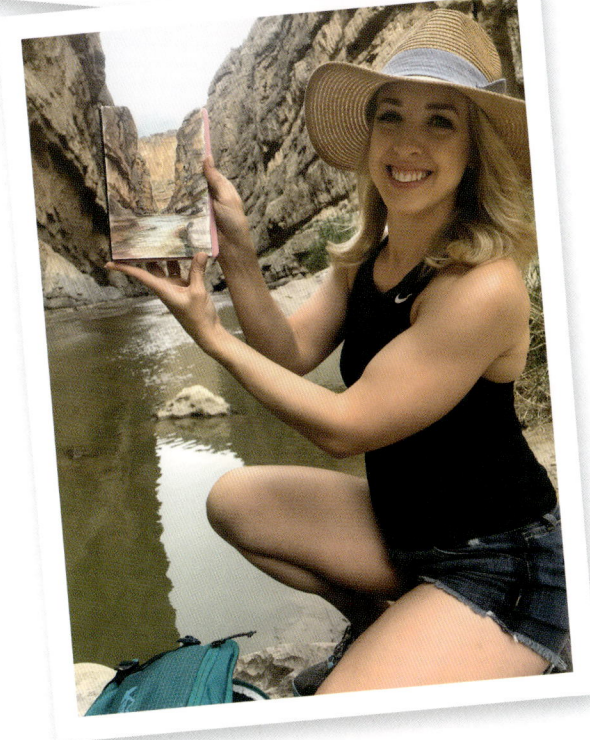

I had the privilege of spending a morning perched on a rock near the river, painting this majestic scene from life. I enjoyed the echoing laughs of people paddling by in canoes and a little spiny softshell turtle that stayed near me the whole time I painted! Fun fact: The rock wall on the left is in Mexico, and the rock wall on the right is in the United States!

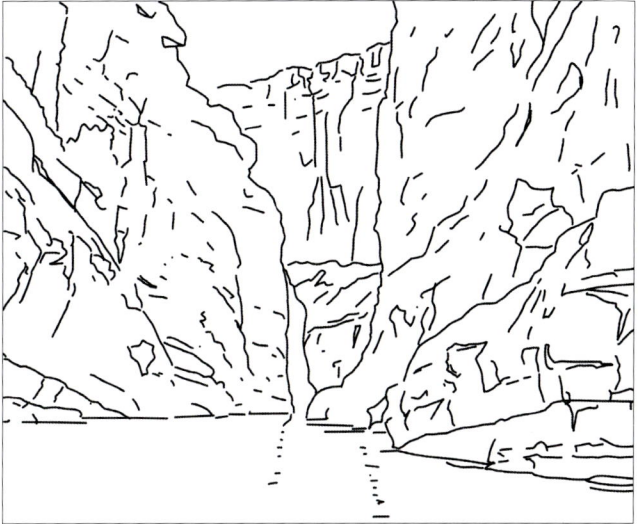

1. Trace or sketch the drawing.

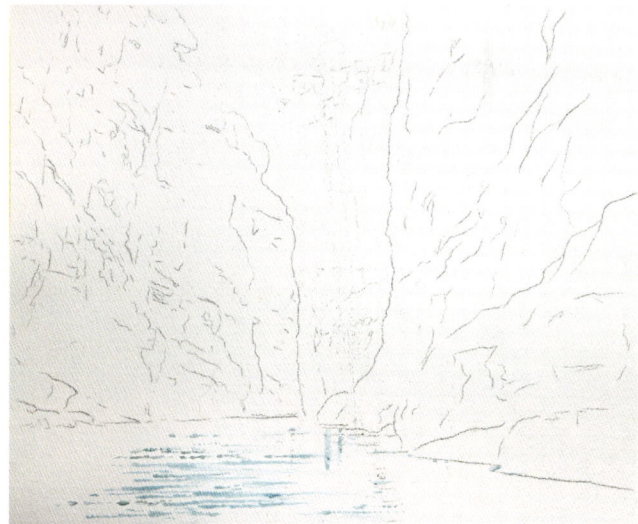

2. Begin with masking fluid to "paint" the shimmering horizontal streaks of light on the water. This will allow you to paint freely over the top while preserving the white of the paper here. Allow it to dry completely.

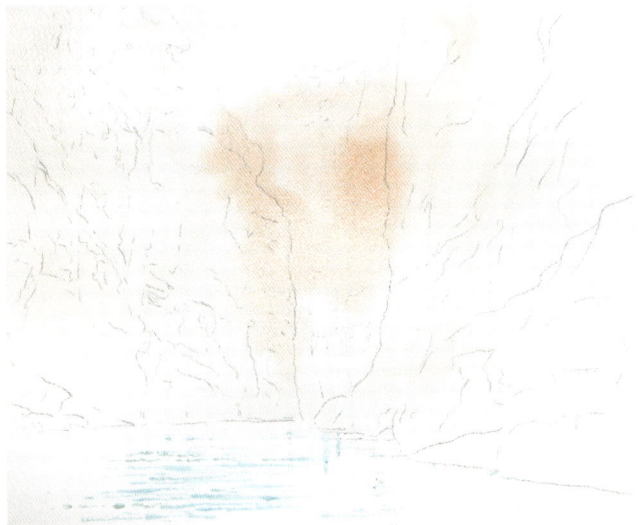

3. Use clear water to prewet your paper. Dab in a tint of burnt sienna over the center of the painting.

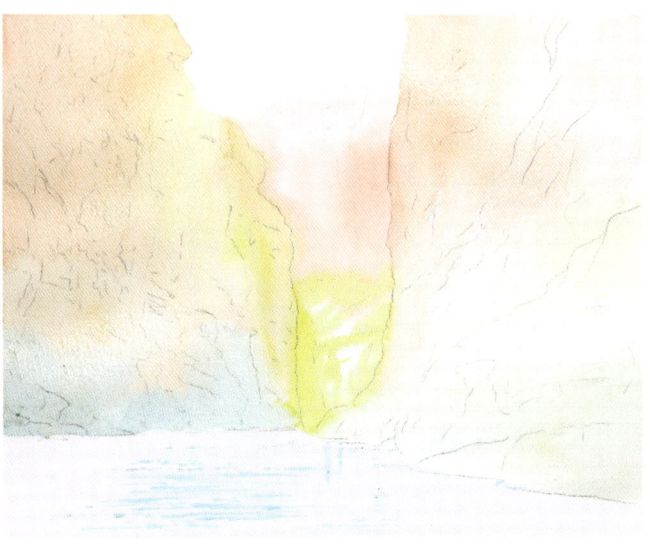

4. While the paper is still wet, quickly brush in some bright gamboge nova between the cliffs and on the left cliff face. This shows the brilliant light streaming in through the canyon. Use a tint of burnt sienna to paint the first layer over the rock faces. Apply a watery tint of marine blue to the lower portions of the cliffs near the water.

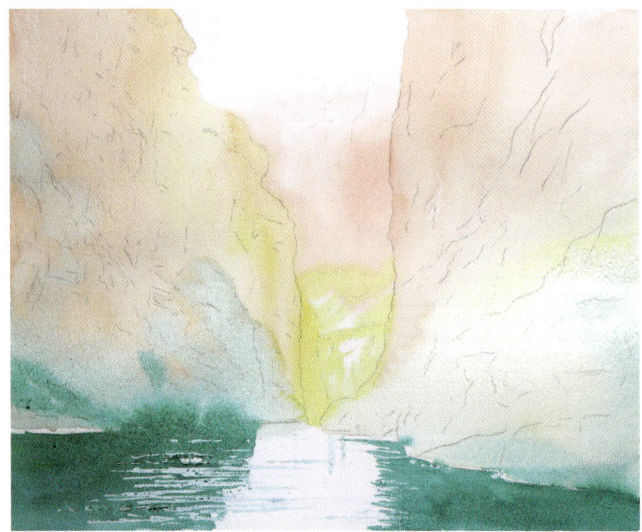

5. Load up your brush with a generous amount of marine blue, mixing in some hansa yellow light to warm up the color. Using broad, horizontal brush strokes, paint the dark green water to the right and left, allowing some of the color to bleed into the still-wet cliffs. Leave the center of the painting untouched but use the tip of your brush to paint around tiny gaps to represent movement on the water.

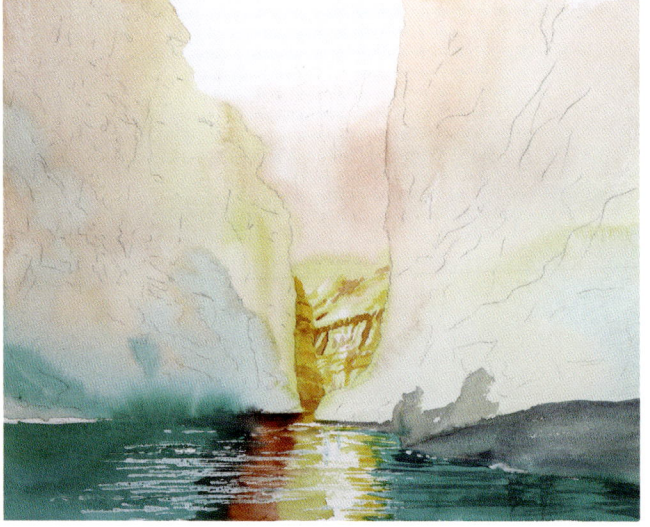

6. Begin to paint in the details in the center of the composition. Use gamboge nova and burnt sienna to create the texture in the rocks. Create the reflection on the water using the same colors. Use indigo to paint the darker reflections and start building up the grey stone on the right.

Scan to watch a video.

7. We will use the wet-on-wet technique to paint a first layer on each cliff. Starting with the right side, soak the entire rock area with clear water. With your biggest brush, begin dropping in creamy paint, observing the reference photo for color changes. Use darker, more concentrated paint wherever you see deep cracks and shadows on the rock. Indigo is the primary color used here, with some burnt sienna to create the brown patches and some permanent alizarin crimson where the cliffs are rising toward the light. Allow the colors to blend side by side on the paper. Do not scrub or overbrush.

Scan to watch a video.

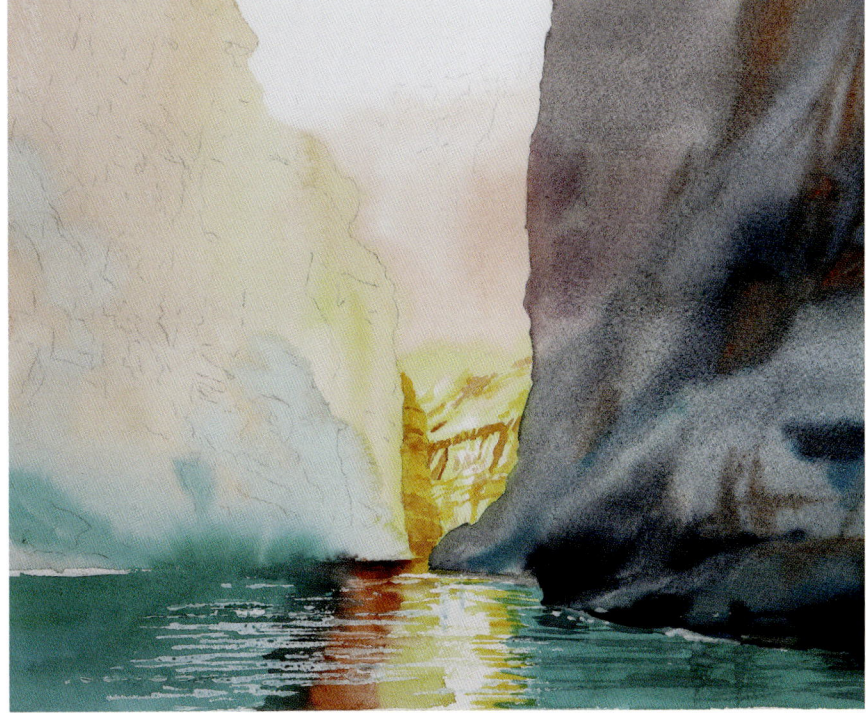

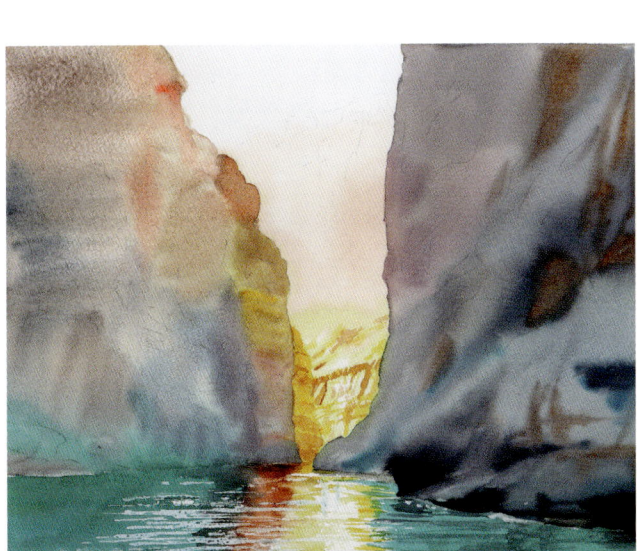

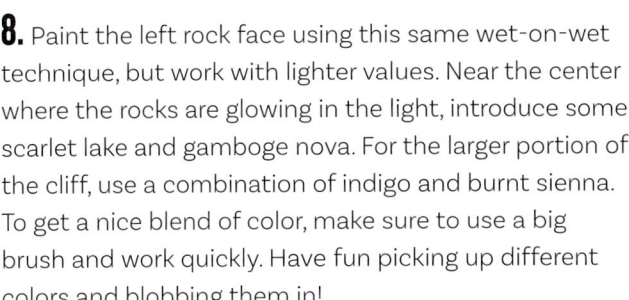

8. Paint the left rock face using this same wet-on-wet technique, but work with lighter values. Near the center where the rocks are glowing in the light, introduce some scarlet lake and gamboge nova. For the larger portion of the cliff, use a combination of indigo and burnt sienna. To get a nice blend of color, make sure to use a big brush and work quickly. Have fun picking up different colors and blobbing them in!

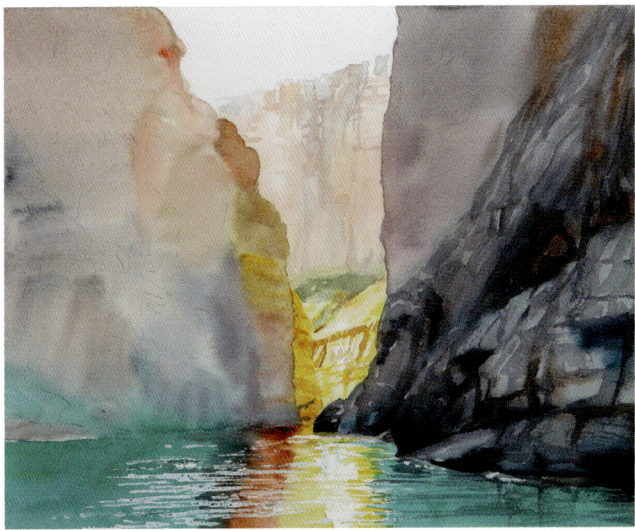

9. With your lightest values all painted in, it's time to add details! Use the reference photo to note where to place your brush strokes and begin painting dark cracks, cavities, and unique features of the rocks. Adjust your values using water. You can use some dry-brush techniques to scrape your brush across the surface of the paper for even more interesting rock textures.

Scan to watch a video.

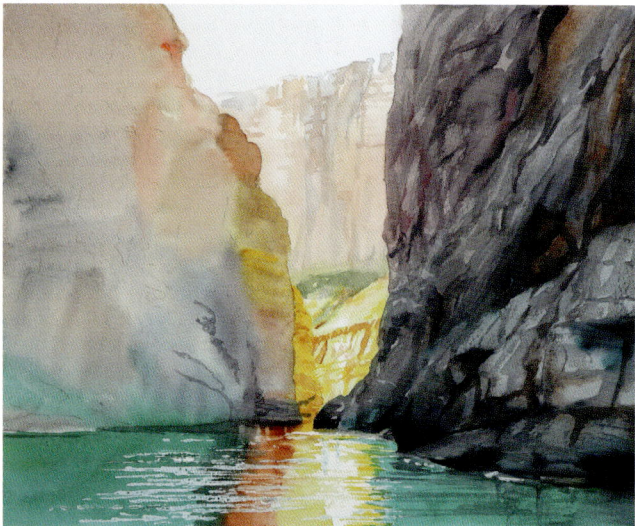

10. Continue adding color and detail to the rock faces. Have fun allowing your brush to dance and sweep across the surface of the paper—avoid picking at the details or lingering too long in one spot. Working quickly will give the painting a fresh and spontaneous feel.

Scan to watch a video.

11. Finish the painting, adding any final details. Remember that you do *not* need to include every bump and cranny! Simpler is better. Gently remove the masking fluid with a clean dry finger or paper towel.

Scan to watch a video.

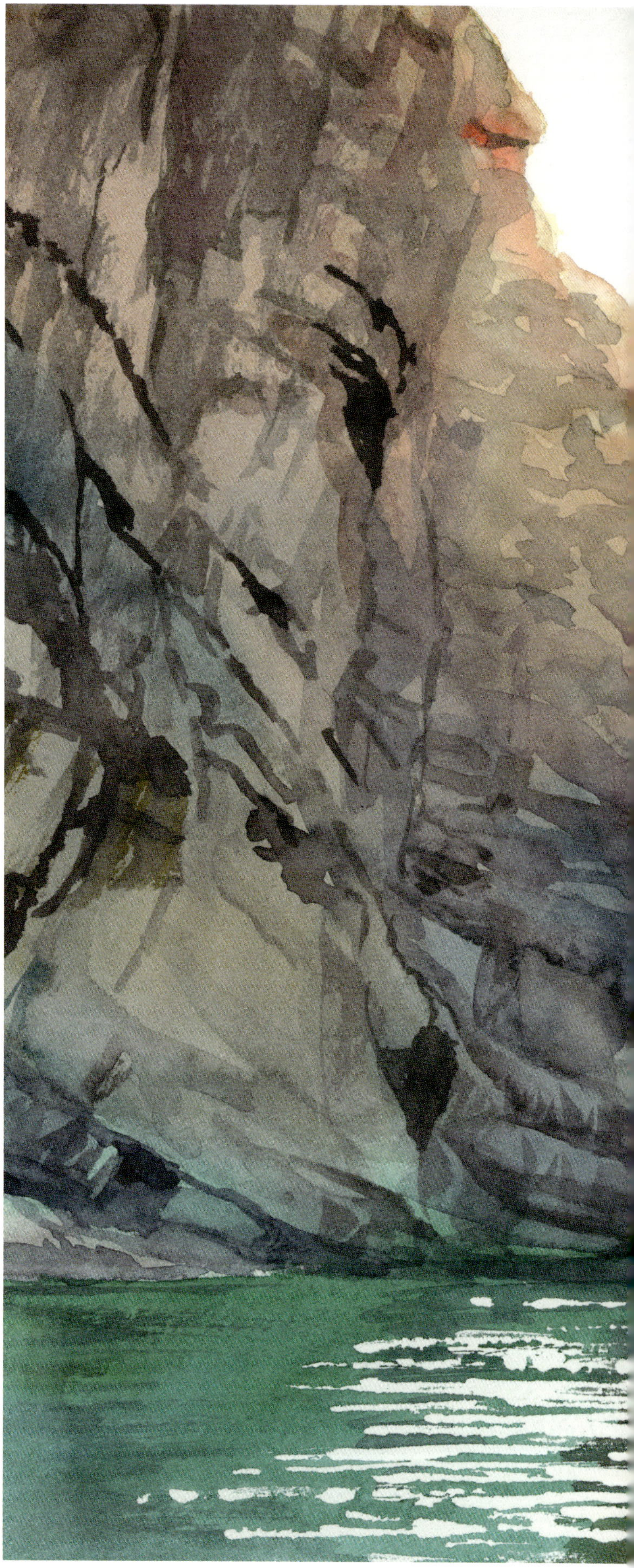

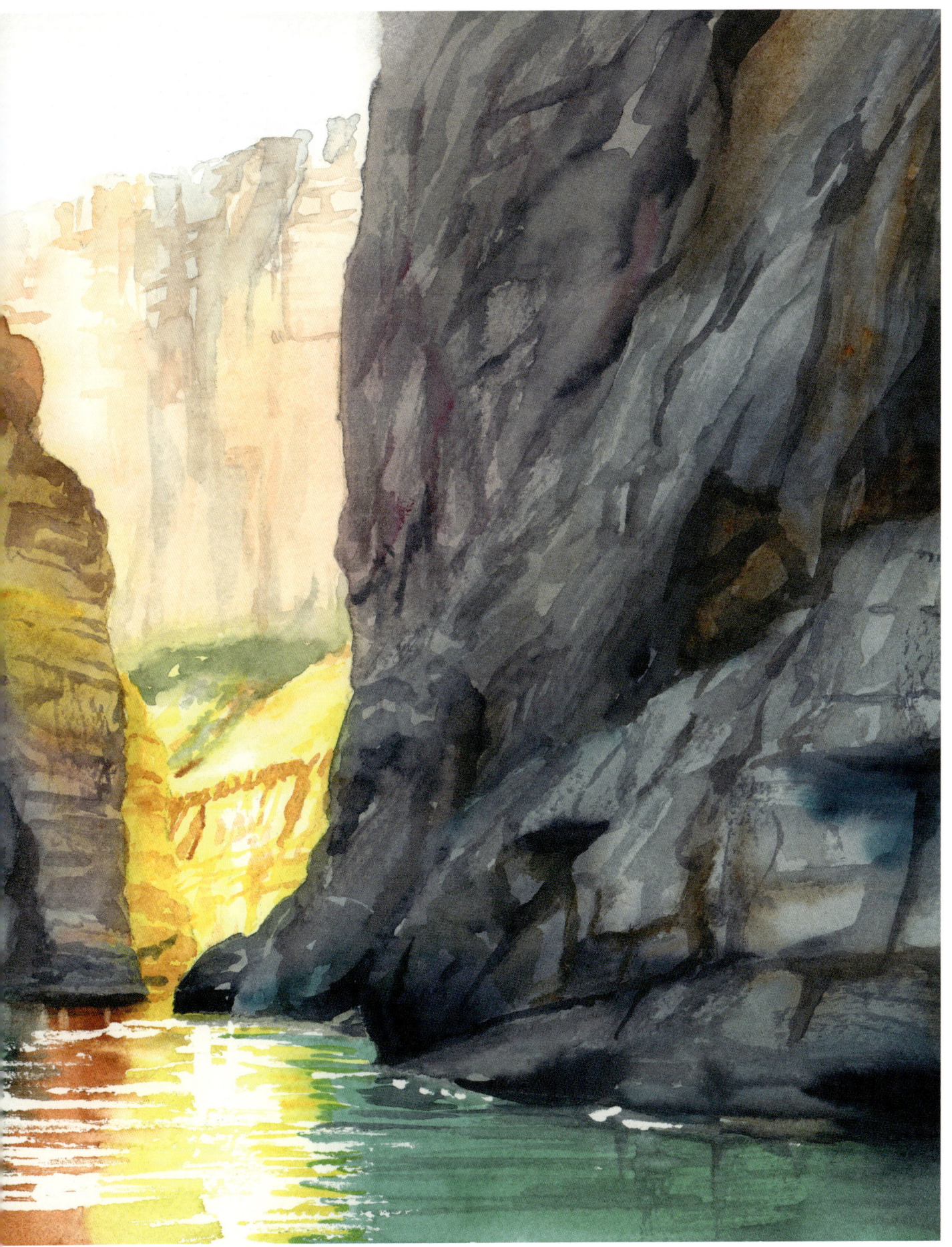

Prickly Pear Cactus

The prickly pear is a native Texas cactus that comes alive from late spring to early summer with gorgeous blossoms in shades of red, orange, and yellow.

Download template and reference photo.

Brushes

Round, sizes 4 and 8

Color Palette

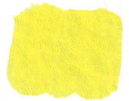   

| Hansa Yellow Light | Quinacridone Rose | Ultramarine Blue | Bleed-Proof White or other opaque white watercolor |

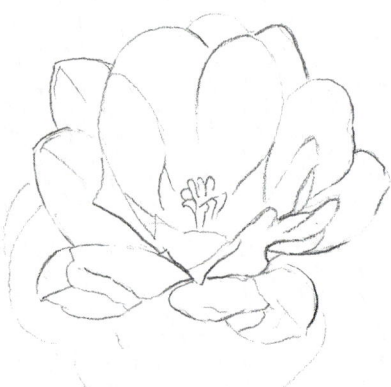 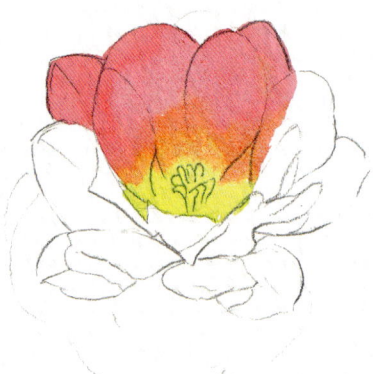 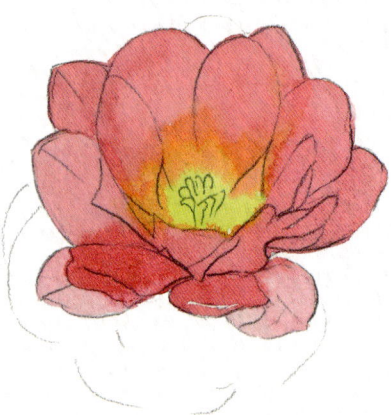

1. Sketch or trace the flower, using a kneaded eraser to lighten the lines.

2. Using your size 8 round brush, paint the center of the flower with pure hansa yellow light, rinse your brush, then paint the top few petals with a medium tint of quinacridone rose, letting the pink slightly overlap the yellow where it nears the center stamen.

3. Paint the rest of the petals wet-on-dry using quinacridone rose. Use a lighter value to paint the outermost petals. Load your brush with creamier paint as the petals turn toward shadow.

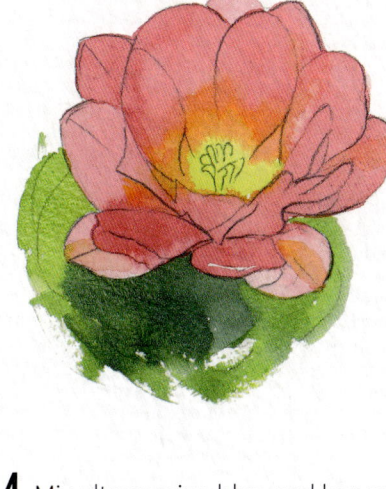

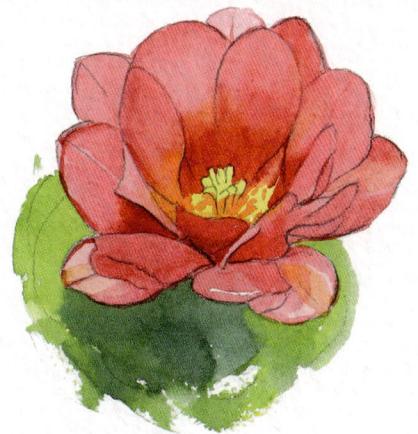

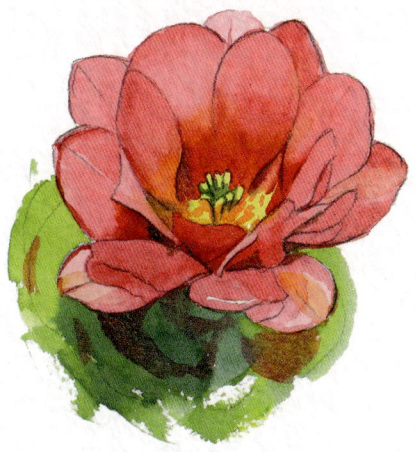

4. Mix ultramarine blue and hansa yellow light to create a spring green. Paint a loose cactus shape surrounding the bloom, using a darker (more blue) version of the mix representing the shadow beneath the petals using quick, curved brushstrokes.

5. Darken the base of each petal with pure quinacridone rose. Use a clean damp brush to soften and blend the edges of your brush strokes.

6. With your size 4 round brush, use quinacridone rose to paint some curved shadows on the cactus. Carefully paint some ultramarine into the dark center of the stamen and add dark shadows between a few of the flower petals.

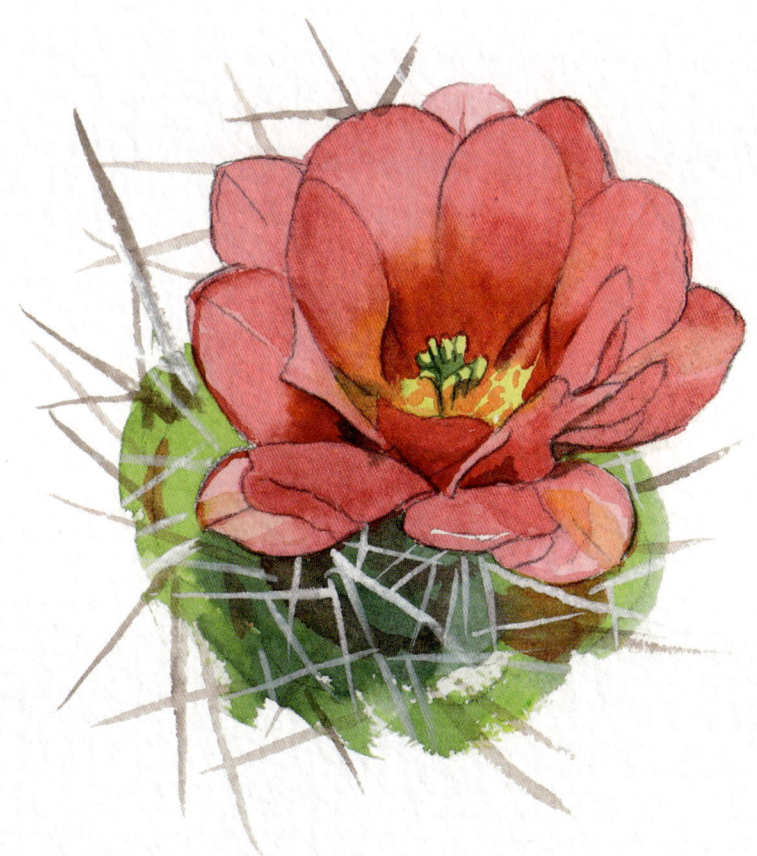

7. Finish the painting with the cactus spines. Mix a soft brown using all three colors to paint the darker spines. You can create sharp lines with decisive, quick brush strokes. Have fun crisscrossing your lines. For the white spines, use bleedproof white or some other opaque white watercolor. The "pricklier" your pear, the better!

BADLANDS NATIONAL PARK
South Dakota

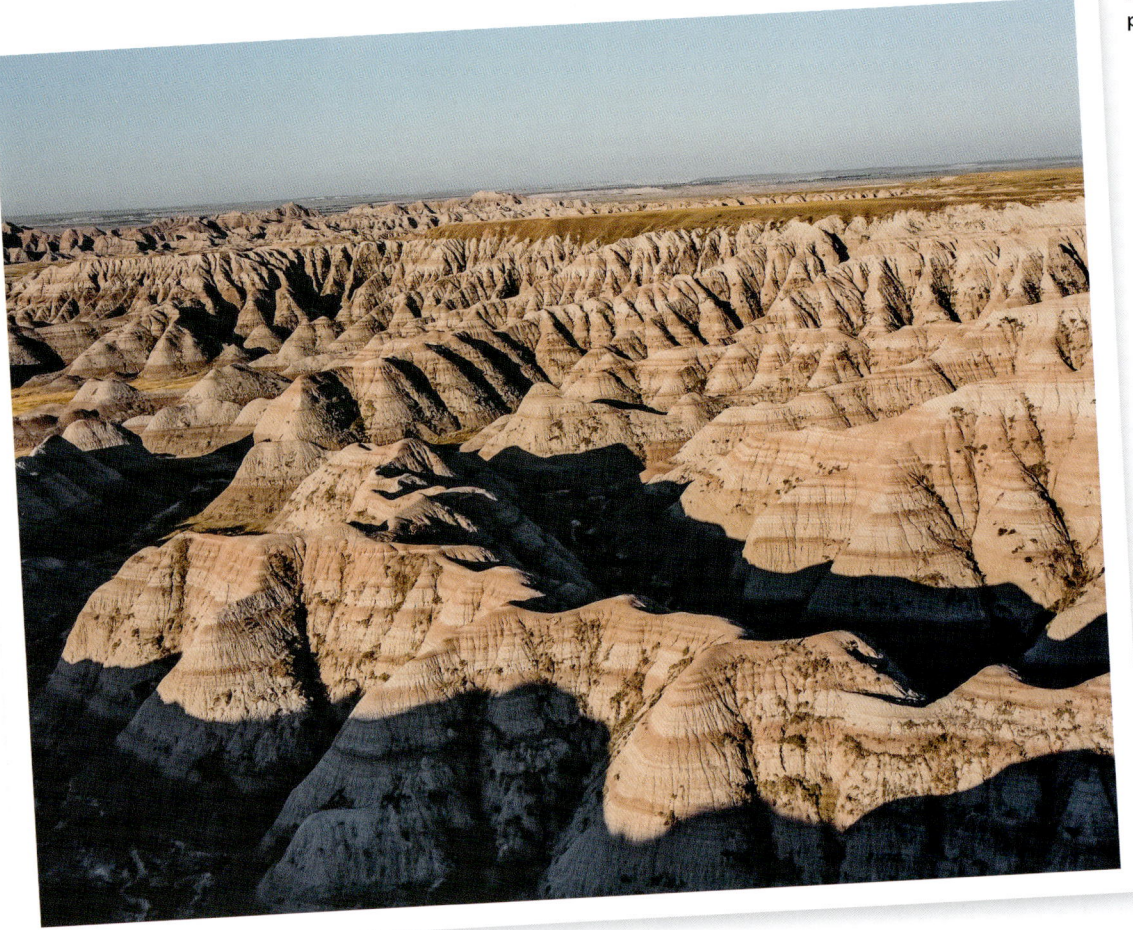

To the Oglala Sioux, the Badlands are considered a sacred place. The astounding beauty and dramatic geological formations captivate all who visit. The park contains one of the world's richest fossil beds, revealing that ancient horses and rhinos once roamed the area.

Brushes

Round, sizes 4 and 10

Paper

Fabriano Artistico 140-pound (300 gsm), cotton, cold-pressed block, 9" x 12" (23 x 30.5 cm); taped to resize down to 8" x 11" (20.5 x 28 cm)

Download template and reference photo.

Color Palette

Phthalo Blue (GS)

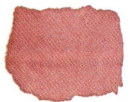
Permanent Alizarin Crimson

Burnt Sienna

Yellow Ochre

Ultramarine Blue

Indigo

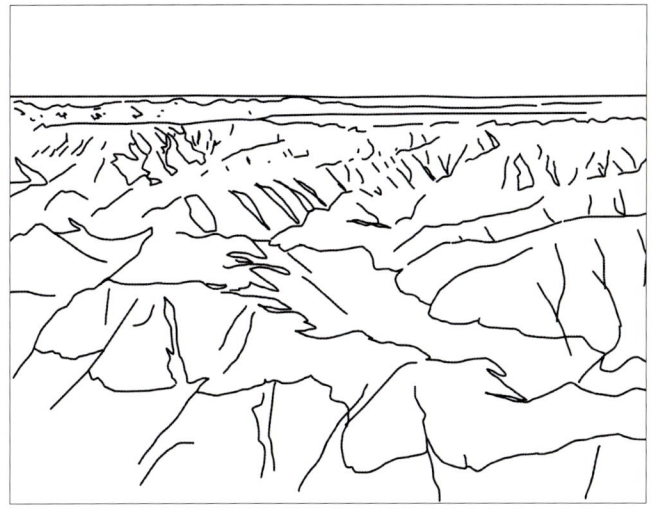

1. Start with a sketch, taking special note of the strong shadow shapes.

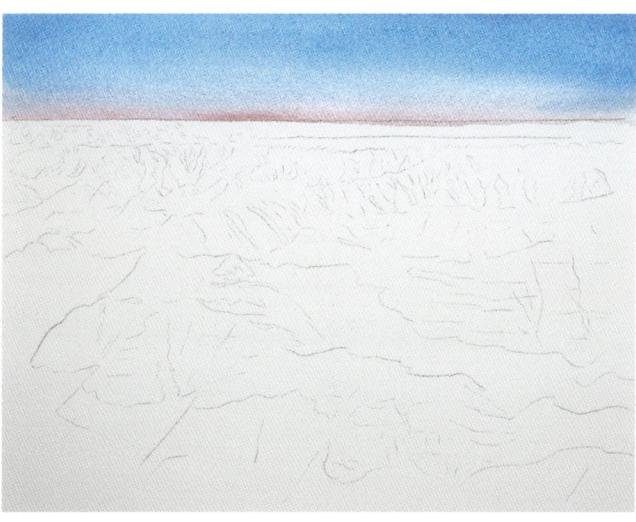

2. Paint the sky using a flat wash of phthalo blue, transitioning to permanent alizarin crimson just along the horizon line.

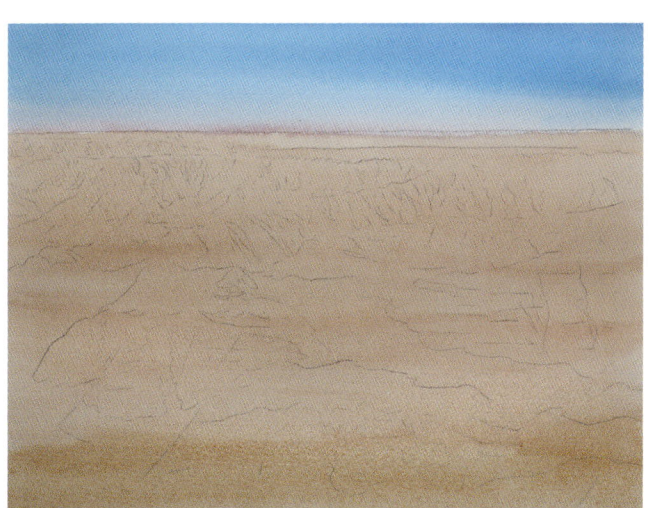

3. Paint a flat wash over the entire landscape using a big puddle of burnt sienna and yellow ochre—mix more paint than you think you'll need. Use your largest brush and start at the top of the horizon line, applying quick, horizontal brush strokes, moving left to right and downward like a typewriter. Allow the first wash to dry completely.

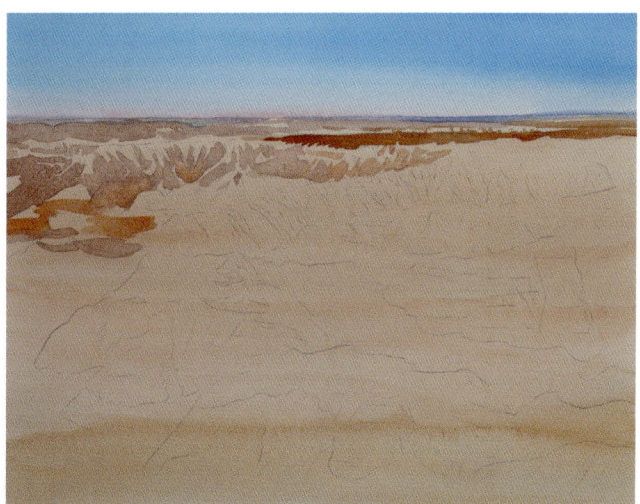

4. Paint a streak of ultramarine blue at the top of the horizon. Prepare two puddles of paint in a milky consistency: one of burnt sienna, and another of burnt sienna mixed with permanent alizarin crimson and ultramarine blue for a violet tint. Begin painting the cone-shaped shadows between the rock formations, alternating between your burnt sienna and violet mixes.

Scan to
watch a
video.

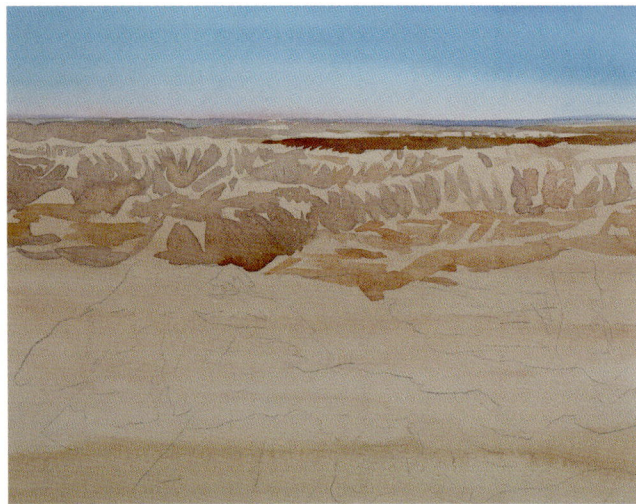

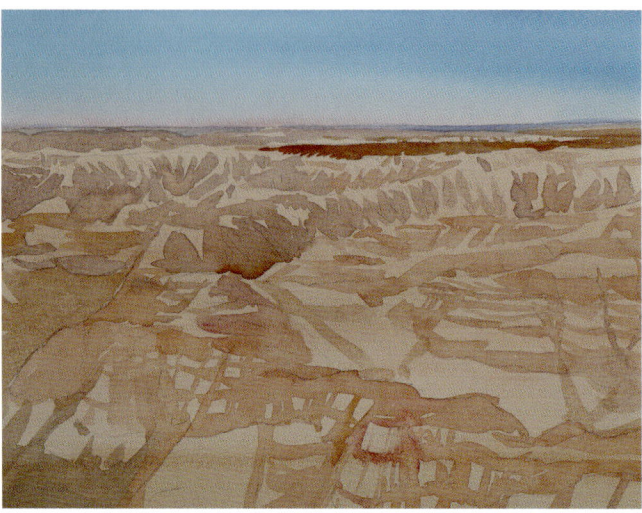

5. Continue using the narrow tip of your round brush to create squiggles and zigzags, indicating the color-shifting layers within the rocks.

6. Finish painting this second layer of carefully studied marks on top of your first wash. By now, the interesting strata and midtones in the landscape should be clearly visible.

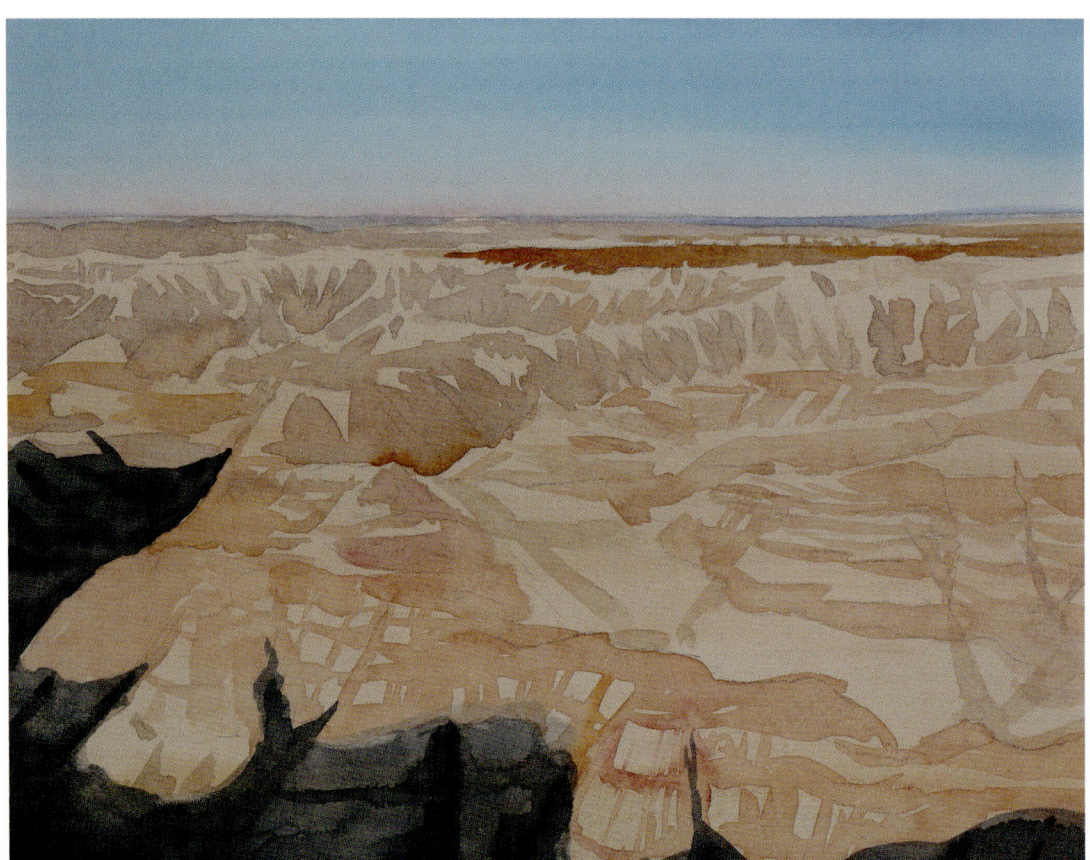

Scan to watch a video.

7. For the dark shadows, mix a generous puddle of indigo to a milky consistency. Aim to paint the shadow shape in one continuous wash. While the area is still wet, add even darker brush strokes using a creamier paint consistency to represent the rock texture within the shadow. Painting these details wet-on-wet will create soft edges.

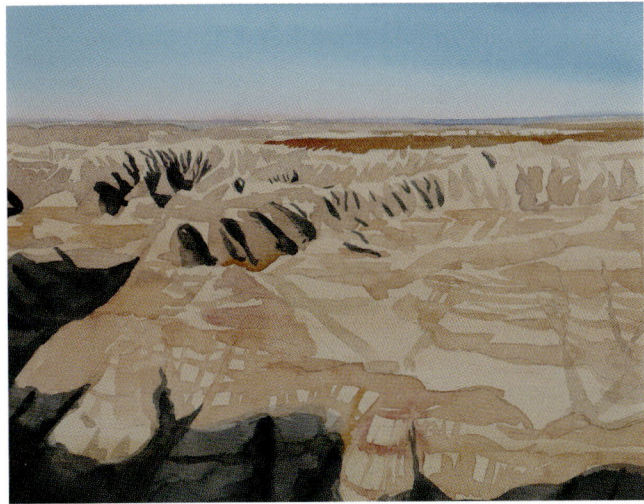

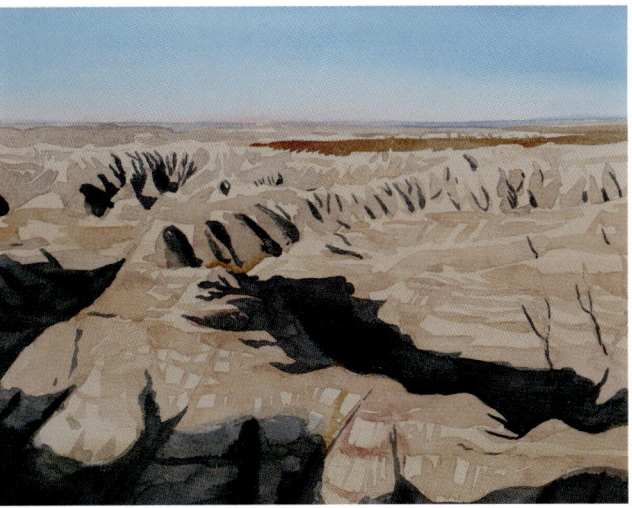

8. Sticking with indigo, begin painting the dark shadows in the distant hills. Study your reference image closely for good placement and switch to your smaller brush for better control.

9. Paint in the second largest shadow shape, ensuring you mix a big puddle of slightly diluted, milky paint—enough to cover the entire area. While it's still wet, use thicker, darker paint to create the deepest shadow effects.

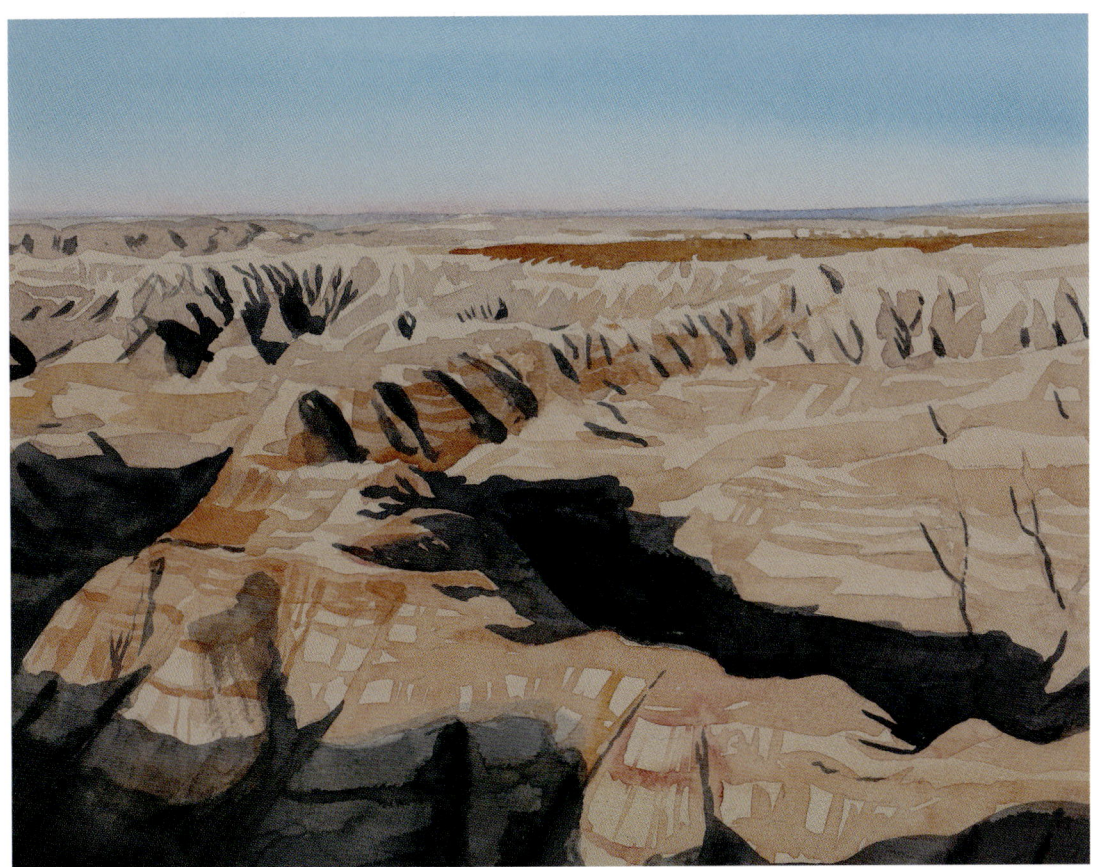

Scan to
watch a
video.

10. With the dark values clearly established, you can now paint more vibrant midtones. Use burnt sienna to enhance some of the reddish rock layers.

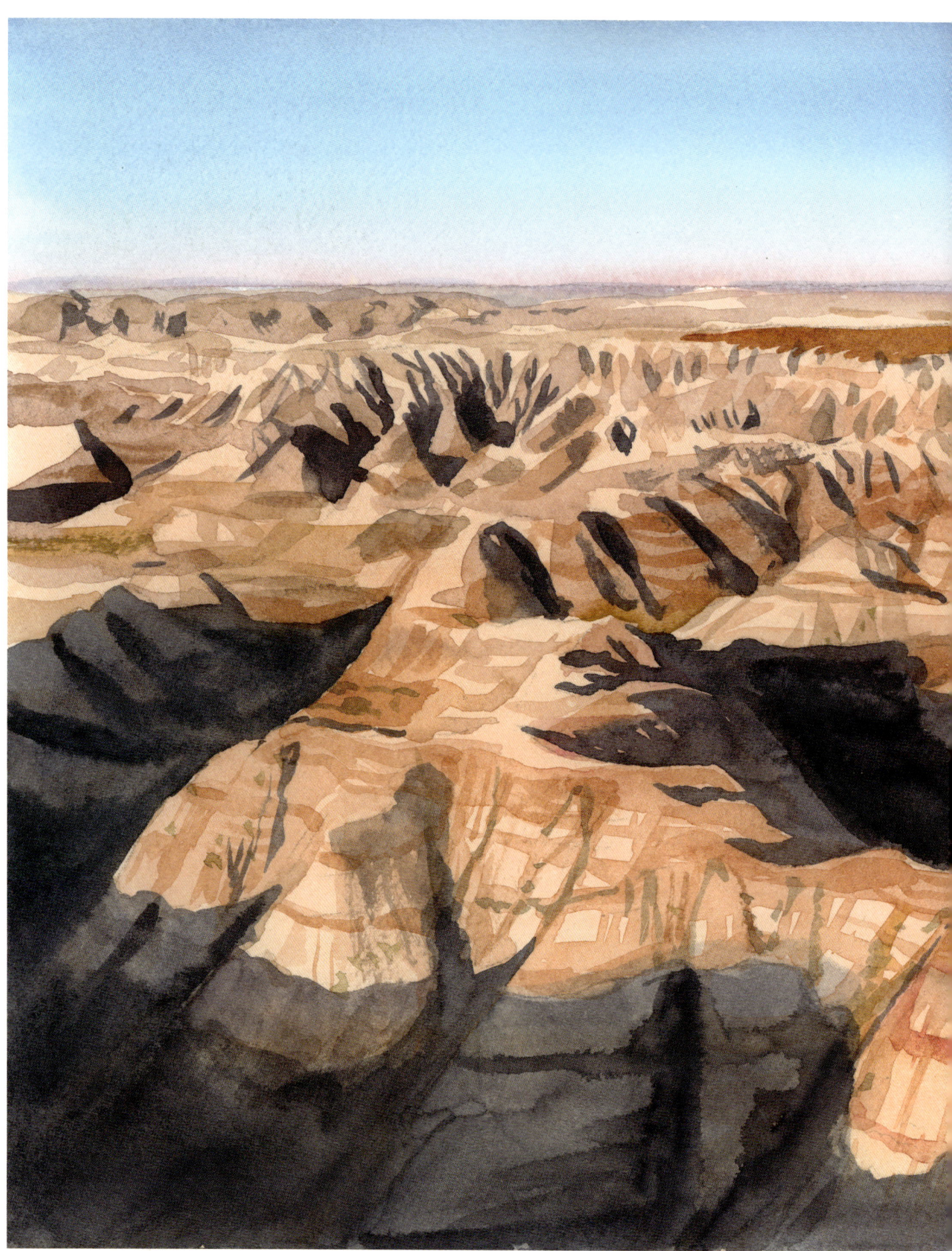

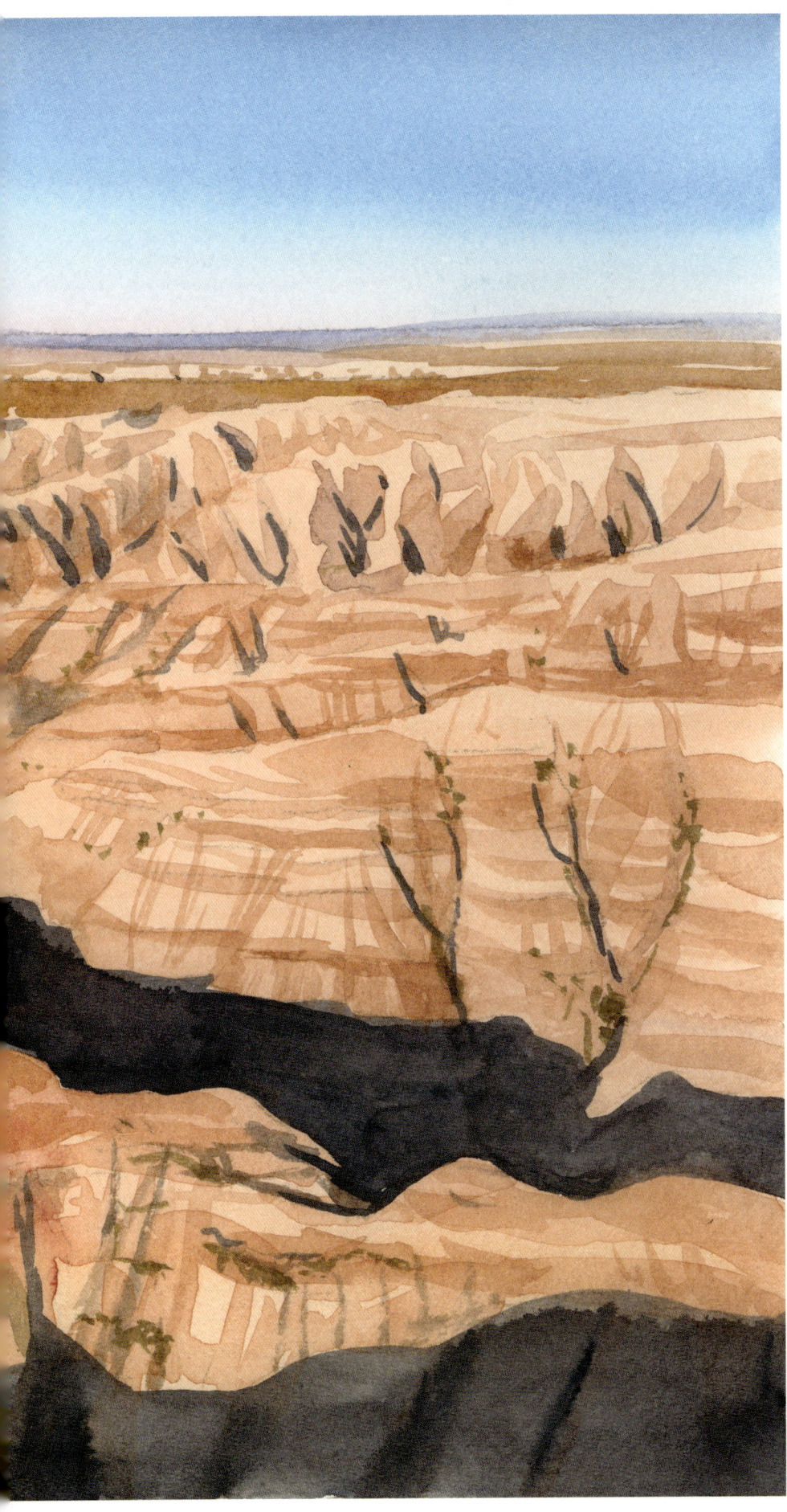

11. Add finishing details with your small brush. Use subtle crosshatching to indicate the horizontal layers of rock intersecting with the downward-sloping hills. Frequently step back from your artwork to better assess your values and overall composition. Ensure your midtone details do not overpower or distract from the main elements.

ACADIA NATIONAL PARK
Maine

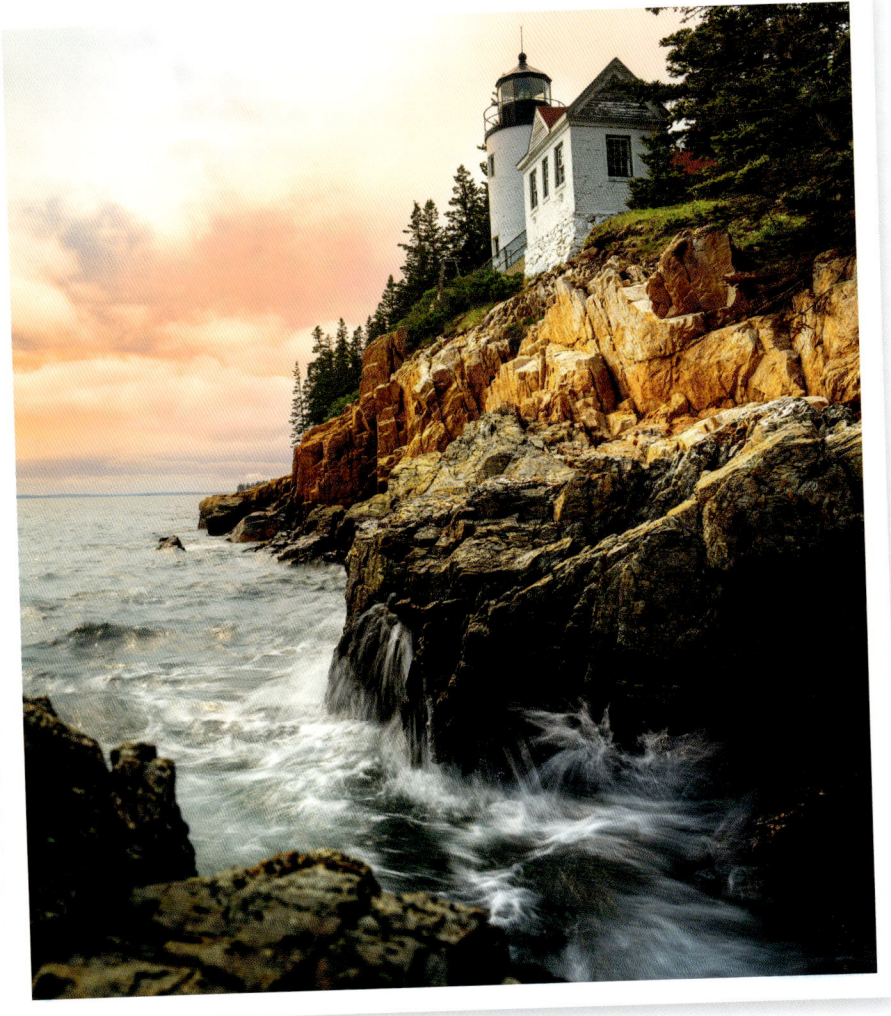

Located along the coast of Maine, Acadia is the easternmost national park in the United States. Originally a colonial fishing village, the island town of Bar Harbor has transformed into a tourist hub where millions of visitors each year enjoy whale-watching, sailing, hiking, and exploring. Acadia is celebrated for its stunning coastal and mountain scenery, making it a magical destination in any season. The image shows the iconic and historic Bass Harbor Head Light, situated on the southwestern tip of Mount Desert Island.

Download template and reference photo.

Reference photo

Brushes

Round, sizes 4 and 10

Paper

Arches 140-pound (300 gsm), cotton, cold-pressed block, 7.9" x 7.9" (20 x 20 cm)

Color Palette

  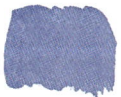 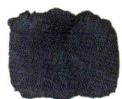 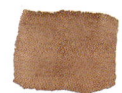 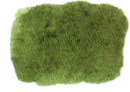 

| Yellow Ochre | Quinacridone Rose | Ultramarine Blue | Indigo | Burnt Sienna | Sap Green | Marine Blue |

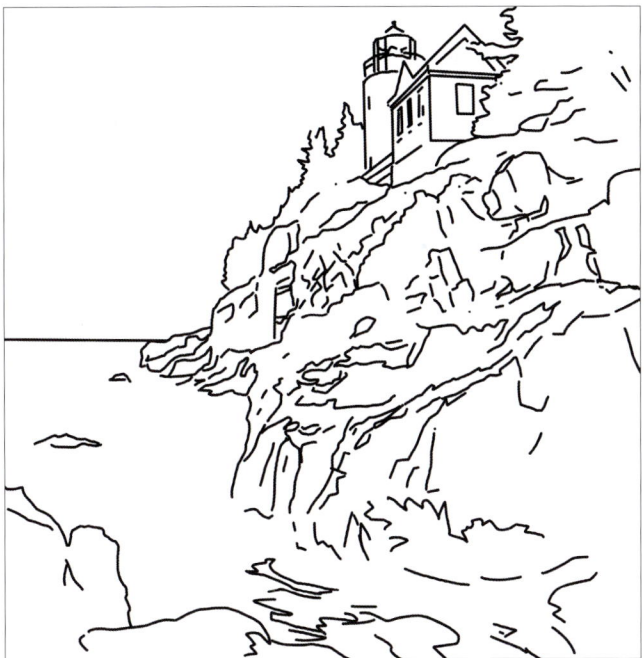

1. Sketch or trace the scene, paying close attention to the light and dark shapes, particularly on the rocks.

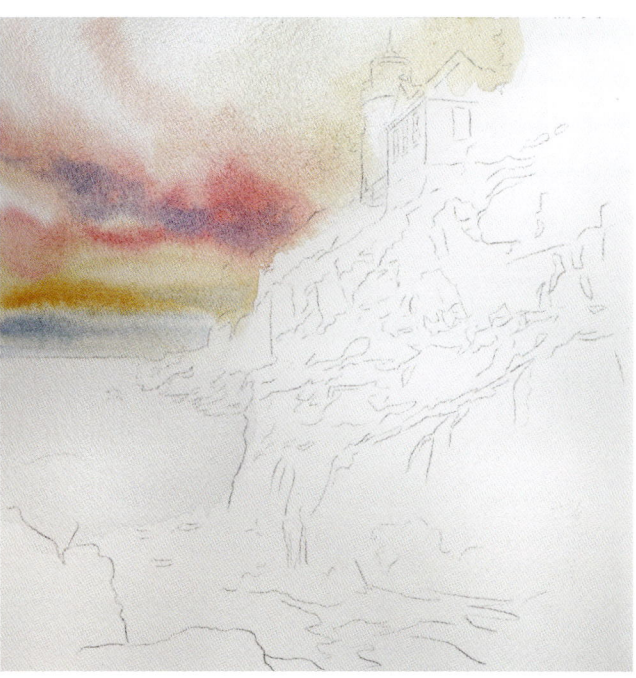

2. Begin by painting the sky wet-on-wet using your largest round brush. Apply clear water over the entire sky area, allowing it to blend slightly into the lighthouse, trees, and ocean. Then, introduce yellow ochre and quinacridone rose to create the sunset clouds, followed by subtle hints of ultramarine blue.

Scan to watch a video.

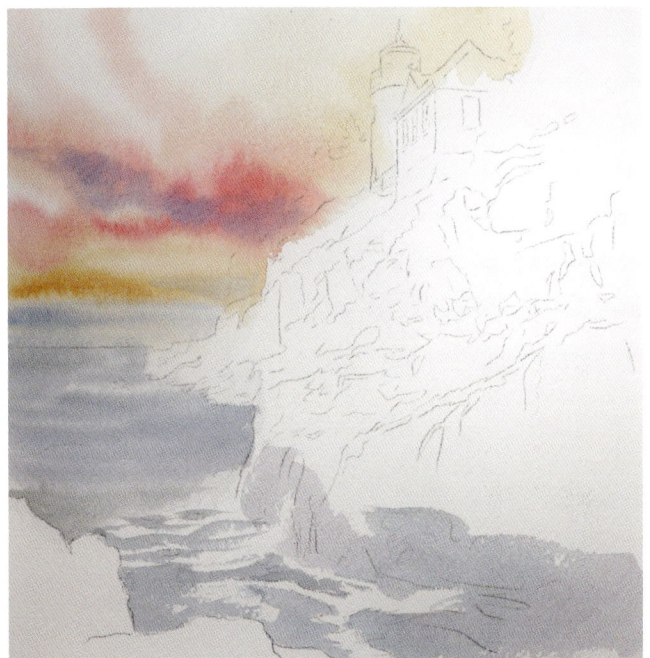

3. Mix ultramarine blue with some of your leftover yellow ochre and quinacridone rose to create a muted slate blue. Apply this as the first layer on the ocean water with loose, horizontal brushstrokes. Use negative painting to leave some of the foamy white splashes unpainted.

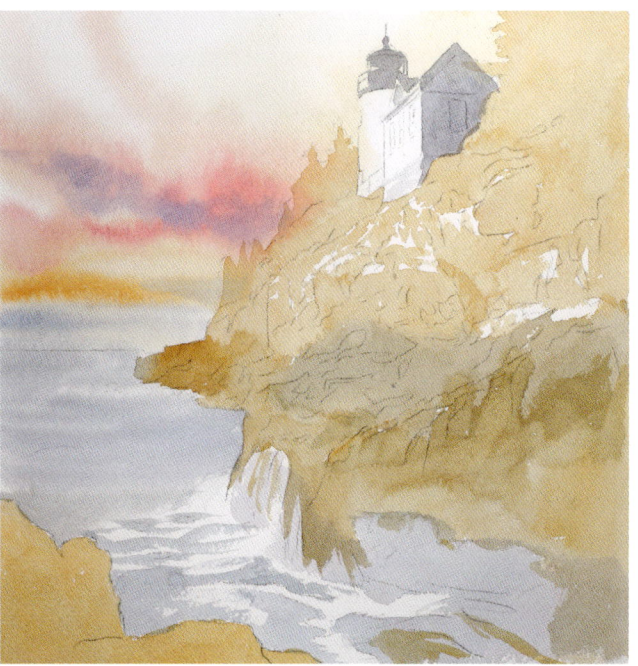

4. Apply a wash of watered-down yellow ochre over the rocks and trees. Then, use diluted indigo to paint the shadowed side of the lighthouse.

Scan to watch a video.

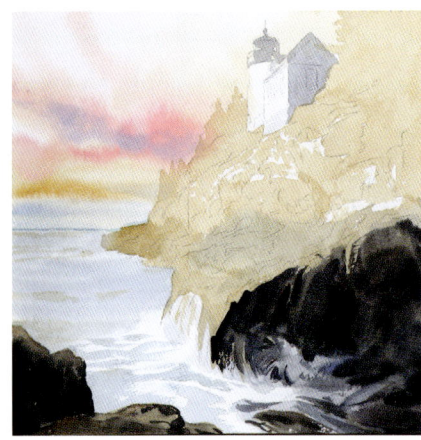

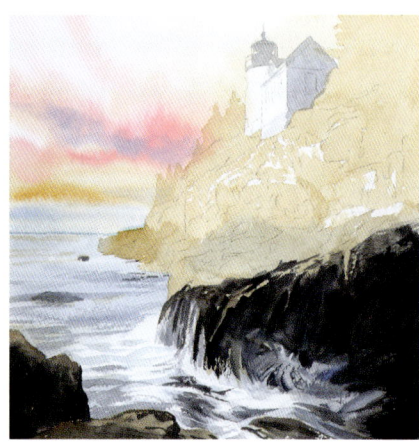

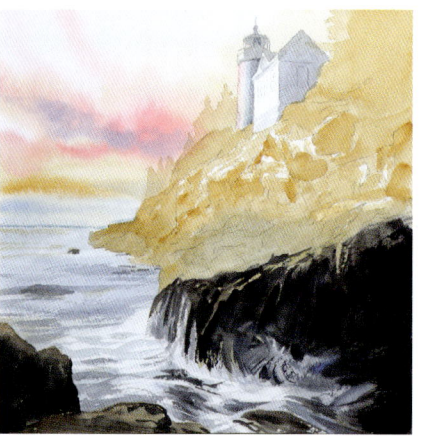

5. Mix indigo and burnt sienna to a milky consistency to paint the rocks. Start by brushing in the dark shadows around the splashing water. Let the yellow from the previous layer shine through on the tops of the rocks on the left.

Scan to watch a video.

6. Use a lighter version of your indigo and burnt sienna mix to paint subtle shadows in the water. Dry brushing can help create the effect of splashing water droplets. Add gentle downward strokes to suggest water cascading off the rocks. Use negative painting to outline the tops of the rocks and any areas illuminated by light. Paint the dark distant rocks in the ocean.

7. Add a shadow to the lighthouse tower by applying indigo to the shadowed side. Rinse and partially dry your brush, then gently swipe along the edge to soften the line, giving the tower a more cylindrical appearance. Apply a second layer of yellow ochre over the rocks.

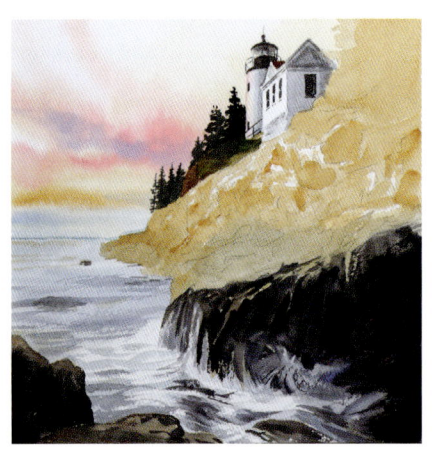

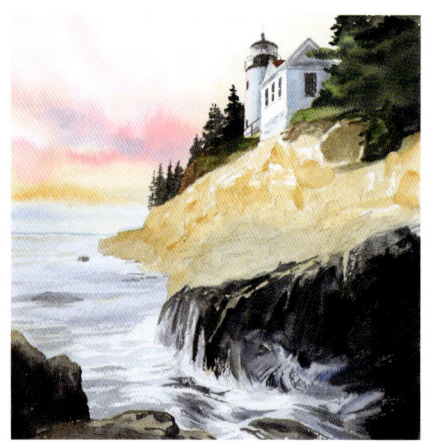

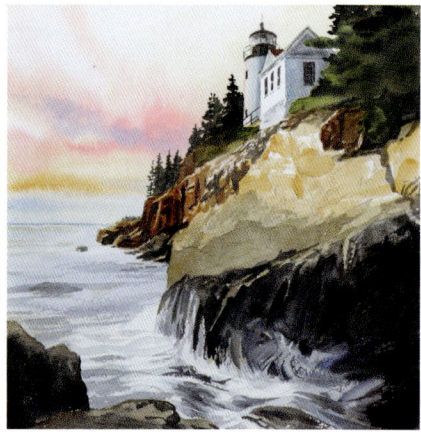

8. Use your smallest round brush loaded with indigo to add the dark window details and railings on the lighthouse. For the grass, apply sap green, and mix burnt sienna with indigo to paint the dark evergreens.

9. Paint the largest evergreen with sap green. While the paint is still damp, drop in indigo using the wet-on-wet technique to add shadows and create the illusion of branches.

10. Using your smallest brush, alternate between burnt sienna and ultramarine blue to capture the warm and cool browns on the rocky cliffs, being careful to paint around the highlights. For the central cliff, apply a murky gray created by mixing yellow ochre and indigo with a little bit of water.

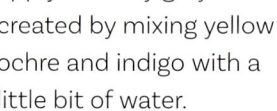

Scan to watch a video.

Scan to watch a video.

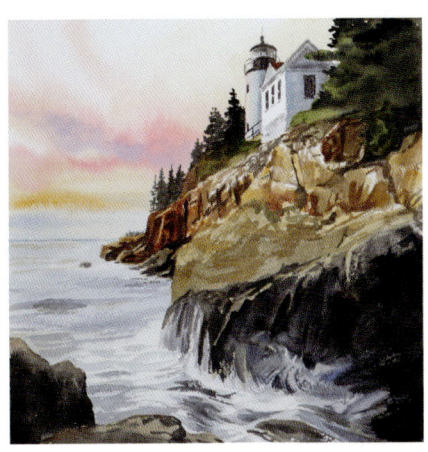

11. Employ the wet-on-dry technique to add burnt sienna shadows, cracks, and texture to the rocks. Keep these midtones relatively light.

12. To complete your artwork, apply indigo shadows and final touches to the rocks. Keep your brushstrokes loose and painterly—focus on capturing the essence rather than replicating the photo exactly. I chose to add a watery glaze of marine blue to the ocean and a touch of yellow ochre to the base of the sky, which helps to unify the colors and values.

Scan to watch a video.

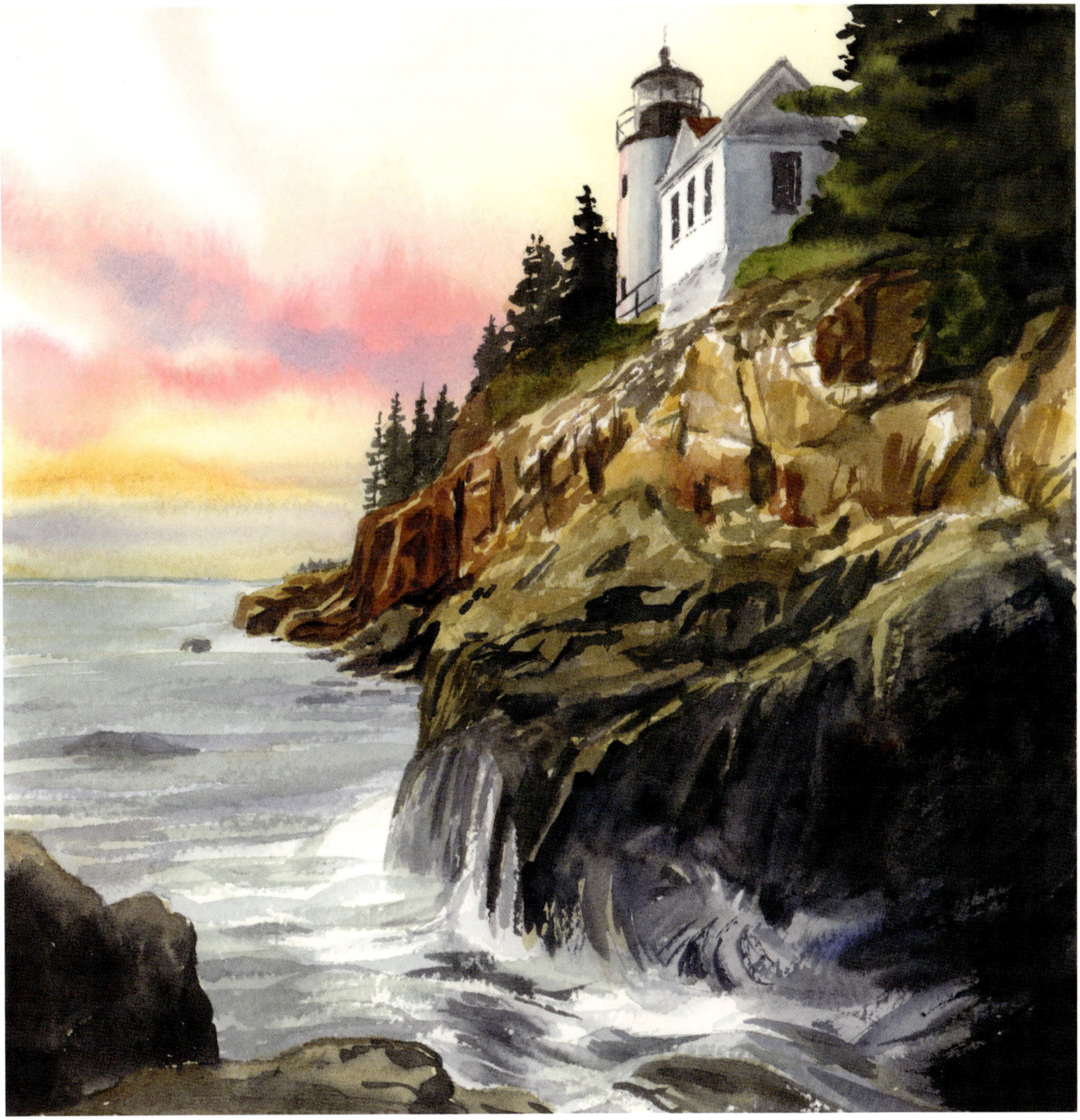

SHENANDOAH NATIONAL PARK

Virginia

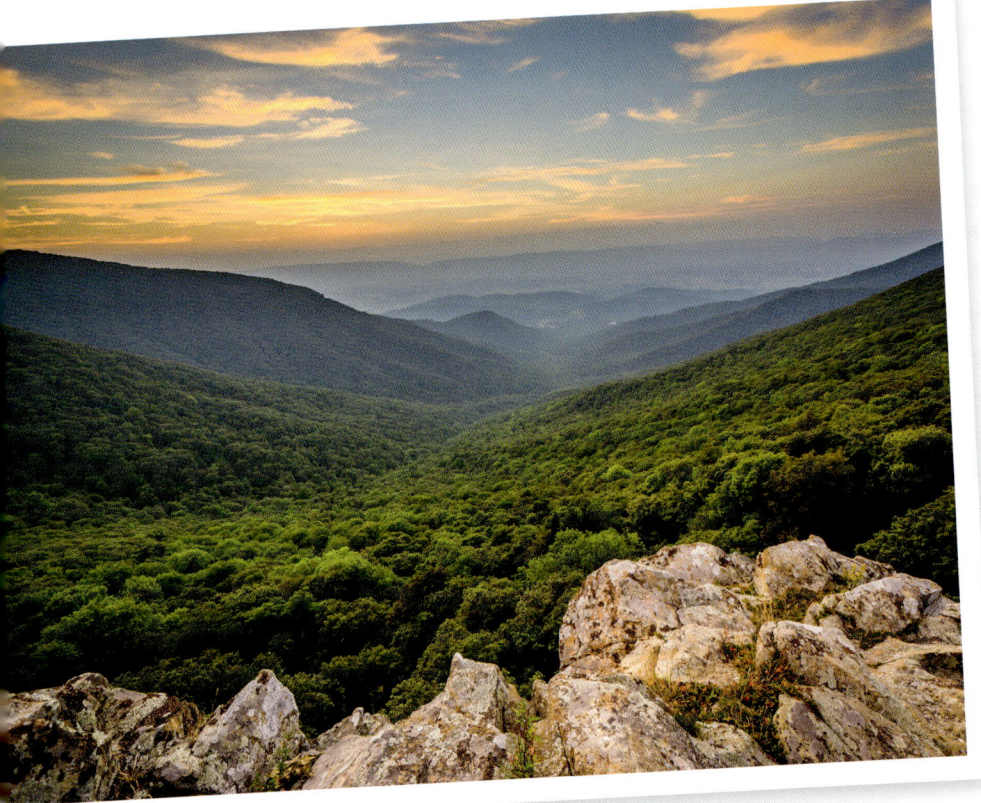

Shenandoah National Park in Virginia is known for its sweeping views of the Blue Ridge Mountains—the perfect escape for nearby city-dwellers! This incredible view from atop Old Rag Mountain is a beloved "hiking gem" inside the park.

Download template and reference photo.

Reference photo

Brushes

Round, sizes 8 and 10

Paper

Fabriano Artistico 140-pound (300 gsm), cotton, cold-pressed block, 9" x 12" (23 x 30.5 cm)

Color Palette

Phthalo Blue (GS)

Hansa Yellow Light

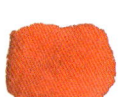

Transparent Orange

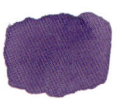

Permanent Violet

Indigo

Gamboge Nova

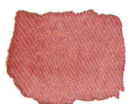

Permanent Alizarin Crimson

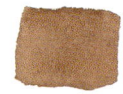

Burnt Sienna

Ultramarine Blue

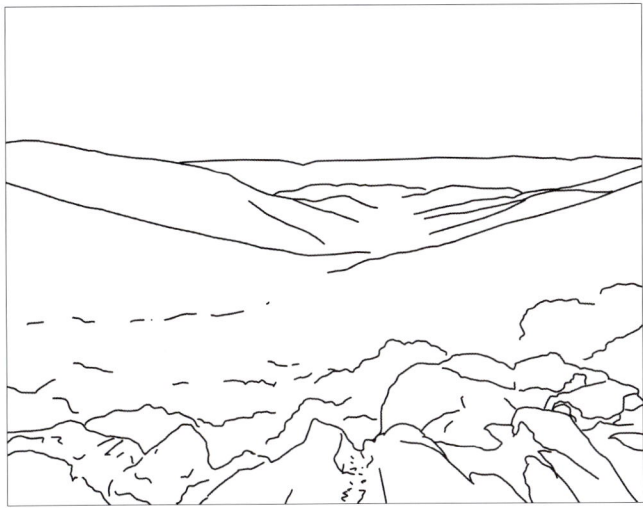

1. Trace or sketch on the simple outline of mountains and rocks—no need to draw the clouds or trees.

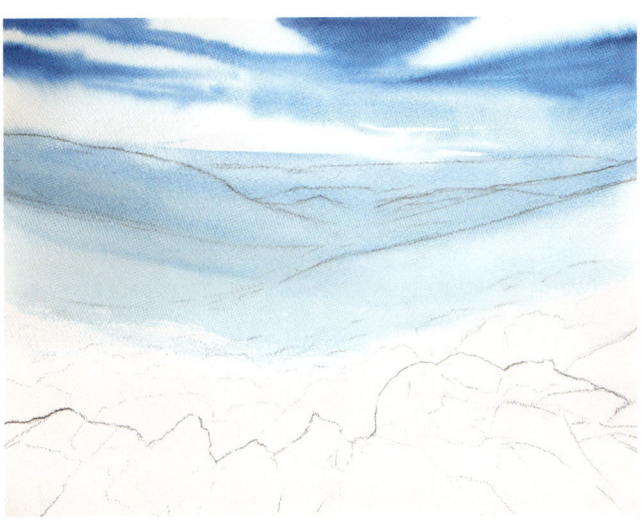

2. With your largest round brush, paint clear water over the sky and into the valley, aiming for an even glossy wet surface with no puddles. Load your brush up with creamy phthalo blue. Begin painting at the top, negative-painting around where the orange and yellow clouds will be. As you work your way down, gradually remove paint from your brush so that you are painting the sky with a lighter value toward the horizon. You can overlap this light blue over the mountains and into the valley. Let this dry completely.

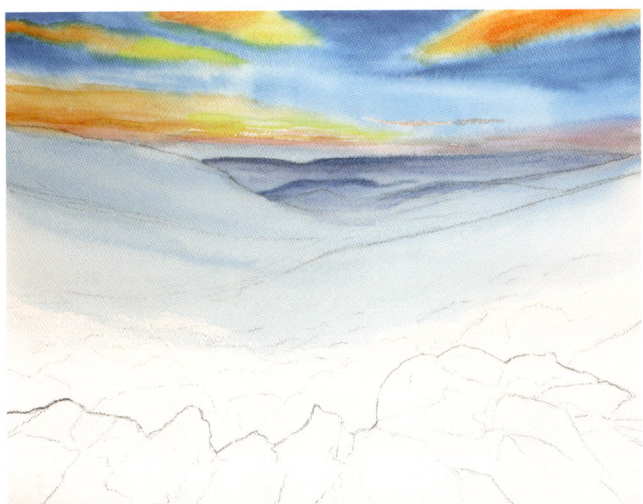

3. Without scrubbing, gently rewet the surface with clean water. Using creamy paint with no excess water in your brush, drop some bright hansa yellow light and transparent orange into the white cloud spaces. If your yellow bleeds into the blue too much (creating green!), quickly soak up the paint with a clean, thirsty brush. Blend subtle hints of permanent violet into the horizon line and begin to define the distant mountains with pale ultramarine.

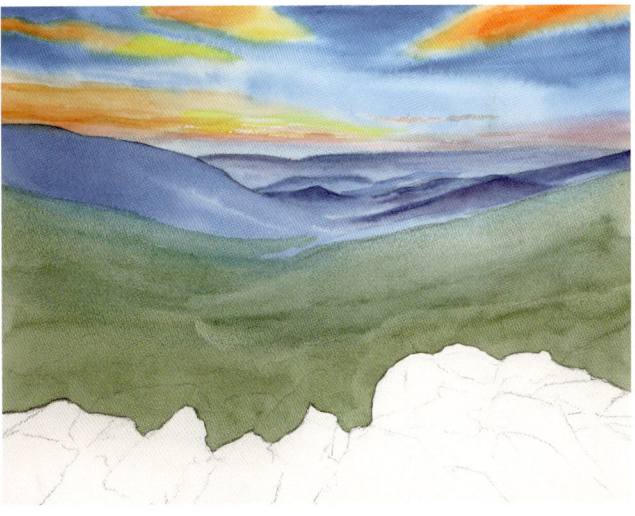

4. Use clean water to wet the entire middle area. Using your largest brush and working quickly, mix up an earthy green with indigo and hansa yellow light. Paint a flat wet-on-wet wash of green over the valley.

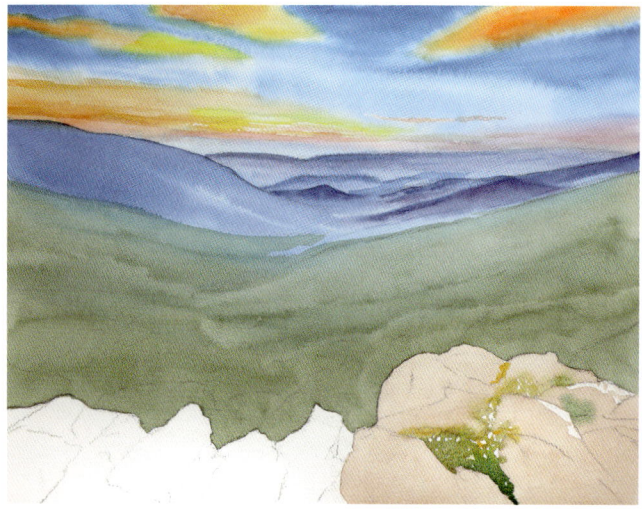

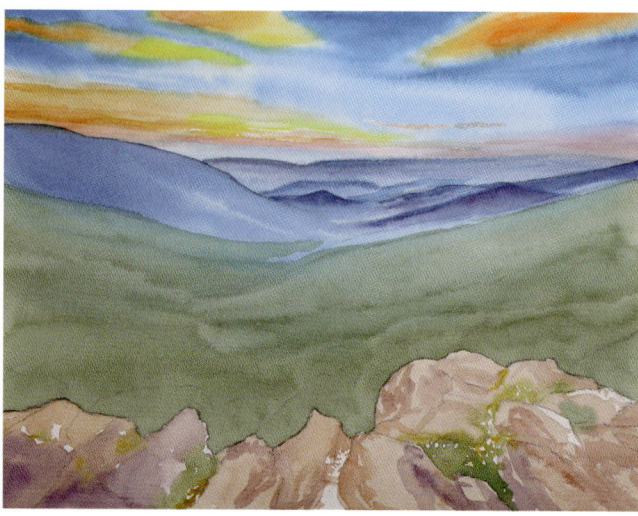

5. You can paint the rocks in sections. Start with watered-down burnt sienna for the rocks, painting around the areas that will be green with foliage. Use a combo of gamboge nova and phthalo blue to paint the greenery in the cracks between rocks. It's okay if it touches the wet burnt sienna and blurs out a little. Leave tiny circles of the white paper untouched—these will later be red flowers!

Scan to watch a video.

6. Continue painting the rocks this way, adding hints of permanent violet. Once your first layer of watered down burnt sienna has dried, you can glaze over it with more intentional brush strokes of the same color, beginning to show the texture and bumps of the rocks.

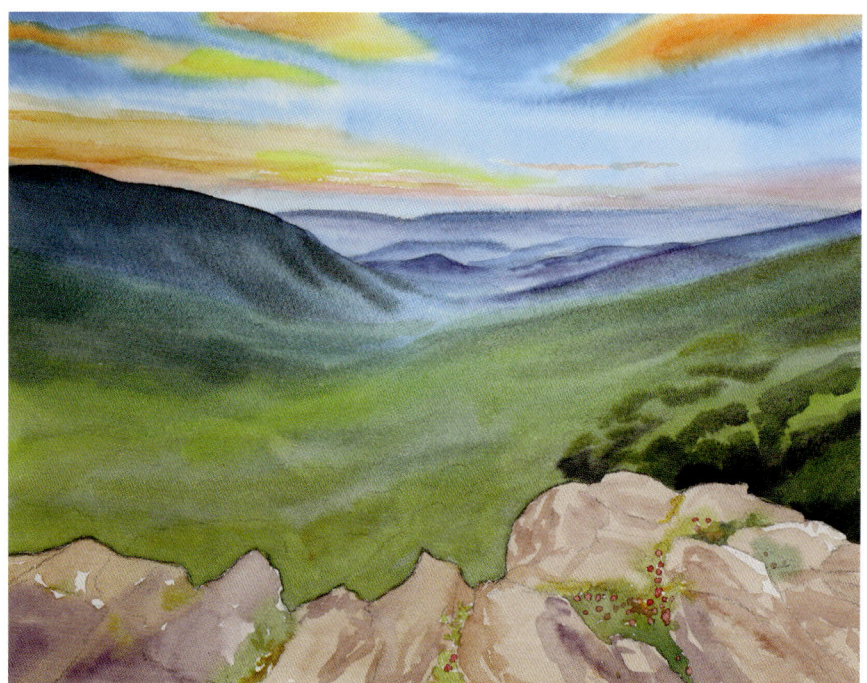

7. Use transparent orange or permanent alizarin crimson to dot in the tiny flowers between the greenery on the rocks. Then, begin painting the trees in the valley. Rewet the whole middle area, including the large slope on the left using clear water. Blob in some gamboge nova and hansa yellow light. Use indigo to darken that slope at the top, using a gentle feathering motion of your brush as you swipe your brush down toward the valley. We want the valley to look almost foggy, so make sure to remove paint and use a lighter value here!

Scan to watch a video.

Scan to watch a video.

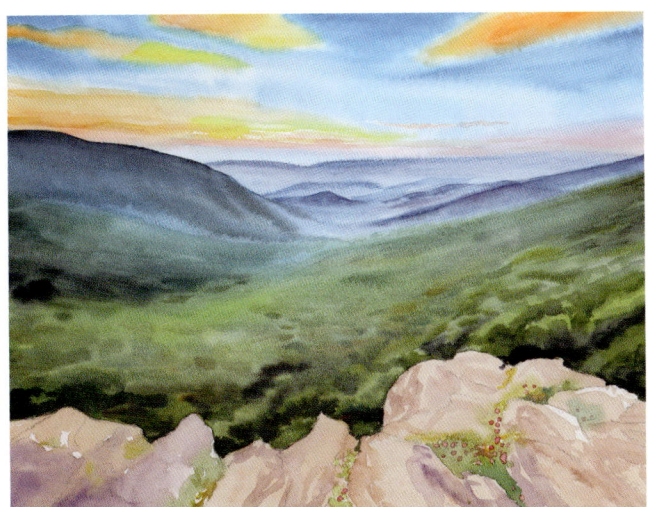

8. Mix indigo and hansa yellow light to create a very dark green. With a quick blobbing motion of the size 8 brush, paint in shadow shapes representing tree clusters in the valley. Vary your values by using creamy paint for the darkest shadows, and a more watered-down version of your green for midtones. Drop in subtle hints of brown and orange using burnt sienna. Work quickly, as these soft trees are best painted in while the paper is still wet!

Scan to watch a video.

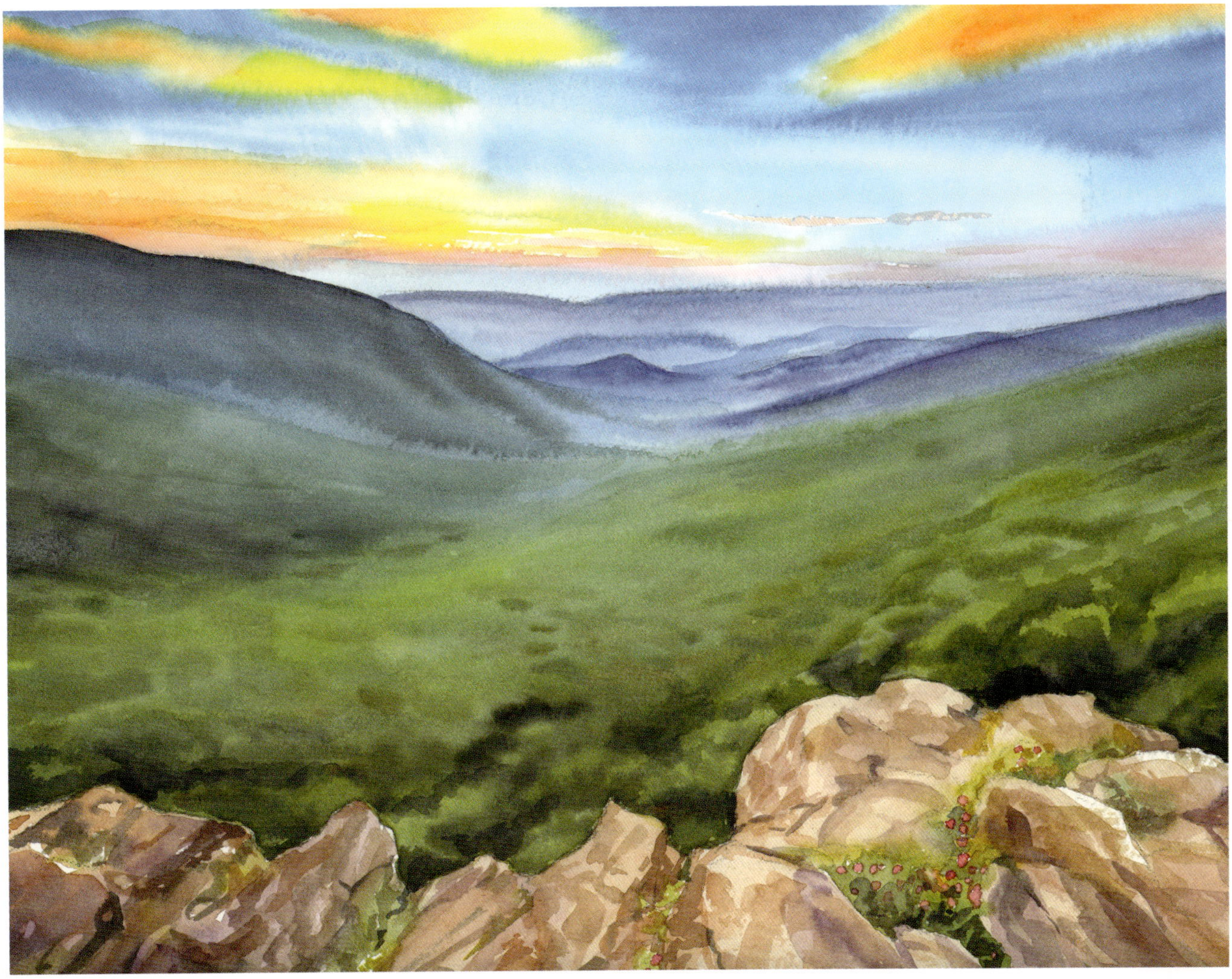

9. Finish the painting by adding more dark details to the rocks. Keep your brush strokes loose and painterly, using light washes of burnt sienna and permanent violet. Mix burnt sienna and ultramarine blue to create a darker brown for the shadows. Leave some highlights on the rocks—be careful not to cover everything up with dark paint. You want your rocks to be lighter than the trees beyond. Use indigo to paint darker shadows within the foliage.

Scan to watch a video.

Black Swallowtail

Black swallowtails are a common butterfly often spotted in wooded areas or meadows—if you've hiked anywhere east of the Rockies, chances are you've seen these lovely butterflies flitting from flower to flower!

Brush

Round, size 4

Download template and reference photo.

Color Palette

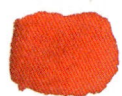     

| Transparent Orange | Phthalo Blue (GS) | Hansa Yellow Light | Quinacridone Rose | Permanent Violet | Permanent Alizarin Crimson |

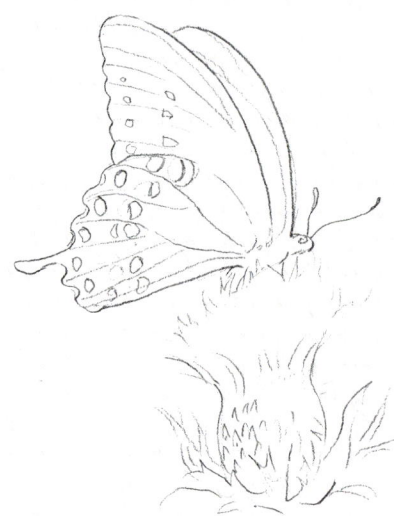

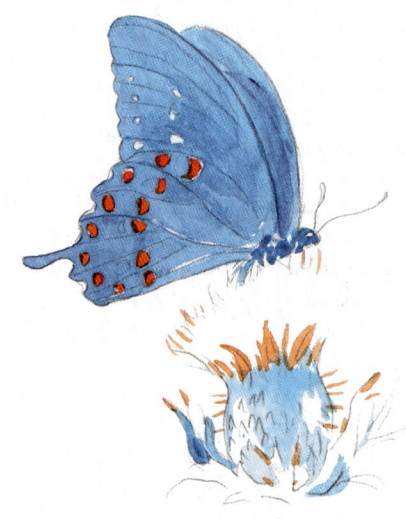

1. Sketch the butterfly, taking note of any important spots, markings, and wing veins.

2. Paint in the transparent orange spots and orange tips of the thistle leaves and base of the flower. Water down some phthalo blue and paint the entire butterfly and thistle base, carefully avoiding the white and orange spots. Let the painting dry.

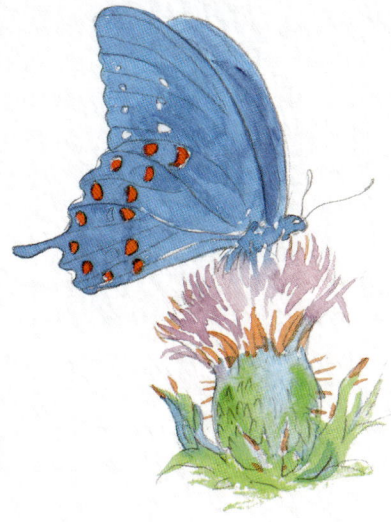
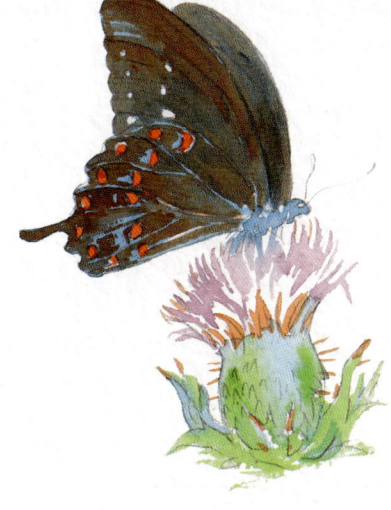
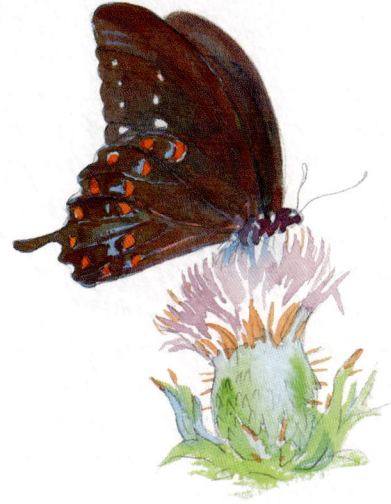

3. Paint over the thistle base with hansa yellow light. This glazed layer will create bright green! Mix quinacridone rose and permanent violet for a soft pinkish purple. With short, quick, curved upstrokes, paint the flower on the thistle.

4. Make sure your blue is completely dry, then carefully paint a layer of transparent orange over the blue in a milky paint consistency. Paint around some of the wing veins, allowing some of the blue underlayer to shine through.

5. Swirl some milky permanent alizarin crimson on your palette, load up your brush, and paint this over the butterfly. Again, avoid the blue, white, and orange spots.

Scan to watch a video.

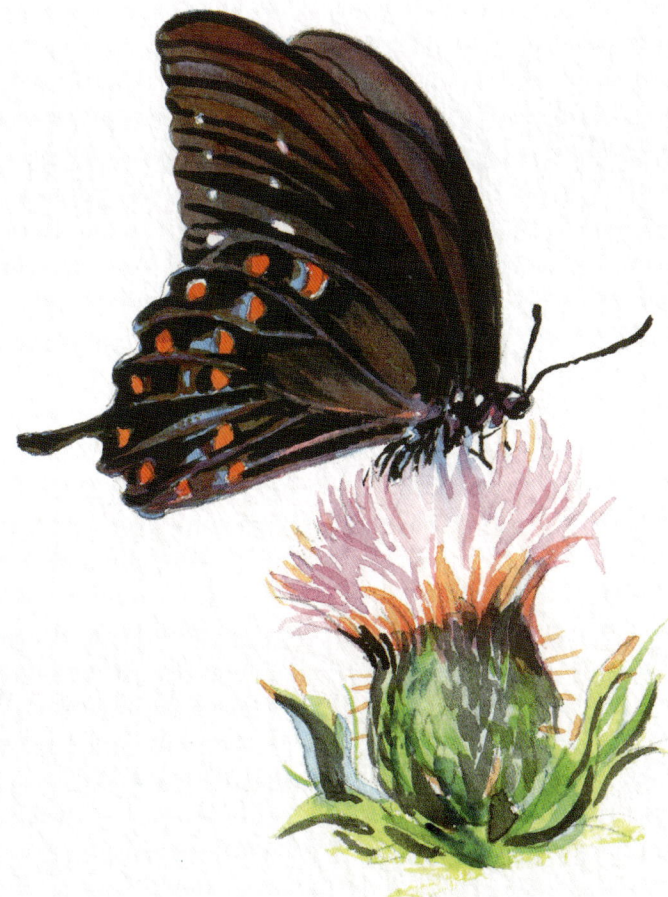

6. Mix up a rich black using a creamy combination of your transparent orange, phthalo blue, and alizarin crimson. Finish the details of the butterfly with black, adding curved lines to show the wing veins, outlining the antennae, and adding dark details to the thistle.

Scan to watch a video.

NEW RIVER GORGE NATIONAL PARK

West Virginia

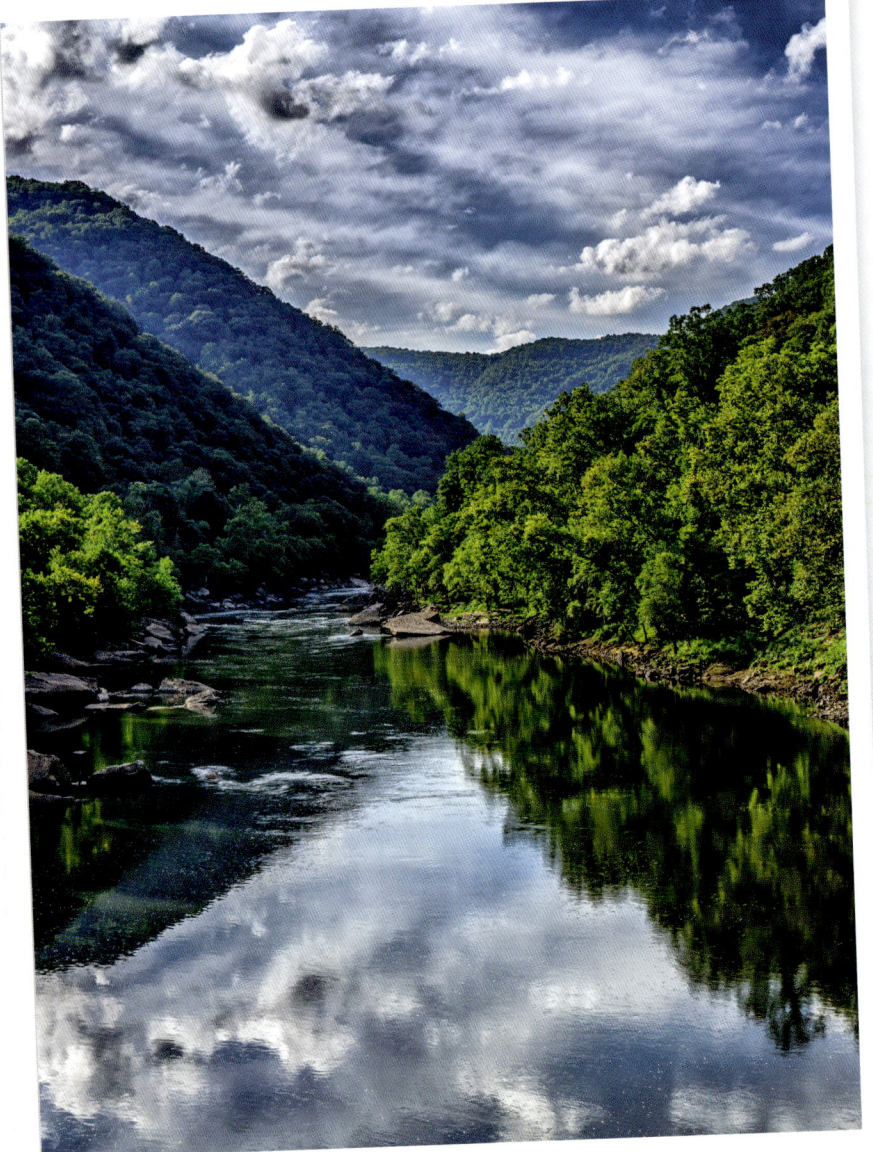

New River Gorge is in southern West Virginia and covers about 72,000 acres (291 square km). The park protects and maintains a deep gorge carved by the New River, one of the oldest rivers in North America. Visitors enjoy rafting, biking, hiking, camping, and fishing in this scenic Appalachian destination! We're using an analogous color scheme of deep blues and greens to portray the lushness of this dreamy landscape.

Download template and reference photo.

Reference photo

Brushes

Round, sizes 8 and 10

Paper

Fabriano Artistico 140-pound (300 gsm), cotton, cold-pressed block, 9" x 12" (23 x 30.5 cm); taped to resize down to 8" x 10" (20.5 x 25.5 cm)

Color Palette

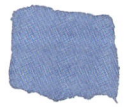
Phthalo Blue (GS)

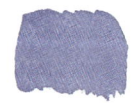
Ultramarine Blue

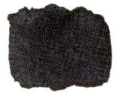
Indigo

Hansa Yellow Light

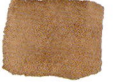
Burnt Sienna

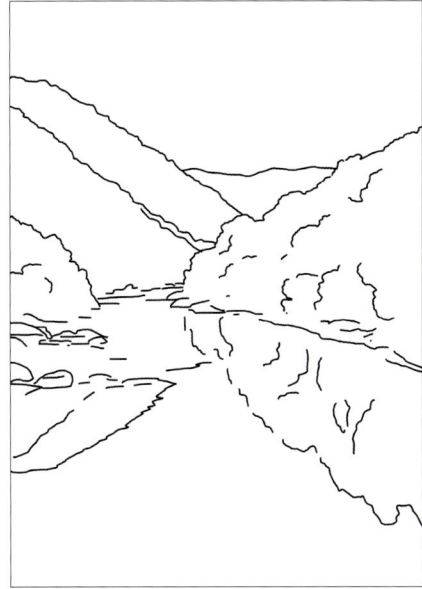

1. Sketch or trace the outline of the slopes, including the reflection on the water. No need to sketch any clouds, as we will create them with paint.

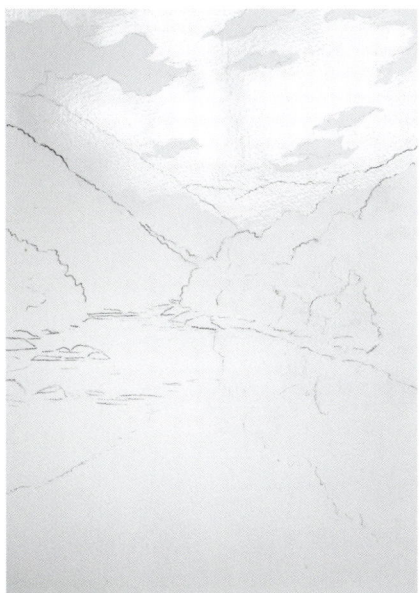

2. With your large round brush, paint clear water into the sky and the first layer of mountains, leaving a few dry patches for clouds.

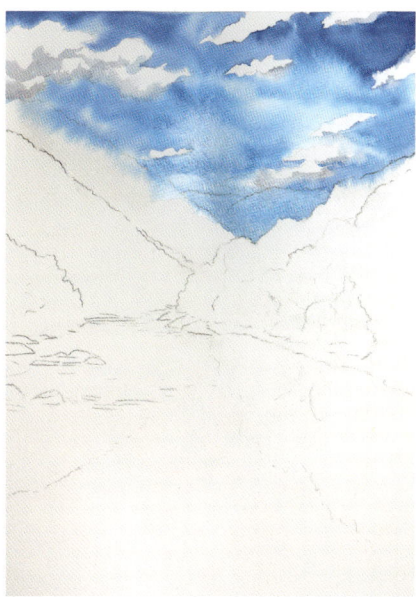

3. Load up your brush with a combination of phthalo blue and ultramarine blue and paint the sky. Start at the top while your paint is the creamiest. As you work your way down, dip your brush in the water to dilute it a little and continue to paint the sky with a slightly lighter value. It's okay if blooms form. Use watered-down indigo to paint subtle shadows under the white clouds.

Scan to watch a video.

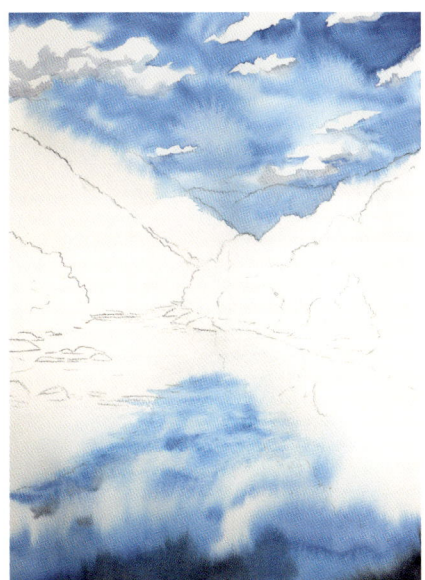

4. Use clear water to prewet the river area—do not leave any dry patches. With your creamy phthalo blue and ultramarine blue mix, paint the sky reflection, avoiding the mirrored cloud shapes. Notice how the reflections look softer than the sky. While your blue water is damp, paint indigo wet-on-wet at the bottom to create a vignette effect.

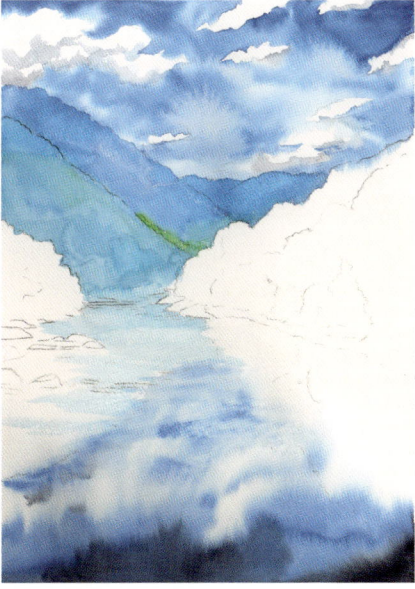

5. Paint the hazy slopes with phthalo blue. Where you see the color shifting greener in the reference photo, use some hansa yellow light mixed with your phthalo blue. Paint a faint tinted wash of this color leading up to the sky reflection on the water.

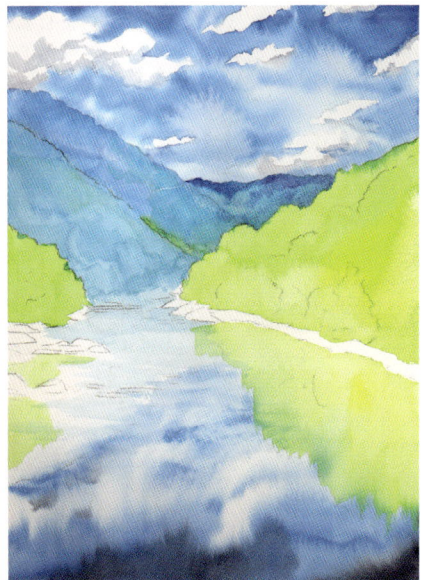

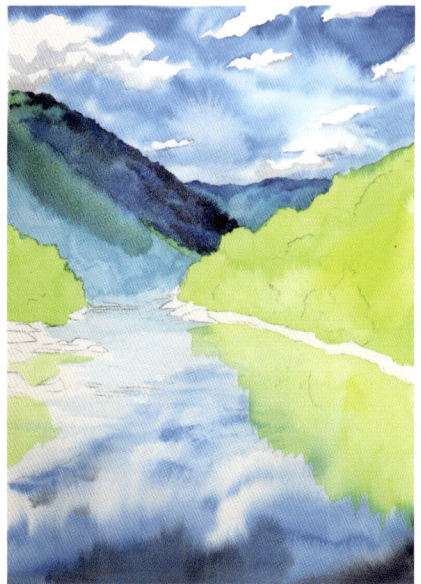

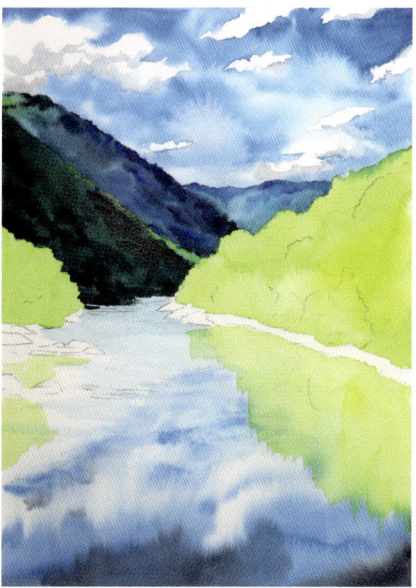

6. Use pure hansa yellow light to paint a first layer on the green hills, wet-on-dry. Paint the same color on the water below, leaving a small gap between the trees and their reflections. Darken the distant middle hill with some subtle ultramarine.

7. Begin to paint the final colors and values of the dark slopes on the left. Use a combination of ultramarine blue, indigo, and hansa yellow light to mix cool bluish greens directly on the paper. Blobby, non-descript brush strokes work great for representing whole clusters of dense trees.

Scan to watch a video.

8. Paint the darkest green slope with a mix of indigo and hansa yellow light, leaving a small gap between the ridges where we can see a sunlit streak of trees.

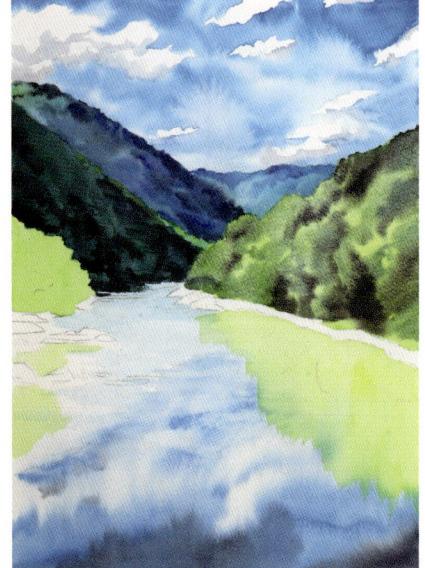

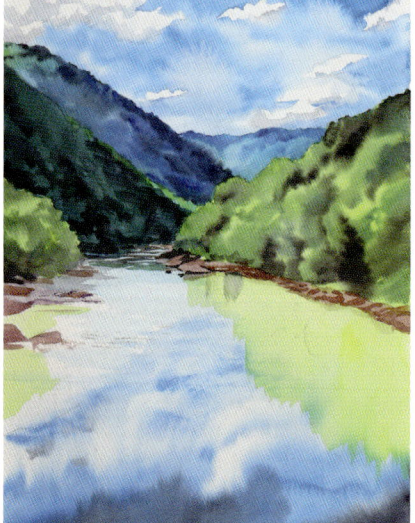

9. Use the wet-on-wet technique to create soft tree textures in the hills closest to us. Prewet the area with clear water, then blob in some creamy indigo for the dark shadows between trees. Use a mix of ultramarine blue and hansa yellow light to paint the mid-value greens. Be sure to leave some of the pure yellow shining through.

10. Start painting the rocky shoreline. Use a medium wash of burnt sienna for a first layer. Let this dry, then paint blobby rock shapes in a darker value. Paint the green reflection of the trees on the water. Take care to mirror your light and shadow shapes on the water.

Tip

....

Turn your board sideways to help you see the symmetry while painting the reflection.

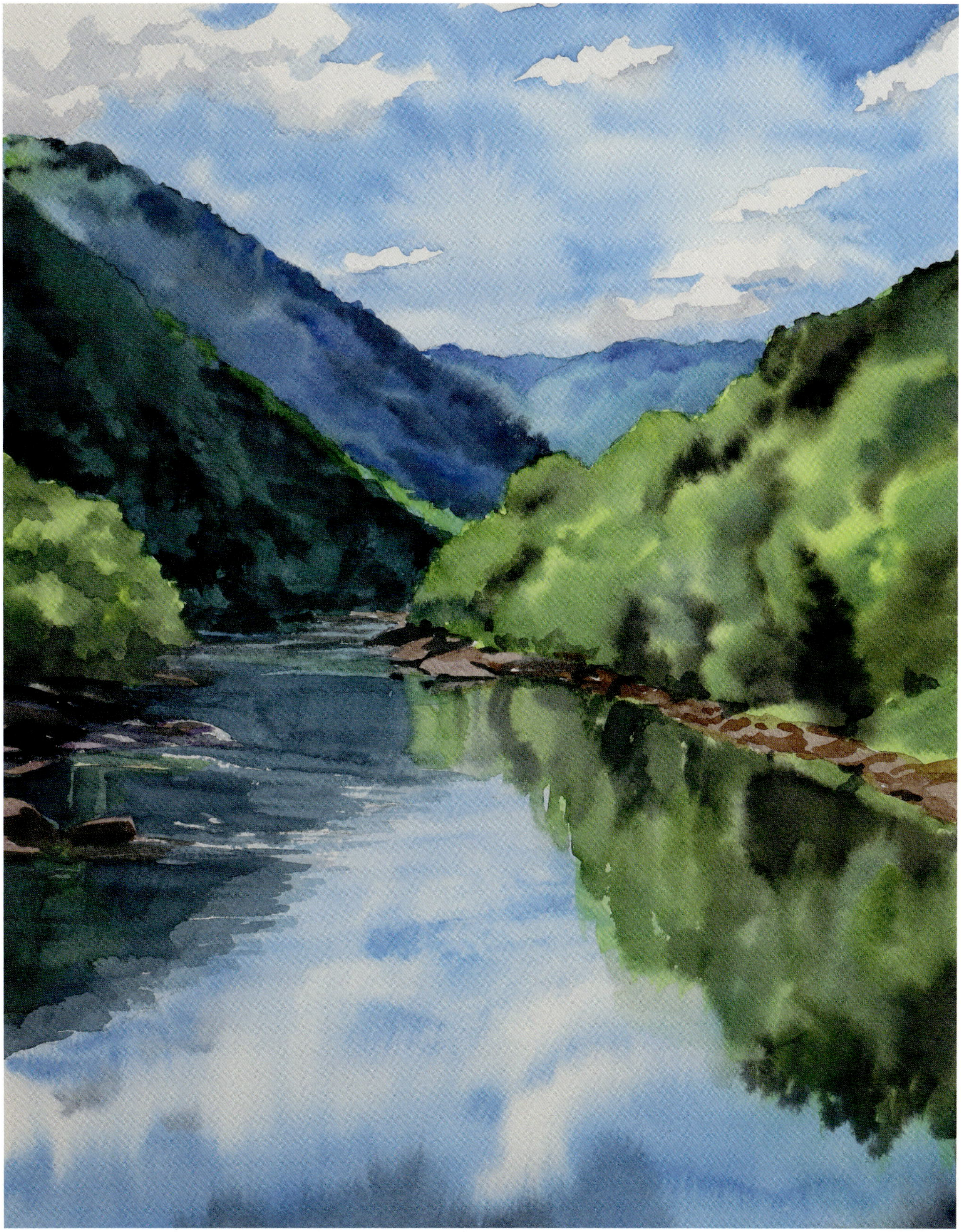

11. Finish the painting with the dark greenish blue reflection on the left side, using the same dark green you mixed up for the slope. Add any final touches, like dark shadows under the rocks to help them look more three-dimensional.

Scan to
watch a
video.

GREAT SMOKY MOUNTAINS NATIONAL PARK
Tennessee/North Carolina

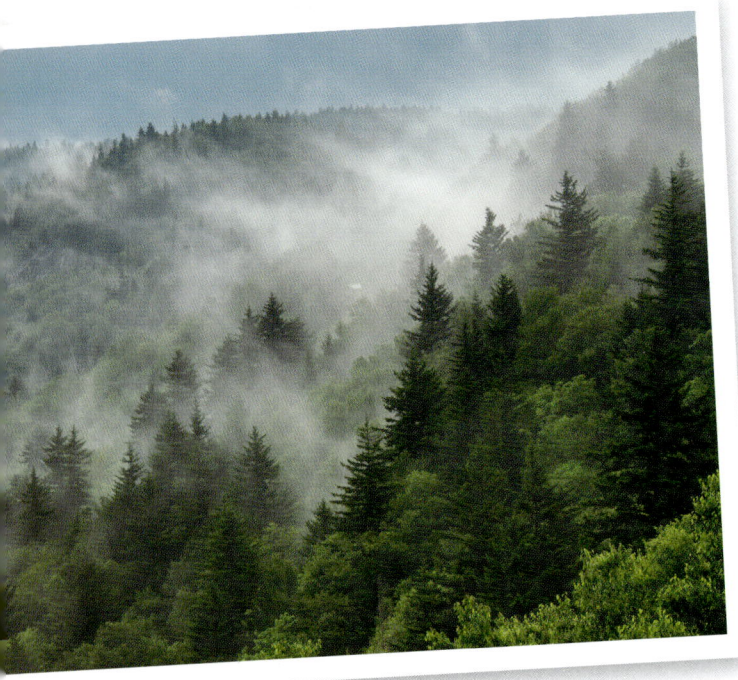

Reference photo

Great Smoky Mountains is the most visited national park and the most biodiverse in the National Park System, home to more than 19,000 species of animals, plants, fungi, and other organisms. In this painting, we will employ the wet-on-wet technique to create the illusion of trees emerging from blankets of fog. There's no need for a traceable line drawing—we'll do all our "drawing" with paint. As a helpful warm-up, try creating a small monochromatic value study. This will clarify the light and dark areas in the image and give you a chance to practice the wet-on-wet technique needed to achieve the soft, foggy effect.

Download reference photo.

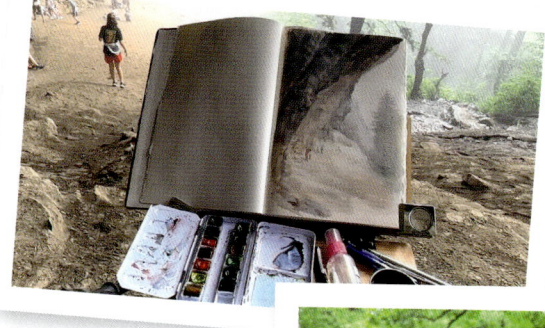

Brush

Round, size 10

Paper

Fabriano Artistico 140-pound (300 gsm), cotton, cold-pressed block, 9" x 12" (23 x 30.5 cm); taped to resize down to 10" x 8" (25.5 x 20.5 cm)

In 2023, I visited the Smokies with the goal of painting waterfalls from life for the first time. It rained the entire week, and this image of fog-draped trees and vibrant green foliage perfectly captures the essence of Appalachia. The landscape was breathtaking—a temperate rainforest teeming with the sounds of rushing water, wildlife, and lush flora. I was surprised by how much I had to adapt my watercolor technique due to the high humidity, which made the paint take much longer to dry!

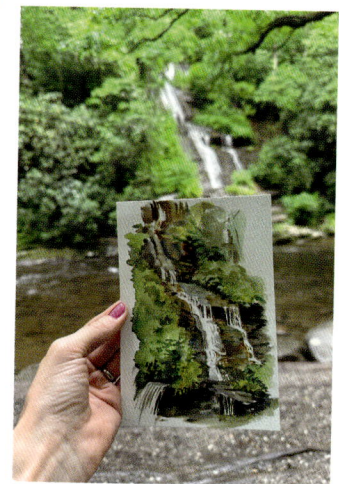

Color Palette

Phthalo Blue (GS)

Indigo

Hansa Yellow Light

Here, you can see just three values: the lightest areas are the sky and fog, while the diagonal line of foreground trees forms the dominant dark shape in the composition. A thumbnail sketch like this helps you focus on simplifying values and shapes without getting distracted by color.

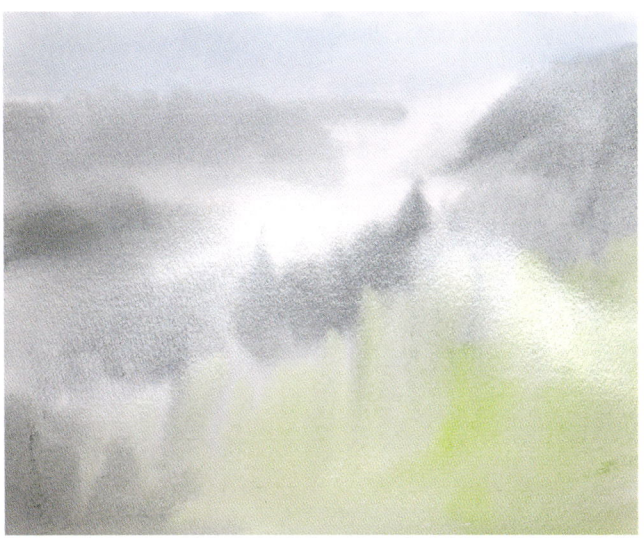

1. Begin by spraying the paper with water and using a large brush to spread it evenly across the surface until it looks glossy wet. Moving quickly, apply a thin layer of phthalo blue to the sky with a damp brush—not dripping with paint. Add watered-down indigo to the tree areas, and hansa yellow light to the foreground. Be sure to paint around the fog and use quick upstrokes to start suggesting tree shapes.

Scan to watch a video.

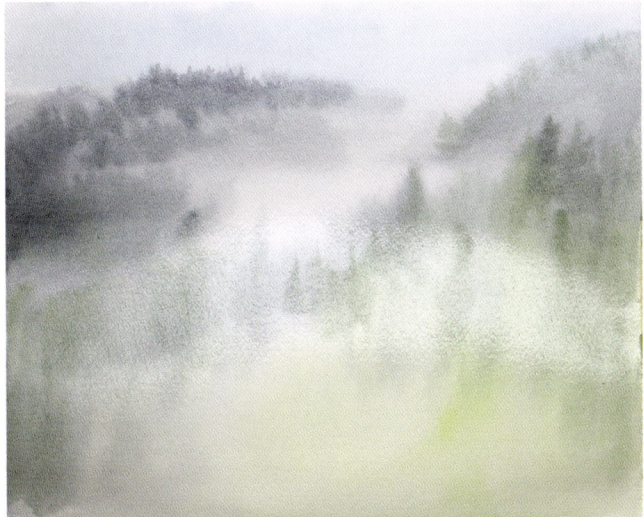

2. Allow the first wash to dry completely—it might be tempting to touch it up but resist the urge! Once the paper is bone dry, apply a second wet-on-wet wash just like the first. With the paper glossy-wet, use milky indigo to paint short, quick upstrokes for the distant pine trees. Mix in some hansa yellow light to create green and start suggesting foreground trees. Since the surface is wet, everything in this layer should "fuzz out" slightly.

Scan to watch a video.

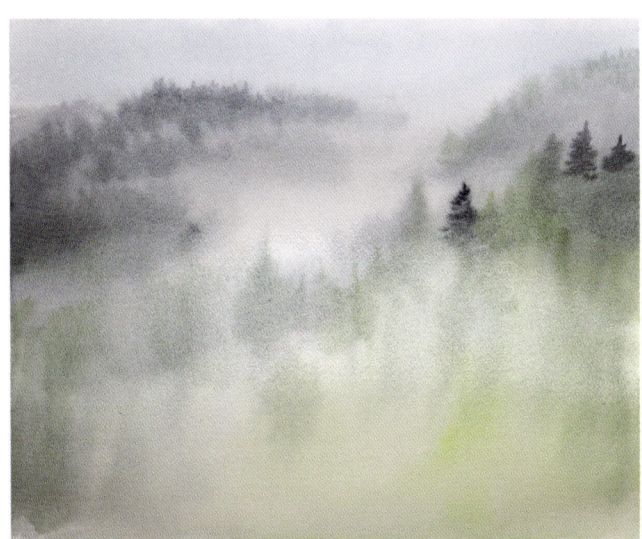

3. As the paper begins to dry, you can start painting darker trees. Begin with a thin vertical line for the trunk, then use quick forward and backward U shapes to create the branches. Make the branches smaller at the top and wider toward the bottom of each tree.

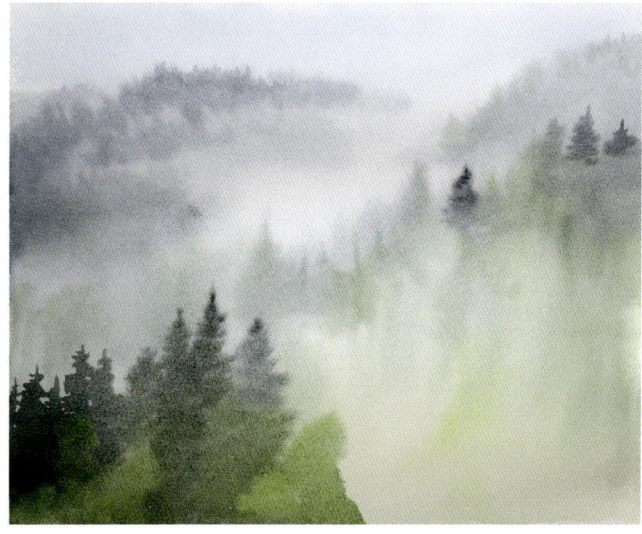

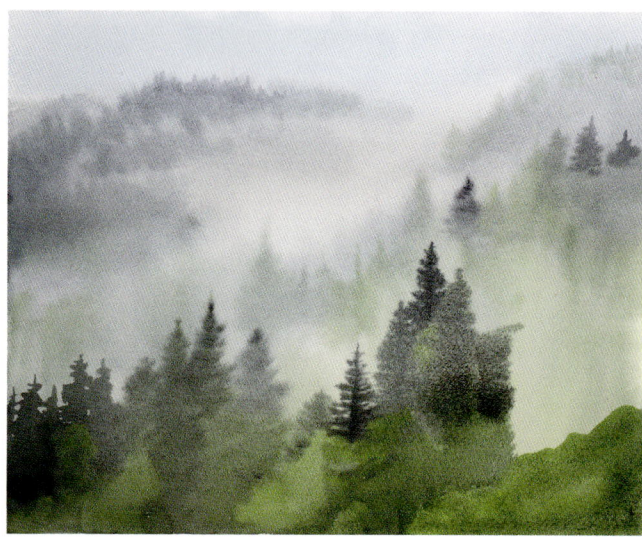

4. As your paper dries, decide when and where to paint your trees. For soft edges, paint them while the paper is still damp; for more defined, sharper lines, wait until it's dry. Use a large brush loaded with indigo and hansa yellow light to paint broad areas of greenery toward the bottom of the composition.

Scan to watch a video.

5. Working your way across the painting, aim to connect all your shapes with the wet paint. Vary the intensity of the colors and move quickly to avoid creating any hard lines.

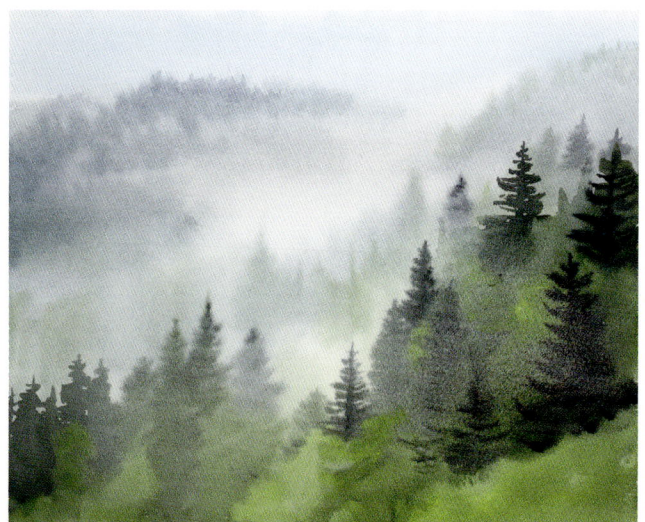

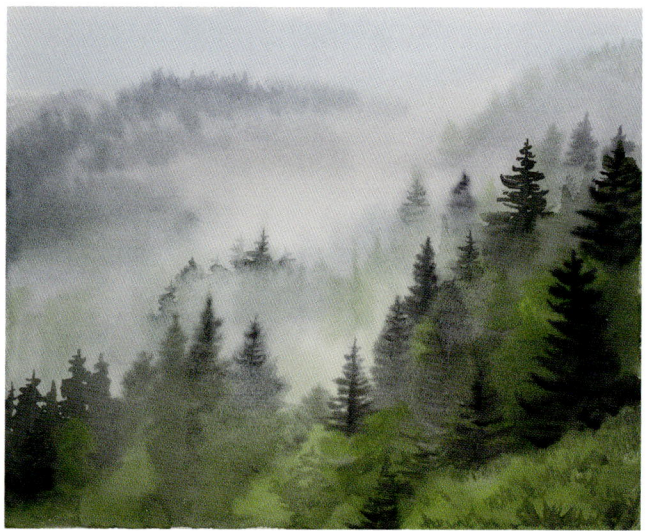

6. Add the darkest and largest evergreens to the right side of the composition. Use your reference photo to guide the drawing and placement of these trees.

7. Paint a small line of foggy trees within the fog by first wetting the paper just below the treetops. Then, paint the tops of the trees, letting the brush touch the wet paper to create a foggy effect. This technique can be used in smaller sections without needing to wet the entire paper again.

Scan to watch a video.

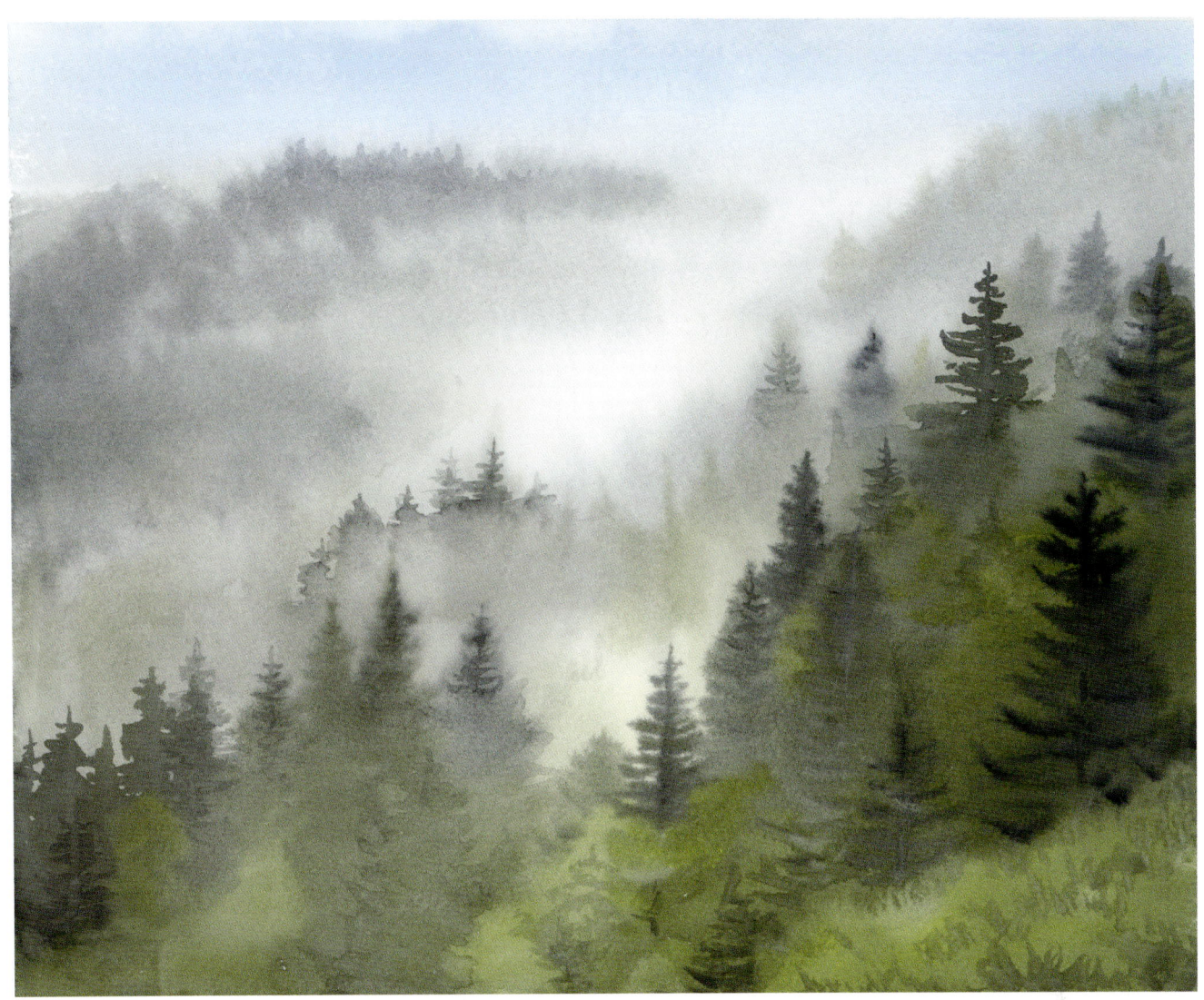

8. Once your paper is almost completely dry, add any finishing touches, such as dry-brush textures in the foreground grasses.

Rhododendron

To see the vibrant, famous blooming shrubs of Appalachia, June is the ideal time to visit the Smokies. The Great Smoky Mountains are home to eleven native species of rhododendron.

Download template and reference photo.

Brush

Round, size 4

Color Palette

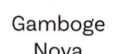 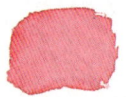 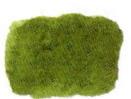 

Gamboge Nova   Quinacridone Rose   Sap Green   Marine Blue

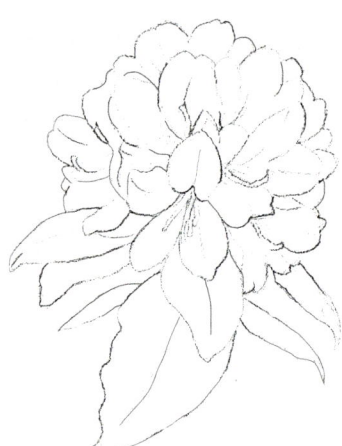 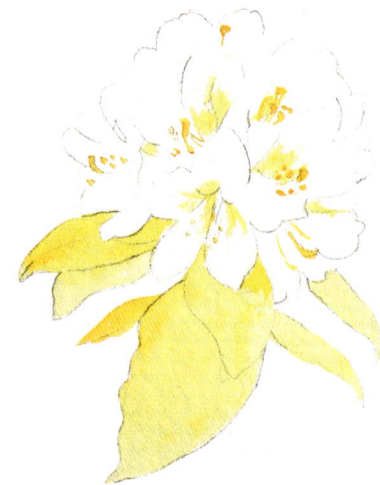 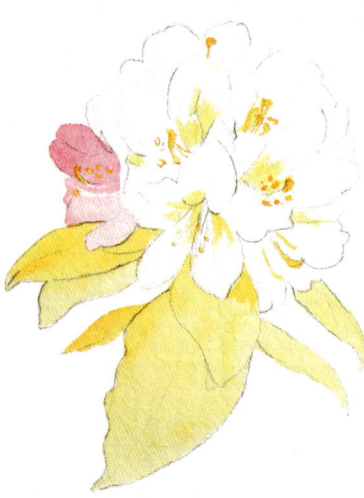

1. Sketch or trace the flower and leaves.

2. Mix up a milky puddle of gamboge nova and apply a flat wash to the leaves. Use the same color for the centers of the flowers and stamen.

3. To paint the flower petals, start with a tinted wash of quinacridone rose. Work just one petal at a time.

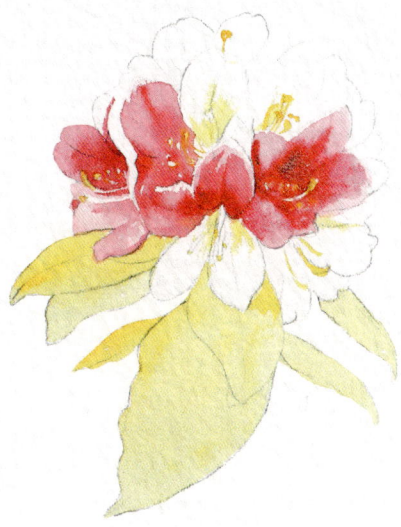 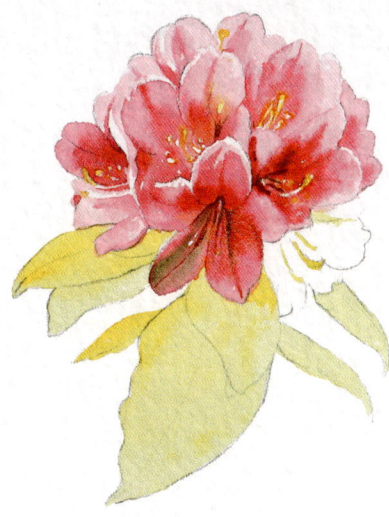 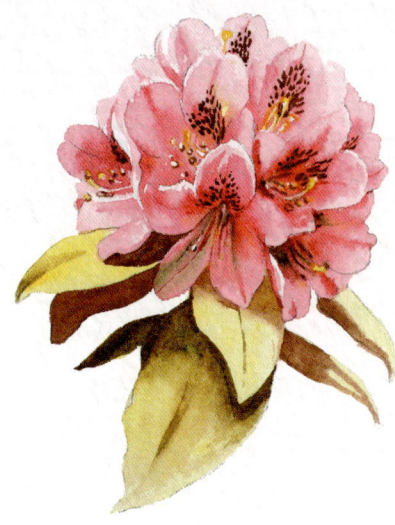

4. While the light pink area is still wet, add thicker, darker paint at the base of the petal. Take care to avoid the highlighted edges of overlapping petals and use negative-painting around the tiny yellow stamen.

Scan to watch a video.

5. To add shadows to the center of the flowers, mix a dark brown using quinacridone rose and sap green.

6. Use your brown combo to paint the shadows on the leaves and dark dots on the petals. Allow this to dry completely.

Scan to watch a video.

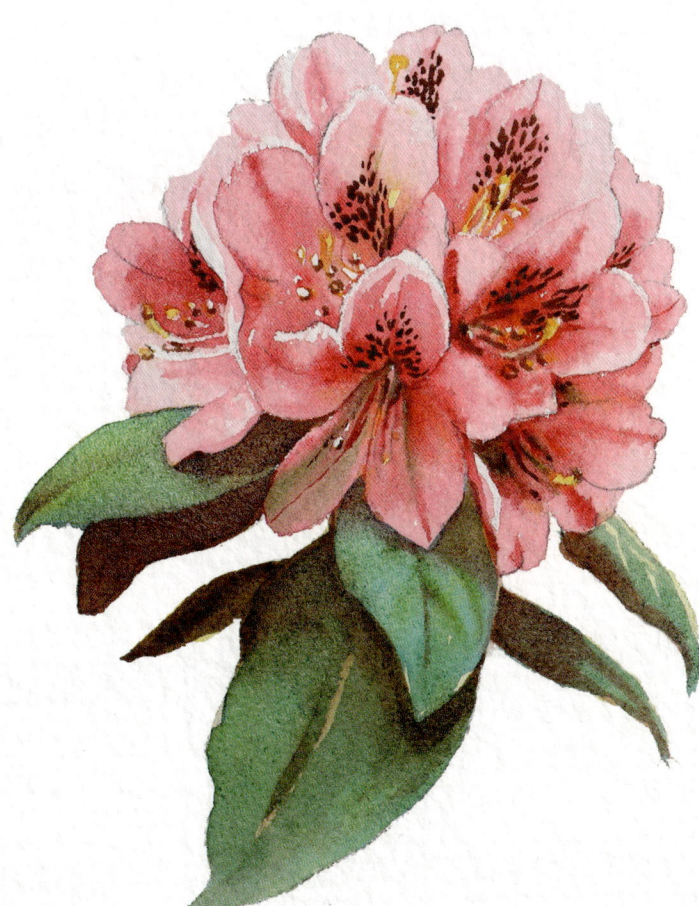

7. Apply a wet-on-dry glaze of watered-down marine blue to finish the leaves.

EVERGLADES NATIONAL PARK
Florida

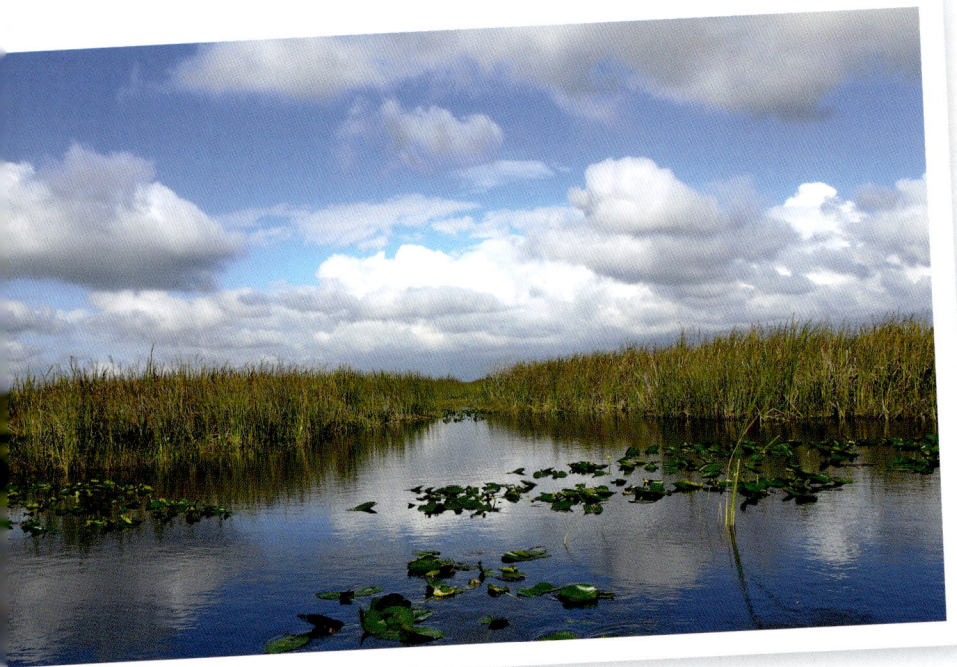

Reference photo

Everglades National Park is a subtropical wetland landscape, home to many rare and endangered species, such as manatees, American crocodiles, and Florida panthers. If you enjoy bird watching or wildlife photography, the Everglades' rich biodiversity provides numerous opportunities to spot unusual and fascinating creatures.

Download template and reference photo.

Brushes

Round, sizes 6 and 10

Paper

Fabriano Artistico 140-pound (300 gsm), cotton, cold-pressed block, 9" x 12" (23 x 30.5 cm); taped to resize down to 7½" x 12" (19 x 30.5 cm)

Color Palette

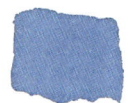

Phthalo Blue (GS)

Indigo

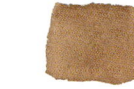

Burnt Sienna

Ultramarine Blue

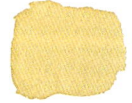

Yellow Ochre

Hansa Yellow Light

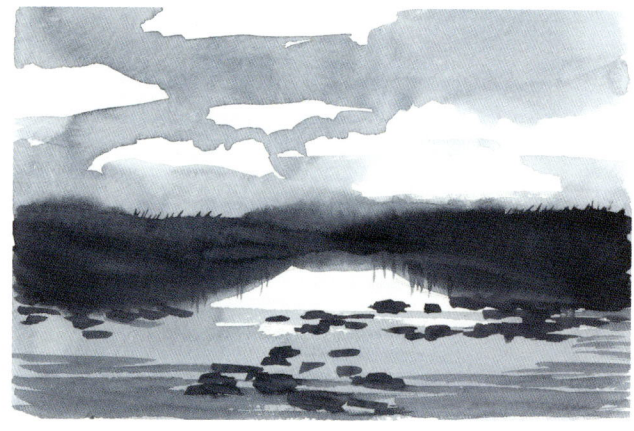

Value study.

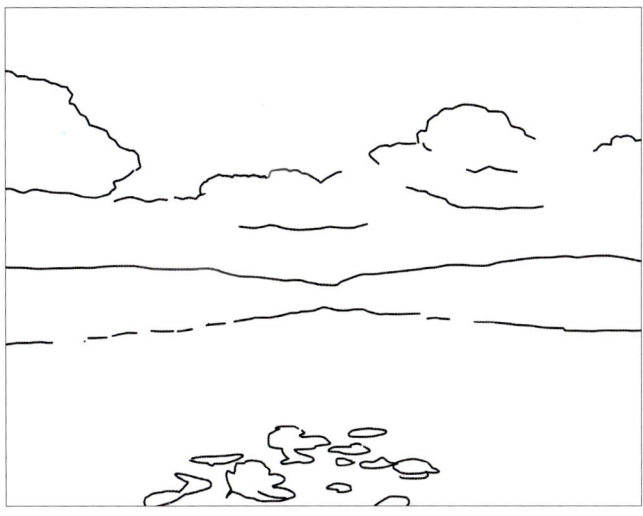

1. Begin with a simple sketch to block in the grasses and main lily pad shapes. It's also helpful to do a quick value study beforehand to simplify the composition and identify the dark and light areas.

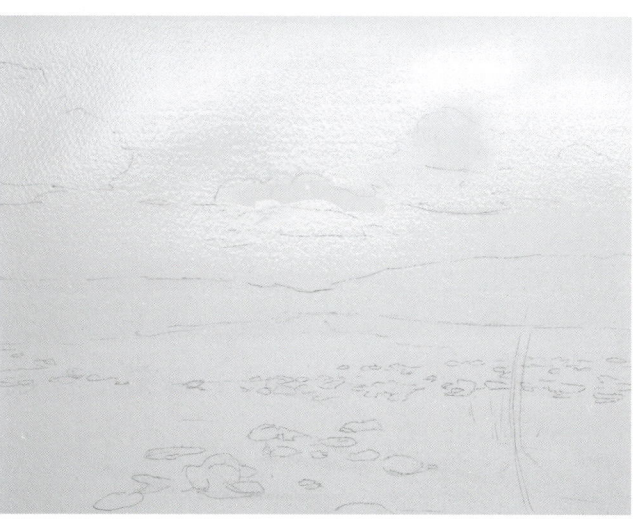

2. Paint the sky using the wet-on-wet technique. Brush clean water over the entire sky area, carefully avoiding the whitest cloud shapes where you want to preserve sharper edges.

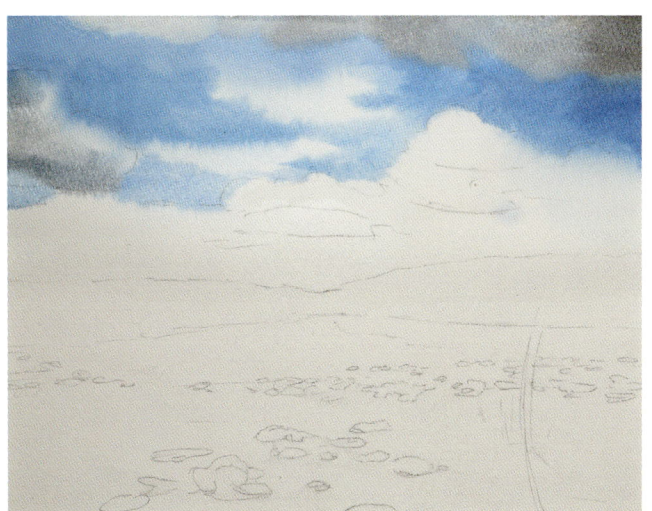

3. Load your brush with phthalo blue and paint the sky, carefully negative-painting around the clouds. Mix indigo and burnt sienna to a milky consistency to paint the darker clouds at the top of the composition.

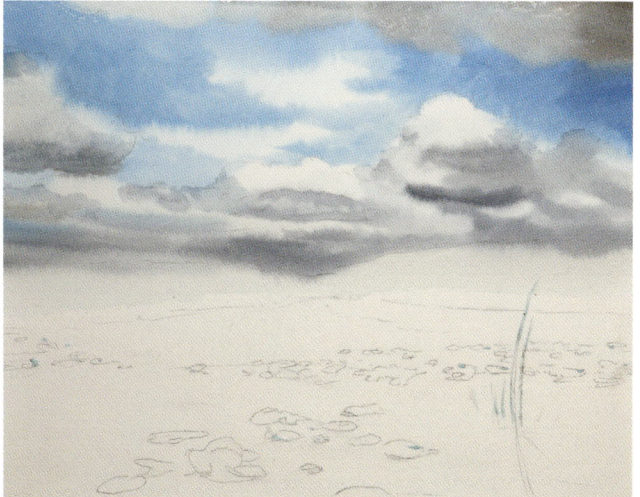

4. Use this same indigo mix to add shadows beneath the low-lying clouds.

   Optional step: Apply masking fluid to a few of the lily pads and reeds in the water to protect these highlighted areas. Let it dry.

Scan to
watch a
video.

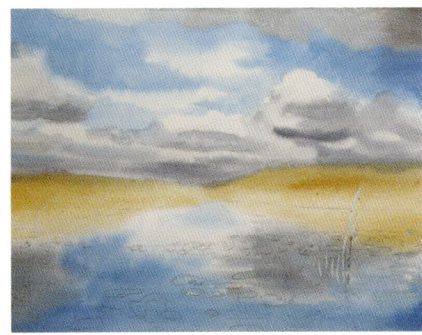
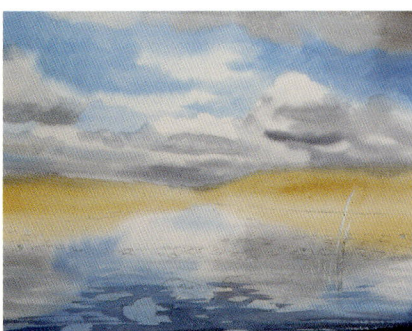
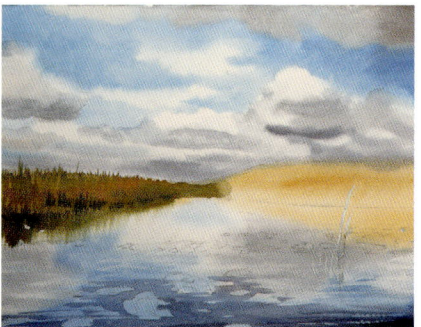

5. To paint the first layer on the lower half of your composition, start by prewetting the surface with clean water. Then, drop in yellow ochre for the grasses and their reflections. Use phthalo blue and indigo to paint the water, capturing the sky's reflection. If your paper is wet, these washes will naturally blend and soften together.

Scan to watch a video.

6. Use a mix of ultramarine blue and indigo to paint darker horizontal brush strokes across the water, carefully avoiding the lily pads and cloud reflections.

7. To paint the marshland grasses and their reflections on the water, use a medium dark wash of yellow ochre. Create a murky green by mixing in some phthalo blue and use quick up-and-down brush strokes for the grass texture. Add darker vertical shadow shapes with indigo. Use the tiny tip of your small round brush and use vertical strokes to paint the pointed, bristly grass overlapping the sky.

Scan to watch a video.

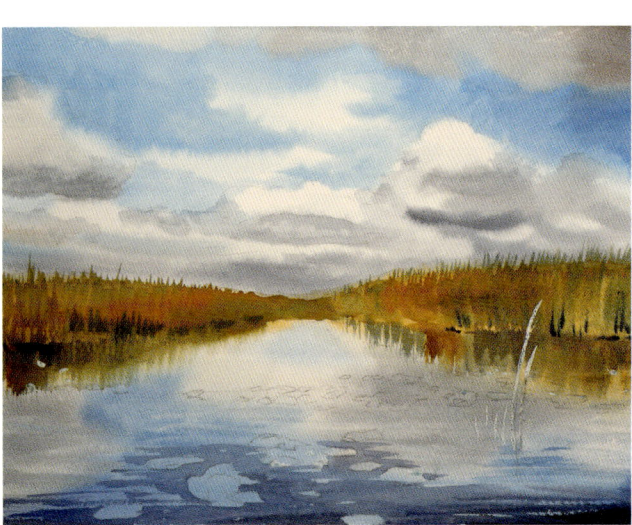

8. Paint the right side using the same technique but avoid making it identical to the left side—some asymmetry adds beauty to a painting. To create softer reflections, use the wet-on-wet technique by prewetting the paper before adding the dark reflections on the water.

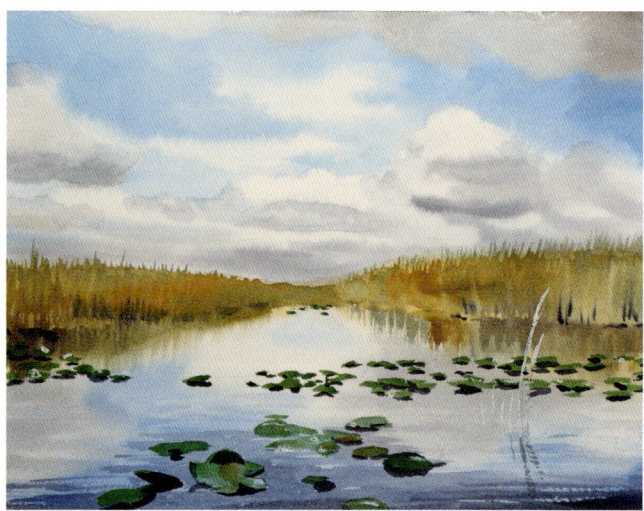

9. Mix hansa yellow light and phthalo blue to create a bright green, then use a small brush to paint the lily pads. Add dark shadows beneath the lily pads with indigo and paint the reflections of the tall reeds on the water.

Scan to watch a video.

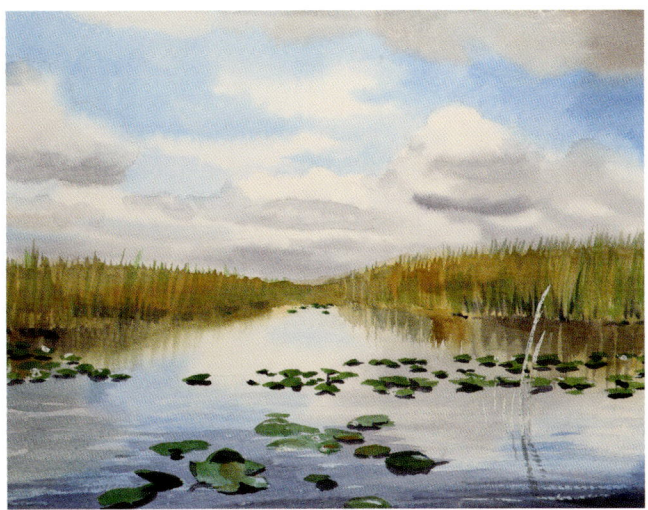

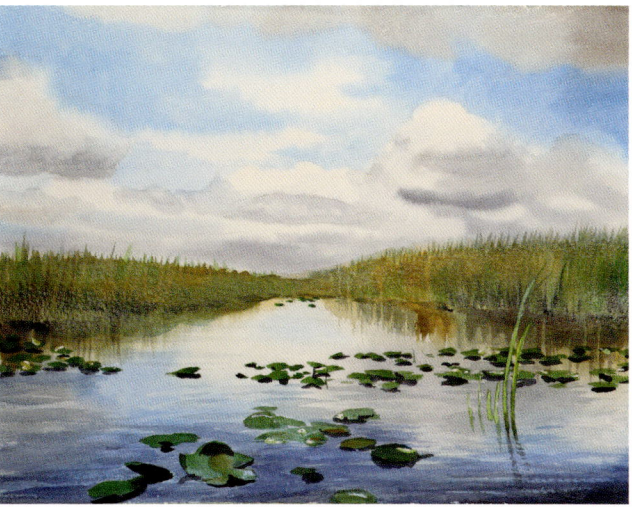

10. Continue adding texture to the grass and water. You can add as much detail as you wish!

11. If you used masking fluid, allow your painting to dry completely before removing it. Paint the grassy reeds green in the areas where you removed the masking fluid. If any of the highlights on the lily pads appear too bright, tone them down with a touch of yellow ochre.

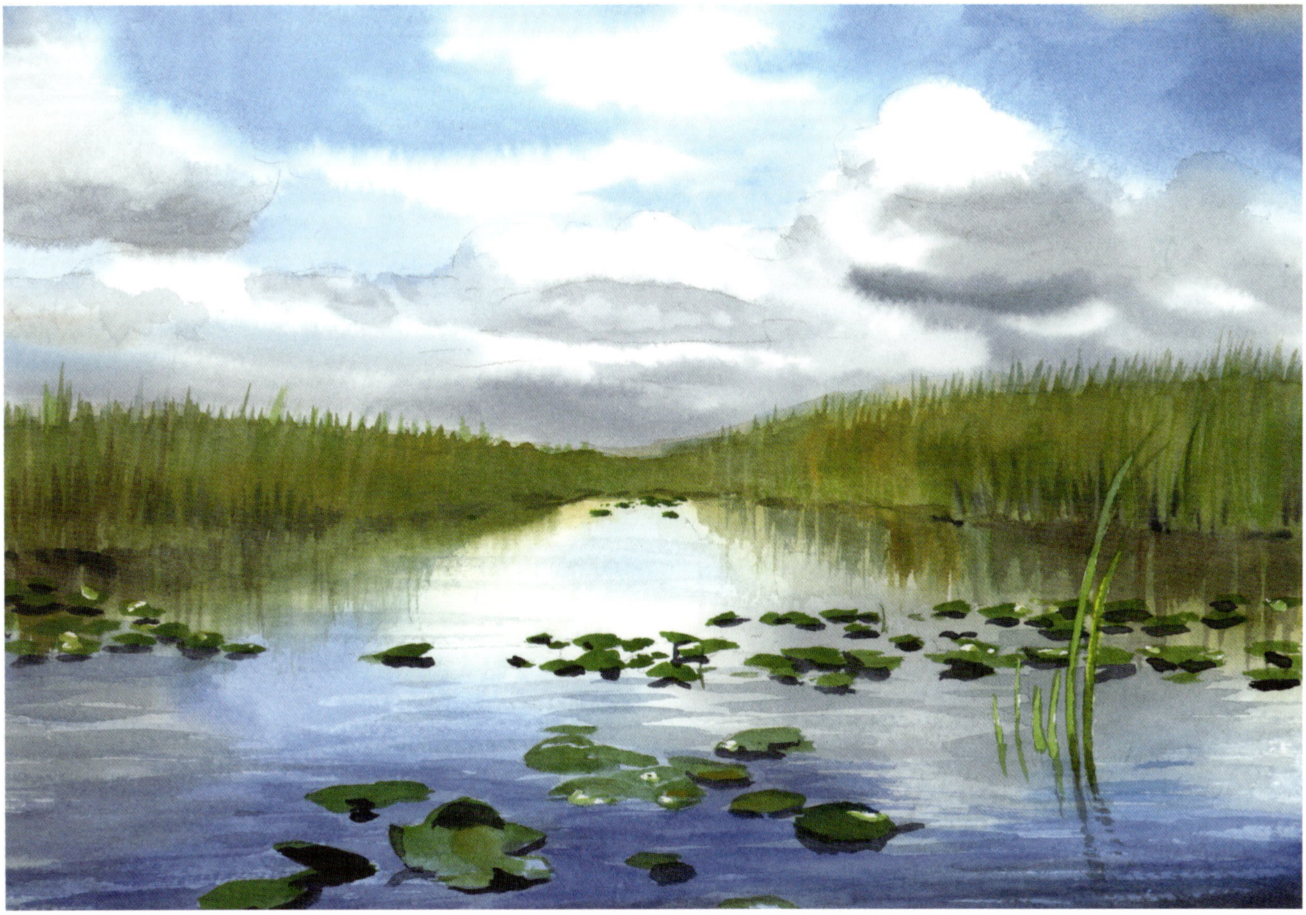

12. Apply a final wash of light green over the grasses, then add some finishing horizontal brushstrokes across the water using diluted indigo.

Alligator

If you kayak through the Everglades, you're likely to encounter one (or several!) of these modern-day dinosaurs. Alligators are an important part of the Everglades ecosystem.

Download template and reference photo.

Brush

Round, size 6

Color Palette

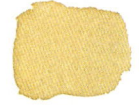  

Yellow Ochre   Ultramarine Blue   Burnt Sienna

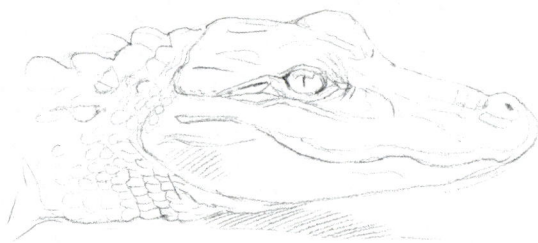

1. Sketch or trace the alligator.

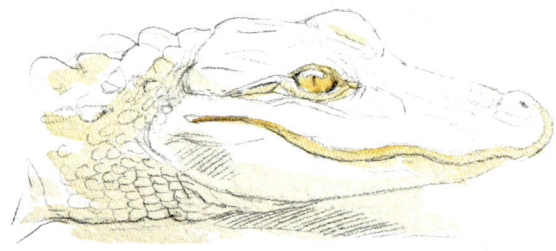

2. Apply a watery yellow ochre to the neck, mouth, and jaw. For the first layer of yellow inside the eye, use a thicker pigment and paint around the highlight.

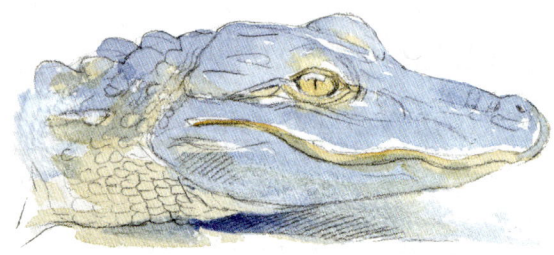

3. While the yellow ochre is still damp, apply a watery wash of ultramarine blue over the head, working close to the yellow and leaving small highlights near the eyes and mouth untouched.

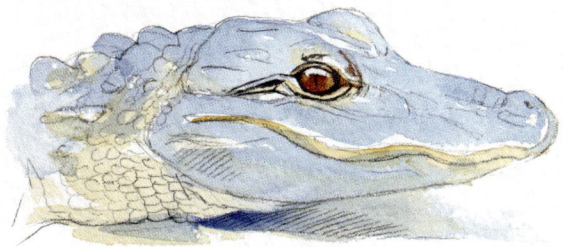

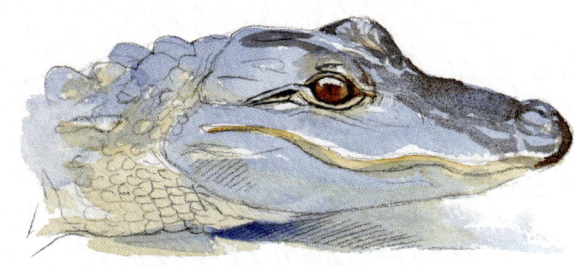

4. Paint the eye darker using burnt sienna. Mix ultramarine blue and burnt sienna to create a very dark gray. Use a small round brush to outline the eye and add dark details and creases.

Scan to watch a video.

5. Apply the dark gray mix as another layer on the alligator. This step involves painting around the lighter blue areas to enhance the shiny, reptilian appearance.

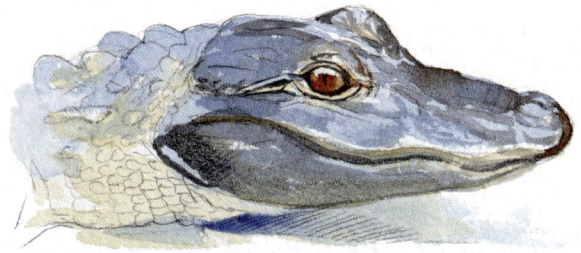

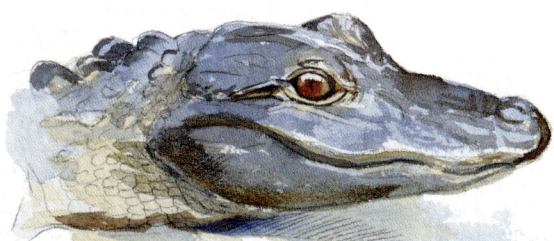

6. Darken the area under the jaw with your gray mix, then add some yellow ochre. Create a black paint by mixing ultramarine blue and burnt sienna in a thick, creamy consistency. Use this to paint the crease of the mouth.

7. Continue layering the dark gray to paint scales and dark details. Add some brush strokes of burnt sienna to the neck and jaw.

Scan to watch a video.

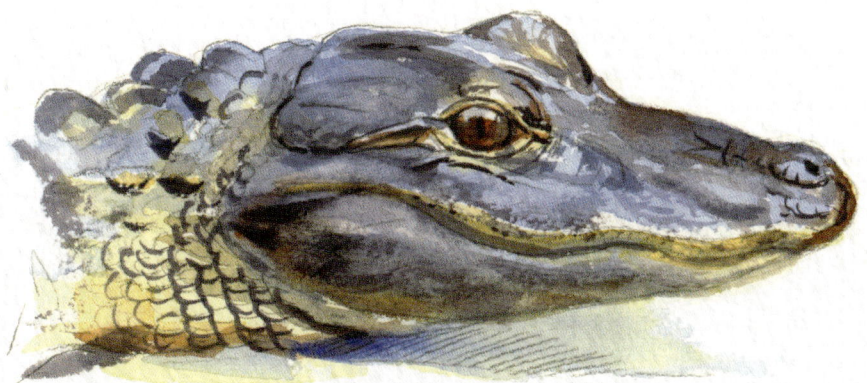

8. Finish the alligator by adding dry-brush texture along the mouth. Use your darkest mix and a small round brush to paint fine-line details suggesting scales on the neck and nose. Apply a final wash of yellow ochre to enhance the color.

About the Author

EMILY OLSON is a Colorado-based artist, plein air painter, YouTuber, and passionate outdoor enthusiast. Originally from Wisconsin, she began her teaching journey through music, studying both music and art in college, and spent 10 years teaching piano before transitioning to a full-time art career.

In 2019, Emily launched her YouTube channel, where she shares in-depth watercolor tutorials, product reviews, and painting tips. She also founded Watercolor Mastery, an online school dedicated to providing high-quality instruction for her students. As a lifelong learner, Emily constantly explores new paints, surfaces, and techniques, aiming to inspire her students with a spirit of curiosity and exploration that she believes is essential for artistic growth.

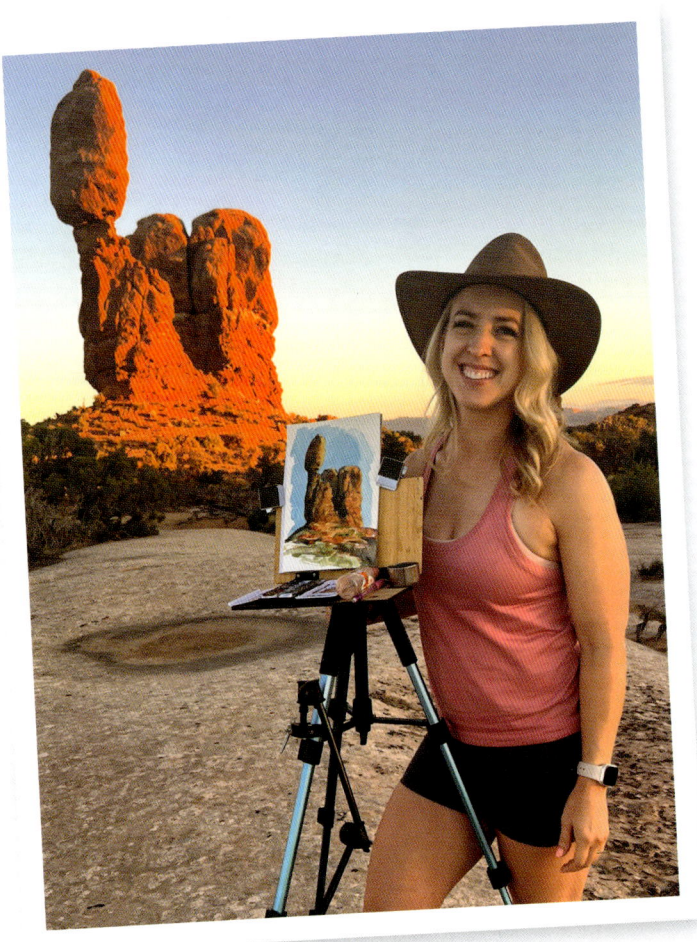

Index